DAYBREAK
INTO
DARKNESS

Rupert Bogarde

DAYBREAK INTO DARKNESS

*A True Story of Happiness
and Heartbreak*

MACMILLAN

First published 2002 by Macmillan
an imprint of Pan Macmillan Ltd
Pan Macmillan, 20 New Wharf Road, London N1 9RR
Basingstoke and Oxford
Associated companies throughout the world
www.panmacmillan.com

ISBN 0 333 90645 4

1 3 5 7 9 8 6 4 2

A CIP catalogue record for this book is available from
the British Library.

Typeset by SX Composing DTP, Rayleigh, Essex
Printed and bound in Great Britain by
Mackays of Chatham plc, Chatham, Kent

I would like to thank Susan Hill
for her patience, wisdom and encouragement.

This book is for Jacqueline Mary Van den Bogaerde, née Wright
. . . and for our children.

In order to respect a simple narrative I have been obliged to compress time, I have also changed the names of people and places where appropriate.

PVdB

Contents

PART FIVE

—

PART SIX

—

PART SEVEN

—

PART EIGHT

PART ONE

1 One Enchanted Evening

19 March 1983

There was smoke and everywhere people were shouting and tearing about. I acknowledged the odd face, but thin on confidence, I found it difficult to talk.

I'd torn my trouser leg off above the knee, my shirt was in shreds and the midget tie that had been such a wonderful last-minute find flopped on the upper part of my pigeon chest like a freshly caught sardine.

I wanted *so* much to blend in.

It wasn't late. I watched my date for the evening hovering not far from her ex, who was writhing with other dancers near the thumping loudspeakers on the other side of the room. It didn't seem to matter. After all, she hardly knew me. She glanced in my direction, pre-occupied.

Shyness sent me outside the marquee to face the cold Norfolk fields. Turned earth that smelled of rain and looked almost edible rose and rippled like a river through the countryside, banking up to stone walls and over ridges into the darkness. Frozen grass crunched under my feet while smoke billowed from the flint cottage chimney and was swiped away, carrying strains of a favourite old song and muffled voices in the cutting wind.

I was back lit from the windows, my ragged scarecrow clothes flailing, throwing shadows across the rough, ice-silver lawn – as if I was in a film, as if this scene was the beginning of a bizarre dream.

I rejoined the party and had a drink by the fire in an attempt to drown shyness. Peter Pan stood warming herself nearby, her blonde hair sparkling faintly. The outfit seemed to fit her body like an advertising poster for fresh fruit.

That morning I'd discovered a barber who had mistaken me for a motorcycle enthusiast. Before he'd managed to screech to a halt he'd cut off most of my hair, and now, looking bald and awkward, I was standing there, dressed like a pervert's dream, next to a lone, slim, brown-eyed blonde.

Miss Pan eyed the remains. 'I'm a lost schoolboy,' I said, when she asked. Her smile showed slightly crossed front teeth and she said that she didn't know they had lost schoolboys in the *Beano*.

'Er, they were invented in a second-hand shop on the way here.' Distracted by her prettiness, I made an attempt to focus.

'You're cold.' She offered a cigarette.

I dug in a heap of clothes for my coat. 'Yes, I think I've got goose-bumps.'

Brown eyes crinkled at the edges. 'You mean pimples.'

A buxom brunette wearing a Viking outfit barged her way through the crowd. 'Jacquie!'

'That's Caroline,' said Peter Pan as Caroline howled at a man dressed as Gnasher-the-Dog staggering towards the beer supply. Then, clocking that the two of us were together, she gave Miss Pan a complicit grin before following Gnasher into the crowd.

Jacquie and I sat on the floor by the fire and she told me about herself as the party spun on behind us. The glitter on her face shone like water, almost as if her cheeks were streaming with miniature tears. I leaned forward, following her voice carefully over a blasting Dr Hook.

'In the summer I run a place in France. It's a restaurant,' she said proudly. 'Caroline's my partner. She's my best friend.' I kept ferrying the drinks and the comic-book characters danced on until the fire was in embers. Jacquie shivered and kept talking. '. . . and my dad used to sit on Mum's lap and watch television,' she finished, and smiled flatly.

She'd sketched a happy childhood around a warm, eccentric father and his capable, devoted young wife. I wrapped my jacket around Jacquie's shoulders. 'I have a younger sister and a brother,' she added, but I was only half-listening now; I was wondering if she'd mind being kissed.

A friend called Hamish, who'd fallen asleep on the rug in a white shirt and braces, roused himself and sang, 'You Gotta Have Heart', accompanied by the end-of-record scratching from the abandoned gramophone, and then fell silent, as if he'd fallen off the back of a punt.

Jacquie spoke more of her father. 'Afterwards,' she said, 'I drank myself sober for weeks. I had to get out, so I chucked everything in and went to France. That's where I began working with Jake, the third partner in the restaurant.' Putting the drink down as if to turn a page, she slapped her hands on her knees. Her mouth, in repose, always fell into a little smile, whether she meant it to or not. Jacquie couldn't close her mouth and look comfortable. 'Are you hungry?' she asked, rising. 'Let's make a paella.'

'What?' I heard myself say as she turned towards the kitchen and, gathering momentum, began searching for ingredients. 'It's nearly breakfast!' I added, looking slightly uncomfortable as she fished through our host's store of groceries.

'You'll love it,' she enthused. 'All you need is rice and a few leftovers.'

I was feeling almost hypnotized, admiring her wilfulness as well as her lovely shape. Peter Pan was *all there*, I told myself.

She stopped, looking right at me while she pulled a blonde wisp away from her eyes. 'Why're you smiling at me like that?' she asked.

I'd had no idea I was smiling although I might have guessed that my intense interest was obvious. 'Because you are,' I said.

Her smile broadened before our host's girlfriend came into the room and whispered in her ear. 'Oh, I see.' Jacquie's face fell. Assuming that my date for the evening had been more serious, she handed me back my coat. 'I've got to go,' she said clinically, then headed towards the door and the dawn light.

'You're not hungry then?' I asked. 'Can I see you . . .?'

The door pulled shut.

Hamish sat up again, still dreaming about singing. 'You Gotta Have . . .' Hamish lay back down.

*

I discovered where Jacquie was staying and asked her to dinner at an Indian restaurant in St Martin's Lane. Her enthusiasm for our evening and her bright, natural manner was matched perfectly by both my lack of knowledge of anything Indian and my terror of not being able to pay the bill.

From the age of thirteen or thereabouts, I'd become convinced that I was somehow not correctly *connected* with other people and life in general. I had an odd notion that I'd been assembled and packed off to life's battlefield with all parts in order, only to find that I'd been switched permanently to 'stand by'. As a child I wanted more than anything simply to be liked, it was all I could do to win approval; a standard characteristic of so many divorcees' children. At the time it never occurred to me that, still repulsed by the cruelty of parental separation, from an early age I might in fact have been only half-engaging; holding life at an awkward distance.

To counter this I'd then bashed my confidence with deliberate physical attempts to look '*wildly awake*', totally '*on the ball*' and utterly '*switched on*'. Doing this I probably often looked foolish, even imbecilic, but that's just how it was. I couldn't stop myself from seeing things the wrong way, or mostly not getting the point at all. Daft humour became a convenient, standard way to escape these embarrassing moments. My love of absurdity has roots that run deeper than any vine's.

'And you're how old?' Jacquie asked.

'Twenty-one,' I croaked, horrified, as my eyeballs, stinging with Madras tears, saw her lower her fork. Her face fell as she considered this news. '*I'm history*,' I thought, but then she broke into a smile, confidence shining out.

'I'm twenty-four,' she told me, then said quietly, 'You don't seem twenty-one.' Truthfully, I looked about nineteen but she'd chosen her words carefully. Doing my best not to lose her, I floundered for more common ground.

'What does your sister do?' I asked, flexing my 'on-the-ball' face, yet trying to look casual as my eyes stole glimpses of her lovely body and my imagination dismantled her clothing, even down to struggling hopelessly with the clasps.

'She's in France, near the restaurant, living with a Frenchman. She came down for a season and never went back.' Jacquie went on, anticipating my question, 'And my brother Stephen still lives with Mum in Norfolk. He's got a few problems.' She didn't elaborate and while I fumbled through worn-out skin-tight cords to pay the bill, the conversation focused again on Jacquie's father.

'I can see that you loved him very much.'

Her hesitation indicated that I'd stumbled into part of her life that was still in the throes of repair. 'I looked after him at home,' she said. 'I was nineteen, doing my nursing training.' She stared at her glass, her mouth set and lifted in that natural smile, but the eyes above were suddenly hollow. 'I left for a while. I just ran away.' The bill and money were whisked off and those routine mints were left for us, arriving as if an antidote to the rather painful subject of Jacquie's father.

'I was his girl,' she sighed, popping a mint and snapping herself out of it. 'Let's go.' She smiled and I leapt to my feet and helped her with her coat.

We drove in her little Citroën to my rented room in a shared Fulham house where it took me until five in the morning and a promise of pyjamas to convince her to stay. Perhaps Jacquie saw something that made her want to make things different with us: hard for me, when all my Neanderthal brain wanted to do at that moment was kiss and wrestle naked with the girl in front of me.

The whole relationship appeared to be something we had both been hoping and searching for. We seemed to connect effortlessly. Jacquie had confidence that I had never known, so very bright. Strength always draws strength, perhaps of another sort, so it might have been my comparative calm that pulled her towards me. My heart was wide open and in many ways I was lost and without direction. We'd hardly kissed, yet whatever it was – lust, luck, spiritual chemistry – it was there with us, drawing us together like pins to a magnet.

It was old-fashioned perhaps, but Jacquie had no wish for a one-night stand. This was a plan, a real chance of something good, and she wanted so much for it to come true. She felt that respect and timing were crucial. To throw herself at me, she felt, would be a stupid mistake. She wanted it to last.

'You're very determined,' I told her. 'The nursing, the restaurant, the pyjamas. So why choose a twenty-one-year-old?'

'My last boyfriend had everything,' she shrugged, 'but he liked control.' Her voice turned sharp. 'I want to be young and free. I don't want to make a mistake.'

I felt relief. If it was youth and freedom she wanted, then I had it to offer in bundles. There was a sexual charge to her enthusiasm, naive and somehow overwhelming.

We went upstairs to bed with shy and almost childish excitement.

'I'm afraid there's only one blanket,' I said. There was no heat in the room either. The fact that she insisted she wore my pyjamas was *almost* understandable. 'I just don't want to spoil it,' she told me, stroking my arm. Amazed, I heard my besotted self agree. I didn't even try to loosen the pyjamas and we curled up together in a gentle kiss. I could see the moon from the window as I felt her warmth across me. The softness and the smell of her hair in the quiet, icy room whispered *comfort*.

Two hours later, leaving her sleeping, I went to work, humping lights about and taking messages in a small film studio in the West End. In my sleep-starved state I was feeling unsure of the girl lying, still untouched, back home in my bed. I'd promised to cook for her when I got home and I was already looking forward to it. I wasn't even asking myself if I liked her. I didn't need to think about it.

That evening Jacquie arrived at about eight. I was stirring the spaghetti and wondering what on earth I could put in the pond of bubbling tomato to make it look like sauce. In the meantime I'd led myself to believe that she probably wouldn't show up. She arrived with a large bag, which she left at the foot of the stairs. 'I've brought my electric blanket.' She smiled shyly, casting every doubt from my mind and scattering any awkwardness to the wind.

I cheerfully threw unimaginative things into my sauce (which, since the news of the blanket seemed suddenly altogether more delicious) and we sat together quietly, drinking wine in the light of the candles that Jacquie had brought. She lit them ceremoniously, seeming to love anything that added atmosphere, relishing the emotion that even the slightest change brought on.

It was a ten-day thunderbolt romance. We were passionate, almost oblivious to the world outside my little room. In those days she met me anywhere, crossing London simply for a stolen moment together, setting the days ablaze. I'd call her from work without reason. She'd previously been staying with friends, preparing for her journey with her friend Caroline down to their summer restaurant in France. However, since the first night with the glorious electric blanket we'd been inseparable and I'd given Jacquie a key. She'd be there, sleeping in my bed or taking a bath, always cheerful.

Hanging up for the umpteenth time, I realized, dazed, that this was madness and I was hooked, line and sinker . . . I'd forgotten myself.

And then the ten days were over.

'No ties,' Jacquie said. 'I can't expect you to wait. Let's just see where we are when I come home after the season.' I looked at her with some scepticism and she returned an anxious glance. 'Please,' she insisted, 'then there are no promises to break.' She tried to look bright as my face fell. 'Rupe,' she kissed me, 'look, I promise . . . I don't want anyone else.' Then she climbed into the overloaded 2CV that would take her and Caroline to France and departed with a clatter, leaving a sudden and powerful silence in my room, a hot blanket and a passion that wouldn't switch off.

2 *Esperance*

One Year Later

Morning sunlight made steam rise from our new duvet as if it were a
compost heap, while water ran down the houseboat windows, making
pools on the sills, then on down the walls to the floor from where it
began its journey back up again via the curtains.

Jacquie, home from a long night shift, was sitting on the bed,
undoing her nurse's uniform.

'You're frozen, Jacquie! Your fingers – look, they're blue.' I
reached and turned the knob on the portable gas fire, our only heat.
'That bloody bike.'

I remembered to take a fresh syringe and measure my insulin dose,
a ritual I was obliged to observe three times a day. The diabetes was a
relatively recent problem and I wasn't altogether used to it, still often
deliberately failing to accept the nuisance. It had been identified
shortly after my elder brother Gareth died, two years earlier. I'd
become frustrated with the constrictions of being a diabetic. I never
had the patience to find food for mid-morning, when the shot would
reach its highest peak and my body would be without the food it
needed and was in danger of literally eating itself. Mostly, in a gesture
of defiance, I suppose, I just pinched a layer of midriff and stuck the
needle in. I'd get a Coke, or I'd find a sweet shop somewhere near
the dangerous time in the day. Forget sandwiches; forget diabetes
altogether, until you have to. It would often turn into a race to find
food or sugar, before the insulin cut me down. I put the prepared
insulin shot ready beside the bed.

The easiest part of diabetes is the mechanical bit. Food quantities, jabbing insulin and timing can almost always be mastered . . . eventually, when one finds the right frame of mind. What wasn't readily explained in those days was the effect that the condition has on one's emotions. In the time before blood-testing was readily available I often went around not quite knowing if I had low blood-sugar or if I was just severely depressed. One could reach a semi-hypo state and simply cruise about, slightly stoned on the sugar starvation, planing on the reduction of fuel to the brain, like an addict. I was lucky that injecting didn't seem to bother me too much.

There were foolhardy moments though, when I'd arrive in a shop with just enough residual control over my body to manage the purchase of a Coke, only to discover that I'd left my money in my other trousers. I didn't want to discuss diabetes with myself and, oddly perhaps, I spoke of it even less to Jacquie. In fact, ever since the man sitting next to me at the diabetic clinic had given me his artificial leg to hold, I hadn't been much interested in going there either. The clinic was old. I only went once. He just sat there; one minute he had both legs, then two seconds later his baggy trouser leg went flat as he pulled an entire limb from the end of it.

'Shhheeeee!' I'd hissed, stunned, accidentally drawing everyone's attention to it. All the other patients were gawking, like me, at the man who was suffering from his system's failure to process sugar. Bravely grinning or perhaps strangely enjoying the attention, he was carted off to have his other foot, the gangrenous one, examined. He was pretty calm, almost wry about that too. I remember going after him to hand back the leg. It was heavy and there was a smell.

I never went there again. Gareth's death and the onset of my diabetes were both almost impossible for me to confront, although at the time I was convinced that I had done so. My condition, at any rate, was a small and manageable pain in the backside. I rarely discussed it with Jacquie and did the minimum to maintain it. I hadn't yet had a serious hypoglycaemic episode so Jacquie had no real reason to try to find out more. She supposed that I was in control and in a twisted sense, I suppose I was.

I was young, athletic and had been told that if I looked after myself, it would be at least ten years before the complications of diabetes stood a chance of affecting me and perhaps they might never do so. At twenty-two this ten-year threshold seemed a long way off. Restraint, I felt, was for when you're old and clinging on for dear life.

Her hands warmer now, Jacquie climbed under the covers. It wasn't yet seven-thirty and the houseboat rocked gently in the wake of a passing refuse barge journeying out to pollute the North Sea.

'It's safer coming home on that bike than on the bus. It's only just getting light now,' Jacquie said, tugging me back into the bed. 'Come on,' she'd say softly, 'you don't need to be on your feet for a while yet.' We would make love and the same would happen when I came home to wake her. How little sleep one needs when one is happy.

I later took the prepared shot and then headed through the hatch to the kitchen and found some breakfast.

Our boat, *Esperance*, seemed to belie her name and to be in a deep depression. Every low tide cut us off from the outside world as her huge tub sank into the sodden beach, disconnecting the telephone line, which only ever worked when she was truly afloat. In some senses, with our focus so fixed upon one another, we seemed to be barely attached to the outside world.

The boat had been my symbolic choice as a start for us when we first decided to be together. It was as transient as the tides that lifted and dropped it day in, day out. If the relationship failed, I felt that this was a place from which we could both walk away, back to dry land, keeping responsibility to a minimum. Now, after a successful winter together, with the prospect of Jacquie returning once more to her restaurant in France, it seemed that neither of us had really thought about what we'd do if the relationship actually proved to work.

'You can't just leave,' I muttered.

'What, darling?' she asked, floating, barely awake.

'I said, when you go, I'll . . .'

'We can phone each other,' she said lamely.

My cornflakes swung past on my home-made hanging table just as a whiff of the rotting cupboards made me clench my jaw shut. 'And what if it's low tide?' I grunted, glaring at the tidal phone.

The first time she'd gone had been almost too long, I'd explained. At twenty-two and having only been together for a few days it was almost unbearable. But she'd just said she expected nothing. 'It's part of a free mind,' she'd said, 'to go and not worry, just to make things happen,' and she did, wherever she went. More carefree than I could comprehend. I saw it as her gift, a magic that could be wonderful, yet ruthless.

I had even gone down to southern France to visit her that summer. It had been my first visit and Jacquie was determined that it should be a success. I felt slightly nervous marching off the plane. It was late in the day and I remember looking shyly at her and then giving her a careful kiss before climbing into the 2CV and being swamped by the incredible heat of the south. It had been our time, just a night and a bottle of cheap champagne in a small room in a pension looking over the rooftops of Castelnaudary before we set off for the restaurant further south.

By then Jacquie and Caroline had been running the place for some months. It was a large stone building with cavernous rooms and smooth concrete floors covered with large Persian rugs. Scattered tired-looking tables and chairs abounded, contrasting with an immaculate new tiled bar and a superb kitchen. Caroline welcomed me brightly with a voice straight out of London's East End. Pale freckled skin shone under dark hair that reached her shoulders. She was about Jacquie's height and every bit as headstrong. Yet there was a sense of order about her, which in contrast seemed to accentuate Jacquie's carefree approach to life.

In the morning Caroline was up at seven and off to the beach for a swim. She was scrubbing the new floor in the kitchen by the time we ambled down into the empty restaurant. We drank a glass of orange juice by the bar as Caroline bustled on. The girls hardly spoke and I had the feeling that either might snap at any moment, but the phone rang instead. It was Jake, the other partner in the restaurant. 'Bloody bitches,' I heard his amused voice echo from the speaker-phone in the hallway. Instructions about outside toilets and plumbing were issued and then moments later Caroline went upstairs to speak privately with Jake while Jacquie returned to the table looking miffed. 'God, she's annoying,' she mumbled, then added sourly, 'it's like being at school. I'll bet she tells him that I've been away.'

'She's been cleaning the floor, Jacq,' I butted in, 'it's hardly mutinous. Caroline's not the bitchy type.'

Jacquie looked at me with an incredulous smile. 'I don't like being made to feel guilty,' she smouldered, looking up towards the windows with a sigh, 'and I wish she was happy.'

Dinner at the restaurant was usually something marvellous. Both girls were brilliant cooks and would change over, sharing the kitchen duties and the bar to avoid any feelings of isolation in the kitchen. Bowls of mussels in curry, *marinière* or cream sauce were often requested. Steak with pepper sauce and fresh vegetables and spicy lamb were the magnificent products of inspiration rather than taken from the few books about cookery that the restaurant possessed. There was nothing that the two girls couldn't invent. They flew between the little tables with infectious humour as the evenings raced on.

Before I knew it, the trip was over. A mixed memory of Jacquie's extraordinary energy, her bright smile and a notion of freedom enfolded me as I made my way through London's bus-exhaust air with salty skin and the sun on my back towards my empty, dreary room in Parson's Green.

'For God's sake, take a few risks,' Jacquie said during one of our long-distance phone calls. 'So what if things go wrong in your life? You've got nothing to lose.' So I'd found the houseboat and at the season's end she'd come home to me, her bags full of wine, *haricots verts*, chorizo, cow hides, endless cigarettes and long, dried grasses. She'd arrived with four holidaying policemen. It was all they could do to help carry the cargo for her. She was as bright as ever and though I could see that the summer and comforts of the restaurant had added a little padding to her figure she was every bit as lovely as before.

Now, all too soon, with the winter almost gone, the time approached when she would leave for France once again. This departure would follow no mere dizzy ten days. Over the months I'd fallen in love, and her carefree attitude towards our separation would now seem almost callous. I was afraid that my judgement had failed me and that it all might have meant little to her.

The swinging table had almost lost its momentum and my breakfast was over. I went to speak but I knew she was asleep and I had nothing to say anyway.

The winter sky spat cold rain and droned with the eerie tone of the Thames flood sirens. I climbed out and locked the door, leaving the little peeling green-painted houseboat bobbing among the dead cats and driftwood.

'I've got another job,' Jacquie announced triumphantly. 'In a wine bar. I thought I was going for the supervisor's job but it's the cooking, buying, everything. And they've got a kitchen like a broom cupboard.' She looked up at the ceiling, acting part delight, part disbelief. 'It was hell today, but they've promised to find someone to help me. I'll get it all running for them, then someone can step in when I go to France.'

At first I was silenced: her nursing was already demanding enough. How could she consider taking on more work? We looked at each other across the swaying table. 'See?' Her fingernail pinged a plate. 'You can cook!' She laughed brightly. 'I've never known anyone to roast a whole cabbage before.' The end of the candle fell through its hot bottleneck and fizzled pale green before guttering out.

'Are you going to stop being a nurse?'

'Eventually, but for now I can do both. Look,' she added, growing irritable, 'I'm fed up with nursing. Besides, I can make just as much money and it's more fun at the wine bar. Oh yes, and there'll be times when they'll need extra help in the kitchen – washing up.' She began to grin. 'It's money, and we need money. They don't pay you anything at your place.'

'I'm hardly going to start as the managing director,' I grumbled. Though I knew it was true: I hated my job and that was that. I just hadn't truly stopped believing in following family footsteps, that a pre-trampled path was the right one. I certainly didn't have the mental package needed to be a film producer like my father. What I was actually doing, working in the organizational side of film production, was far from clear. I suppose I hoped that something there would strike me and I'd get some kind of calling. In the meantime my creative spirit was choking to death while I wandered about trying anything I could, hoping fate's magic lightning would strike and send me on the right path.

'Only the odd evening, Rupe.' Jacquie reached across, holding my hand. 'Just washing up. Come on, a few dishes. Then we could go home together.'

I'd previously worked for a year or two in Chicago on a building site enjoying the sweltering summers and glacial, howling winters. One day off a week and it paid good money. I'd had a huge pick-up truck, a girlie, a waterbed and a nice apartment . . . but the girlie got bored and went back to her ma and pa in Arkansas. So at twenty-one I gave up the truck, drained the bed into the street, killed the Americana in my life and came back to London and my family. My brother Gareth, after all, hadn't been gone very long. Perhaps that's really why I came home. Then after a year as a trainee film editor I'd mistakenly looked for and accepted the present job. I was a small sprocket in a modest engine that produced TV commercials. I'd quickly discovered that I simply didn't fit. I looked very young and couldn't organize myself out of a bucket, though I certainly didn't want Jacquie to hear that this was how I felt. She would have insisted that I quit at once and jump into the jobless void. I could only picture the concerned look on my father's face. I'd stay put, keep my mouth shut and the peanuts rolling in.

The wine bar was in the heart of the City, in what looked like a Chicago gangland basement.

'Jacq,' I yelped, 'there must be two hundred people in here tonight.' Dishes flew out, still warm from my sink. 'This is insanity.' For a second or two she stood skinning a salmon beside me. 'Last week they said you were managing the kitchen,' I hissed, 'but you *are* the kitchen.'

That evening she wore her hair up. I remember the neat bun darting about in the steam like a shark's fin in a crowded jacuzzi. Oblivious to the confusion, she seemed to delight in the stress. Amanda, the overwhelmed commis chef, stopped for a moment and wiped sweat from her face with her wrist, then shot back and forth to the bar with trays and began slitting baked potatoes clumsily, burbling maniacally as she nodded to herself: 'Oh God, oh God. Help! Help!' Jacquie remained calm while Xavier, the scrawny, pushy French barman, squawked impatiently through the hatch from behind his greased moustache.

We left the bar sometime after one in the morning.

'Jacq,' I asked, 'how on earth will you be able to get up at seven and do a shift at the clinic?'

'I'll be fine.' She wrapped a scarf around her neck. 'It's just so nice to do something I like.'

'But you're an intensive-care nurse, for goodness' sake. Isn't that unsafe?' I was worried that her fatigue could affect her work as well as exhaust her, but Jacquie's standards were high when it came to nursing.

'Look, Rupe, don't judge me because you need more sleep than I do. This is how I am. Anyway,' she said reassuringly, 'I said I'll give up the nursing.'

'Jacquie, is this bar job for money, or what? What is it, for the excitement?'

The following week I'd worked on a TV commercial featuring a scene on a front porch that had been built in the studio. It was a night scene, the scenario quite simple: a young woman comes out of her front porch to take her dog for a moonlit walk. It was the lighting cameraman's eighty-second birthday and it became obvious that we wouldn't be finishing until the eighty-second take was done.

The lights were finally turned off, twenty bacon sandwiches and armfuls of cola later, at two in the morning. The crew were bored, the clapper loader exhausted and the prop man was snoring happily, delighted with the overtime. Pedalling home towards the houseboat through the freezing quiet of the early hours, I felt an intense, depressing rush of nothing whatsoever, of pure meaninglessness. I stopped the bike on the side of the Embankment and watched the black, curling water slip seawards. I was without a future, I sensed, and the girl was leaving. The stars seemed distant and bitterly cold. I'd be fired in a few days if I didn't quit first. How desperate I was to find my own strength, just to make a small mark and demonstrate who I could be, to achieve or create something, anything, of which my loved ones might approve.

3 Sundays

'So what's wrong with Sundays?' I leaned out of bed and propped myself up with one hand on the floor, the other reaching awkwardly to turn off the TV.

'Nothing.' Jacquie tuned away. 'It's just like the end of all the good things.' Then she rolled over and lay flat, fixed in a melancholic gaze towards the drizzly scene through the side window. 'Just like the autumn. I can't bear it. It's depressing, everything's dying.'

It was a side to Jacquie's nature that I'd only slowly begun to see. It was like wandering through a meadow together, reaching the heart of the long grass, far from the boundaries, only to discover that we'd drifted into the centre of a minefield. I stroked the lean yet curvy lines of her body, close enough to the heat for the gas fire to send one side of my face pink. 'There's a lot to look forward to. It's the beginning of a new week, there'll be other things happening, not just work.'

'Don't say you like Mondays, for God's sake.'

'I dread Monday morning, but things have to go on. There's got to be an autumn to make way for spring, otherwise what would there be to look forward to? Be optimistic!' I said, insufferably bright, and kissed the middle of her back. The ending of certain things were sometimes fearful episodes for Jacquie and, depending on her level of confidence, even changes of the seasons seemed to affect her profoundly. A dinner was a disaster if it ever failed to go beyond midnight, a party a flop if the early hours weren't in sight. She was fantastic at making these things happen and bitterly disappointed should she have to surrender when they didn't.

'Jacquie, you can turn your hand to anything. You never stop. You can do anything. It's a gift, a real gift,' I'd plead. 'Be positive.'

She didn't move. 'I hate it,' she said, 'you see things differently. To me it just feels like everything's finished. There's no more fun: no life. It's all come to an end and there's nothing left to look forward to.' I felt a strange sense of pain for her, a feeling of hopelessness, and yet this only went to strengthen my devotion. She turned to me, curling up, resting her head on my stomach. 'Anyway, I only look forward,' she said.

'Oh? You don't like to see the lovely things you've left behind?'

'What? So I can mope?' Her frown persisted while she drew circles in the steam on the window with her finger. 'You love the autumn. You love the colours and the calm. You don't feel emptiness. It's like the old people in the hospital.' She sighed. 'I'll never let myself get old like that.'

'Jacquie, everything has its end. Darling, what's this about? Life is good.'

'Yes, well, I worry,' she said.

'You said you never worry about anything.' I kissed her.

'I worry . . . worry that you'll leave me.'

Jake had recently arrived from Paris on a business trip and stayed with us on the boat overnight.

'Come on, Jacquie,' he snapped, 'get your arse in gear or I'll be late for my meeting.' His jacket was beautifully pressed, the tie straight and the tired face still not ironed from sleeping virtually on the houseboat floorboards. It was a far cry from his lovely Parisian flat, yet Jake didn't complain. 'Hurry up!' he barked again at Jacquie. 'Bloody bitches.' This apparently charmless muttering was in fact an expression of affection for the girls but one that made his authority over them and the restaurant quite obvious. Jake was in his late thirties; dark-haired, tall, handsome and decisive. He had a drive for winning that went beyond competition, didn't smoke that much, hardly drank and always seemed able to hear the unspoken. Jacquie's mother had once spoken of roses arriving from Jake and I suppose I had then assumed the rest; that Jacquie and he might once have been together. It really made little difference to me, and Jacquie never spoke of it, just as I rarely mentioned previous girlfriends.

I took my insulin, the cold skin bending in and popping out as the overused modern needle broke through. I then ate some bread, sufficient, I estimated, to keep me going until I found the usual shop or sandwich bar. An absurd risk but the kind of folly that characterized my reluctance to accept the condition. That morning we were all setting off in the same direction. We made our way out of the boat and dashed to a hired Mercedes that Jake had left on a double yellow for the night.

In the car they began a conversation which startled me.

'WHY THE HELL DON'T YOU STOP BEING SO STUPID AND GET RID OF THE MESS IN THE RESTAURANT FOR GOD'S SAKE?' Jake bawled, accelerating and pushing at the driver in front. 'ALL THE DEAD ANIMAL SKINS HANGING FROM THE BLOODY WALLS, AND COW HIDES AND SHIT. IT LOOKS LIKE A BLOODY PIGSTY IN THERE.' The car changed lanes and shot forward like a bullet.

'STOP IT, JAKE,' Jacquie shrieked, 'YOU HAVE NO IDEA WHAT IT'S LIKE TO POUR YOURSELF INTO THE PLACE. IT'S MY CHOICE. WHY'RE YOU BEING SUCH A WOMAN?'

'JACQUIE!' he shouted, almost exultantly. 'DON'T BE SO STUPID AND GET OFF YOUR HIGH HORSE.' The Merc thundered on while I clung to the back of his seat. 'IF YOU WEREN'T SO STUBBORN YOU COULD BE SO MUCH MORE SUCC—'

'DROP US HERE,' Jacquie barked. 'Bye, Jake, and thanks.' He bade me a warm yet polite goodbye and the car sped away.

'What on earth was that about?' I asked. 'Do you always treat each other like that?'

''He respects me for it,' Jacquie said coolly, not wanting to say more. 'We have an understanding.'

'An understanding? What kind of understanding?'

'You've got to let people know how you feel and what you think,' she explained. 'Otherwise they walk on you.'

At work the subtleties of office politics defeated me. My unhappiness there was beginning to show cracks in its wall and subsequently I was useless.

'Oh! You mean that they only served Moët at Timothy's wedding?'

snooted the company PA, in her à la mode earrings and her dressed-for-success skin-tight kit. I dreaded being in the sights of this ruthless vampire. My 'on-the-ball' face didn't work here at all and I hated myself for the way that trying to look engaged made me feel like a prostitute.

It was a world in which I could gradually hang myself with my own naivety. I remember almost floating down the stairs to the little film studio. The noise was getting on top of me and the film crew seemed to have stopped temporarily. It all seemed very strange. But that was in the early days, when if the diabetes got out of control I poured with sweat and shook like a bomber going down. I fumbled with the wrapper of a boiled sweet and drank Coke until finally my brain sat back down in its socket.

I decided, as I sucked back the sugar, that not only had I failed to master the diabetes but that – and at the time this seemed more serious to me than my health – the job was a blight. It did not occur to me then that happiness in work would influence my health. I actually expected to be unhappy at work. My upbringing was proof enough that anything to do with money usually caused misery.

I gave a week's notice, feeling as if I'd called time and jumped just before I'd been pushed.

It was late when I plodded over towards the City to my washing-up duties at the wine bar. It had been raining again and the little black cobbled streets shone in the street light. The place was three-quarters empty, with only the die-hards left to go. Xavier looked up with his beady eyes for almost a whole second and let out a foreign-sounding grunt. I nodded, almost honoured, then addressed my pile of pots and pans while the girls cleaned up the little kitchen and chattered.

Amanda had gone home before I tried to explain my jobless predicament but when I began I was interrupted by loud voices from the bar. We rushed over to find a tired stockbroker propped up in a chair, sweating and very pale. 'Eee sinks it's ees 'art,' Xavier flatly expliquéd.

Jacquie and I walked home in silence, just listening to each other's footsteps and looking at light reflecting over the river. We'd just taken the poor wretch with the ailing heart to a hospital somewhere nearby and since then I'd completely forgotten about being unemployed. It didn't really seem important any more.

'I'm sick of this misery,' Jacquie moaned eventually. 'What are we doing here? I'm sick of your job and our chemical toilet.' She laughed and shoved me sideways. 'Why don't we go to France together this time? You could find something to do. There's loads of work, I mean, you could run a bar,' she grinned, adding 'Xavier' by way of explanation.

I watched and listened while she reasoned the whole thing out. 'Instead of making cups of tea you can serve pastis!' Her brown eyes sparkled, scrunching in the corners. 'It's the same thing, only less humiliating.'

I stopped walking. 'It doesn't get you anywhere either.'

'It'll get you to France . . . with me.'

I kissed her. 'You created your restaurant in France, Jacq. It's not my life.'

She didn't seem to be listening but pulled away a little. 'Listen, I phoned the hospital. Someone explained a lot about diabetes. You told me it was fine, like you don't even have it. I haven't studied any of that since my training. But I know you're supposed to be careful, it can blind you or you can get gangrene. You haven't been straight with me.'

'I haven't bothered you with it, have I?'

'That's not the point,' she snapped. 'You don't bother with it yourself.'

'Is there any sugar in French wine?'

She rolled her eyes. 'Don't try to change the subject,' she added, fighting a smile. 'France might be good for you. And I won't have to wash backsides or do the tooth round.' She leaped up on a park bench and began a balancing act while I sat and grabbed one of her legs, relieved that she didn't go on about the diabetes, that the subject had changed.

'But I'm worried,' I began. 'Whatever will we do at the end of the season? We'd have nowhere to go.'

She stepped down and stared, tapping her foot, arms folded in a schoolgirlish way. 'Don't tell me you're planning your retirement already! Look, you've got to start going on your instincts.'

I felt inadequate, never having really trusted my instincts since they'd been mangled in the blender along with my parents' phobias. Jacquie was still enthusing. 'Well, what d'you think?' From her stage on the bench she pushed down on my shoulders. 'Think our old green car will make it to France?' Her long blonde hair made a tunnel between our faces and then she suddenly became serious, and with a wry smile, stepped down and began to flap her arms and hop in the cold. 'Rupe, I've forgotten to tell you something that I've done for the wine bar.'

'What? Why are you smiling?'

'There are more than two hundred pies in the kitchen.' She laughed, skipping further up the street. 'They're on our bed too. There wasn't enough space.'

I took a big icy breath through my teeth and focused on a light on the river far, far away. 'How many? How could you possibly have found the time to do that?' I spoke softly. 'And where are we going to sleep?'

But she was still there, up the street, hopping and flapping her arms. 'What about France?' she insisted. I had a feeling, nothing logical for once. It just had to be an instinctive decision, like walking out of my job just now. I wondered if she'd realized that I'd been listening to her every word.

4 *For Harold*

Seagulls saw us off, flinging themselves out of the sky, swooping above the wake, smooth and silent as we watched Dame Vera's white cliffs shrink under a dull sky. It was 12 March, and would have been Gareth's twenty-fifth birthday.

Uprooting was always slightly painful for me. This time I felt numb and was later unable to recollect much about it beyond feeling an odd weight on my chest and a sense of loss. Yet in truth the only thing I wanted was sitting right beside me. 'You like to stay put,' Jacquie smiled, seeing under my skin with annoying ease.

'I react differently to change from you, that's all,' I said, avoiding telling her that I was anxious. We had very little money and I didn't trust our battered car. We'd bought it for £100 from a lugworm digger.

'You're afraid,' she jabbed at me.

'I know what can happen.'

''You'll change.' She shrugged. 'Things will force you to fight back. I *had* to. Nothing comes unless you fight for it.'

Along with the money from the sale of the pies to the wine bar and our cooking and washing-up endeavours, after all bills had been paid, we'd managed to raise £250. We should have waited until April perhaps, before departing. There'd be no work in south-western France's Roussillon area in March but we'd been far too excited and unemployed to stay in London and find more money for rent.

Down in the hold I was ripping a piece of astro turf from under the gas pedal. I'd pinched it from the porch film shoot and used it to refit the floors of the car. I'd even done the boot. I reckoned our outward appearance leaned towards a Bonnie and Clyde image: we were rugged, exciting. I settled back in the seat, gripping the racing steering-wheel cover, held in place with knotted plastic string, while Jacquie climbed on to the pile of clothes massed on her seat before we drove off the boat.

There is something wonderful about stepping on the gas and leaving it all behind. For some it's impossible to kick the habit. For others, walking away loses its thrill as age and responsibility shrink the escape routes into passages into which one can no longer squeeze without pain.

The grounding factor for me is, and has always been, love. I would happily stay in one place forever if that's what it takes, so long as my faith remains. At twenty-two I was oddly aware that those who can't kick the habit often end up simply leaping through rough seas from one cluttered cage, only to find themselves trapped in another. To me, that seemed the most dreadful prison of all. That day, young and with incorruptible faith in each other, and the sea before us smooth as glass, there was not a cage or a ripple in sight.

Driving out into the light was confusing. I had the odd feeling that I'd driven through French Customs unnoticed. I was anxious. I had no idea if the car was even roadworthy, let alone insured.

'You're biting the inside of your mouth,' she said, once again reading me like a book.

Bordeaux loomed ahead in the darkness and further along on the coast campsite gates opened into a vast area where great trees whistled in a fierce wind, hiding a velvet starlit sky. Sleep came after we'd sat up, wrapped in our jumble-sale belongings, listening through the howling to the crisp voices of the BBC World Service.

We spent a couple of days wandering through the long grass in the sand dunes and idling under pale skies. I began to relax and, having stolen away from work, I suppressed odd feelings of guilt. Though it was cold lying in our tent and the skies were clouded, a childhood memory of summer holidays gripped me, reaching out from when we were together, my elder brothers and I.

I found myself reliving the sounds of squelching gumboots, and floats clicking against fishing rods over little shoulders. Following the older ones back to that childhood house through the long grass on the roadside with the green and the air melting together in the rising summer heat. Three boys in the Sussex countryside; there'd be food on the table, there always was. She did well, our mother, though she never had that much to manage on. The two older boys would gut the trout, looking to see if it had eaten anything unusual, then they'd spray river mud off each other with the hose, standing next to the dovecote where Harold, the old black lab, used to sleep before he went away.

Harold and my father had things in common. They both *had* to go.

I'd searched the cottage from top to bottom but Harold had eaten my hamster, which had lived in the stuffing of the sofa for ages. I'd seen the tail disappear down Harold's great throat and my heart briefly broke. I'd thought perhaps that the hamster was the reason why Harold had been ousted. No use asking my brothers. They only ever talked to each other and besides, at two huge years older, they were already rotten, I thought.

With Dad it was another story. A story that they were capable of comprehending and I was not. Like Harold, Dad too had gone. My search this time had been far more dramatic. I'd even said prayers or at least our mother had encouraged me to say them. But he didn't return. Perhaps that's why the prayers hadn't worked, because they weren't my idea, though my heart went with them each time. Anyway, it didn't matter, because nothing stopped Mum from crying, and me therefore being led to believe that old Dad was all bad.

Some time after he had gone I used to watch this programme on our new, old black-and-white television in the days when I'd started school. Following each near-disaster the lost American space family would switch the ship's switches and turn all the knobs to AUTO-PILOT and suddenly everyone could relax. It was all over. Amazing. Spreading my four-year-old arms wide, I'd close my eyes to slits and run, flying in the school's playing-field, down along by the big oak trees like a bomber through the valleys. Flipping all the switches to AUTO-PILOT, nothing could touch me, nothing, and it didn't matter if Harold never came home, never ever, even though I knew in my heart he was good.

A screen had come down, arresting my development. The child-hood cottage became my world, alone there, on the edge of the woods. The elder boys grew up almost abnormally fast, while I, too young to find my way, stayed back with Mother, protected and partly isolated by her inability to accept the breakdown of her marriage. For what seemed an eternity, I remained a child.

We'd left Bordeaux, setting off late, and now the Corbières mountains loomed in the distance. Great jagged rock shadows reached from the vineyards into the sky at staggering angles while the dawn slowly traded Bordeaux's green verges for the arid, red earthen, gorse-covered landscape of the south.

As we entered the Roussillon the sun began to climb, eventually giving us our first view of the Mediterranean. A cluster of flamingos picked around, wading in a huge, shallow estuary. They lifted off over rows of oyster beds, barely visible through the sun's reflection on the water. We stopped for a moment, opening the car door and breathing cool air, heavy with the smell of dew and sun after rain. I saw that Jacquie was sweating and beginning to cough.

'You're overheating.' I said, stroking her face. 'I've got to get you to a proper bed.'

'It's freezing in here.' Jacquie turned the heat up to full blast, her pale skin beading with sweat. 'Did you see the flamingos?' she asked, making an effort to sit up. I nodded. A bumblebee floated past. 'It's like coming into paradise,' Jacquie sighed.

5 Meeting Mr Merlin

We were next to the foothills, the fingertips of the Pyrenees. One could see where they turned to jagged rock, tearing down from the hillsides, crashing over the beaches, away into the dark blue water. Perpignan was quiet, the sun bright yet soft across virtually empty streets. As we carried on, seeing the palm trees gently fanning in the warmth brought a feeling of gentle awakening. After the flinty camp-site in Bordeaux, the sensations softened the town's rough edges.

A big old Peugeot estate spluttered next to us at the lights, the roof rack loaded with clothes in cheap chequered plastic hold-alls and old bicycles attached with bits of electric cable and string. Inside, the creased, dark-skinned father and huge family looked across at us.

'They're North Africans,' Jacquie explained, 'they'll take that car down to Algeciras and across to Morocco, then south. If it gets the whole way without being hijacked or breaking down they'll make a killing on it.'

We all seem to think of France as European, but you would hardly know it by wandering through the back streets of Perpignan where the North African influence is truly alive.

We headed out of town, south in the direction of the Spanish frontier, and eventually arrived at the campsite close to a village called Argelès. Behind a bamboo-flanked passage we drove between a dilapidated arrangement of old concrete and caravans, stopping beside a wooden shack.

Although the sun shone through the bluest sky, rain spat at us as we hauled ourselves out of the car. We stood, surrounded by hedges and peacocks, while stray animals began to appear from every gap along the bamboo.

Jacquie blasted her nose into a limp handkerchief as a thumping sound came from the wooden shack, followed by a ripping of fabric. Then there was a bigger thump and the door burst open. A man with one leg in plaster to the hip crutched his way over, a vast stomach flopping beneath his filthy vest. The strays fell upon him but he ignored them, his crutches wading through and landing dangerously close as they fought for position.

'*Bonjour*,' said Jacquie.

He stared vacantly while he reached into the pocket of his oily blue mechanic's trousers and scratched his balls and the cats caressed his plaster and single, high-laced combat boot.

'Monsieur Merlin?' Jacquie asked, doing the unfazed nurse bit. '*Nous sommes des amis de Michel*,' she continued. He put his hand in his other pocket and Jacquie sighed, expecting to be subjected to another scratching, but he spared us, pulling out keys, then silently turned and made his way across the site, his entourage in tow.

A tiny caravan was hidden in the bushes in the far corner. Although it lacked electricity among other things, it was far better than a tent. It faced an area where the peacocks congregated. A lizard, which had been sleeping on the ceiling, belted for cover as I poked my head in.

Jacquie sat down on the grass. 'I need sleep,' she mumbled. I ferried things from the car and tucked her up. 'I'll teach you French,' she said, 'and about the Catalans – from bed.' In a matter of moments she was asleep. Once peace had returned, the lizard made his way back into the middle of the ceiling, and as soon as I'd decided he wasn't poisonous, I went looking for aspirins and food, driving along a deserted street in the centre of Argelès Plage. Obviously nothing happened there in March. There were signs swinging in the wind under empty apartment blocks facing miles of sandy beaches scattered with gutted telephone kiosks. I found the only shop. Neither of the two people there spoke French and I, the only customer, couldn't understand a single word, nor identify half of the meat in the *boucherie*. There were impressive rabbits hanging from the ceiling and the odd hare next to the chickens, all of them strung up by their feet above round baskets of salted sardines which looked dry and inedible.

A young woman asked me something in a language that I presumed was Catalan. She was my age, tough and dark and with a shapely figure. She clasped a chopper and manipulated a pig's head with the other hand. '*Jambon*?' I tried. She merely slammed the chopper through the head, so I pointed instead. After some brains were slopped on to a plate and both sides of the halved head were placed so as to grin through the glass counter, she coolly cut me my ham. It was a dry reception, but no worse than it might have been in any hick town elsewhere.

A large woman behind the cash register sold me aspirins, her scarf cutting into the fat at the top of her throat. She made little effort to converse and, forgetting to apply my 'on-the-ball' face, I left feeling slightly foolish and drove through fierce wind and rain under a clear blue sky to the little caravan in the bamboo near the sea.

'Oh shit, it's going up.' Jacquie passed the thermometer in an effort to distract me as she pushed away her tray of food. I started to worry. We'd been there for five days.

'It's always at night, isn't it?' I whispered. 'That's when it gets worse, at about this time. It's too cold.' But she was almost asleep again.

Frequent electric storms lit up the gentle, vine-scattered slopes of the Albères foothills to the south-west. In those long evenings after dinner I'd wash up with the strays at the latrines, then settle down, blow out the candle, and watch the skies explode while the rain on the tin roof made comfort of the silence. I rested, quiet in the shadows, while she slept on, flushed, exhausted. In the early hours when she was restless we'd talk. 'Sometimes,' she said, 'I think I'm here for a reason, and then I look at my family, my brother, Stephen and his problems – and my mum. She's always tried so hard. I mean, it's not like I can ever do anything. There seems no point to any of it. And my sister, we're so different.'

Jacquie's sister Linda lived only a short distance from where we were, in a small flat with a local man, and would sometimes work at the restaurant. 'She's more like Mum than I am.' Jacquie sighed. 'I'm sort of on the sidelines.' She coughed and rolled over while I covered her up. In the shadows I could see and almost feel her smile as she joked, 'I'm the black sheep.'

It rained for more than three weeks, but after a few days I began to search for a doctor. Jacquie lay in the bed protesting, damp with sweat. The steady rain had left us with few clothes that weren't soaked. Our things hung from string across the sink or dripped around the tiny caravan, sagging along the curtain rails, dribbling down on to the floor. The nights became progressively harder. I'd hear her cough, her lungs rattling like the sound of the brakes on a steam train. Then she'd relax, her stomach muscles strained and sore. She hardly complained, but feeling her fragility in the darkness I became convinced she wasn't getting any better. This seemed to be the brink of pneumonia and I was afraid.

'You're thinking of your brother.' She spoke gently. 'You're worried. Look, it's not going to happen to me,' she spluttered, 'so stop it.'

'It's been almost two weeks, Jacq; you have to see someone. Forget the money. I'll call your sister.'

'Linda can't help. Anyway, I know what to do here just as well as she does.' Perhaps it was a big sister thing but for whatever reason Jacquie was adamant. She could handle it. 'Look, they're struggling as much as we are, Rupe,' she pleaded. 'I'm never ill and we can't affor—'

'You're going,' I snapped. 'Tomorrow. Then, if you won't ask your sister for help, maybe you can phone Jake about us moving into the restaurant a little earlier. At least it'll be dry there.'

'He'll get pissed off if we go too soon.' She coughed.

'But Jacq, you own half of it!'

'Only nearly a quarter: remember, I gave Caroline half of my part. And if Jake tells her we've been down here sponging off the place for ages, she'll just side with him.'

'But you gave her the shares! She's your friend. Honestly, just look at the state you're in. She'll understand.'

Jacquie pretended to ignore me. 'It's her German blood,' she said. 'She's quite tough about those things.'

'Shouldn't we ring Linda anyway, just to let her know we're here?'

'We'll ring her from the restaurant,' Jacquie agreed with a sigh. 'I know you're right about going there sooner.'

*

I found a Belgian doctor in a village nearby. The sign said 'Homeopath'. For a moment I thought we were to be confronted with some sort of loopy nature cure. In the street outside, the buildings were ancient, bowed and crumbling stone or harsh render. We sat in a cement waiting-room, surrounded by 1930s brown and yellow Spanish tiles, amongst a group of people with various sharp pins sticking out of their necks, ears and noses. Someone put a log into a small stove which had turned the whole ceiling brown and the walls yellow, giving the impression of a mountain hut somewhere in Peru.

The doc appeared, wearing a comfortable old sweater, and ushered us into a very modern, white, warm consultation room where we were seated on comfy chairs before a huge desk. Many questions later he examined Jacquie, who was sitting in a slump. He spoke kindly, taking his time. He seemed young, but wasn't. Half an hour passed as he chatted. We were a good deal less damp and much warmer. He'd begun to write a long list on a prescription pad, then stopped, looked at us both through the upper part of his bifocals, and let out a slight sigh.

Seeing the warmth returning to Jacquie's face, I began to understand why he'd kept us so long. My own hands were burning with recovered circulation.

He rewrote a shorter list and told us where to find the pharmacy.

'Are you insured?' He seemed to already know the answer.

Back in the car I pleaded not guilty. 'But he wouldn't take the money.'

'Couldn't you have given him a tip?'

'A TIP! He's a doctor, not a bell-hop.'

'You were just too shy to talk money,' Jacquie spluttered. 'You sometimes have to be more aggressive with people, Rupe.'

We stayed in the caravan for a month while from bed she slowly introduced me to the customs and the language of our day-to-day needs. Her illness retreated but only over time. In order to keep Jacquie in bed I had been thrown in at the deep end, obliged to shop and feed us with little more than fast-food experience in both.

6 *The Old Mill*

The old car rumbled along the little tree-lined avenues, carrying us towards the restaurant, passing fields of sandy earth and lettuce. Eventually endless rows of fruit trees turned the roadsides pink and the ice-cream peak of the Canigou Mountain appeared, breaking through a distant haze as if it were afloat. I had my arm hanging out of the window in the cool morning air and felt the heat of the sun on my shoulder.

The road narrowed as we approached a thin railway bridge across which only one vehicle could pass at a time. This marked the boundary of the village of Una. On the other side an old pick-up approached, and its driver's intention to be the first through grew obvious. As if preparing to charge, his truck almost swaggered into the middle of the road.

'They always drive like that here,' Jacquie informed me casually. 'It's your right of way, so go faster,' she insisted. 'Go on. Put your foot down. Hurry.'

'But he'll kill us,' I said, watching the whiskery old farmer approaching. 'He thinks he's jousting!'

Jacquie grabbed at the wheel, thumping the horn, forcing the car to swerve as I struggled to correct it. We shot across the road, spraying gravel, then levelled off.

'WHAT ARE YOU DOING?' I shouted.

The truck driver shook his fist at me, yet he hadn't even arrived at the bridge.

'BASTARD!' Jacquie shrieked, leaning over in front of me, slamming her hand on the horn once again.

'GET OFF, FOR CHRISSAKE!' I yelled. 'WE'RE GOING OFF THE ROAD.'

33

The car's tail slid sideways, stopping us directly before the bridge and filling the inside with the stink of thick sand and lugworm dust from the floor. The old man honked, still shaking a bony fist as he passed.

'UP YOURS!' Jacquie screamed. '*SALAUD!*'

'GET OFF!' I pushed her. 'For fucksake, Jacquie, get OFF! What the hell was that for?' Irritated, she snapped back in her seat. 'What were you doing?' I glared, then shifted down and we set off.

A few seconds passed before Jacquie pointed to the village camp-site. 'They've got horses there,' she said, calm now. 'The riders come up to the restaurant sometimes.' There was a silence. 'You just can't let people walk over you, Rupe,' she told me flatly as her attention was drawn towards the restaurant emerging to the left. 'There it is. We're here.'

I had almost forgotten what the restaurant looked like. I was still rattled by the episode back at the bridge. We pulled up in front of its tall, steepled wrought-iron gates. A huge padlock and rusting chain entwined with creeper hung through the railings. Dry leaves banked high up against the front door of the building, the wind gently carrying them around the courtyard. Jacquie ran across the street to a neigh-bour to get the key while I wandered around looking up at the magnificent old mill, admiring the rough mortar and stone walls, beautifully cornered and arched with huge red clay bricks.

We carried our few things inside and set them down in the middle of the dining-room. The wooden ceiling, six yards above, echoed every sound as we crossed battered, fake Persian carpets laid over rough concrete floors. The crude lime and river-sand walls showed the haphazard boulders set inside them as if one was looking at giant slices of fruitcake. On the smooth cement floor at the base were grains of mortar that had come free over the long winter months.

A spiral staircase wound up from the hallway to a tiny landing and two doors. One led into an apartment for the owners and the other towards rooms for the staff. I carried the bags through the first to our room, then opened the big windows and storm doors, watching the sun stream through in great golden bars as it caught the dust in the air. That same smell of dust and hessian filled my head, reminding me of my romantic first time there the year before. Most of the furniture had come from an auction in Norfolk. An old upright piano stood against one wall, a dartboard on another; a *chaise longue* in green velvet and a variety of tables, all of different ages and styles, made the room complete. There were also books, of a jumble vintage, probably a lifetime's collection; a reflection of an English way of life from thirty years ago transported and locked away in this little village.

Light reflected on the ceiling, changing with the gentle breeze through the trees, all so wonderfully quiet. Someone spoke across a fence somewhere in the gardens below, while a swallow scratched and then swooped out from under the eaves, sending loose mortar tinkling against the faded blue shutters.

'Isn't it lovely?' shouted Jacquie, puffing up the stairs from the hallway and the telephone. 'Jake doesn't mind as long as we get it ready for the season. He'll be here in two weeks. There's a job maybe, but you'll have to talk to him.'

I smiled, bouncing on the mattress. I was amazed to find that after so many months unused and in darkness the fabric wasn't even damp. 'I'll bet you get the creeps staying here on your own.'

'I hardly ever do.' She shook her head. 'I don't even like the dark. It squeaks.' She motioned to the bed.

'And how did you find that out? Anyway,' I said, 'I don't care how. I was lucky to find you. I don't mind sharing with the past. It's now that counts.'

'My father found you for me,' she said, kissing me. I said we'd found one another, but she shook her head. 'He did, Rupe, I'm sure of it. He found you because you were as alone as I was.'

We had a late lunch, sitting on huge logs in the courtyard. More birds clattered from under the old roof and the occasional tractor or car passing would slow down as drivers peered to see who was parked in front of the old mill. A woman appeared through the gap, stopping immediately inside.

'Gisèle,' said Jacquie cheerfully. '*Entrez.*'

But Gisèle stood her ground. This watchdog neighbour from across the street was in her late forties, stooped and greying, showing the effects of the sun and years of earthy struggle on her prematurely wrinkled everything. 'You've taken a lemon,' she accused in a heavy, tongue-rolling, scowling Catalan accent, holding her chin high. She had been asked to keep an eye on the place and hold a spare set of keys in case of emergency. 'A lemon's gone,' she huffed. 'There were five.' She nodded at the small lemon tree in the corner of the court-yard. I could barely understand Jacquie's answer but I got the impression that it was some remark about having gin and tonics.

Gisèle looked up, like someone might shortly after being coshed. 'Is that your fiancé?' she asked, dropping the previous conversation like a red-hot dinner plate and putting her hands in her pockets. She leaned forward for a second, squinting as she inspected me. 'I saw your sister yesterday,' she continued. Linda had come down to the restaurant for a season a few years before. She'd never really returned to England for much more than a visit. To Gisèle's horror Linda lived in sin in the neighbouring village. Linda cleaned and her boyfriend Frank ran a swimming-pool business. 'You know,' said Gisèle, tapping her foot with a look of intense enjoyment and disapproval, 'she's still living with *that* man.'

To the fascination of the whole village, Jacquie and Caroline had participated in most of the mill's heavy restoration work, spending weeks chiselling away at the stuccoed walls on the local builder's scaffold while his workers sand-blasted whatever the two couldn't remove, leaving only the original stonework. The village men, being predominantly chauvinist, spoke of them in a friendly but derogatory way, suggesting that the girls might be lesbians. Women in this part of the world didn't behave like brickies. Up at the café there had to be some other reason for the girls' determination and individuality. *Why weren't these pretty women chained to a bloody stove somewhere, for goodness' sake? What's wrong with the world?*

But this was not really France. This was French Catalan country, where values hadn't changed since Napoleon and the village was still trying hopelessly to prevent itself from falling into a coma. All things con-sidered, as the girls were young and attractive, if nothing else, the idea that they were lesbians probably kept any belligerent local wives at bay.

*

The following day a gleaming white Alpha Romeo growled up to the forecourt, stopping near the gates. Linda stepped out, blonde, petite and incredibly neat, followed by Frank. Behind, across the street, Gisèle stared motionless through the upstairs blinds, frozen, her scarved silhouette black as the Grim Reaper himself.

'Frank,' said Frank flatly, reaching forward with a home-tattooed arm, almost crunching my fingers to dust.

Champion of French kick-boxing from Perpignan to Marseilles, Frank had a particular way about him. He was brown and gypsy-Latin, mid-thirties, flicking his filterless Gauloises in the rose bushes. His flares barked 'Saturday Night Fever' while he coolly eyed the court-yard. I noticed a small scar on one side of his face.

Linda was tiny in comparison, slender, evidently running harder on her nerves than Jacquie. She still had a Norfolk accent, whereas Jacquie's was virtually undetectable. Linda struck me as sharing her sister's conventional and immensely practical streak, but little else in the outward sense. They had a drink, but didn't stay long. Frank had things he had to do. We arranged a lunch. There were kind words from Linda and then the Alpha chewed into the street and they were gone.

The days passed slowly. We'd wake to the sun and the birds singing through the open windows, then toast a stale baguette and sip coffee sitting up in the ancient bed. 'I love the mornings like this.' Jacquie creased her face in a yawn as I rose and began putting on my clothes.

'What's this?' I asked, pointing at a tall wooden box behind the bedroom door.

'It's a giant bottle of champagne,' said Jacquie, 'for when the restaurant goes into profit. Jake bought it.'

'Is that going to happen soon? I mean, you're the one that does the books. How much of the loans is left to pay off?'

'Jake arranged it. I don't know, Rupe, we owe a lot.'

'Who's we?' I asked, tying my shoelace. 'And are your shares written down anywhere?'

'Jake always took care of that.' Showing signs of irritation, Jacquie slipped out of bed, threw on a dressing-gown and sat back down to brush her hair.

'I think I understand,' I said, treading carefully. 'So I guess you can sell those shares if things get nasty and you want out?'

She looked at me, shrugging. 'Things won't get nasty. Anyway, how can you sell shares that aren't worth anything? That's what Jake told me. We'll have to wait until the restaurant goes into profit, that's all.' She spoke in a hopeful tone, yet her frustration was obvious. 'We need time,' she said, 'to make it a success.'

I wasn't easily convinced. After all, the restaurant had been going for some years by then. There was a silence which seemed to grow hostile. 'You really believe that?' I asked. Outside, I heard the sound of next door's chickens and chuckling water as suddenly, set free somewhere, it travelled along the gullies, searching for a garden to feed.

'Jake wouldn't lie to me.'

'He wouldn't necessarily tell you when you can cash in your shares either.' I tapped the bedstead uneasily, wishing we hadn't got into this, aware that it wasn't my affair.

After the death of her father, Jacquie, aged nineteen, temporarily abandoned her nursing studies before her exams, left Norfolk and got herself on a train to Paris. She had only one phone number, given to her by a friend, to be used if she was in trouble. Wearing a pink jumpsuit, she arrived in one of the roughest areas of the city. She had £100 to her name and did her best to find the cheapest accommodation she could. People were sleeping and pissing in the corridors, she told me. She was afraid and lonely. Isolation has a way of wearing one down and Jacquie, especially fragile at that stage, needed people. Eventually, as her fears grew she dialled the number. The voice on the other end was Jake's.

'Look,' said Jacquie defensively, 'Jake taught me everything, how to dress and how to sit up and hold my knife and bloody fork. He saved me from misery.' There was another silence while Jacquie simmered down. Jake had helped her, found her work and to some extent focused her and taught her how to use her strengths and, alongside her mother, had encouraged Jacquie to complete her nursing training. 'It's a business agreement and I don't want to see it fail,' said Jacquie tensely.

'All right, all right. So it's business.' I shrugged uncomfortably, aware that she was still irritated.

'Oh, you'll never understand,' she snapped, then went over to the window and I followed, still listening. 'It's like a gentleman's agreement,' she added, again looking away from me.

'But I *do* understand,' I said, attempting to show compassion, 'you were lovers. There's nothing wrong with . . .'

Jacquie turned and slapped my face hard. 'DON'T YOU EVER SAY THAT!' she shouted.

I reeled a little, shocked by her ferocity, my face stinging. 'SAY WHAT?' But as things sank in and anger took over, I headed for the door, humiliated.

'Oh, no. Don't go,' she began, 'I'm sorry. Look, I'm sorry. It's just that we weren't. It never was like that. Never. I don't want you to ever think that.'

'So you slap me? Jacquie, what the hell is your problem? Who cares what happened before?'

Accompanied by his beautiful girlfriend Simone, Jake strode up through Perpignan airport Arrivals and shook my hand warmly. 'How are you, Rupert? That bloody woman behaving herself?' he said, hugging Jacquie.

We headed back to the restaurant and gave the two of them a simple dinner, which Jacquie had cleverly devised from the last remains of our supplies.

'It's not bad for three francs.' Jake looked at the bottle of wine with the stars on its shoulders. 'When I think that yesterday I was drinking a bottle that cost a hundred and it wasn't any better,' he mused. Later Simone went to unpack and I slept, leaving Jacquie and Jake to discuss the coming season.

In the morning Jake had risen early. There were fresh croissants on the breakfast table, sitting still warm in a bag from the same *boulangerie* that had accepted almost all of our last loose centimes. Croissants had been a luxury for some time. I gave a sigh of relief. Jake had arrived just in time and his kindness would not be forgotten: Jacquie and I had four francs left.

Caroline was due to arrive any day now and we'd have a week or less to prepare before the restaurant opened.

That evening we had a barbecue beside what had been a hole in the garden behind the restaurant. The hole was once intended to be a small swimming-pool. Among others, Jacquie's younger brother, Stephen, had been given the task of digging it on a summer working visit. Sadly, with his psychiatric problems still unrecognized, Stephen had gone home after a quarrel. The project had been abandoned for almost two years and since my arrival, I'd transformed the hole into a fishpond.

'Y'know,' I said as I took out a phial and syringe from the fridge, 'we should give him a chance to try it again. Maybe he was just too young.'

Jacquie looked up as she carried a salad across the narrow kitchen, putting the bowl down and pouring dressing in. 'You don't know, Rupo. Stephen doesn't do a thing that he doesn't want to. I mean, he's eighteen and still Mum brings him tea in bed.'

Stephen had suffered greatly, ironically because his behaviour bordered on normality. Living on the edge without drugs or psychiatric help, he was somehow managing to get along, but it was their mother, Barbara, who took the brunt. It was she who made it seem to work, who encouraged and must have prayed, unable fully to comprehend the problems that Stephen faced. He was taken as delinquent, unmotivated, sullen, yet it was clear that in many ways he was clever enough. 'He's just lazy,' Jacquie told me with anger in her voice. 'He gives up on everything. It's pure selfishness. He doesn't give a shit about Mum.'

The hard labels flew around and stuck to Stephen's name. Sadly, most of us were too blind to think and look at the way he really was. Only their mother, perhaps, had a notion of how things were or could be different.

Both types of insulin were now in my hand. I'd had an aperitif and it had gone straight to my head. The cloudy one last, I told myself, pushing the syringe into the clearer, faster solution, then blindly pulling back the wrong dose. I checked it by drawing up the rest of the dose from the cloudy bottle to the correct number on the syringe, which in turn made the mixture utterly incorrect, then pushed the needle under my skin.

Jacquie flew about with her usual sparkle. If the occasion was a dinner or a party, her behaviour was infectious, charming, somehow more alive than the event itself. The barbecue took its time and half an hour later we still hadn't eaten. By this time the alcohol in the virtually sugarless red wine had blocked any reserve sugar from being released from my liver and I had forgotten the need to eat. It also obscured the warning signs from others and myself. I'd nibbled on some bread but it was no match for what was coming. I seemed, and was, drunk and sleepy. The huge amount of rapid insulin I'd mistakenly taken was by this time in the faster stages of its time release and looking for the food that wasn't there as it steered me towards being eaten from the inside out.

Melancholic, my brain progressively starving of its fuel, I kissed Jacquie on the stairs.

'You going to bed, Rupe?' she asked. 'I won't stay late. I'll be up.'

'Okay, sure,' I told her. 'I'm smashed. I just can't stay up any more.' I turned, climbing the big sweeping spiral stairs. 'G'night, darling,' I mumbled as she headed back to join the others.

Above in the shadows I thought for a moment that I saw my brother. 'Gareth?' I mouthed his name. A ghost? I wondered. No; a memory. Tears filled my eyes and I sighed, over-emotional, as my brain jumbled its interpretations. 'You're drunk, an' he's dead,' I told myself. Then I fell into a heavy sleep, clothed, crashing into the pillows like a bomber thundering and smashing through a forest.

First there was pain in my arm, then voices. I recognized no one, saw nothing. I was aware of being dragged from a cosy, warm, soft-lit passageway. I didn't want to go. There was blood in my mouth and when the shot they'd given me had worked, it occurred to me that Jacquie was sitting beside me. The windows were open and outside it was dark, perhaps in the early hours.

Jake had gone to the doctor for help and shortly Simone arrived with cheese on toast and honey. 'Eat it, Rupe,' said Jacquie, 'the injection releases the sugar from your liver. You need to replace it.'

The bread got stuck in my tongue while dizziness left me in the quiet. Jacquie held my hand, unaware that she still clasped the syringe that had revived me, tears streaming down her cheeks. 'I couldn't stop it, Rupe,' she cried, 'Jake had to hold you down. You've bitten through your tongue,' she added.

I wanted to speak but I felt awash with confusion. There was blood on my toast.

It was my first encounter with the hideous side of diabetes. It had been diagnosed six months after Gareth died. Now I was in my second year of managing it. Overwhelmed by stupidity and lack of respect for my brother's parting gift, I wept with shame. 'Is he okay?' I heard Jake's voice. 'I had to climb the doctor's bloody fence and the fucking dog attacked me.'

The following afternoon, with the summer on its way, we lay on the beach.

'God,' I groaned, 'I feel like an old man.'

'Serves you right.' Jacquie kissed me. 'It's a first, Rupe, don't worry. Perhaps you'll be more careful now.'

'If I had that problem,' Jake slapped his knees, 'you can bet I'd have every machine to do the tests and every doctor on the phone until I got it right.'

'Mmmm.' I nodded sheepishly. By this stage my tongue had swollen to vast dimensions. The sunlight hurt. I thought I might die, not from the effects of the insulin reaction but from being the ass that had provoked it.

'Oh, listen to you, you're all talk.' Simone laughed. 'You'd never pay a doctor.'

Jake hesitated. 'Yeah,' he grinned, 'and you can be sure that from my deathbed I'll be haggling with the bastard for a reduction.'

Caroline arrived at the restaurant in a rusting blue Renault. 'Hello, darlin',' she said, as she unloaded her things, embraced Jacquie and kissed my cheek. She and Jacquie seemed similar in many ways although there was an underlying friction in their relationship that seemed to revolve around Jake and the running of the restaurant. Gisèle appeared, making her way across the street, glancing up at the adjacent shutters like a cautious stoat, lest she be seen by her neighbours to be chatting with *les anglais*.

Frank and Linda arrived a little later on. Linda was obviously pleased to see Caroline. Seeing the two chatting, I imagined a winter without speaking English and instantly felt I understood Linda a little better. Again, she and Caroline seemed to display their Norfolk background in a way that Jacquie had somehow become detached from. Jacquie and I stood apart, strangely alone.

Frank looked me up and down as if I was a piece of meat, then eventually nodded to Linda. 'Frank says he's got some work for you, building swimming-pools maybe,' she said with a cautious smile, 'after the summer.' I thanked him as best I could but the exchange was brief. Frank didn't waste words.

The first of the tourists wandered into the restaurant and the summer began.

In the mornings I peeled potatoes and cleaned what seemed like thousands of mussels. In the afternoons, following the lunchtime service, we went to the coast and put printed restaurant fliers on the foreign cars now crammed beside the beaches.

The empty winter flats overlooking the sea at Argelès had filled this last month, their balconies now bulging with towels, lilos, flabby thighs and budgerigars. The dusty roads were no longer quiet and crowds of people buzzed about. We attracted a good many English to the mill, and even my family descended. I recall my half-brother and sister, who were children then, running on the beaches and sitting in the cool of the restaurant as my father snapped photographs and shone with admiration for Jacquie.

Through all of this Jacquie and I were inseparable, both driven by a feeling that fate had willed us together. 'It's meant to be,' said Jacquie, as I rubbed her shoulders between a ferry-load of dirty plates. 'I know it, Rupe, you've made me so happy.'

The restaurant spun along, infested with hyperactive squeals from cola-addicted children as they crawled over their bewildered, brain-dead parents, like wasps on crushed peaches. In the mornings Caroline would be up at seven, sometimes earlier. With tremendous discipline, she'd be out for a walk, get the bread, and then start cleaning, both inside and out. We would descend to find the chairs on the tables and Caroline scribbling at a list, the whole scene bleached in magnificent morning sunlight, the doors open and a gentle breeze floating in, carrying a hint of roses from the courtyard.

With a cup of coffee, Jacquie would attack the books.

The atmosphere between the girls was often cool. Quietly, I'd ask Jacquie why they couldn't try to be nicer to one another. 'The thing about Jacquie is,' said Caroline dryly, 'she could jack this place in tomorrow, and within two months she'd have another one going in the bloody Bahamas.' She took her list and went into the kitchen.

It was a trait that Jacquie admitted to, in jest perhaps, but anyone who really knew her could discern the sting of truth. 'She's jealous,' said Jacquie, hardly looking up. 'Just don't get involved.'

'You know,' I went on, trying to switch track, 'this summer will be over before we know it. If we want to stay we'll have to think of something.'

'We'll be all right,' said Jacquie, looking back towards the kitchen almost uncomfortably. 'We're together, aren't we? That's all we need.'

7 Jezebel's Lions

During our first year together, in our time on the houseboat, Jacquie had introduced me to a woman called Jezebel, an odd Turkish psychic who read the leaves.

I'd contemplated finding a psychic who might be able to give me news of Gareth. One of the reasons I didn't was because Gareth used to say that if any of us brought anyone into the house who fooled around with tarot or Ouija boards or any of that stuff he'd throw them into the street. Perhaps some tactless would-be clairvoyant had informed him that he'd never make twenty-four.

While I have no doubt clairvoyants like Jezebel can see things, I do not believe that this information is necessarily heaven-sent. Like buying hotdogs from a street vendor: most of the time you don't know where the stuff comes from or what poisonous things it contains. Some of us, it seems, are more open to the supernatural than others. Jacquie, for example, was like a blank page. At the receptive age of twelve or thirteen, after experimenting among friends with the Ouija board Jacquie became infatuated with the game. Her parents quickly put an end to this after repeatedly finding her downstairs alone in the early hours playing endless word-games with the dead.

Jacquie's mother, Barbara, initially discovered Jezebel and had gone to her for answers after the death of Jacquie's father. A friendship had developed and Jezebel was visited infrequently. I remember my regret as I walked from Jezebel's London council house living-room, after a terrifying crystal clear dive into the past, that I had allowed someone to pry into our future, leaving us with her blinding influence.

'You'll live in Spain. There's a house, with pillars,' she said. Wrapping her white shawl around herself, Jezebel looked at the soggy grains in my coffee cup and spoke kindly, deep in thought as she ran them around, letting them find their own place to settle. 'You,' she said, looking into the cup, 'you are going to do beautiful things.'

I wasn't sure if I was buying it all but her unsettling remarks about my turbulent childhood had me thinking of my elder siblings. We were an unusual lot, we three brothers.

Gareth was the eldest and toughest. He was tall, good-looking, amusing and unavailable. He'd been known, later on, to drive girls wild with a stubborn, granite silence. In his teens Gareth had taught himself to sew on an old machine, making skin-tight jeans and bits and pieces to go with his accent, the urban camouflage that stops you from being a target. The working-class voice stuck to us all like a South London postage stamp. With Gareth it was different because the voice was his own, no divisions, no vocal cultural shift once home and away from the kids in the playground. Gareth was the pathfinder and this rough accent was a part of what he was trying to be. So dyslexic he could hardly write, he had an extraordinary respect for anyone that achieved anything, or was trying, though he was utterly intolerant of those he considered to be fools.

The charming side of Gareth's character made for fabulous scholastic achievements. Like when my father discovered that Gareth had somehow managed to convert almost all his lessons at school into continuous periods of art. This comedy aside, he was an ordinary lad, nothing more than that. The fact that he had so many friends was enough. His teachers liked him and drank with him. They came to his funeral.

Gareth's words of love and encouragement still creep up on me in the strangest circumstances. In moments when one accidentally stumbles in thought, I find him there.

With no father about and a mother suffering in her own way, Gareth had been obliged to learn quickly from his own experience. You could feel safe with Gareth. On rare occasions when we were a little older, and drunk, he'd tell us brothers he loved us, and Brock, a year younger, would tease him mercilessly as only brothers so close in age could. The two of them seemed, in the light of our childhood struggles, to be one.

Brock, the clever one, was far more secret and self-disciplined. As children growing up in the countryside, we all had the chance to open life's doors at the same bumbling rate, but as we grew, it occurred to me that someone had woken Brock up early and quietly slipped him the instructions.

'Jacquie and Rupert,' Jezebel announced. Writing our names on a little piece of scrap paper, then placing it between the pages of an enormous Bible, she informed us that coming to our aid was a sacrifice: it was going to make her very ill. It turned out that all the males in my family were cursed years ago and for an unknown reason. However, Jezebel remained superficially benign. 'As long as you stay together, you'll be safe,' she assured, with a smile that promised purity with only a hint of menace from almost thyroidal eyes. *'As long as you stay together'* – unforgettable words.

I left, my young mind smouldering, frightened, as if scars that were still too raw to contend with had been opened. I had a sense of violation, dimly identified with those early years somehow choking at the back of my throat. Childhood had been awkward, even distressing. With Gareth gone, I was forced to turn back in time if I wished to find him, and that, I felt angrily, had to be of my choice alone.

I'd asked Jezebel if Jacquie and I would grow old together. She took a peek at my palms and replied with a cheerful smile, 'You're going to live for a long time,' then, throwing in the diabetic disclaimer, she added, 'as long as you take care of yourself.' She pointed out that there was something else wrong with me. With or without diabetes I was privately a very nervous individual. 'What is this? It's like you're so strung up inside it's terrible. How can you live like this?' she asked, her face contorted.

Jacquie howled with laughter. 'There,' she said brightly, thankfully believing none of this. 'You're a nervous wreck – but you'll live forever.'

'What about Jacquie?' I asked.

Jezebel kept smiling as I looked at her intently. 'Come on, Rupe,' Jacquie told me. 'You shouldn't ask that.' Jezebel was holding the thin coffee cup, the grains still peppered around the inside. Now she turned it in her hand as she searched her thoughts for the correct response. Her eyes didn't stay on me; they looked away. 'You are lions,' she said, 'run and play while you are young.' I often wondered what awaited Jezebel's 'lions' when our youth came to an end.

'I've got an idea,' announced Jacquie, as we ate croissants and drank coffee in the restaurant courtyard. She watched as I took a shot of insulin. 'Let's work with English diabetics.'

'What, start a cripple club?'

'No. Holidays,' she continued, 'all the latest testing gear, and good food. You're not a cripple, are you? And I'm the nurse.'

I thought about the complications, which seemed endless. 'We'd have to raise some money. I could write to the bank and maybe some drug companies. It's going to be bloody hard.' This was an insane understatement, though the idea was to be the most exciting that Jacquie and I would probably ever have.

Diabetics are pinned down in subtle ways – it's much more than the inconvenience of injecting insulin and the fear of what can happen if you don't. While looking, feeling and behaving in a perfectly normal way, they carry around with them an invisible agenda of time-related restrictions. The idea of holidays planned around people who truly want to embrace physical challenges under sensible supervision, who wouldn't have to feel awkward or embarrassed about syringes and insulin in the fridge, who could share experiences, even screw up, all with a trained nurse in unobtrusive attendance seemed brilliant. The guests could then get on with enjoying the usual South of France pleasures like anyone else and we could provide things for them to do that would challenge their view of diabetes, that would prove to them that they literally could be and do anything.

There were roses everywhere in that courtyard, the smell of promise. 'You can do it, Rupe,' Jacquie beamed. 'I know we'll be okay. We're here together for a reason. Seriously, Rupo,' she hugged me, 'let's try.'

I bought some paper, did naive sums and began a campaign, starting with a letter to the bank; then letters to any businesses that I thought might help. If they couldn't help financially, I asked that they write to my bank in a demonstration of faith. It amazes me still today how people would rather send a cheque than have to struggle with writing a letter. Two or three weeks later the postman delivered the first of the replies.

I was standing in the kitchen when Jacquie handed the letter across and looking at me apprehensively went to get us a drink. I remember the surfaces around me, all clean and the bright sun cutting through the home-made skylight with surgical clarity. I tore at the envelope, pulling out the single page, and struggled to read it fast enough.

She put her coffee on the table and leaned over the page. 'They've said YES,' she howled. 'Oh, God!' Bringing her hands to her cheeks, she made a face as if she'd just won a beauty contest. Her arms flew around my shoulders, crushing the letter. Laughing, we danced in a ridiculous circle and I ripped the backside of my trousers on the edge of the cooker.

'Jacq, wait a minute,' I said, 'it's just one answer.' Though it was clear to me, burning with excitement, that we were off the ground.

'I knew it would work,' said Jacquie, 'you're good luck. You make us lucky. Now d'you see?' She cheered. 'You've *got* to *go* for things. You just never know what life will do until you try.' She pulled at the rip in my trousers. 'So what are we going to do now? Start looking for a place?'

'Yeah,' I said, suddenly finding myself awkward. 'If we're going to do this, I mean, have our own place and all, then don't you think we should go all the way with it?'

'What d'you mean?' she asked, her expression a mix of seriousness and humour.

'I mean,' I rummaged in my mind, 'I think we'll want children one day and I just think that we haven't got any reason in the world not to.'

'Do what?' There was a silence while she looked at me, searching my face. 'Are you asking me to marry you?' It was a subject we'd talked about so many times before. We already knew that it was going to happen; it was only a question of time. 'Aren't you supposed to have a rose for me and be on one knee?'

I ran off to the courtyard and found one, then belted past Caroline and back in. 'You didn't give me a chance to get that far, Jacq, it's not fair, I wasn't . . . .'

She kissed me. 'I'll marry you whenever you want.' She smiled, putting her arms around me. 'I can't wait to tell Mum.'

8 *Vincent's Gift*

Beautiful golden evenings welcomed the end of the grape harvest, or *vendange*, as it's called. The tractors that filled the long avenues in the shade of the plane trees, towing overflowing trailers of green and black grapes, were becoming scarce. And in those last days of September, the light at its most magical made long shadows of the workers heading gradually north, following the ripening of the grapes in cooler regions.

With few tourists left, the restaurant was gently wound down, and in an attempt to increase our chances of finding work we'd begun French lessons with a retired children's teacher called Jacqueline. She had a boyfriend called Vincent who would sometimes be there when the lessons began or ended. He was a Catalan farmer, older than all the trees in his orchards and overflowing with wicked, gentle humour and charm. At seventy-five, Vincent was a man in love with most living things. He had lived in the area all his life and in the palm of his aged, earthy hands he now held an incredible network of helpful and influential friends.

'So you want to be a nurse here?' he asked, holding Jacquie's hand. 'You got papers?'

'Yes, but I don't know where to start.' She blushed slightly.

''Don't worry,' he smiled. 'I'll take you Monday. They know me there. It'll save you waiting the rest of your life.' He rose and kissed her warmly on both cheeks. 'You can be my niece.'

As promised earlier in the season, I was employed by Frank as a helper in his swimming-pool business. I was never really sure if he and Linda hadn't helped us out in order to keep us going. It had to be a kindness at that stage. I couldn't keep pace with him, nor did we even remotely understand each other's speech. Frank seemed to be in perfect shape but after two weeks of watching him work in a soup-thick cloud of resin vapour, I began to wonder why he wasn't dead. The walls of the pool closed in on us like oven doors. We worked like dogs, stopping only for the single event which all Frenchmen seem to take more seriously than death: lunch.

My first working lunchtime was spent in Frank and Linda's little flat. He sat at the table waiting for Linda to serve us. She spoke some impressive, sharp words in French, like the angry shouts of a wrestler before submission to a deaf opponent, then fed us, telling me not to worry. There were boxing medals and trophies along the walls. 'Champion boxe française', one read, and then a list of various gruelling encounters, newspaper cuttings and ribbons. Frank assured me that he had taught Linda the art of self-defence. It seemed obvious that she might be using it on him sooner than he expected. I was given a tour of the gun collection and an explanation of which tattoo meant what, while Linda tore into the washing-up like a shark.

In the meantime good fortune had paid a modest visit. We'd been given an old mobile home, a gift from friends at a defunct holiday company who kindly wished to help. 'We'll have to find somewhere to put it,' Jacquie announced, 'but it's ours. Our own place.'

Finally, no matter what, we'd have somewhere to stay when the restaurant closed and winter approached. It would be madness trying to live in that huge place during the winter. It would be impossible to heat and besides, Jacquie didn't think that Jake would appreciate it. I also believed that we should somehow be under our own steam and I felt that Jacquie wanted the same. Maybe old Vincent might find us a field to put the mobile in. It didn't matter to us where it ended up, or that there were whole windows missing from its wrecked frame, or even that nothing inside worked.

'I thought you'd need some company while I'm out nursing.' Jacquie was excited. 'Vincent's got me a job. I'm replacing the village nurse.' She reached into her bag and retrieved a tiny puppy. I looked at the dog, then at Jacquie's smile. 'Now,' she said delightedly, 'with the animal quarantine laws we'll *have* to stay in France. At least, until it gets old.'

'You mean until it dies,' I said, looking at the puppy and making a subtle point.

'Yeah.' She shrugged, unfazed.

Early the following morning she left me with the dog while she went out on her first round of French country nursing. The local nurse had hurt her back lifting an old man out of bed and needed time to recover. She suggested, however, that I went along that afternoon to see how and who to lift should the patients be too heavy for Jacquie alone. It was the first of many visits, where Jacquie's loathing of autumn and her horror of endings in general became strangely understandable to me.

That afternoon we cheerfully wandered up an alley, then across a vegetable garden and through a little wood before arriving at a tiny, tin-roofed bungalow. A woman answered the door, holding back a huge, frenzied Pyrenean mountain dog.

The living-room had a giant steel-framed hospital-type bed in it. An old television set crowded one side, leaving just enough space to get around the bed. '*Ça va, Papy?*' said the woman. 'I've brought you a little English girl. She's coming to look after you for a while.' An old man perched in the bed stared over, making no real move to speak or show emotion at all. Jacquie put her bag down and sat next to him.

'*BONJOUR,*' she smiled, all cheerful.

He stared at the bag, then fixed his gaze on Jacquie, blinking his wrinkled eyelids every so often, ever so slowly. His unbrushed grey-brown hair caught the sunlight coming through the net curtains, making him wither into a rough, straggly, unshaven face. There were deep lines in the face, as though he'd been laughing forever, only they didn't move now. The bed reeked of eau de cologne (often used by the local elderly in the prevention of bed sores) and stale sweat, which made me fight the need to retch.

'We're going to make you all handsome.' Jacquie helped him sit up and his eyes followed her as she went into the kitchen and fetched a bowl of warm water and a towel. She undressed him and cleaned him up, pulling the baggy clothes from his limbs as the unused muscles swung from his bones like empty hammocks. After putting him in comfortable pyjamas and a dressing-gown Jacquie asked me to lift him up. I bent over, sliding my arms under his knees and behind his back, then lifted. He put his arm around my shoulder and we stood there while she made the bed. I smiled and joked with him but he just stared, weightless, smelling of the old furniture in my grandfather's house.

We put him back in bed and shaved his incredibly tough beard.

'*MACARBUNDEAO!*' he shouted repeatedly in protest.

After brushing his hair Jacquie went and got a mirror. The man looked at himself. For a moment I thought he might smile but he lost it somewhere. He seemed to be waiting for something. His wife had died a year before, and shortly afterwards, in perfect health, he'd gone into the little room, climbed into his bed and taken his place in the queue, deliberately shutting down. He'd stopped almost all communication and let his body go to waste in the hope that eventually, if he was relentless, in a great quiet moment, he'd flutter out the window of his own living hell, like a sparrow.

His granddaughter arrived from school. 'Papy,' she cried, 'you look magnificent!' Wandering in, she ran her finger along the side rail of the bed and cheerfully sat close to the edge, holding his bony hand and chatting without looking up at his face, as if it wasn't necessary, as if they were both blind.

How hard for him, I thought, as his head gently turned and his eyes looked upon her, switching from a gaze to her hand on his. How tempting it must have been, to give up his place in the queue and reach over, embrace life, and stroke the beautiful face.

'God, he's desperate, Jacquie,' I said, as we left the house.

'Tomorrow,' she said, having switched off, far from the suffering, 'tomorrow we'll start looking for another place and I won't have to do this any more.' This was terminal care. I knew it would have a painful effect. Every day, like waking from an awful, recurring dream, Jacquie would now play a similar role to the one she'd taken with her father, Ernest.

Ernest had died from cancer at home. Worried and frightened, as a trainee nurse Jacquie had done all she could to make him comfortable. The district nurse would come round on her bike. There was morphine and there was pain; Ernest had pain, but what was conveyed to me by Jacquie was the underlying horror in which they all lived as she watched her dad slowly fade away. People forget; in that house there were five suffering and only one set free in the morphine. Jacquie's willingness to stay with him to the bitter end was mixed with confusion. Barbara quite understandably began to prepare herself. This was love in the extreme and Jacquie had perhaps failed to see what Barbara was doing in distancing herself.

So many misunderstandings, so many misplaced emotions: Jacquie knew, when Ernest finally lost his dignity, that this was the end. He looked at her and gently shook his head. Her love for him was to blind her to the enormous grief that her mother, sister and brother endured. Everyone has their own way of working these things through. Much later, when Jacquie returned from France to find the house had been cleared, she was outraged. She felt that her childhood had evaporated in the turn of a page and was still very angry with life itself. Ernest, who used to wander through the supermarket with Barbara in tow, sneaking all the wrong things into her and anyone else's trolley basket, was now gone forever. Jacquie had always been close to him and his death had left a void in her life. Intellectually very capable, she lacked the tolerance to handle living in Norfolk with her siblings and mother. There had to be something there over the rainbow.

While I spent the day with Linda's Frank and the glass fibres, Jacquie carried on, mostly with death. The region, like other southerly areas, was where many people hoped to spend the autumn of their lives. It is hardly surprising that Jacquie's feelings for this time of year were so bitterly obvious. Even so, love and the embers of summer made a perfect remedy for this awfulness and these short inter-missions in our time together seemed to have the effect of flinging us towards each other with equal passion.

We seemed oddly to be acting in our own side-show, bigger than life; a safe but bizarre dream, where, despite the approaching autumn gales, a warm sun and the thrill of change carried us forward blindly like bullets from a gun.

9 Sainte Marguerite

We could pull the mobile home up in front of the restaurant at the end of the season and I'd repair it as best I could. I was lucky; the last plumber to visit the restaurant had abandoned a tool kit. Late one warm afternoon Jacquie and I and the young mutt were going down to the sea for a swim.

'And don't forget the chicken legs for tonight,' Caroline reminded us as we left. Things were okay between the girls just now but it would be good if we remembered the chicken all the same. Reaching the coast, we ran out over the warm sand, throwing our towels into the air and crashing into the surf. Few people were left on the beaches in September, yet the water was the warmest and the weather the calmest of the whole summer. We floated about, watching an old man trying to pull up the sail on a huge windsurf. Exhausted, he eventually dragged the board up and sat on the beach nearby, chatting to us in an open, slightly bizarre way.

'Michael,' he introduced himself. 'I'm almost seventy years old,' he puffed, tapping the board. Then he patted his chest. 'I'm a White Russian.' His eyes seemed to twinkle above a wry smile. The tight, short curly hair on the very top of his head was indeed whiter than white. We talked about his home in the mountains about two hours away.

'The château is mostly derelict but we live in the farmhouse,' he told us. 'You must come and visit.' He smiled again, handing me a phone number written on a bus ticket. 'Call me. It's a wonderful place, truly wonderful.' He cheerfully made his way up the beach. 'Come and see us in the mountains,' he shouted back. 'You never know, my friends, perhaps we can help each other.'

We decided to spend an hour or so looking for a house in the small villages along the foothills and so said our goodbyes. Michael remained on the beach, snoring under his newspaper. We'd see him again and he'd help us. Call it what you like, fate, destiny. This accidental meeting must have been a special dispatch from heaven.

On the way to get the chicken legs we took the road running alongside the Pyrenees, heading away from the coast. We'd heard of a beautiful village tucked into the foothills somewhere in that direction and had hoped to look for a house there.

'You've overshot,' said Jacquie, 'why don't we go up there?' She pointed to a private-looking road some distance further on. 'It goes in the same direction. We're going to have to be quick or the shop'll shut.'

'I'd like to call the dog Kansas,' I said, imagining a country-style, master-and-dog walk somewhere as I followed her instructions. We chugged up the lane, which after a few hundred yards turned into a valley of its own. A municipal sign announced the community as 'Les Chartreuses'. There were a hundred or so select, clean, modern houses, perched on spots about the forest hillsides amid scattered cork-oak trees, which descended to a small riverbank in the near distance. After a fork in the road we entered a cul-de-sac.

'I doubt we'll make it at this rate,' I mumbled. This must have been a special day in life's great plan. Turning the car around and heading back, we found ourselves looking over to one side at a dilapidated medieval chapel.

'It's beautiful,' said Jacquie.

We left the car and wandered through the yellow grazing flowers in front of the building. A ten-foot-high thicket of brambles with branches as thick as rope kept us from looking too closely at the whole building.

'Can you imagine living here?' Jacquie scampered around, touching the rough masonry. 'Oh, Rupe! This has got to be it.'

A square-cut stone doorway led into the shell. Rock pillars held damaged arches, which in turn supported a crumbling, vaulted, rough stone ceiling.

Apart from the doorway and two holes in the walls there were virtually no openings. Light shone from one of the holes across the chapel to the battered round abside (the dome-shaped end of the chapel), which had lost its altar and become a part of the wine-making process at some stage. The walls, stained brown-purple from wine a hundred years past, had heavy iron rings protruding here and there. Dust floated through the rays, which, touching the stones, turned them golden-hot in the darkness. A curate's house stood joined to one side of the building. Above the door a marble plaque showed the date, 1724, when the curate's house had been added – at least 600 years after the construction of the chapel itself. Jacquie appeared through the big stone doorway. 'You think you can manage the work?'

'You mean "we",' I said.

'You're the expert.' She tried to look indifferent and averted her gaze. 'You're the man.'

'I've never really built anything in my life,' I blurted. 'Anyway, we don't even know if it's for sale. Jacquie, this isn't a fairy-tale, for goodness' sake. I mean, we'd have to actually rebuild it.' We went next door into the curate's house and climbed a rotting wooden ladder to the upstairs. There was a chair in front of metal barred openings and we sat for a moment, overlooking the valley. It was huge. It could take us forever, I felt. Some of the repairs looked over-whelming. I examined a row of flat, earthen tiles on a ledge. 'It really must be worth a fortune. We don't have anywhere near what it's going to be worth.'

Two older members of my family had recently offered to help us. They'd received my letters and had decided with great faith to give us a little money and offered to countersign in order to help us borrow the rest. It wasn't a huge amount, even then it was less than the price of a small car, but to Jacquie and me it was an absolute fortune.

'We'll miss the chicken!' she gasped, grabbing at her watch.

We followed the road up and around until we passed a little sales office in the middle of a cluster of modern rabbit-hutch-like apart-ments perched on the mountainside. 'Let's go and ask about it. Come on, Rupe, otherwise we might not get another chance.' The chicken nagging, we climbed out of the car and headed for the office.

After a hearty handshake and being ushered in by a man who, for some reason, reminded me of a stoat, I caught a glimpse of a giant swimming-pool and tidy tennis courts from the window. All this was neatly arranged in front of the partially sold litter of rabbit hutches and this alone convinced me that the price of the chapel would be ruinous. The cool but cheerful man sat before us nodding enthusiastically, as if encouraging us to speak.

'We've come to ask about the old chapel. You see,' said Jacquie, her automatic smile working wonderfully well, 'my husband is an historian.' Awkwardly I both grinned and frowned, then attempted a knowing nod as she went on. 'We want to restore it and bring young people to it.'

'It's not for sale,' the man said bluntly, gutted that we didn't want to buy a rabbit hutch. He seemed to re-evaluate his options, contemplating us as if at the same time he was shuffling cards. 'The man who owns it will be here in ten minutes,' he said. 'How much you got?'

Chatting about it in the chapel ruins, we'd optimistically given ourselves a year to fix the whole thing up and so had held £2,000 of our savings back for materials and living expenses. Youth and spirit seemed to tell us that it would all work out. The decision had more to do with faith in one another than practicality. 'You'll be all right,' Jezebel had said, 'as long as you stay together.'

We offered as much as we could and the man laughed. 'He'll never sell it for that. Anyway, you can wait and ask him yourselves.' He motioned to the door. 'Outside.'

'Historian, huh?' I smiled after he'd politely and coolly shut us out.

'Well, it sounded better. You've got to go on your instincts.'

The man he had spoken of was a property developer. This man didn't just own the chapel, he was the kingpin in the creation of the entire community of houses burrowed into the mountain around us.

We sat in the sun worrying about the chicken until a car pulled up and a well-dressed businessman in his late forties walked past us and into the place. Time passed uncomfortably while from outside we listened to the stoat, occasionally getting a glimpse of his flat expression through the adjacent window.

'If this goes on any longer we're sure to have missed the chicken and Caroline'll kill us, Rupe. There are a lot of people coming tonight.'

'For God's sake, how can you be worried about chicken? We'll plead; we'll bang on the butcher's door. I'll roast my bloody self.'

We were ushered in and I tried to look as much like an historian as I could. The developer conducted the meeting as if he had never spoken to his partner, obliging us to start from the beginning. He put his fingertips to his lips in a praying motion, watching us as we sat like coiled springs, throwing a mixture of naive dreams, transparent white lies, hope and money like breadcrumbs at his feet. He sat forward, making a note of our price, and then showed it to us to be sure. 'This isn't old francs you're talking about?' He stopped for a moment, looking at Jacquie. 'I mean, you've been nursing the old people here and they only think in old francs.'

'No,' Jacquie answered, 'that amount would be nothing in old francs.'

'It is nothing,' he agreed, commanding an awkward silence. 'But it's okay.' He smiled.

'You mean you'll . . .' Jacquie began.

'I mean,' he said, shrugging, enjoying every moment of our delight, 'we have a deal.'

He merely asked that before signing we waited until his *notaire* had studied the chapel's deeds to assure that it was in no way restricted or classified. I felt slightly nervous about this but kept quiet and we set a meeting for the following week to sign the promise. He put forth a positive handshake. 'My name is Boris,' he said, 'Boris Freshtin.'

We bumbled down the hill, past the ancient chapel with its red tile roofs and crumbling bell-tower. I hadn't noticed the huge oak tree in front until then. It was one of the biggest and oldest trees in the area.

'I can't believe it,' I said, stopping the car nearby. I grabbed Jacquie's hand to look at her watch.

'The shop's closed,' she said quietly, staring at the ruin, over-whelmed by what fate had thrown in our path. 'I feel sick.'

We never learned precisely why Boris sold us the chapel at such a fraction of its worth. But close to the truth is the fact that he had children our age and perhaps simply wanted to give us a break. There is no doubt in my mind that he was sick to death of those on the mountain who would have squabbled over it like dogs and then turned it into a mausoleum. There were also faint intentions to bulldoze it looming on the horizon. After all, it was sitting in a prime location.

We'd have to work like dogs to pay the money back and it was going to take forever, but it was a start, a wonderful beginning.

The last licks of amber sun had lifted from the sandy walls and the old building seemed to have faded into the shadows of a deep sleep.

PART TWO

10 *A Roof above the Forgotten*

With the season now over, Caroline had gone home to England and her family in King's Lynn. Jacquie didn't really say much after Caroline's departure, her thoughts strangely private. I felt the same sense of loss that I always did when change came around. There was a mix of pleasure and discomfort, like when I was little: the first days of wearing new family hand-downs.

Caroline and Jacquie's friendship would always suffer, it seemed, as long as the restaurant had them working, summer after summer, competing in what seemed like sibling rivalry over the running of the place. It dawned on me later that their relationship was perhaps more convoluted than, in my naivety, I had ever envisaged.

Jacquie climbed into our borrowed four-wheel drive. 'It's lunchtime,' she said. 'There'll be nobody on the roads. This is probably the best time to go.' I shunted into gear and pulled the huge, hideous old mobile home off the restaurant forecourt and down through the narrow part of the village. It had been sitting for a month while I'd repaired it. A few faces stared from the village bar, mouths opening as we steamed past.

'Slide your window open,' I said, 'and listen for that dodgy wheel.'

'Didn't you fix the extra bolt on?' I reminded her that it had snapped off when I tightened it but I'd got some washers for the other two off the wheelbarrow. I'm not sure how reassuring this was. The vineyards were empty now, turning red-brown, summer's green shifting to rust. We left a long tree-lined avenue, heading away from the coast and on towards the base of the foothills and the chapel.

There was a thump. Jacquie leaned out further. 'It's making a hell of a noise now. What happens if the wheel falls off?' We passed by well-kept houses, painted pink and cream, adorned with Spanish pottery, garden gnomes and subterranean sprinkler systems. I told her we'd drag it if we had to.

Near the chapel I backed into a space above a tiny brook, where cork-oak trees scattered themselves down to the foot of the rising forest on the other side. Climbing out, I felt soft rain. A small funnel of smoke made its way up into the cloudless sky from the bungalow 200 yards opposite and an odd feeling of calm settled about me.

Jacquie squeezed my arm. 'It's so lovely.' She looked around, then began a little hopping dance in front of the chapel. 'Well, we're here.' She gave me a preoccupied smile and wandered off to explore. I settled the feet of the mobile into place and caught up with her upstairs in the curate's house. 'We've got to call Lance,' she said. 'Post office closes at five.'

'Just a few more minutes, Jacq, and we'll go. You know, I think we should start on this house first.' I pushed on a tile that hung loose from the roof. It fell. Two others crashed on to the weak floor-boards. 'These beams are stuffed with worms. In fact,' I said grimly, pulling at another part of the ceiling, 'the whole roof is alive with them.' More loose tiles thundered through from above, leaving a huge hole.

She stared back. 'You're not going to tell me that the roof's dead? Oh, God. We're really going to need Lance now.'

The post office jutted out on a corner in the village, with cars pulling in all around it and people barging towards its counters in disorderly haste.

'The booth's over there,' the woman said icily.

'Struth,' I shouldered my way away from the counter, 'why're they all shoving in like that? Anybody'd think they were fighting for the last crumb after a nuclear strike.' We squeezed into the booth.

'You always get uptight in crowded places.'

'I'm not pissed off,' I grumbled. 'I just can't stand the selfishness.'

Jacquie fumbled in her purse for the phone book while I read the carved graffiti. 'Anyway, the French think that we're stupid to queue.'

She began to dial Lance's number. 'They think we're all far too stuffy. Do you want to speak or shall I? You're the man.'

'True, but, *he's* a man.' I said, 'You're a woman. He'll definitely warm more to you than me.'

She put her hand over the mouthpiece. 'But he's already promised us they'd help.'

'It doesn't mean a thing,' I whispered, 'it's only a promise.'

'Hello, I'd like to speak to Lance Fumpf. Thank you.' She puckered her lips. I bent to kiss her neck. 'Hello, Lance? It's Jacquie. Yes, we've just moved in. Oh, it's a mess. You do?' She smiled, giving me the thumbs-up sign. I scratched through her bag for a pen. 'Yes, we'd love to. We'll be there for the twentieth.' She wrote the date and an address in London, a drug company HQ, where we were to meet Lance. 'And to you too,' she finished cheerfully. 'Goodbye, Lance.'

She turned to me. 'He said he wants to "*Help us with a capital H*". He wants to meet us and talk about the whole project.'

'Well,' I said, feeling suddenly hopeful, 'he said that they'd help last time. Maybe this is it.'

'I hope so,' Jacquie said faintly, 'now the roof's fallen in. We're depending on this bloody Help with a capital H, aren't we?' Her fingernails clicked on the top of the little counter. 'I suppose we'll be showing all their products to the diabetics that turn up.'

'I don't mind. I just hope that he thinks the idea's worth throwing some money at. We can last a few months but we've got so much to build. We can't sleep under the roof like that. It'll fall on us. We need Lance, Jacq. It's nothing to a big company like his. It's pennies, but for us it's going to mean everything.' Then I leaned towards Jacquie, sounding as polite as I could. 'I don't think we're very welcome here.' A woman tapped impatiently on the little booth window and we made our way through the human thicket to the counter.

Jacquie asked cheerfully, 'How much for the phone call, please?'

'*VINGT-SEPT FRANCS,*' the woman shouted rudely, as if saying it louder might make us understand. She glanced at her colleague, who looked up at us, then back to the woman again in what seemed a rather unsavoury understanding. We were obviously the brunt of some vile gossip, I supposed, and people are generally cowards.

Sitting behind those bars anything could be safely said. We were foreign, alone, an easy and vulnerable target.

Jacquie's eyes opened wider. 'I'm English. I'm not deaf.'

I leaned towards her, sounding as polite as I could. 'I said, I don't think we're welcome here.' Then firmly, 'Come on; grin, and let's just go.' But I had an awful feeling that it wasn't going to be like that.

Jacquie began a fake smile. The woman produced an equally insincere grin. So suddenly sarcastic and hostile was it that I felt as if I'd taken a mouthful of rotten meat and swallowed before I'd had time to react. Jacquie's voice cut the air like a fire extinguisher, though somehow less venomous than it might have been in English. 'You're supposed to supply a service, why can't you do it and be polite instead of making people unhappy?'

'Jacquie,' I begged, 'it's time to go.'

'What d'you know about what I do?' blurted the woman, jowls shuddering. 'Who d'you take yourself for?'

'It's obvious,' hissed Jacquie. 'You don't do anything, NOTHING. Did you go to school to learn how to be mean like this?' The woman hurled a stream of abuse long before Jacquie came to the end of her sentence, while others in the room snapped sharp, vulgar words that I didn't understand. I yanked Jacquie, still shouting, out of the building. I remembered what she'd said at the bridge, about standing up for myself. I also felt annoyed that she just couldn't stop herself and think about the long-term damage.

'Those bitches,' she snapped, 'why'd they have to be so fucking rude?'

I told her to get in the car. Angrily, she chucked her bag into the leg space in front and we pulled away towards the *tabac*, trying hard to avoid smacking into anyone, yet incapable of paying attention to the road. 'Okay,' I began, 'they're bitches. We both know they're bitches, but those bitches can make us suffer. You almost went off your trolley in there. They're going to hate us now and they can screw with us seriously if they feel like it.'

'No they won't,' said Jacquie bitterly. 'You'll have to go in now. They think you're Mr Nice with the bitch wife. Why didn't you say something?' She lit a cigarette and wound down the window, chucking the match.

'I tried to stop it, didn't I? Don't make me out to be the bad guy when you can only hear yourself. You didn't have to make such a big deal out of it. Those people have nothing else to do but work in that room all day.'

There were tears coming. She looked away from me. 'You shouldn't just let people treat you like you're in a prison camp. Just because they've got a little power they behave like Nazis.'

'So they don't give a shit about anyone. So use them.'

'You don't understand,' she snapped, 'you were being bloody pathetic.'

'YEAH? Well, I didn't LOSE CONTROL OF MY FUCKING SELF.'

The *tabac* wasn't much better. Icy faces. I wandered back to the car feeling hollow and we drove home in silence. 'What did you expect?' I asked, as we pulled up in front of the chapel and sat looking at the dog leaping at the windows of the mobile home. 'It's a little village. It'd be the same anywhere.'

'I know.' Sadly, she smiled at me, making me feel like hugging her, breaking the silence. 'My dreams are always smashed. I always think things will be magic when they're not. When I was a girl I thought that the Queen was like an angel, that she had magic slippers and little people who did everything for her and she looked beautiful, like a fairy-tale.' Jacquie began to smile and she dried her tears with her sleeve. 'Then I saw her. We were on an outing with the school. She got out of a big car and walked right past us. She looked just like my Auntie Margaret. I was heartbroken. Don't laugh, I'm serious.'

We'd settled down and were tidying up the mobile home when a thin man with a white beard marched up from the road. 'What are you doing here?' he asked, looking quite upset.

'We're going to live here,' I said.

'We've bought the chapel, we're going to renovate it,' Jacquie added.

'But that's impossible!' said the man. 'This land belongs to everyone. Boris should never have sold it.'

'Well, he has,' said Jacquie. 'It was all done properly at the *notaire*'s office in Perpignan.'

It would have been a bad time for him to behave aggressively as under the circumstances we'd almost had enough and would have been up for a fight.

'This is our land,' Jacquie added politely but firmly, 'and it's going to be our home.'

Frustrated, the man departed. He informed us that he would be checking this at the planning office and he did not seem to be at all happy.

'It's the scruffy mobile and the old car,' I told Jacquie as he walked away. 'He probably thinks we're bad for the neighbourhood.'

It was late, after dinner, after dark. We were sitting by the light of a candle, listening to the radio, recovering from the fumes inhaled over the food we'd eaten in the smoky light from the petrol lamps. The *tranmontana* was blowing hard. It warned us: we were still ill equipped, fragile. I ran through the local stations, turning the dial slowly. For a moment the radio spoke to us in English, Capital Radio miraculously skipping across the heavens, and we listened, frozen with nostalgia as it faded, leaving us with the wind and the hollow feeling I'd had earlier in the day when walking away from the post office.

'Jacq?' I stroked her shoulders, feeling the curve of her neck. 'When something happens, like today, it's as if, well, you're so angry, you almost turn on yourself.' She looked up, defensive, and I continued, 'It's as if you're willing to smash yourself up. Like you wanted to stop, maybe, but you can't stop.'

'I know.' Sighing, she squeezed my leg, 'I don't know why . . .'

The following morning there was a thump at the door and the white-bearded man who had called the day before was standing there, with a far more friendly look on his face.

'Hello.' He nodded, looking around at the empty cement bags, pallets, the acro jacks and finally the frozen hose, which was standing upright, swaying like a cobra. 'I'm Hugh. Remember? Your neighbour from up the road.' He spoke in English.

'Oh, good morning. Would you like a cup of tea?' I heard myself say, feeling nervous, anticipating a dispute about common land or ownership or some awful unknown by-law that would steal our home away from us. Instead Hugh did the opposite; he invited us to drinks. To our delight he also suggested that we could take a bath while we were there. He pointed to his house and departed. I imagined him envisioning the horrors we might inflict on his wonderful, hedge-trimmed, lawn-sculpted neighbourhood. Stunned by this kindness, I closed the door, looking for a saucepan so we could at least wash. 'I bet they want to find out what on earth we're doing here.'

'I want to get the cement out of my ears and nails,' said Jacquie. 'I'll tell them anything, anything they want to hear. That's nice; a real bath,' she smiled, almost laughing, 'that's really nice. Make-up, I can wear some make-up!'

11 Meeting the Pillars

It was getting dark by the time we wandered up to the house for our bath and drink. 'I'll bet they'll be beautifully dressed,' said Jacquie, puffing as we climbed the hill. 'The women will have spent hours getting ready.'

Our fingernails were black and broken, our hair knotted. After a day removing vast sections of the rotting roof, sometimes a foot deep in decomposing leaves from the great oak, we were filthy. The road curled steeply round, overlooking the opening to Les Chartreuses in the valley and out to the vineyards beyond. I felt tired but warmth carried through me, my face flushed from the work.

'French women are always well groomed like that,' she continued.

'Don't worry how you'll compare with them. You're young. You'll probably be the youngest woman there and *that* doesn't come off on cotton wool at the end of the evening.'

Hugh's wife, Jott, welcomed us in with a warm smile and a soft '*Bonjour*'. She was younger than her husband and had an aura of gentleness. The house was built into the slope and split on to various levels, much like a modern impression of the stern of an old ship. After a brief tour we were shown the bathroom and Jott handed over warm, folded towels. 'Here,' her voice petted us, 'just call if you need anything,' and she floated away. I began to relax and look around at the clean surfaces, gleaming taps and the bath, thoughtfully prepared. We undressed quickly, silently cherishing the sensation of warmth and luxurious space.

'Someone's already here,' I said, having heard the doorbell and reckoning we'd better not submit to the temptation to linger.

'Don't worry.' Jacquie kissed me. 'Let's just enjoy it. It might be ages before we have another bath.'

Hugh introduced us to an olive-skinned, dark-haired, unmistakably Latin woman in her thirties called Marie-Antoinette. Marie's husband, Louis, rose to shake our hands, which prompted everyone else to do the same. A very self-assured English woman, slim, a few years older than Marie, reached across, smiling. 'Hi, my name's Dorothy and this is my husband Eddy.' Eddy, a tall and solid, broad-shouldered English-Brazilian with a warm but fleeting smile, squeezed the blood out of my hot, bathed hand with distant politeness.

Jott came in carrying a bottle, which Hugh opened ceremoniously. 'To welcome our new neighbours,' he smiled as he filled the glasses and a gentle barrage of questions lifted off.

Marie chatted with Jacquie in French, while Louis, a calm and warm-hearted man who worked as a croupier in the nearby casino, spoke of his favourite English game, blackjack, and offered a slim cigar. It was his night off, Marie explained, leaning closer, smelling of perfume and clean clothes. She spoke to me carefully and clearly but without being patronizing. She told us that her father once had a farm in Algeria. She was a *pied-noir*, the name given to those from Algeria who lost their roots and their homes when the country claimed its independence. The conversation that we struggled to comprehend was translated by Dorothy with lightning speed while her husband Eddy kindly offered to advise me on the building of the first of the chapel roofs.

'You'll need timbers for that roof,' he told me. 'Wood's expensive. They have to bring it from the north.' Eddy knew about things like this. He'd had plenty of practice using his own hands and the strength in his back while constructing the plastics factory that he and Dorothy had struggled to build up over the years.

'We've got some friends,' I began to explain.

'Michael and Janet,' Jacquie added. 'He's a White Russian. We met him on the beach.'

'They've got a château and they've invited us to stay with them. There's a huge forest. They said they'd help us with wood.' I had taken over the story.

Eddy looked astonished. 'I see,' he began, 'you met these people on the beach and they . . .' He hesitated, eyes fixed on his glass.

'Only Michael,' said Jacquie. 'He's sixty-five. He was on a windsurf.'

Stunned by this, they listened as we explained that we were about to buy an ancient Land Rover and would be shipping the wood down from the mountains ourselves. Eddy was clearly troubled either by the immensity of the task or the idea of Michael's eager generosity.

'Well,' Dorothy said, looking tired, 'I admire you.' She tapped the table softly with her hand. 'Come on, Eddy.'

We said our goodbyes and set off for the mobile home, stopping in the darkness outside Marie and Louis's house half-way down the hill. 'I think Marie's going to be a good friend,' said Jacquie.

'She's nice, Jacq, you need a friend here.'

'Everybody's your friend.' Jacquie sighed, leaning on me in the darkness as the ground became uneven. 'Friendship's something you don't really worry about, it just happens.'

'It's not true. I don't really have many friends, I'm happy just with you. Why are you saying this?'

'I'm afraid,' she replied, 'afraid you might find someone else.' It was lovely that she felt trusting enough to be this vulnerable and truthful with me, but I couldn't understand why this was an issue. 'You'd tell me, wouldn't you?' she asked unsteadily.

'How could there be anyone else?' I wondered where this was leading but she smiled briefly and moved on.

'Rupe, d'you ever think about Jezebel and where she said we'd end up living? She said the house would have pillars and the chapel does.'

'Yeah, but she also said it was in Spain.'

'This *was* Spain. I was talking to Jott; the French fought the Spaniards back across the mountains. The chapel's Spanish.'

'Were they called France and Spain then?'

'Oh, stop being negative. Jezebel was right,' said Jacquie, 'she saw it. She knew we were going to get this place.'

12 *Michael and Janet*

The little curate's house would be an easier beginning than facing the renovation of the chapel cold turkey. I'd be able to experiment. It would also be our first real home.

We were driving to the mountains, intending to cut down the trees that would replace the timbers in the little roof. The windows were square and the roof constructed with wooden beams. Beside it, the 900-year-old architecture of the chapel depended entirely upon arched stone and the massive forces that its weight provided.

If our newly acquired, rattling old Land Rover reached any speed, conversation became difficult. It was almost too late in the year for us to head into the mountains and we were in a hurry to get to Michael and Janet's. Once the snow came it would be months before we could have access to the forests again. We'd grown weary of the paraffin lamps in the mobile home and the cold gusts creeping in between the boarded-up windows.

Jacquie sat back, thoughtful, looking straight along the road. 'Janet told me that they'll stay until they've got us sorted out. You understood, Rupe,' she shouted, 'that they're going to leave us with the farmer?' She shifted her handbag against the crack between the door and the floor to block the cold. The Land Rover throbbed away, my hand resting on the big stick, silencing the muffled alarm-clock racket it made when left unheld.

Various Land Rovers had played a part throughout my childhood. I wasn't sure why I liked them so much but I only had to see one and memory would throw a scene from the past into my lap. They all had three seats in front. The gear-sticks in every one buzzed. I grew up sitting on cushions on the seat in the middle because I was the smallest, listening to the stick go quiet and watching the hairs on my father's big forearm and his wrist-watch shake as the gears clicked. It was the Land Rover's premium position. I could put my little arms around his gear-shift arm, then rest my head above his elbow. That was great. That was about as close as you could get. If you were blubbing then he'd put his hand on your knee and cuddle you as he drove and you knew he was there, and at least for a while he was mine.

Every third Saturday my brothers and I used to wait outside our cottage, the three of us listening, guessing if the next engine coming down the road would be our father in the Land Rover; waiting for the weekend to start, each of us excited. My brothers' excitement was always less obvious than mine. I never knew what my needs were or why I was so wound up. Then it was fishing, down first to 'Dennis the tackle man' for lugworms and on to Newhaven pier or over to the chalk-carved Long Man at Wilmington on the Downs. Then the long sleepy drive to London and our father's rooms where the orange lights in the street flooded in at night so darkness was never so black.

Then each third Sunday night we'd watch the tail-lights flicker red as they drifted away through the trees and we'd wait until we couldn't hear that familiar engine any more. My brother Brock was silent. Gareth might say a word or two, but we were all listening until the very last sound of the tyres on the road was gone.

They never showed a thing, those two, at least never much to me. Heroes never do. In the darkness our mother's voice beckoned and I would open my eyes super-wide so they might not drip, and feeling angry, try hard, ever so hard, as we carried our things towards the light.

We left the cottage when I was eleven years old. Brock and Gareth had run away to live with Dad and I joined them shortly after my mother had had the breakdown.

Parental separation can happen, I'm sure, with a minimum of upset, although I've seen so many perfectly strong people crushed under the weight of it. Deception, loneliness, hatred, violence of every kind and despair, we all know what so many of our children live with, yet sadly we're only just beginning to see people's minds as the fragile machines that they are – only just. Mental illness can be remarkably subtle. Most people will at some stage in their lives be driven to the edge; you never believe when you're young that it's really just a matter of when.

My father and stepmother Lucilla's London house was a doorway to the future, full of light and sound. Change forces you to grow. Most of us hate it, but it can be tremendously healing. It was a strange and eventually a very happy time. We had a half-brother, Ulric, and a baby sister, Alice. Life was on the move and at the age of eleven I had been determined to forget the jumbled emotions from those childhood years at the cottage and so close the door.

I hoped more than anything that we'd make it; that Jacquie and I would manage somehow to survive life's struggles and build our home. Never had I felt more positive about anything. We'd be married in a few months. A home, two of us, indestructible, like nothing I'd ever known in the past. These simple things, naive thoughts though they may seem, were incredibly important to me.

Eventually a white-green valley stretched before us, forming the flat shape of a loch with the mountains towering above on all sides. We'd been climbing for some time and the bare trees on the roadside hung sad and heavy with frozen droplets.

Michael's château was impressive, internally derelict yet relatively intact from the outside. Its turrets' great black points were covered with fish-scale slate reaching to the sky, sharp and daunting. Broken blackened windows stared across the icy grass loch, high above arrow slits, resembling sad mouths cut in thick stone.

Janet, aged about fifty, emerged from a doorway in the farm buildings and walked across the courtyard with a sausage dog in tow. 'Hello!' she shouted cheerfully. 'Michael's still in bed, I'm afraid.' Her shrug seemed to accentuate her Welsh accent. 'It was so cold this morning. He just hasn't got the energy when it's like that.'

Michael's room was scattered with various boxed memorabilia of their previous lives. There were English plug sockets on the walls and an old-fashioned heater in the middle of the room beside the bottom half of a set of children's bunks. 'Now come on, my darling,' his voice rang out. The chicken he'd been holding so gently saw me and left his arms, heading for the light. Then, making an effort to turn his stiff neck, Michael reached out with joy. Half sitting up, he wore a military greatcoat over pyjamas and blankets. He beckoned, half shouting. 'My dear fellow! Come in, come in. How are you?' I looked at the chicken and back at Michael. 'Yes, I know, I expect you think I'm potty.' He frowned. 'We've been having trouble with a fox and she's a bit upset.' Then breaking into a smile, straining to turn and get up, he cheered, 'But never mind, what d'you think of the château? Isn't it lovely? Lovely, lovely, isn't it? Simply wonderful place.'

Evening came and we watched the black-and-white TV. Michael translated for Janet who felt that French, perhaps because of her age, was beyond her. 'What'd he say?' she asked, drowning the dialogue. Michael cocked an ear and squinted at the screen. 'Sorry. I didn't catch that bit.' I imagined that they must've only heard half of any film they'd ever seen together.

As Michael dozed by the fire, Janet explained that an arrangement had been made for Jacquie and me to stay with the farmer and his family in the next village. 'Another three weeks and the whole place'll be under snow,' Janet added, speaking of their imminent departure for England. 'Thank God we're going,' she said wearily. 'He's too old for this.'

We slept in a deep-sprung bed covered with linen that might have been in my grandmother's house. I lay with Jacquie's back against me, curled around her, hoping to block the cold. She spoke quietly. 'It's killing them, being up here.'

'They're together, at least. That's what's keeping them going.' We were deep in thought, silent, before Jacquie spoke again. 'It's just like Jezebel said. As long as we stay together we'll always be safe.'

In the morning we headed up the mountain to the area of forest that Michael had decided we could cut. A mist roved about, trapped in the bottom of the valley and around the château itself. In the light it seemed colder, touched with menace. Staring down on it as we drove up through the woodland, I felt as if the black-topped building was aware, set in its tree-lined coffin, of a slow, living death. Michael didn't come far into the steep forest but stayed on the roadside waiting for Jean-Luc, the farmer. He pointed to trees that were a yard or more thick at the base. 'They should do for your roof.'

Eventually an old blue tractor sounded across the valley as the smoke from its vertical exhaust pipe marked its path through the trees. It pulled up nearby and Jean-Luc climbed down, jumping the last few feet in his ex-army boots. He reached and shook Michael's hand. He seemed a serious man, although there was something mischievous about him. Hard-fisted but friendly, he was much smaller than me but moved with tremendous nervous power, his brown eyes twinkling like a ferret's, sharp in his patchy, worn face. It became clear, listening to Jean-Luc, that he knew what he was doing and was more than willing to help and to lodge us. Michael had obviously been helping him out in some way, and more to the point, Jean-Luc was clearly hungry for a share in the cut trees.

Michael took us down to the sawmill where a fat man with taped-together glasses struck a deal. Cut posts for Jean-Luc's fences and wood for the barns at his farm would be provided, along with beams for our roof and planks for the curate's house. All this would be handed over in return for Michael's trees. Michael himself would get nothing from the exchange.

'I'll bet that man's going to make a killing out of this,' Jacquie huffed, thinking about Michael and Janet. 'They're all profiting from Michael's gift to us.'

'Jacquie, you don't think that we're not?'

'I just think that they'll take more than they should.'

The fat man agreed to pick up the trees from the roadside. They had to be cleaned, peeled, and lowered to the road before he'd come. Jean-Luc explained that he was too busy to help but he'd lend us the tools and teach us how to prepare the trees.

The fat man peeled a plaster to inspect a nasty gash in his thumb, then stuck it back down, looking bored.

'He's the mayor,' Jean-Luc thumbed towards the fat man, who now looked irritable as well. Jacquie coolly assured him that we knew he was busy.

'I've got the sawmill,' the mayor boasted, 'and I do the taxi. It's the only one in the village, so what you want?' He shrugged. Everyone there seemed to shrug. I was transfixed by the way the filthy mayor's chins rippled, bringing the words out of his mouth like an escalator.

'I want nothing,' Jacquie shrugged back tersely, 'just a roof.' Her face was pale with irritation.

'I'd like to work more in politics,' the mayor added for no apparent reason, then rubbed his face with the back of his hand. 'But I haven't got the clothes.'

It was obvious we couldn't tell a cubic metre of wood from a mountain goat. I understood only that I'd get enough wood to build my roof and floors. Most of the bartering had relied on Michael. Jacquie understood the language and could converse, but as a woman, she was handicapped: anything she said in her English accent was amusing and not to be taken seriously. The mayor, distracted by apathy, somehow managed to shake our hands, so we could only suppose that business had been correctly concluded.

Returning to the château, Michael opened the doors. 'I wish you could come up here and help me fix this up.' He smiled. 'I just haven't got the strength. Ah,' he motioned to the drive, 'there's Jean-Luc to pick you up. He'll take care of you. Janet and I must be on our way to England by midday. If it snows we could be stuck up here.' He wandered off to make his last arrangements.

'Everyone's in on it.' Jacquie went further into the old château and we sat in the quiet.

'That mayor's a bastard.' I agreed, but pointed out that Michael, who was no fool, might find him useful at times, remembering Michael's charm and his remarks on the beach the day we'd met. He'd specifically said that we might be of use to one another.

'Why didn't you help?' Jacquie snapped, still smouldering about the fat man.

'I didn't even know what the agreement was until you translated half of it. What would you have liked me to say? I can't just whip out Excalibur for no reason and start lopping off heads.'

'Well, I'm going to tell the fucking mayor what I think, for Michael's sake. The mayor's a thief. You know what's going on. Why should we help him rip off our friends? You don't give a shit.'

'Okay then, I'll go and tell Michael that we don't want the wood,'

I told her. She stared at me, silent for a while. 'Don't you think Michael has some idea what's happening?' I asked. 'He's bloody clever enough. You're willing to give up our roof because you don't like the mayor. Shit! It'll screw us. Come on, Jacquie, stop. Please, darling. Oh,' I sighed, 'don't cry.' I reached out to comfort her.

'Don't patronize me,' she snapped, pulling away. I felt sick with irritation and confusion. 'Jacquie! If you choose to burn this bridge there won't be another. We've spent almost everything we have on this trip. You can leave now and you know I'll leave with you, but don't make enemies for Michael just because you're on your high horse. This is a trip for wood for fucksakes, not a suicide mission.'

On one level I felt that my own weakness had brought us to this, that somehow perhaps Jacquie was right, that I should have been able to beat up all the bad guys, get the wood and the girl and go home. I felt a deep sense of frustration and some indefinable shame. My confidence was wearing thin. 'So I've decided,' I announced, pretty sure she'd fight for control, 'we'll go home. There, now the pressure's off you.'

'Then you'll blame me for the roof not being finished.'

'You'll have to live with that, or turn a blind eye to the mayor.'

'Then we'll stay,' she muttered, the tears gone.

13 Enough for Love

Jean-Luc's village included a row of houses with upper storeys bulging obscenely over narrow streets of worn tarmac. The tractor billowed smoke and chugged up this corridor. We followed, past the stone fountain where an old man in a torn, dirty jacket shouted from a bench, leaning forward on his stick, addressing a small herd of goats.

Through the narrower parts dung coated the road, the tractor tyres throwing it in the air as they slipped on a corner, drawing us eventually into the light of a little courtyard.

A boy about sixteen years old, wearing a beret, threw his stick aside and closed the gate behind us, nodding to his father as Jean-Luc came to a halt. Two gleaming tractors stood before us, tucked into a large barn where long beans dried in their jackets hung overhead. On one side a stack of several cages housed the laying hens. Alongside, their noses twitching, rabbits peered out through holes in high-stacked recycled beer crates.

I watched a small van as it pulled into the neighbouring farmyard. It rolled low to the ground, its load thumping, squealing, forcing the suspension to squeak as it came to a juddering halt. The contents tumbled inside.

'I'll show you the animals.' Jean-Luc pointed to the nearest of the barns and we waded across the small courtyard through a sea of ducks. Goats tied to hoops jutting from the walls tried to move aside as our young dog Kansas chased the birds.

The two barns and the house formed a 'U' shape, a sort of fortress with the gate at the far end, closing out the identical farm on the other side of the street, where the squealing van stood. The barn door scraped open and the sensation of warmth from the manure and the dim light closed in behind us.

'God! Cows!' Jacquie's voice blended with the din. 'So many!' Joyfully she made her way to the first stall. A new-born calf, only hours old, stared back at us. The building glowed golden with the reflection of the electric lamps on low beams and straw.

Jean-Luc made motions with his fingers to his lips. 'Delicious!' He pointed at the calf.

'You're not going to eat that,' Jacquie pleaded, 'it's just a baby.'

'You like to *eat*, don't you?' He laughed, his mischievous black eyes sparkling, nudging her elbow as he gripped the calf by the chin, bending its head round to face her.

We made our way to the end of the courtyard. 'Those your dogs?' I asked.

Jacquie looked at me with a wry smile, anticipating my next question.

'What happened to his eye?' I went on regardless.

'I ate it.' Jean-Luc grinned evilly at Jacquie. In the next barn the noise grew louder.

'How many animals?' I shouted. 'In here, HOW MANY?'

'TWO HUNDRED.' He glared back at me. My expression had angered him, triggering a tirade about rights and how the animals were protected and monitored by the state. Obligated and now a bit nervous, we nodded back in enthusiastic agreement.

We were shown to our room in the unfinished part of the house. A row of black cows watched as I closed the door downstairs with a large bolt. Upstairs was in darkness. The window shutters sealed by cobwebs in a cracked frame allowed only thin streams of light to lance across the planked floor so that we could see our bed and the parts of walls better left untouched. The cows clumped about below as we sat down, making the rusty bed-springs screech.

Jean-Luc was now in the courtyard, calling shrilly to the half-blind dog. Somewhere through the rumble of the farm children laughed. We looked at each other, grinning, alone at last. A magical, childish feeling briefly enveloped us as we cuddled on those springs in the cold, dark room above the cows. Jacquie blew in the air, then mimed a sulky kiss. 'I'm cold.'

'Come on, Jacq,' I encircled her as much as I could, 'you'll be warm. We'll be fine.'

'I couldn't bear to be ill here. I'd die,' she said as I encircled her reassuringly.

'Nobody is going to die,' I insisted, but she shook her head.

'Everything in those barns is going to. I like Jean-Luc, really I do, Rupe, but I feel death everywhere here. Everything is on borrowed time, like most of the people I look after.'

As dusk approached we were given hand-crafted wooden forks and had the healthy task of mucking out the barns, then loading the muck-spreader from the wooden barrows that Jean-Luc's father had made. The elder son, Arnaud, wandered in from the fields. Jean-Luc spoke in blunt sentences to the lad and his brother as Jacquie, in her tight jeans, staggered between them with her barrow full of manure in the last of the afternoon light.

'I told them,' Jean-Luc smiled cheekily, 'you have to work, if you want to eat.'

'That's not what you said,' snapped Jacquie with a smile as the two sons laughed at their blushing father. 'But thanks for the compliment,' she added.

The family ate and cooked in the one downstairs room off from the hallway which was filled with logs, axes, walking sticks, dung forks and the rougher clothing worn by all. By the kitchen door a large pedal-driven grinding stone in a wooden frame stood waiting, ready to sharpen everything and anything.

We shared the simple bathroom and the bed – although the family knew we weren't yet married, it didn't matter to them. We were so foreign anyway, so strange, outside any normality of theirs. Nothing but strange behaviour was to be expected from *les anglais*. Although we were taken in and kindly treated, we were also somehow far apart, a novelty, strangers.

Before dinner most evenings I took Kansas for a walk in the fields behind the house. It was a way of obtaining silence, away from the kindly small-talk of the crowded downstairs room. The sky a vast, absolute black above me, a sniffing dog here, a goat or perhaps a rat scuffling about. Inhaling, one could taste the air, like ice water. Through the darkness the occupant of the overloaded van in the adjacent yard puffed and thumped impatiently.

I followed Kansas back into the hallway, past the grinder, and pushed open the cloth-edged door to the kitchen. Mimi, the grandma, was watching a large sixties TV resting on castors. She sat on a wooden chair in the middle of the room, the screen a white fizz. Behind her thick-lensed glasses one sore eye wept heavy tears which tumbled down her creased, pleasant face. Her body was the size of a ten-year-old's and she moved cautiously, seeming as brittle as fine balsa.

'She sees poorly,' Jean-Luc's wife, Henriette, told me, 'but she understands the sound.' Mimi dabbed her weeping eye while her ancient husband sat in close and loud conference with Jean-Luc and Arnaud around one end of the kitchen table. A light-bulb above the kitchen part of the room dimly illuminated the huge plaster and wood chimney breast and the dark and yellowed walls. The few decorations flickered in the light from the fire, its heat tremendous, the only source of warmth in the house. The younger son sat with his feet on oblong newspaper packages, tied with string. They lay on a steel plate upon which the logs burned. I imagined that the packages were there to protect one's feet from the heat of the plate, which was at least half an inch thick and jutted out about a foot above the floor. Bright yellow tape had been stuck to the edges of the metal where it protruded. The tape smouldered slightly.

Jean-Luc prepared himself at the far end of the table while Henriette and Jacquie passed bowls of soup. The table was the stage for most of the family entertainment, followed closely by the TV which, after the bowls were in place, was rolled up close and meticulously tuned by Arnaud. The wooden chairs on which we sat were old, the only seats in the house. Mimi sat on my left, glancing at me suspiciously out of the corner of her damp eye while her husband, Papy, comfortable in his hard seat, used his worn folding knife on the bread.

'So tomorrow we cut some wood.' Jean-Luc looked at Papy. 'Papy will prepare the tools for you.'

'*C'est bien!*' Mimi announced, holding her spoon, her voice shrill as the buzzer on an intercom.

I looked at my bowl, minestrone, thin as turps but delicious. Mimi smiled at me, raising the spoon delicately to her mouth to copious appreciative sounds around the table. A large droplet rolled from her eye and plopped into her bowl. Rabbit followed, in a thick tomato sauce, then cheese. This Jean-Luc and Papy set upon amidst great discussion over the agricultural fair to be held soon in Paris: Arnaud, it had been decided, would accompany Papy.

'You like coffee?' Mimi asked, pulling herself with immense strain to her feet. There were voices and nods from around the table.

'Hey, Papy,' Jean-Luc announced, perhaps to draw our attention from the old woman. 'I got to cut your hair before you go to the "Grande Ville".'

'And you, my son?' Henriette glanced at Arnaud, then kept talking while her attention turned to Mimi. 'You've got to be ready for those Parisian girls!'

The grandmother made her way across the room at a painful pace and lit the gas under a blackened coffee pot that she'd left already prepared on the makeshift stove. With slow precision she turned to the fireplace and the cups hanging nearby, stopping suddenly, looking down, searching for the smouldering yellow tape so as to protect her shins from the steel plate.

Sure of her position now, Mimi prepared the cups on a tray.

'I'll go and help.' Jacquie started to get to her feet.

'No.' Henriette's voice was firm, her hand on Jacquie's arm. 'Maman will prepare the coffee.' Politely, she gestured for Jacquie to sit down, then touched Arnaud's shoulder, sending him to the fireplace to fetch something. With dignity and great effort, Mimi came to the table, setting the tray down silently.

Arnaud handed me one of the string-tied newspaper packages from the fireside. It was hot and heavy. 'It's a brick?' I asked, looking up.

Jacquie watched me as the boy replied, a little smirk forming on her face. 'It'll warm your bed,' he said.

I could almost feel another kind of warmth from Mimi's smile. 'Would you like some sugar?' she asked, so alive.

I woke early. There'd been a hell of a noise even earlier. Slumbering through it, I'd dreamt that Jean-Luc had been feeding pigs but I couldn't remember having seen pigs on our tour of the barns the evening before. I dressed and went downstairs where I found Kansas scratching to get out. She darted into the courtyard, then up the alley beyond before I could stop her. Jean-Luc passed by, wearing gumboots.

'Your dog is on heat,' he tried to explain.

'I'm perfectly warm.' I smiled, seeing my breath crystallize.

Jacquie appeared and seeming embarrassed, Jean-Luc decided to leave me in my ignorance, picked up a shovel and grinning, headed for the barn. I noticed the van that had been parked opposite pulling away, riding high on its springs, empty now.

'God, it's cold. I'm hungry,' I said. 'I'd better take my shot.'

'No, maybe you should wait. Better see what's for breakfast first, in case you jab too much.'

Walking into the kitchen, I saw the table piled high with the freshly butchered carcass of a pig. Gasping, Jacquie arrived close behind. 'Oh! Did you do that?' She looked at Henriette, then at the head and the white tongue on the table.

'No, Jean-Luc. He does it for some of the other farmers.' She packaged various cuts and morsels in plastic and went into the hall-way where a large chest-freezer stood under the coats. 'In return we keep some for ourselves.'

It took me a moment to realize that the snorting and thumping creature in the van parked across the road the evening before was about to watch me have breakfast: in an abstract sense. I looked at the freezer. 'These are high-tech peasants,' I said.

Papy sat nearby at the grinder and began pedalling, sharpening a curved blade attached to the end of a long stick. The sound of the steel on the stone allowed Jacquie to speak candidly. 'Peasant,' she said.

'What?'

'*Peasant*,' she looked at me, 'for goodness' sake, it's the same word in French.' Jacquie looked across, smiling pleasantly at Mimi.

'*Café?*' Mimi asked.

'Henriette,' I began, 'do you have any bread?'

'Oh yes, Henriette,' said Jacquie, 'Rupert needs to eat. He's ill. He has diabetes.'

'No, I'm not ill,' I snapped. 'Now, Jacq—'

'Stop it, Rupe. I know you're not.' Jacquie stood in front of the newly dead pig and me. 'He has diabetes,' she repeated.

'*Ah! La diabète!*' The coin dropped and Henriette looked at me as if I had only seconds left.

Jacquie started to make me a jam baguette while Mimi shuffled the coffee towards the table as though it was in suspended animation on a trip across the galaxy. Henriette switched into the 'tragic' mode and began a long, painful account of various cousins who had died or whose lives had been destroyed by diabetes while at the same time she fondled the dead meat.

'Jacq, I can get my own breakfast.'

'All the women do this up here. I want to,' she gave me an archly doting look, 'darling husband-to-be.'

Mimi finally made it with the coffee. 'Is there any milk?' I smirked.

'Yes, anything,' said Jacquie sickeningly, beating Mimi to the fridge by a mile. I noticed that the butchered pig's head had its tongue out next to the top of my plate. Seeing this, the old woman laughed soundlessly, stretching her toothless face back, using every available crease, yet no sound came from her, just bubbling from her lungs.

'This is a Fellini film.' I bleated, 'she's dressed like the Grim Reaper, you're behaving like Venus in a Turkish bath and I'm sitting at breakfast with a dead pig in a room full of sharp knives.'

A short time later we were in the forest with Jean-Luc, high above the château, climbing from the road to the first tree, carrying chainsaws and two of the long sticks with the curved blades that Papy had prepared.

'This one?' Jean-Luc tugged at the old and powerful saw which eventually phutted and died. Then he shoved the choke back in a little, tugged again and it burst into life, fierce. The chain spun, sending a streak of resin into the air as he turned towards us, almost idiotically triumphant. The saw ripped into the base of the huge tree as he leaned, tugging to one side. Skilfully, he sliced a wedge from the tree, which took up almost a third of the base, then threw it to me. We began counting the rings while the tree stood precariously, like a speared bull in an arena. He moved behind and cut until sounds of breaking timber filled the forest. The trunk twisted as it lost its strength. Branches fell from above as the tree creaked, stumbled and swiped, clinging to wood alongside before thundering to the ground, its limbs slamming deep into the leafy earth.

The forest canopy showed a wound, open to the sky as the sound of the fall echoed on. Jean-Luc picked up the long-handled blades and beckoned, leaving the saw muttering on the fresh-cut stump. 'It's easy.' He slid the blade along the fallen trunk, sending a thin strip of bark three feet long into the air. Underneath, the cream-coloured wood shone, clean and sticky. I swung, feeling the skin on my hands tighten on the worn stick as the blade dug in, removing a chip a little larger than a cork.

'It's something you have to learn,' he grinned. We chipped away pathetically as he felled a second tree, making another hole where light crept into the wood. The saw stalled as he looked back to see if we were still admiring. 'You'd better get the bark off these quick.' He looked up. 'It's going to snow.'

Jean-Luc left us after he'd cut a third. It was cold under the trees and we weren't equipped in any way. All of the trees were to be stripped of their bark and the prospect of snow seemed equally daunting. In spite of this, we wouldn't be leaving the mountain without the wood.

Some time later Jacquie and I were talking about children.

She began to smile, because I was trying to encourage her to look upon the idea favourably. Hacking at the huge trunk, her hands wrapped in the ends of her woolly sleeves, she said, 'I never thought I'd have children at all before we met.' We were working, sweating, occupied, so maybe I failed to register the significance of this remark. Jacquie had said once before that she didn't want children but life has a way of changing people. I couldn't see us going through life without them.

We left some hours later as the first signs of sunset arrived, heading down through soft earthy woods, having finished less than one tree, chip by chip. 'I'm going to be useless tomorrow,' said Jacquie.

'Don't worry,' I huffed, feeling blisters on the sides of my thumbs, 'there are gloves at the farm.' I paused for a moment, but not in a pregnant way. 'I think we'll be fine' – that phrase again only used when things weren't looking favourable. I started the engine and adjusted the heater. 'As long as it doesn't rain like this too often.'

As we pulled away from the roadside the tyres spun. 'Temperature's dropped, road's frozen.'

A normal kind of conversation resumed as we headed back. 'We'll run out of clothes.' Jacquie squeezed her damp sleeves on to the floor of the Land Rover, yelping at a piece of broken skin. 'I wonder what's for dinner.'

'I've got this feeling that it's going to be pork.'

'I doubt it.' She looked at me with her explaining look. She knew I'd ask. 'Because you can sell pork, especially good cuts like that.'

'The food they eat is good.'

'Yeah, it's fine, but that's not what I'm trying to say. Rupe, you have to open your eyes sometimes.'

'No, I understand, so it's rabbit.'

'Or maybe chicken.'

Up on the plateau outside the farm it seemed colder than ever. Everything was frozen. I felt the sting as the water on my hands hit the air. I'd taken a step towards the house when we heard the dog. Jacquie headed inside to the fire, while I followed the barking towards the alley as fine snow began to fall.

'Kansas,' I yelled, 'for goodness' sake!' I tried to pull the two dogs apart. 'Shit! It's okay.' I attempted to sound calm as the bigger dog went for me. 'It's okay. Don't worry, babe, I'll sort you out.'

I rushed to the house and burst into the kitchen where I grabbed a saucepan. 'QUICK! Kansas is frozen!' I stammered, turning the hot tap as fast as I could while others around the room stopped what they were doing and looked up in surprise.

Jacquie stared at me, stunned. 'She's frozen to another dog.' I yelped. 'I'll take this warm water, maybe it'll melt enough to get them apart.' The entire family watched as I rushed out with the sloshing pan. I could hear Jean-Luc speaking. There was a clatter of followers behind and laughter. The dogs were still there. I threw the warm water over them. The big dog growled, stared up at me. I could have sworn his panting face twisted into a sly smirk.

Jacquie put her hand to her mouth, her eyes creased. Jean-Luc howled, slumping on his elder son's shoulder. 'Oh no,' I gulped, looking across at the others, dropping the pan in sudden clarity. 'They're screwing, aren't they?' A silent moment passed while I registered my naivety. 'But they were in a different position when I . . .' The others were all laughing by now. Jean-Luc fell to his knees, holding the top of his head with his hands, then began pointing, his face streaming with helpless tears.

Jacquie shook her head with a warm smile. 'You didn't know? That they got stuck together?'

'Yeah? Well, I bet you didn't either,' I mumbled.

The others made their way back towards the house through the falling snow. 'You're cold, Rupe,' said Jacquie, 'come in.'

'I will. In a minute, okay?' I needed a moment to pick up the remains of my dignity.

'Hey, English,' Jean-Luc turned back, 'you want a drink with us?'

Dinner was packet soup and a delicious bowl of unidentified tail. We ate well, the bread, from the village, soft but crusty. I chatted, my spoken French improving. It seemed that because I'd made such a human mistake about the dog, I'd somehow become more acceptable and less of a foreign entity, although I wondered whether perhaps it was just the plentiful wine.

Something was generating tremendous warmth here, even then as my own weakness or ignorance had been displayed. I'd grown fond of these people, because they shared an identity and drew their strength from themselves as a family. The simple nuts and bolts of life were exposed here, no gloss, no family composite on a mantelpiece, just barely enough, enough for love. Coming out of the kitchen, past the grinder and under the stars with our warm brick, I heard thumping again in the stillness. The mysterious van stood on the other side of the gate, parked in its usual place, loaded down, its doomed occupant incredibly heavy, uncomfortable on the freezing metal.

I felt the effects of the day soothed by the wine and made my way into our part of the house, locking us in, nodding to the cows as we clambered blindly upstairs. Darkness was something that truly frightened Jacquie. The holes in the floor and the gaps in the stairs were suddenly alive with the unknown. There were rats, undoubtedly, slinking about in the corners. This was a place in which Jacquie could never stay alone. She clambered into bed and we cuddled, kissing and listening to the sound of the animals below. Sleepily we made love. Then I listened to her heart calm as we lay in silence. She curved her arm, putting her hand on my chest. 'What are you thinking?' she asked. I could sense her smile as she spoke in the dark. 'Same as me?'

'I was praying that it never stops.'

For the next fifteen days it snowed lightly, growing steadily bitter as it created a build-up of quite nasty ice. The road froze and slowly the winter began to steal the ground from us. We worked, still chipping until with time I got the skill, the hang of it. In all we'd managed to remove the bark and chain-sawed the branches from fifteen huge trees. A professional might have done the same in two days. I'd chosen one particularly straight tree, felled it and prepared it for transport. It was smaller than the others and would make two superb beams to support the new roof. On the very last day the fat mayor appeared for his booty, shouting rude instructions from his huge logging truck. Before taking the first load down the mountain he called us over by banging rudely on the side of the truck door. He leaned out of the cab, irritated even by this small discomfort. 'I'll give you dry planks and beams,' his chin rippled, 'when you like.' He shunted the ancient thing into gear. It leaped and then with a hiss rolled down the hill, its claw-like mud-caked tyres crushing the stray branches in its path.

We watched the huge trunks rumble down the mountain, a hissing of air brakes on every turn. 'He's a bastard,' Jacquie scowled, 'screwing Michael like that.'

'So, he's a bastard.' Neither of us could go on much longer, stoned on kerosene in the caravan every night. 'That bastard's got our wood and he'll probably screw us too. I'll bet he gives us just enough to build the roof and floors but bugger-all else. I'm sure that amount of raw wood makes up five or six roofs. But, Jacquie, if we don't piss him off, we'll have our roof. Please. Don't let's blow it now.'

Our way of dealing with these problems was almost bizarre, the balance rather beautiful. She had the experience and the confidence I lacked, and I offered stability, which to Jacquie stood out like an island in the sea. Though she dominated, she was strangely aware of her vulnerability, and so in difficult moments she'd often listen. As Jezebel had said, together we'd safely find our way.

Back at the farm, Papy greeted us, sitting in the middle of the kitchen with a towel wrapped around his neck as Jean-Luc appeared holding an electric shearing machine. 'You leaving today?'

He turned on the shearer and drove it up his father's neck and over the top of his scalp, leaving a bald stripe in its wake. 'You're going to miss those trees, huh?' he laughed, as Papy bent one ear out of the way. 'Be careful, there's ice on the road.'

We drove down the mountain with eggs from Henriette and a blessing from Mimi. I stopped at the place where the smaller tree trunk I'd cut for beams lay in a ditch and we managed to tie it to the steel rack above the roof. When we arrived at the sawmill as agreed, Jacquie said nothing while the mayor grudgingly helped me load up the timbers. She smouldered, staring coldly through the car windows while I hurried, hoping the mayor wouldn't say something obnoxious which would make her bite his head off.

Now, back at work on our curate's house with all the wood in place, I saw that building this roof wasn't going to be simple. In the middle of this puzzle, Eddy and Dorothy called with an invitation to supper.

'I've got him on a diet,' Dorothy announced with some satisfaction. 'Yes,' she said cheerily, 'he'll be starving by then, so don't be late. Eddy has sour cream and egg for breakfast and then nothing all day.' She laughed. 'Not until dinner. Of course, it's self-defence,' she added.

Later that evening Eddy reached across to me and taking a pencil from my pocket, he made a sketch on a piece of scrap paper. 'About that roof of yours,' he began . . .

I only realized the true mammoth scale of the roofing problems when the sheer amount of materials and equipment needed became apparent. I was having problems dealing with the peculiar askew square of the little curate's house walls, but this was nothing in comparison with what was to come. Standing balanced on one of the walls, looking across the stone division to the chapel and its 7,000 half-broken tiles with weeds flooding out and great troughs where the solid vaulted stone structure below had receded, I felt overwhelmed. How could I possibly ever complete this? I didn't even know what quantities of soft lime cement to mix with my sand. I didn't know which kind of sand. Rough? Grainy? Silver sand? River sand? Soft? Also, it didn't look safe to walk on the stone roof. If falling through didn't kill you, then the tons of rock falling along with you certainly would. I really hadn't a clue what I was doing. I simply imagined that the solution would come to me, and having a brain that can jerry-rig almost anything, I charged on. Unfortunately this absurd faith took some wearing down. Then there were the other obstacles, financial and physical. I was one man. In order to build a roof this size and set the tiles in place, one needed a crane or block and tackle to lift the stuff up and a cement-mixer of one's own. We could afford neither. Buckets of cement were the only answer. So while Jacquie did her nursing in the surrounding villages, sometimes replacing other nurses or even going into Perpignan itself to do a night duty shift, I would carry on, up and down the ladder, mixing the cement in an ancient wheelbarrow donated by Michael and Janet.

Eddy's sensible advice was often ignored the first time around, only to have me reappear days later at his house some miles away with fingers bleeding from the acid lime and a tired look in my eye. The roof was beating me, and deciding to start with knowledge first this time, I'd listen to Eddy.

Nearer to home there were Louis and Marie-Antoinette. My first memories of Louis are when he came to help me remove a rotting beam from the curate's house. 'It's like paper,' I told him naively, but neither he nor his chainsaw believed it for a moment. Again experience is everything. It was Louis who befriended the workmen nearby and got them to lift the new beams up to the primitive curate's house first floor, balanced on the huge bucket of their mechanical digger. Many evenings, when Louis had left for the casino, Marie would invite us up and send us for a bath and then offer us dinner. Louis and Marie had a daughter, Emmanuelle, who was about twelve, the same age as my sister Alice. Emmanuelle would join us, sit for a little while and speak school English, better than any French I could muster. The differences between Emmanuelle and my sister were alarming in some respects. Emmanuelle was an only child and comparatively careful with her studies, whereas Alice was learning to cope with a London school and to camouflage her accent so she didn't get beaten up and called a snob on the bus. Looking at Emmanuelle and the immediate world surrounding her, I felt that this wasn't such a bad place for children. Nice schools, beautiful countryside, the Mediterranean not more than a few minutes' drive. What else could anyone ever need?

Eddy and Dorothy, though further away near the next village, were just as thoughtful. Tools were lent and Eddy would sometimes allow me to repair my cars on the factory forecourt. I changed the engine in an old Renault there once and could never understand why a whole bucketful of washers remained after I drove it away. Again, in those early days I used my runtish nature more than anything else to solve problems. I remember using this home-grown approach on a Citroën, and then weeping alone in the rain outside the factory because I couldn't put the two-cylinder heap back together again. My blood-sugar had dropped, I had eaten all the sugar I'd had and my hands were bleeding from slipping with a spanner on decaying nuts in the cold. The food I'd brought was not enough for this exertion, thus I could no longer rationalize and get the parts to go back and so had to wait for someone to show up, hoping I wouldn't be too far gone by then to ask for food. It sounds irresponsible but it can happen to anyone. You can be so blindly driven to achieve that you forget everything else. I also loathed the way diabetes slowed me down, and fought the feelings of hypoglycaemia, fending them off until the last possible second before giving in to find food.

Eddy would lend his huge van to collect quantities of sand, gravel and cement, offering dinners and advice without ever trying to steer us from what must have seemed to him and Dorothy, in the midst of our efforts, to be a daunting or even worrying situation.

On the day that I finished the little curate's house roof, Marie-Antoinette had asked us to breakfast. Jacquie's nursing work had gone desperately quiet and it had become obvious that our struggle to survive hadn't improved. Growing concerned, we'd even asked Marie if she knew where we might find work. She pulled her door open. 'Shhh,' she motioned, holding a finger to her lips, 'Louis's asleep. He finished at the casino at five.' As she ushered us in I listened for her *pied-noir* accent but noticed nothing. I hadn't realized until then that it was the hands in the air, the almost theatrical delivery and the extreme changes in pitch and expression that makes the *pied-noir* culture so unique. As this dawned on me I began to see Marie differently. She could laugh at herself. She would explode with delight, only to howl with laughter at her own reactions. It wasn't an easy house in which to keep a straight face. This wonderful spirit also went in the opposite direction and although thankfully I never experienced it, Marie was not one to cross.

We sat in the kitchen while she made coffee. '*Eh bien . . . excusez ma robe.*' She glanced down at the lovely embroidered fabric. 'You like it?' She smiled. 'It's Arab. I wear it round the house and for the pool. They have good ideas sometimes, those Arabs.' The child of a successful farmer, she and her family had been forced out of Algeria during the war of independence, their huge farm and most of their possessions lost, bought for pennies. Marie knew what it was like to come to a strange land. This was probably the reason why she could understand our situation. Returning to France, a stranger in his own country, her father had bought a snack bar in nearby Canet-Plage. Marie told us that she wept when first she saw him pick up a broom and sweep the little floor. She looked at us thoughtfully, pouring the strong black coffee into small cups. 'You remember I told you about a farmer?'

Jacquie nodded. I nodded too, imagining, as usual, that we were talking about something else.

Marie continued, simplifying, virtually carving her words in the air for me. 'Every year I help an old farmer. Maybe I could ask him to give you some work? His name is Joseph. Some people call him something else because of his face. I don't think he's ever washed his clothes.' She looked at me and I had a notion that she felt that the farmer and I made a good match. She began to laugh. 'And good God,' she grinned, 'does he have a face!'

I asked what was wrong with it.

'It's the sun, he's spent his life in the sun. I wish I could say that it was wrinkled from having a good time.' She began to clean her immaculate kitchen and prepare Louis's late breakfast. 'I don't know if Joseph will agree,' she said. 'I'll just ask.' We gratefully accepted.

'Now, *mes enfants*,' she looked at us both, 'I've heard gossip about you. You know, via the *téléphone arabe*' – this unlovely phrase translates as the grape-vine. 'It's going around the village. So I think you should be ready and don't let talk upset you. I've got to admit, what you're doing is a little unusual and they don't know you.' She shrugged. '*Courage.*' She faintly smiled, then offered me a cigarette. 'There are some grand houses up here. You didn't know what it was like before you came, did you? How could you have known . . . ?'

I shook my head, baffled.

'It's just,' she added, 'well, people get jealous. They think the old chapel belonged to them.'

'But these are wealthy people. They could have bought it ten times over . . . Why didn't they?'

'Good God!' She laughed again, at my naivety this time. 'They never got the chance.' She put the cigarette out on a piece of Spanish pottery. 'I think Boris did something good. He gave you a break.'

14 *Skull Face*

When Marie-Antoinette had said, 'People call him something else,' I hadn't understood. I'd realized very quickly though, exactly what she'd had in mind. In the village he was known as 'Le Singe', or 'The Monkey', although privately I named him Skull Face.

I wore gloves but even so, I couldn't feel my fingers. I was relying on the gloves to stop me from falling out of the trailer, and growing slightly uneasy about the pain. Looking ahead, I saw the back of Joseph's neck, the skin rough-shaven like a plucked chicken's, and the backs of his ears, burnt brown and probably freezing – his thin clothes seemed barely warm enough. Wings of plane trees lifted overhead as we rumbled through the early mist while I prayed for sun. Joseph glanced back from the tractor, then resumed his hunched position, rather resembling a demon. His bony hand pointed towards the field he intended me to work in as we left the road and bounced over hard verges before stopping.

'You,' he squawked as if there were several of me, 'you'll wait here.' His limbs hung tired on his bony, almost boyish frame. The darned shirt, sweater and aged overalls seemed quite normal, but it was his head, that face, that did it for me as it did for everyone, every time. It made one feel that death was on the doorstep, no matter how alive his pure Catalan accent told me he was.

He motioned to the churned field. 'I want to plant apricots here. They don't mind a few stones but we'll have to get the big ones. Are you listening, *you?*' A mound of tree roots and stumps had been cleared to one side and burnt, the middle still smouldering. I nodded and helped unhitch the trailer. He climbed back on the tractor, wincing as he lifted one foot over the gearbox, opening his mouth, tilting his head to the sky, eyes closed.

'Aaaagh, *putain!*' he swore at the clouds, offering me a glimpse of a sparse selection of teeth, mostly solitary and all brown. 'My knees, my God!' He looked sharply at me. 'And your wife, where is she?'

'In bed.' He asked if she was sick. I shook my head.

'I don't know,' he wagged a finger, before driving off to fetch the plough, 'you're all the same, you foreigners.'

I spent most of the time on foot, following Joseph and his tractor through the troughs as the blades of the plough carved the field into order, ripping out stones that I could barely lift aside, ready for humping on to the trailer. Often he'd stop and try to help me but it wasn't always pleasant. 'You're skinny.' Ironically he placed his hands on his own bony hips. 'Are you sure you're not hurting yourself? Watch your back.'

I told him I was fine but he wasn't worried about me; he was afraid. 'I had a woman got injured and then she made these threats.' He picked up a stick and threw it to one side, shaking his head. 'She said she'd go to the authorities. She made me pay.' He knelt on the soil, close enough for me to smell his breath. 'You're not going to do that to me, are you?' He'd been chewing ripe mountain ham.

I got closer to the ground so that all I could smell was the clay earth and worked on at lifting a big one. 'Of course I wouldn't.'

'*Bon.*' His sigh was heavy with genuine relief. 'Well, it's nine o'clock. I'm going to eat. It's a pity the ground is so wet.' He carried a cloth bag from the tractor, searching for a dry spot. I suggested the trailer. He shook his head.

'I'll lift you,' I offered. 'It's your knees, isn't it? You sit in the water and it's going to get worse.'

He looked around suspiciously. 'Okay, but you be careful.' Then he put his arms around my neck as I lifted him to the dry trailer surface. 'Oh, son of a whore,' he moaned, 'if my sister sees me now.' His arms tightened and I feared that he would choke me. Clinging like a limpet he snapped, 'Once, I was strong, stronger than you!' I understood that this frail yet strong old man might not like being physically lifted by a younger one, but I was gagging. '*Attention!*' he screamed, as I put him down. '*Animal!*' he grumbled.

I unwrapped my honey sandwich while he produced a baguette,

a paper-wrapped chunk of purple, stringy ham and a bottle of red with the stars embossed around the glass neck. Then he fumbled in his pocket for an ancient Opinel knife. 'How old d'you think I am?' he asked.

I looked at his face, his eyes sunken so deep that under his eyebrows there were cavernous shadows, the skin brown as old oak, and said that I didn't like these questions.

'No, seriously. What age d'you give me? Here, taste this. It's mine,' he said with pride as he handed me the rough bottle, 'my wine.' Most of his face hung from his high cheekbones, as if a paper bag had been stretched over his head and tied upside down around his neck. One or two visible teeth set the lower jaw apart and helped to define the form of a skull.

'Phew!' I swigged from the bottle and the sharpness hit my throat. 'You're asking me a question there.'

'*Allez, vite!*'

'You still going to pay me after this?'

'That depends,' he muttered.

'Okay. Fifty years old.'

'No, come on, I'm serious, I'll pay, you have my promise. Be honest.'

'Hundred and thirty-five?'

His jaw swung open like the drawer in a café where they dump the old coffee grounds. 'I must be some sort of masochist,' he cackled. 'I'm seventy, good God, and young for my age. And you can stop smiling like that. It's like those Spaniards – you can trust no one nowadays. This month I'll teach you something. I'll teach you how to cut the vines and you'll see what it does to have my years.'

When I asked if that wasn't supposed to have been done in the autumn he looked sad. 'I didn't have the courage,' he said, breaking his baguette and laying a sliver of ham inside.

'Then it's not too late?' I asked. 'Don't you want some butter with that? It must be dry.' An Englishman to the last, I suppose.

That afternoon I waited in Joseph's farmhouse where I was introduced to his sister, Yvette. 'Ah, you must be the husband of the little nurse.' Yvette, dressed in black, actually spat on my face in the middle of the word 'nurse'. I didn't like to react and wipe it off, so I left it and prepared for foul weather. 'She's kind, your wife,' said Yvette, 'she's got a good heart.'

'Yes, she's lovely,' Joseph added. 'You're lucky.' Yvette's expectoration was clearly an accident. I nodded, and asked if either of them was married.

'Me, no.' Joseph looked at his sister. 'Her, yes, but she left him. He wasn't nice.' He shook his head. 'When we were young we listened to our parents too much, and now, we're alone. It's not like nowadays. It was like that for everyone then. You did as you were told. Our mother was poor; we were a poor family. She was frightened.' He sighed. 'She told us, "You be careful, don't let some stranger into your lives."' He rubbed the smooth tabletop with his sleeve. 'I remember, when I was eleven, I had to carry the flour from the village. On my back I carried it, till I couldn't feel my legs. I watched her suffer, my mother.'

We sat silent for a moment while Joseph recovered himself. He tapped his knuckles on the table. '"You go and marry," she said, "and they'll leave you, they'll take it all, everything you have, all the inheritance, the good things we've saved will be lost."'

'And you listened to that?'

'She was formidable, our mother.' Yvette spat assent.

'So why didn't you just move away?' I asked.

'What for?' said Joseph, spreading his arms, displaying the room with its browned wallpaper leading to a blackened ceiling with a single bulb hanging down above a huge, shiny, cash-bought remote-control stereo television.

'We've got everything here,' said Yvette. The two stood there, perfectly happy, and Joseph, with his arms like that, seemed just like a bird that had never known the meaning of flight.

My father's second marriage had no great significance for me. I was nine and like a frightened pawn I wanted everyone to be happy and didn't really understand much about marriage anyway. I was just glad that I didn't have to be there on the day and wear itchy clothes.

I was also fortunate enough to discover later that I had an

extremely gentle, loving and thoughtful stepmother. Ulric, my half-brother, was now thirteen and my half-sister Alice eleven. Ulric had come to the chapel with my father to visit and celebrate Jacquie's twenty-fifth birthday.

We looked critically around the chapel. It would be a first time for them, and Jacquie and I wanted to make it marvellous. It was raining slightly, blowing from the Spanish side of the mountains, although there wasn't a cloud in the sky.

'That's a hell of a ledge.' My father peered over, looking at a platform that we'd excavated into the hillside behind the chapel. I explained about the bulldozer with the huge claw on its back, how it had taken two days to create the ledge. I also feared I'd upset Louis as I'd wrecked his chainsaw cutting all the trees back.

'You can have it serviced for him,' my father said calmly. I didn't answer, ashamed, unwilling to admit that I hadn't been able to afford the repairs. I'd make it up to Louis somehow, I promised myself.

'How on earth did you get the caravan down there?' Dad looked further down to the ledge and the river below. 'And that extension cord, it must be a hundred and fifty yards long.'

I muttered something about our new luxuries – the fridge, radio, TV . . . I so wanted him to be impressed. He chose to keep silent. Our fragile situation was obvious and I would so easily have been knocked down by his words, such was my admiration for him.

He turned towards the most chaotic section of the chapel, clearly noting how much had yet to be started, let alone completed. 'Rupe, there's an awful lot of work to do, old son.'

I was relieved that we were distracted by Ulric, who raced through a hole in the chapel wall calling out, 'It's great, Rupes. What's the puppy's name?'

'Yogi. We only got her a few weeks ago. She's Jacquie's dog. Kansas is mine.' Yogi and Kansas leaped about in the rubble.

My father looked at the curate's house, the new chimney, the mud floor and the window-frames that Louis had taught me how to make. There were pipes and tools on the floor upstairs along with a plastic bathtub that I'd brought from England. 'Did you make the stairs?' he inquired, inspecting, slightly bemused. I explained, with some pride, that I'd had to dig into the wall for space. I'd hoped that doing this would somehow make the steps less steep.

Somewhere in the dry part of the chapel, next to the stacked pictures and the belongings with no place to go, Ulric had found our wind-up gramophone and was sitting outside the curate's house dragging the cork out of a bottle of wine. He'd removed the middle seat from the Land Rover and set the gramophone upon it above the dust. He looked like a young Noël Coward in the making. He was only thirteen but already had a grasp of the style.

Having filled our glasses with wine and his own with some innocent cola, Ulric leaned back on an abandoned crimson foam seat, dumped from Louis's casino. He then dug in a little drawer for a fresh gramophone needle while Jacquie, my father and I filled the primitive new fireplace with old pallets and cement bags, anything that would burn. 'One Enchanted Evening,' the gramophone sang as the sun's last rays faded from the hillside trees above the chapel and the dogs frolicked in the dust.

'Tomorrow, I'm going to take us all for a smashing birthday dinner,' my father announced, hugging Jacquie while the cold chimney fired sparks into the sky and smoke pumped from the unfinished windows. 'I've brought you some beautiful curtains. You've been given them along with a huge carpet. It's all in the back of the car. It's not a real present for you, Jacquie,' he added ruefully, 'but they might be useful somewhere.'

'It's always quiet on my birthday,' Jacquie said, with a smile that did not quite hide disappointment. I knew she craved excitement and there in the Pyrenees, at the end of winter, there was little to be had apart from a dubbed American film or a delicious dinner, and even less that we could afford.

Ulric and Dad departed on a Sunday, my father attempting to hide concern that we'd never survive in such a harsh, poor region. He wanted to lighten the load, do anything to help, but the chapel was huge, a millstone of vast proportions, and he was deeply troubled for us.

Back on the foothills, Skull Face pursued me to the umpteenth vine. He'd been following me, breathing on me, all morning, as if, like an insect, he'd become more active in the spring sunshine. 'You've got to *feel* it as well,' he added. 'The movement, it's everything.'

'What? How? I *am* feeling it.'

'I don't know *how*,' he glared. 'You just learn to understand how the sap rises, then cut it so it flows.'

I observed the stem and the little shoots, trying to follow the life flow of the plant and cut it as he'd shown me. This, apparently, was 'the movement'.

'Well, it's better,' he sulked. 'Of course, I'm going to die before we finish this row. Now try, oh no! No! No! What are you doing? In God's name! And you, the *amoureux*, have you bought a ring yet?'

'Yes, I've bought the rings. Joseph, we must have done a hundred rows. I'm doing them fine. We could have done two hundred if you'd cut some.' I was enjoying his curiosity about marriage, feeling sure that he'd lived an entire lifetime devoted to almost nothing but the fields.

'You're injuring them, look!' He shook his head in frustration and then proceeded to hack at the adjacent vine, glancing back to check my progress. 'How can you afford a wedding ring? Oh no. Look. Look, *bon Dieu*, you're getting it all wrong!'

'You can't keep doing this to me,' I groaned. 'She wanted an ivory wedding ring, twenty-seven francs. She wouldn't have a gold one. Mine's gold and it's so thin that it's almost transparent.'

'Look at what you're doing! Good God.' He slapped his forehead. 'I'd be better asking my sister. Are you not an imbecile?' I felt a fury coming on, as if we'd reached a point in our relationship where a stand-off was inevitable.

The old man watched as I placed the jaws of the cutter at the base of the entire head of the next vine and, glaring at him, slammed the handles together. 'Ahhhgh!' he screamed, the blood in his shrivelled face draining. 'You've killed it! Assassin! You did that on purpose. Assassin!' he gasped, stamping about in the dust. 'Where in heaven did you come from?'

We moved to the next vine while his temper burned furiously but he said nothing. Some colour returned to his face so that it no longer resembled crushed brown paper. 'Okay, okay, *c'est bien*.' He patted my back. '*C'est bien*. Perhaps I misjudged you. *Calmes-toi*; I think you've got it,' he said, reaching to pat my shoulder then, changing his mind, awkwardly withdrawing his hand.

We worked the mornings together, gradually picking up speed and usually, in the afternoons, Joseph went home to rest.

'Joseph?' I said, as we sat eating our lunch under a cherry tree. 'I'm learning to dance the rock and roll. *Le rock* . . . in a class, with Jacquie, in Perpignan.'

'A man,' he glared, amazed, 'in a dancing class! It's embarrassing. You're not ashamed?'

'It's fun. All the young here know how to do it. If you can't dance the rock, you never get to dance with anyone. It's boring.'

'You're insane,' he said, closing his knife up and shoving his bottle back into the dishcloth bag. 'You must be sick. Any man knows how to dance. It's natural for men, and besides, you already have a woman.' There was a moment of silence, where his thought process seemed to be travelling to a conclusion like the sap in a beautifully cut vine. 'You mean . . .' he stared blankly, 'one woman is not enough?'

It was an afternoon in April, just after they'd accepted a bottle of pastis and joined the electricity up with no questions asked, but before they'd connected the phone in the curate's house. (Louis had told me to have a bottle ready for that too. I wanted some extra cable.) We'd gone to the post office to speak to Lance Fumpf, our drug company sponsor. We were excited, having received another promising letter from him affirming his original support. So much seemed positive. Incredibly, we'd managed to survive, building, nursing and working the fields together. Surviving, though, over our first year is about all we'd been able to do.

The woman at the counter icily pointed to an available phone booth and we settled in to make the big call. 'Here goes, Rupe.' Jacquie dialled the number while I nervously read the graffiti. 'Hello, Lance,' I heard, 'well, it's about the chapel. Yes, it's coming on fine. Well, that's just it, we need some help. You remember you said that you would help us? Well, we're at a stage now where we . . .' I stuck my ear to the phone, hearing him faintly. *'I'm sorry, but I'm afraid there's nothing left for this year. Everything's already allocated. You see, there are so many who need it more, but when you're finished,*' Lance added cheerily, *'we'll send you equipment, syringes and things perhaps.'* His careful voice made the position horribly firm and clear. Stunned, Jacquie thanked him, then hung up. 'Help with a capital H' had been Lance's opening gambit when we'd first met. Now Jacquie quietly uttered, *'Help with no capital,'* and we sat in dreary silence for a moment until someone tapped on the glass. 'I'll go and pay for the phone,' I insisted, unwilling to experience a further skirmish with the post-office gossips, the queens of the *téléphone arabe*.

'We're screwed, aren't we?' Jacquie put her hands over her face.

'No, babe, not yet. Come on,' I looked at her, feeling daunted. 'We'll just have to build it ourselves, alone.'

'It'll take years,' she said, defeated, slightly aggressive, tears coming.

Coincidentally and perhaps providentially, we had decided that I would finally go and visit my mother. I say 'we' because without Jacquie's determination to put an end to the ten years of silence I doubt that the reunion with Mother would have taken place so early, if at all. Years ago she had sold up and moved to Andorra, a principality about four hours' drive from the chapel. She ran a little business, but apart from this I knew little.

'We can't live where we do and not let her know,' Jacquie had said often. 'She's older now, Rupe. You're older. Things have changed. It would mean so much to her. You'll find that she's forgotten all about your father.' I had never really forgiven her for the confusion and fear in my childhood and I was anticipating any conversation getting out of control and the rash behaviour that used to follow. But Jacquie was right. Things should be different.

We'd gone up over mountain passes and through the valleys on the way down into the heart of the tiny principality. I was still preparing myself as a child might; it was the only point of reference I had. I hadn't spoken in the car since we crossed the frontier forty minutes before and Jacquie was aware and making kind allowances for this. I had an address and a number but had chosen not to telephone, wishing to see my mother as she was, unprepared. I wanted some kind of control and in not allowing her time to form ideas, I knew I'd have a chance of a conversation without preconceptions taking over.

Mother lived in a tall building in the town. We'd found it easily. I remember pressing the number in the lift and my heart pounding as if I'd raced through the mountain pass on foot. I was listening to every sound, smelling the Spanish cooking from the other flats as the lift clicked between floors, passing voices behind closed doors and the faint mumbles of televisions and children. I wanted some familiarity, some idea of what to expect. Jacquie stood next to me, smiling, looking very smart. 'Will you just relax?' She clutched my hand. 'You're going to meet your mother for goodness' sake, not the Pope.'

'The Pope would be easy,' I said, 'he's predictable.' The doors swung open into a corridor with dark wallpaper and a smell of polish and detergent. Mother was there.

'Hello, Mum.' I smiled.

It's freaky, hugging someone that you've hugged a thousand times before a decade out of time, yet feeling the strangeness of the very first time. Even Mother's perfume seemed familiar, yet her body was harder and more angular, the softness gone, dissipated in some other room, alone, along with my childhood.

'Rupert,' she said, utterly overwhelmed. 'Well, well,' she flapped. 'Well, what a surprise. Come in.'

She had blonde hair, cut to shorter than shoulder length. She looked as though she was coping with the sudden apparition of a ghost. Mum had always been pretty. A decade had not aged her greatly despite her self-imposed estrangement from England and all that it must have taken out of her to survive there. I wondered if she was lonely, knowing the answer already and knowing also that attempting to interfere would bring disaster. She was pale, probably from the shock of seeing me standing there. I now deeply regretted this surprise, but I knew the possible reactions and was trying to protect both of us.

She ushered us into the flat while I clocked every object that I could. I wanted to see what she had brought with her through time and what parts of us were there. Her clothes, everything about her was as I had expected. I kept remembering that she was a good and capable mum and this in turn brought about a sense of tremendous guilt for the distance I'd taken. I kissed her cheek, then brightly introduced Jacquie, whom she greeted with a warm smile, asking almost immediately how long we'd been together.

I'd hoped she might ask some humorous question like, 'So where have you been for the last ten years?' but shocked as she was, she said very little. We were both thrown by the very foreignness of being together and now there was much to ask and say, yet so many minefields to avoid. Her hatred for certain relations and my father and stepmother would be the first thing to ignite should we accidentally stumble in that direction.

'This is my office.' Mum showed us into a room with a large, sparsely ordered desk behind a window with filing cabinets across to the other side of the room. Everything was in its place and neatly presented. She ran a small business from home.

'Things are quite tough,' she smiled, 'but I manage.' She looked away, her face softening a little. The room was as I imagined the inside of my brother Brock's brain to be. It was easy to see who had given him his meticulous nature.

'Come upstairs and sit down,' Mum said.

There were carpets everywhere and the apartment was warm. Very few things seemed to be out of their allotted place and I could feel the practical, sensible, comfortable nature that my mother had all around, and tinges of the emotion of times gone by made a target of my conscience. Her flat towered above the dingy narrow mountain streets, and bright light streamed in as if it were breaking through the canopy of a forest.

I watched her, my eyes glued to her. She wore a blue sweater, a tweedy-looking skirt, tights and sensible shoes. The chair was comfortable and there were things from our childhood cottage scattered about: a picture here and there, a stuffed creature set in a glass case, which evoked mixed feelings of fondness and sorrow.

I always felt that the old cottage was haunted. It used to terrify me. Years after we'd left, Brock told me of how he used to have his ribs tickled while lying in his bed alone in the darkness. It was a strange house. I couldn't blame Mum for selling it and getting out.

'Would you like a drink?' she asked. For a moment I thought she might be shaking.

'I'm afraid there are some people waiting for us,' I lied, losing my nerve for a minute. I just began to feel uncomfortable and upset. Jacquie shut me up with a simple glance and asked Mum for some water. As she headed for the kitchen she asked softly after Brock.

It must be a terrible thing to have all of your children sever their contact. Mother had sadly inadvertently managed to do this all by herself. An acrimonious separation had turned into years of psychological trauma and the result was children who preferred to turn the taps off on love to protect themselves. At first I couldn't physically write to her. I'd sit there with a page or a card in front of me and was unable to make my hand push the pen, *physically* unable, without tears. Ironically it was Lucilla, my stepmother, who urged me to try.

I told Mum that Brock was fine and that we lit candles for Gareth in churches whenever we were able. I knew she was hurt too – pneumonia, of all things to die of – but she would not see it that way. There had been rash accusations. We were swords, we children, and this tragedy had been an opportunity to lunge at my father's heart. Subsequently, I had no wish to share my thoughts of grief because I feared how they might be used later.

She returned with drinks for both of us, saying in a sad and pleasant tone that she also lit candles, but the blame for Gareth's death predictably and inevitably arose. 'Well,' said Mum, 'I was absolutely sure that your father and that woman never fed you all properly and of course his friends . . .'

'Mum, don't.'

'Yes, but if your father had taken a little more . . .' She began to wind up. I noticed it immediately: the rushed speech and the inability to hear.

'Mum, *please*,' I said, sharp, defensive, winding up like a cobra. 'Gareth was ill, *that's all*.'

'Okay,' she said quietly, 'all right, Rupert, all right.'

I was grateful that she was controlling herself and sensed how she was resisting a wish to dredge up the old grudges and thus try to manipulate me. I was surprised at how quickly I could become angry and I hadn't realized how much more in control I would be. I was no longer a child.

Despite the distance from England, Mother seemed to be in a place that worked for her. The more I looked at it, the more her new life seemed appropriate. She obviously managed well but looked tired. I hoped that she had found some peace.

Mum turned to the obvious courtesies. 'And you, Jacquie,' she asked, with genuine curiosity, 'what does your father do?'

Jacquie's gift for adapting to any situation, her ability to read people so well and I supposed Jake's superb tuning of her upwardly mobile social skills, made me burst with admiration. 'Oh, he's dead,' she said.

'I'm sorry,' said Mother. Then, more delicately, she asked what he'd done for a living.

'He was in oil.' Jacquie smiled and Mother gave a relieved glint of approval before getting up. 'Would you like to see some pictures of Rupert when he was little?'

'I thought your dad drove a truck?' I whispered, as my mother went to fetch them.

'He did,' murmured Jacquie, 'for Shell.'

The photographs were wonderful, and Mother turned the album pages delightedly, apparently unaware of the way they would affect me. Black-and-whites, happy faces; Brock and Gareth and I, arms linked in a magical, preserved innocence. My 'on-the-ball' face smiled fixedly as my heart bled with love and sorrow for the dead son and childhood promises that I felt had never truly come to be, and a strange, cautious, loving understanding, . . . for Mother.

With something of a hurrah, we'd moved into the curate's house during the warmer months so that I didn't have painstakingly to build all the windows at once. My hands had hardened and certain building skills were very gradually sinking in, but carpentry took me a while even to grasp. Another summer of work in the vineyards and orchards came to an end while I practised my plumbing following the advice of the man in the DIY mega-shop in Perpignan. I fitted a bathtub (bought in King's Lynn for £6) and a sink salvaged from the remains of a demolished hotel up the road. The only part I couldn't face finding and refitting was the lavatory, so at great expense we bought a new one and jerry-rigged a ragged plastic cistern to fit. When the maiden attempt at plumbing the curate's house bathroom was finished, I rushed downstairs where Jacquie was sitting expectantly and turned on the mains. There was a hiss as the pressure mounted in the new, still-gleaming copper pipes, and then silence. 'There,' I said triumphantly before noticing the stream of water pouring down the wall and the drips gathering speed as they fell from the ceiling in several places. Jacquie began to smile infuriatingly.

'If it doesn't work,' said the same man on a further visit to the DIY shop, 'don't get angry. After the fifth try, you have a cigarette. Then, if the joins still leak after that, who knows?' He shrugged. 'Instead of killing yourself, you go for a walk. You just keep walking,' he said with a mad look. 'It stops you from freaking.'

Then, over a long, wood-burning winter, we managed to equip the chapel itself with most of the simple comforts until January when it snowed and the firewood we'd bought ran to nothing. As it always has been there in the Roussillon, in very bad weather the roads and electricity fail at the same time. Friends in Britain and elsewhere had sometimes assumed that all was invariably warm and sunny in south-west France, season after season. We looked out at the white coat that covered the mountainside and, through dense clouds, glimpsed helicopters where they were fishing old people out of houses without heat or light. Jacquie's tiny nursing clientele had suffered in the freak cold spell. Many had died.

'If I can't get out to work we'll starve,' said Jacquie.

We made the last of the four-franc coffee and looked for breakfast. I was always anxious about these things. If I took the insulin shot and there wasn't enough to eat it might be a hideous end to the morning. But it would be shaming, I felt, to go to the neighbours for food like that. So I drank a glass of sugar-water and ate some stale baguette, then waded through the snow and into the forest to find dead trees that might be still standing which I could cut for fuel.

'Everything's going to be fine,' we'd tell one another, kissing in bed, with a single candle burning amidst the smell of dust and sodden logs, while above us the light danced and inspired over the beams that had once come from Michael's great wood.

This was a situation that would repeat itself at least twice more in our battle to build the chapel. We were fortunate to have found our friends. I had little to offer the local community in order to break into that mysterious regional economy. Every single man was a hack builder and I didn't play rugby or spend much time in the café. Jacquie on the other hand was well liked. She was the little nurse and her brave endeavours over the years saved us from failure without a doubt. At the end of one January we began burning the furniture. Then, by hand, I sawed through some railway sleepers, which proved so toxic that eventually we threw them burning into the snow. Grimly we wondered what to do next.

'I know!' Jacquie shouted. I remember her springing to her feet and rushing upstairs and could hear her through the ceiling as she thumped about in the bedroom. Returning, her face beaming and her arms loaded, she announced, 'We'll burn our old shoes!' While I loaded them into the burner she went across to the chapel and rummaged about in some boxes. Somehow she found pasta and old packet soup from the days in the mobile home.

'Tra laa!' She arrived back. 'We're back in business.' She made the dogs bark as she laughed. 'Come and dance the rock with me, Rupe, come on!' The shoes sizzled and the radio had us leaping about. We couldn't afford the dancing classes any more but it didn't matter. 'You can do it,' Jacquie laughed, as she spun about, 'you'll be able to go up to anyone in the room and dance with them; you'll never be standing there on your own.'

Many times when we'd been invited over to Eddy and Dorothy's house for dinner, Eddy'd lean across the table with a suddenly kindly face and murmur discreetly, 'You know, if you need a little help I can lend you some.' Sometimes we'd both been sorely tempted to say yes but had left happy, our bellies full, climbing into another banger to head home. Nothing would stand in our way. A foolish attitude, perhaps, but we were determined to go it alone.

*

Months later, shortly before we were due to head home for our wedding day, we were sitting quietly at the table in the little curate's house, staring and fretting. Things had finally bottomed out.

'Jacq, we've been broke like this before. It'll be okay.'

'But it *isn't* okay. We're still on packet soups and instant mash.' She sighed. 'At least we bought the wedding rings.'

Feeling responsible for our dilemma, I looked around the room as if a solution might just appear in the air. Being a man does this. You are traditionally programmed to feel that it's *your* problem when the money runs out. It's got nothing to do with equality. It's a human instinct to wish to provide and be needed. 'Darling,' I said, 'there are no other jobs. I don't know what to do to make it better.'

'Even if we can't get home for the wedding,' she looked towards the window, away from me, 'oh, it's not your fault. Look, we should get some dog food, though.'

Two days later, feeling wretched, we telephoned Marie-Antoinette. 'Marie? Could we come up?' Arm in arm we climbed the hill to find Marie already at her garden gate.

'Marie,' Jacquie spoke at once and held out a little box, containing a small collection worth a quarter of what Marie wore on one finger, 'do you know anyone who might want to buy these?'

'And we've got some beautiful curtains,' I added, holding up the things that my father had brought.

Shedding a tear Marie laughed. 'Come on,' she said. 'Are you hungry?' she asked, without waiting for a reply. Then her face set, almost darkened. 'How long has this been going on? You know Louis and I wondered how you could manage.' Food appeared and as she spoke, I felt a strange, humbled feeling, something like homesickness. 'Those curtains are beautiful,' she went on. 'Now, eat, eat.' She excused herself. 'I've just got to make some calls.'

15 Hand to Mouth

Our 1964 two-cylinder Citroën chugged over the bridges, twisting through the Fens towards my future mother-in-law's Norfolk house. The last hour or so had seen the tiny engine running on vapours, all that remained of the cash from Marie-Antoinette's sale of our curtains and Jacquie's little box of jewellery.

She'd found friends to buy whatever belongings we'd felt we could sacrifice. In truth, only Marie's determination had dispatched us to England and our wedding. She had also taken great care to make the sale of our items as genuine and blunt as possible, avoiding the humiliating notion of charity and insisting that we suffered no loss of face.

'When we get back to the chapel I've got this money-making idea,' I announced.

Jacquie stamped her frozen feet and stuck her hands in her groin for warmth, taking on a bossy tone, 'No other projects, Rupe, you've got to finish the chapel. I can do more night shifts.' She looked out across the grey of the Fens, searching more than ever for solutions to the chapel's completion and finding none. Rain began to speckle the windscreen. 'I might go to see Jezebel while we're home. She's not coming to the wedding, and after all, it's hope I'm looking for.'

I did not think then about why Jezebel didn't wish to come to the church and see us, the two she claimed to have found for one another. It never occurred to me that she might not feel comfortable there. I was young and my faith in people's better nature was unusually and foolishly strong.

'Still, I know we're lucky,' said Jacquie. I suppose this was quite a sweet thing to hear from your bride as you lurch and splutter in a terrible car on the way to your wedding. I expect I smiled but I still had some worries.

'I know,' I said, 'but I'm afraid of the future. All I've done is build our house and look after the vines. God! I'm in my mid-twenties, the chapel's not even half finished and when we're done, I still won't have a job. I'll hit thirty as a dumb but shit-hot handyman.'

'Yes, well, you can look at it like that,' she said, with a mixture of weary patience and irritation. 'You'll also be the director of your own holiday company.'

'You're far better at that kind of thing than me,' I said, but Jacquie's thoughts were already elsewhere.

'We've got to have a party before the wedding,' she had decided, 'maybe a get-together with all the guys or something.' She scrunched her eyes up and swayed a little in the seat, her smile bright in the cold as the car tugged around the dreary countryside like a rotting sponge cake on a spring. I pulled at the wiper knob and waited for the blades as they slowly gasped across the screen. There would be more than 200 people to look after. Bill, my best man and oldest friend, was coming from Chicago. We had the vicar to see and the hymns to choose and so many other things to arrange. The whole wedding was already a marathon event, with a massive reception in King's Lynn's finest hotel. It was impossible to imagine how we'd be able to fit another party in. I asked if her brother would be at home.

'Stephen?' she asked glumly. 'He'll be wherever Mum is.'

Of all the things I did during our wonderful time together, one of the most stupid, I felt, the most arrogant, was to judge Jacquie's background by the rules I'd acquired in my own. My needs could never run parallel to hers, although in those days we believed that even our dreams ran in synch. When Jacquie's father died her mother Barbara was left with little money and few options. She had Stephen who was barely adolescent to bring up and Linda had not yet flown the nest. Jacquie often felt that her mother overcompensated and smothered Stephen in the absence of the father. It may well have seemed that way but there were other more significant things happening. Every mother knows her child and Barbara was trying, under difficult circumstances, to cope with the gradual onset of Stephen's illness. Jacquie felt bitterly that Barbara's mothering and Stephen's hopelessness meant the two deserved one another. Looking in from the outside it seemed that way too. Long before Stephen was diagnosed I felt compelled to write a letter telling Barbara that I felt that overprotecting him was a mistake. How was he supposed to grow up? I regretted this enormously when finally the truth became apparent and a proper diagnosis was made.

'We're not like you,' Jacquie had told me. 'Everybody kisses and cries in your family. I love it, and your dad, it's almost ridiculous the way you all go on.'

I only remember one or two instances of Jacquie discussing her father with Linda or her mother. Nobody really seemed to talk about him when they were together. It just upset things, but it did not mean that there wasn't love. It was just a different way of dealing with things from anything I understood.

'You know, Rupe, you could learn to be harder,' Jacquie would often tell me. This, I knew, was true, and yet this learning to be harder on my part would be the death of her.

'One in three marriages don't make it,' she said as the little Citroën neared its destination.

'One in three?' I said, sighing a little. 'You're talking like Jake again. For God's sake just trust, this once, just this one time, that fate will be kind.'

Jacquie looked at me intently. 'I know what you say is right but what we have is my *everything*. If we fall apart, Rupe, my faith in life will go.'

Stephen sat in the living-room of the tidy modern brick house on an estate on the perimeter of King's Lynn. He was watching TV across from the new electric fire with the glowing plastic logs. 'How are yer?' He nodded as I shook his hand, his accent heavy Norfolk. 'Are yer ready then?' He winked, referring to the wedding.

Stephen was around twenty, slowly passing through that stage of growing up during which some general clumsiness is excusable. He was ill equipped yet emerging into a cold world that would take its time to see past the confusion in his life. Their mother, Barbara, welcomed us. 'You like prawn cocktail, Rupert?' she asked, in a milder but still pronounced Norfolk accent. Food appeared and plates departed with impressive efficiency, while Stephen sat, absorbed by the television. 'Cuppa tea, Stephen?' Barbara bustled about, trim, strong-willed, immensely practical. She removed the lock device from the phone in the hall and rang someone about the wedding flowers.

Barbara worked on a market stall most Tuesdays. I admired the independence she maintained. She was brought as a child to Norfolk from London during the East End air raids and although she'd become a countrywoman, her practical devotion to her own suggested that she'd never lost her East End values and ties. I admired that too. In the morning there'd be coffee on the bedside table. 'Come on, you two,' she'd say, her short curly hair perfectly in place, 'got a lot to sort out today if you want that weddin'.'

'Mornin'.' Stephen sat at the breakfast table wearing a jogging outfit.

Jacquie looked across, slightly irritable. 'Aren't you supposed to be at work?'

He'd been doing well to hold the job down. It was hard, up early, dirty: 'There's money in muck,' his stepfather had said. Barbara had remarried, to a man called Ron who farmed potatoes on a huge scale and was a self-made success with tremendous drive. Unsurprisingly, he found Stephen's lack of initiative frustrating.

'More bacon, Stephen? Come on, finish that last piece of toast,' said Barbara. 'Rupert, how'd you like your eggs?' Food appeared as fast as it was possible to eat, and just like her daughter Linda, Barbara tore into the washing-up like a shark, clearing the table in seconds. 'Go on,' she said, pushing the last rasher of bacon on to my plate, urging me to finish it off as she emptied the teapot into my cup.

Stephen had gone. Pop music thudded faintly through the ceiling from a ghetto blaster on hire purchase, the conditions of which deal he hadn't been able to grasp when being helped to fill out the forms.

It was a chilly May morning and the church was packed with a mixture of television and advertising people and a majority of Jacquie's family and friends from the heart of Norfolk. Everyone got along wonderfully despite the enormous cultural divide. The wonder of a wedding is that people don't care – there is always enough goodwill to send a ship to the moon. My brother Brock drove the little blue Citroën and Jacquie appeared in a flowing white dress that my stepmother Lucilla had made over many months. A thin blue trim ran around the dress and a veil swirled in the wind as she entered the church looking truly lovely. A trail of frozen bridesmaids were to follow, including Caroline and my sister Alice, shivering under the grey skies.

Jacquie seemed to shine. It really was one of the best days of her life. My Uncle Brendan, a vicar in Northern Ireland, came across to conduct the service, and fire and brimstone rocked the inside of the church while innocence washed over every moment. My best friend sang 'Forever Young', the words of which would come back to me so many years from then with a terrible truth and dark irony. It was a happy, happy day, yet like all young grooms I shook the hundreds of hands and danced and stammered through my speech with complete oafishness and some terror. The reception went on endlessly and Jacquie was having so much fun that she wouldn't leave until threatened with being the dregs of our very own wedding.

At the Job Centre

Two months later, we were back in France and desperate to find work.

'I told you, Rupe,' said Jacquie, 'Jake said my restaurant shares were worth nothing. It was all eaten up by the interest, everything gone.' She became fractious when I said that I could accept that the shares were worthless but was hurt about being excluded from her discussion with Jake. 'Look,' she said, 'it was a private agreement, private, between him and me. I told you. Anyhow, we came here for jobs,' she added, snapping us away from the subject.

'I know that.' I smiled politely at the man behind the counter. 'But they've only got one job available and that's for a man.' I tried to reason things out. If Jacquie owned half of the restaurant, then surely she should know exactly when the game should be up.

'Rupe,' she insisted, deftly changing direction, 'you've got to finish the chapel. We'll survive, so let's not fight over this.'

We went to the car and sat in silence while I tried to figure how the huge investment she claimed to have had in the restaurant was suddenly gone. I could not understand why there wasn't going to be a huge bust-up between them over this. All the pride she'd had in the place. This news, I imagined, was devastating for her. How could it be that she'd lost the bloody lot without even knowing it was going to happen? She seemed simply to embrace the situation with painful acceptance.

'Jacq? Does Caroline know?'

Jacquie refused to speak further. I was mystified and by now frustrated. 'Well, I'm going to see about this washing-up job. Who knows? It'll keep us going at least.'

'I bet you'll be out,' her eyes didn't look for mine, 'every evening after you finish, eyeing up all the nubile young tourists.'

'Why are you saying this? I can't just stay at the chapel. What d'you expect, that for the rest of my life I'm going to do nothing because if I step outside I might run off? What about the video business I want to start? You said you think it's good. I'll have to go out and work for that, won't I?'

'This is different.'

'Listen, I'm getting irritated with the heartache over the restaurant and yet the way there are no explanations and all this bullshit about me running off. How many girlfriends have I had in my life? Maybe five? And how many men have you dumped? Would you like me to make you a list? Now, what is going on?'

She only shrugged, still tense. 'Nothing; nothing's *going on*,' she replied bitterly, though I knew it wasn't directed at me.

The seaside restaurant boasted 600 covers a day in three barbaric sittings. For the punters it was heaven, I suppose, to have food and comfort available well into the early hours and a soft sandy beach only a few yards away. It was a short season and everyone was there to burn the midnight oil and make as much money as they possibly could. Workers realized very quickly that money could be made, but they couldn't do much except slave. Life quite simply went on hold. On my first night I washed over 1,000 plates. It was two-thirty when I finished cleaning the floor and sat amid the tin tables in the forecourt watching the last of the inebriates stagger their way back to the endless tents and mobile homes along the coast.

A bright moon shone down and stars scattered a sky without a single cloud. It was warm too, though raining. My hand was cut as I'd dropped a glass in the sink. I wasn't going to heal for a while because my hands would be sodden for weeks but it didn't seem to matter and anyway, the money was okay. Someone kicked a bottle down the walkway. It skimmed and chipped then smashed on coloured paving-stones that couldn't be seen in the day for crowds. Music blared as a night-club door burst open, taking some seconds to swing shut and leave the fluorescent street alone, running into the darkness of the beaches beyond. I had a feeling that I should be somewhere else, but this would be okay, I decided, for a while.

'Two *vin rouge* for the six,' a voice flashed past. Two months had passed.

The restaurant owner, Hector, wrote on the bill for table four, then scribbled it out and began scrabbling impatiently for the six. 'I can't go on like this,' he puffed, only half intending anyone to hear. He mopped his brow, stuffing the handkerchief back into a pair of faded shorts that creased too tight around the crotch.

'That's twice now!' the neurotic chef squealed, his spindly and rather grubby fingers grasping at a blur of stainless-steel objects. His dark hair looked like the fuzz on the top of a coconut, his eyes like currants on spotty white skin. '*Merde*,' he hissed, 'I did it again. I'm really burnt this time. Did you see?' I scrubbed maniacally at a pot the size of a baby's bath, reaching beside to unload another batch of steaming plates from a huge machine, condensation from the ceiling dripping on to my head and back.

'Look at me!' the chef cried amid shafts of flame.

'The eleven, good God!' screamed his commis. 'I've sent them the food for the three!'

The vulgar but incredibly good-looking girl leaped on to the counter, her face dripping in the heat, eyes scanning. 'Oh no! They're eating it. Cretins!' Her chin jutted out 'AY! You. You ordered steak!' Her husky voice continued, screeching across the crowded enclosure, 'SINCE WHEN DID STEAK COME WITH FINS?'

'Another steak for the three.' Hector's wife, Rosie, spoke calmly, standing at the front of the kitchen. She tapped on the counter, unfazed. 'Dalida! Get down.'

Jacquie had joined the restaurant staff shortly after me and we'd been there together for nearly two months, lodging in the big house above the restaurant with Hector and Rosie. It was just too far to go home each day. We could have just afforded to but if we were to save to buy materials for the chapel, then stay we would.

Sitting at the tin tables after hours, we were watching a drunken English lad pick a fight and lose to a boy who practised the same kick-boxing art as Linda's Frank. This one incident aside, out there in the avenue it was remarkably peaceful. It was further down by the bigger clubs where the testosterone flowed that it wasn't so easy at that time of night.

'Another week, Rupe, and we can go home. Pity. It's been really great.'

'You find this fun?' I laughed weakly, noticing the smell of sweat on my shirt.

'Did you read *The Prophet*, the book your father gave us at the wedding? It's really good when you feel desperate. Think of all the money we'll have made. Living here has helped us a lot. Come on. Smile. Rupe, someone's looking after us. We've been in France all this time and we're still together and safe. We're lucky to have enough to eat. I know you get disheartened. Life can be horrible but we're still lucky. Those cold sores will go. It's exciting, Rupe, it's like a ticket to have fun.'

I began to loathe this reminder that because we were still functioning and together then we must be happy. I shook my head. 'I'll see Joseph when we get back and I can go pick grapes for him. I don't mind working hard, Jacq; I just can't live like you, with so little sleep. I'll do that video thing I told you about. I'm sure it's going to work.' It had come to me that in lodging here Jacquie could sustain an atmosphere of almost permanent excitement. The fury of the restaurant kept her speedy all day and then the hunt for thrills in the clubs kept us going until so late each night that exhaustion pulled the curtain down.

'As long as I get five or six hours I can manage.' Jacquie spoke briskly, like a nurse, as if this situation was something apart from her own. 'Anyway, your tiredness is the diabetes.'

'It's also human. Almost no one has that kind of energy. Jacq, every single night we're out till three or four. I'm ugly,' I motioned to my fat lip and the sores on my lower jaw, 'I'm tired. You're supposed to cope with five hours' sleep at sixty, not when there are so many reasons to be in bed.' This statement annoyed me in itself because it reminded me how ugly I was becoming.

'Oh, stop being so ungrateful.'

'I'm grateful all right. And I don't mean to be negative. It's just that, Jacq, things are strange with you. You know we haven't even slept together in over a month.'

'Look at the way we work,' she snapped, then sighed, paradoxically pleading fatigue. I pointed out that this was a matter of priorities.

'No,' she said. 'I love you, Rupe, but I need to unwind.'

'So unwind!' I said, feeling bitter, trying to avoid saying anything that I might regret but wanting a row just the same.

She looked for distraction. A man in the bar across the road stumbled, pushing his drunken friend back in his seat.

'It's not your thing, is it?' I asked.

'What?'

'Sex.'

'All right,' she said impatiently, 'let's go to bed then.'

'Like going to bed tonight will sort it? Why don't you tell me what's up?'

Above us the lights on the front of the restaurant went out, drawing Jacquie's attention to the brightness of the surrounding bars and clubs as if she were a moth.

'Look, I need to have some fun,' she insisted, staring angrily. 'You just don't appreciate the chance we have.'

'If you had to stay back, Jacquie, washing up in the kitchen, would you still be so enthusiastic?'

'We'll just go to bed then.'

'You go,' I said coldly, frustrated that she refused to understand.

'Look.' She leaned on the table as if she were lecturing a spoilt child. 'I've said I'll sleep with you. What more do you want?'

I slumped back in my chair. 'That's just great. Fifty nights out in a row and every night you're after the wondrous big thrill. What are you, sixteen again? You're doing the same shit over and over and over again. I mean, what didn't you find out yet? And suddenly for some reason you think a ten-minute shag is going to fix it? Come on. What's wrong with being just the two of us?'

She got up and marched off towards the bars as Hector cleared the chairs around me.

'You sleep soon, my son,' he said, 'you don't look so beautiful. Not like me.' He scratched his balding head while pouring a beer, left it on the table before me, cleared the remaining plastic flowers from the surfaces, coaxed a smile and bade me goodnight.

At summer's end we'd returned to the chapel and little by little, our situation changed.

A Chinese nurse in the village had Jacquie on call most days, so as the months passed we were able to buy things that were structurally important for the building. Nursing, it seemed, was lucrative. Jacquie spent a lot of time making her house calls and as the days progressed, we hardly saw one another. It was probably the perfect solution. Jacquie was surrounded by endless change once more, with new households to visit all the time and a certain amount of human drama to provide an interesting flare to events now and again.

Slowly, in the time spent alone, it dawned on me that I'd become utterly dependent. It's frightening for anyone, regardless of sex, to know that you've given up your ability to live without another's help. For a couple with children it's another matter, and perhaps that's what the chapel and I subsequently had become for Jacquie: surrogate children.

Working on it, which was taking years, also had the undesirable effect of expanding my worst imaginings and fears. Time alone triggered many dark thoughts. 'What if I get to the end of this and the diabetic project doesn't work?' Nothing – no training, no future. When I dared to air my fears, Jacquie was practical. 'If you want to go back to the fields with Skull Face and earn a hundred a week, then fine. I can get four times that for a weekend. You'll break your back and we'll never finish the chapel.'

I'd started on a project that I felt might help and give me something of my own to aim for. The idea involved running videos on the screens in the many night-clubs in the area. Most already had enormous screens or elaborate television systems. It dawned on me that these clubs when combined could function together as a little TV network. Through various contacts, I'd been able to find the first action footage I needed to start the thing up. In return for a little advertising footage thrown in, a major company had financed the cutting of the material and a cheap plane ticket. I'd spent two weeks staying with my parents and Ulric and my sister Alice while working in a little video edit suite in Soho. It hadn't taken me long to get used to the editing machines and really anything would do, racing cars, planes, saucy broads, boobs, bums and explosions. Anything that would draw the dancing public's attention to the club's screen for a moment.

The first few clubs were delighted with the idea, although there was a tendency for the club owners (often quite unsavoury characters) to demand more material or simply to be too crooked and short-sighted to be trusted to return the video-cassettes.

It was high summer, over a year since we'd worked for Hector and Rosie. This particular night was the eve of my second run to deliver the cassettes and Jacquie was unhappy. We were sitting on the stone flowerbeds that I'd built around the walls of the chapel and the sun had just gone down.

'It's beginning to work.' I cheerfully shook the cassette. Perhaps the struggling wouldn't be necessary for much longer.

'Yes, but that's *your* thing.' She threw a pebble for Kansas. I pleaded that it was ours, that we could do this together. She could slow down on the nursing and we'd be able to get help fixing the chapel up, people to do a far better job on it than I could do by myself.

'But I love the things you're doing with it,' she insisted. 'I don't want you to start working all the time.'

'Come on, Jacq,' I said, confused. 'It's not the time now to say you don't like what I'm up to.'

She complained that she didn't want me working nights.

'So what?' I shrugged. 'You work nights all the time. I help you, don't I? Do I complain? Never!' I caught a stony glance. 'Okay, sure – except for some of the dead people. Come on, Jacq, I'll only be doing it once a week, remember.'

A lovely smell of lavender floated about from the big earthen pots that Eddy and Dorothy had given us as a wedding present. Jacquie got up and marched towards the front door.

'Don't just walk off,' I pleaded. 'How can I fix a problem if I don't know what it is?'

She stopped and turned, chewing on the inside of her cheek. 'You'll be out there in the evenings while I'm stuck here,' she said bitterly. 'Like the little wife. You'll run off with some hot young holiday screw.'

'Jacquie, give me some credit. If you don't want me to go alone, then you share it with me. You come with me; we'll distribute the tapes together. There are twelve night-clubs that are willing to run my films so far. It's our own TV station if we do it right.' I tried to hold her hands. 'Come on, Jacq. I'm happy, I've got you. I don't need anyone else.'

'I know, I know,' she nodded, casting her gaze away, 'I just feel like it's your thing and suddenly I'm not going anywhere.'

I looked at her in amazement. 'But you're the one, babe. You've fed us for God knows how long now, everybody in the village knows you. Now there's a chance. It actually works in a small way. They're screaming out for more tapes. Come on, there's something good for us in this. If you're behind me nothing'll stop it.'

Coldly she turned and went into the house. 'I need the car until at least nine. You'll have to leave after that if you want to drop the cassettes to the clubs tonight.' The door closed, leaving bitterness hanging in the air.

The evening came and we fought. 'There's no gas left in the car. No fucking, Jacquie, WHY THE HELL ARE YOU DOING THIS?'

We were to fight every evening for a month until the hopes of making it all work drifted away. Since it seemed to threaten our marriage, I eventually abandoned the video project entirely and once again buried myself in the chapel's construction.

I had made the shocking discovery that Jacquie was willing to sacrifice almost anything in the battle to have our chapel. I was slightly disturbed by this, but without her, I told myself, what was there to fight for? I adored her. She had become and remained everything: she was the reason for it all. She was my confidence, my life. I seemed to lose something at that time, the threads perhaps of my own self-worth.

In the next months I devoted any hours that could be worked to the chapel, becoming almost fanatic and far more careless with the diabetes. Subsequently my understanding of my situation became muddled and equally unhealthy. I eventually found myself losing the skin on my face. Opening up in small areas at first, it advanced, wouldn't heal, then began to seep. I became feverish and looked like death. Jacquie took me to the village's new young doctor, Jacques, who treated me, put me on vitamins like horse pills and prescribed disturbing injections. I did little but sleep for two weeks.

'He said if we're not careful you'll have a breakdown. What's happening to you?' Jacquie asked in fake surprise, that natural smile of hers now seeming caring but almost sinister as she fed me intravenous antibiotics while my head spun around in the air above.

'I got my hopes up,' I told her.

Much later, after a slow and difficult winter, we'd put the curate's house up for rent in an English newspaper and had some luck. It was now June, and the first punters were due to arrive in a couple of weeks. A great deal of preparation was needed.

Since the abandonment of the video project Jacquie had spent a lot of time making sure that I felt positive about the chapel. The dispute had left a rift that would be quickly healed but long in the forgetting. More than likely the whole thing would have struggled anyway but the fact that Jacquie would not help me succeed in achieving anything outside of the building of the chapel left me some-what confused. It was a building, I told myself, nothing more than a building, and there will be other places in our lives. You don't sacrifice a relationship for something so transitory.

People, even the French themselves, dream about the South of France. On soft sunny evenings the long shadows evoke feelings and churn up memories of endless summer. The truth, of course, is far from this. The little summer bungalows of the meagre retired and the straight rendered stone buildings of the rich still howl in the icy *tranmontana*. A cold wind blows there in the south just as hard as it would anywhere. And health, good luck and success are still just as elusive as in cooler climes.

When Jacquie was nursing I would often work for Skull Face. Depending on his mood he'd have me spraying filthy carcinogenic chemicals on grass in the orchards, or driving the tractor or cutting and pruning the trees. He'd often lecture me about the vines and how reliable plants were in comparison to modern people, who were rotten, disgusting, undependable and slovenly through and through.

'You'd come to my funeral, wouldn't you?' he asked one day. I assured him I would. 'I want to leave this world in my sleep,' he said. 'That's how a man should die: peaceful. Not like my brother.' His elder brother had died in pain before Jacquie and I had really known them. Jacquie had administered the last of the care.

'I want to go in my sleep,' said Joseph once more, his face showing me he was certain that it wouldn't happen that way and, like a little boy, he was afraid.

At home there were still many things to achieve before our renters could move into the curate's house. While extracting some lovely French doors from a hotel due for demolition at the local thermal spa of Le Boulou I'd discovered an ancient cast-iron bedstead. The thing itself was cumbersome and grotesquely ornamented, with bunches of pewter grapes, vine leaves and flagons decorating every inch. Hideous or not, at first glance I felt it was a shame that this magnificent example of Napoleonic extravagance would soon be buried in rubble. A small ornamental cherub had pole position in the topmost centre bar. I decided that I could not manage to lift the entire heavy piece and so just salvaged what I could, carefully wrenching the cherub free and sticking it in my pocket. It had been painted white, but with a little elbow grease I'd eventually removed the faded white paint and returned it to its original chipped pewter. I felt it should bring us luck. It now occupied a place of honour in the middle of the main beam in the curate's house downstairs room. Though not particularly religious, I liked the idea of the cherub being near the heart of the building, as if it were watching over us.

The future renters would be here any day and we were beginning to show signs of nervous acceleration in the race to be ready for them. The water supply to the main part of the chapel wasn't complete and one evening I'd been hurriedly soldering with a huge blowtorch in virtual darkness. We were still actually living in the curate's house. The chapel itself now had half a kitchen and I'd promised myself that before bed I'd have finished the soldering of pipes and turned on the water. We could then move in officially the following day. Jacquie was busily moving kitchen things and covers, ready to set up camp on the chapel's newly completed upstairs.

'We've got the mezzanine, the bathroom, and it doesn't matter about the kitchen being a mess. It's enough, Rupe. Don't worry,' she said, rushing about. Things seemed to be easier now with the prospect of a little rental money coming in, and the pace was lessened to some extent.

There weren't any windows, just holes in the huge four-foot-thick walls, and we were back to one extension cord again. 'I don't care. Do you?' I asked. Jacquie shook her head and smiled too as she looked at the mass of double plugs crammed into the battered wire.

The whole affair was ramshackle. The beams supporting the mezzanine were made of railway sleepers that Linda's Frank had found, with double-track ones to span the width of the building. The smaller sections were salvaged rafters from another demolished hotel nearby, as were the patio doors and most of the uninstalled electrical fittings. There was, however, one beautiful aspect to the chapel's renovation. The plastering of the whole inside of the building had taken us months and in doing it we'd sacrificed a great deal of our skin. We'd finished the last bag a few weeks before and, though dusty, the chapel no longer looked bleak. Above us the whole stone-arched, vaulted ceiling sang out in a coat of pure fresh white, like the feathers of a dove.

The heat from my blowtorch travelled well along the rounded walls, better in fact than I'd realized. I was trying far too hard to get the water sorted that night and without thought, almost inevitably, I'd allowed the heat from the powerful flame to travel and meet an upright beam, one of Frank's railway sleepers standing many inches away. The heat began to sizzle the heavily treated wood in the darkness beyond my immediate area of vision. In my slightly manic determination, amid sizzling flux solder and a sea of burnt matches the deadly nearby smoldering went unnoticed.

The copper and tin joins held, so, happily and quite unaware, we headed next door to bed, leaving the chapel and its newly plumbed kitchen to sleep under fresh, perfect white plaster arches.

We woke before eight. From the bathroom window of the curate's house I thought I saw a cloud of plaster dust blowing from the chapel doorway in the *tranmontana*. I'd left the chapel door open to help clear as much of the dust as possible and so was unsurprised and carried on, turning my thoughts to the day ahead.

I brushed my teeth, then made pancakes for our breakfast. We ate cheerfully, excited about our move into the chapel, enjoying the slowness of the morning, taking our time in the cosy little house, while next door the blackened new plaster fell in sheets from the ceiling as the tumbled mezzanine blazed.

Walking into the building with the wind behind me, I had no notion of the fire until it registered, almost as if in slow motion, like a bomb going off in my brain. Flames licked between the water pipes that hung in the air, the timbers gone. Thank God, these were not the timbers from the next-door curate's house roof that were burning. The chapel roof at least, being solid stone, was safe. The railway sleepers and thousands of floorboards, which I had cut to fit every curve of the chapel's walls, were gone or scarred and thus only good for salvage and repairs.

I dropped to my knees in the dust, watching a shelf tumble down where others had fallen, setting light to those below. I felt like the first trout I'd ever caught as a child probably felt, eyeballs bulging, mouth open in horror, senses dulled with shock.

'Rupe,' cried Jacquie, 'how can we do all this again?' Tears streamed down her face. She looked like a little girl. Plaster dust from my hands stuck to her wet cheeks as pathetically I tried to wipe them.

The irony was that the joins in the water pipes had held. I'd done them well. Had they burst, perhaps the fire would have been less severe. We hugged for a moment, kneeling together, somehow pathetic, in the middle of the burning chapel. Then, crying angrily, I attacked the smouldering boards, yanking the beams out of the walls, my thick cloth gloves burning.

'WHAT IS IT? WHAT IS IT THAT YOU FUCKING WANT?' I shouted towards God.

I was young then and my floor was on fire. It also occurred to me that I should have put the lucky cherub in the chapel instead of the curate's house. It crossed my mind later that perhaps God hadn't appreciated the railway sleepers and the oafish way that I'd been putting his place together. 'Okay,' my spirit roared, 'we'll do it again and again.' I screamed, my eyes stinging from smoke and angry tears.

It later came to me that the fire might have been an accident, simply one of those things, but at the time, like my own mother, I couldn't accept it that way. Reality had momentarily left me. This wasn't just life. It was someone's *fault*. There *had* to be someone else to blame.

'How bad is it?' asked my father from London.

'Well,' I muttered, 'we've lost the floor and most of the beams. I think some of it can be saved. The plaster though . . .' I said, dazed. 'It's not the money. It's the energy . . . I mean, to pull it all down and start again. I had scaffolding back then.'

He was very calm. I knew there was nothing to be done, but the phone call somehow put the drama into perspective. My father, blissfully rational, expressed no panic.

Jacquie seemed able to brighten and shift up a gear within the day. 'We'll just have to get on with it,' she said. 'Don't worry, Rupo, I'll find us some help.' Determined, again using the nurse's tool of shutting it all out, she steeped her whole outlook with optimism and went off to the phone. It was a difficult time for her because she spent her days rushing from house to house, trying to keep the aged and dying as comfortable as possible and then returning exhausted to a home which seemed to be similarly desperate. For this I admired and adored her.

Within a week, with the help of various friends that Jacquie had contacted, we had repaired most of what had taken us months to accomplish alone. Pepe, a waiter from our summer at Hector and Rosie's, appeared. 'I 'ave broken my hankel,' he announced in equally fractured English, hobbling in wearing a modest plaster cast, a tool kit under one arm. 'I can't stand to sit at home and talk to myself, and besides zis, I ham han electrician.' His grin faded as he stopped to inspect the huge, melted pile of double plugs and the burnt extension cord.

Hillary and Tony from Essex appeared in an environmentally friendly car. Slightly ill at ease, they unloaded a bag or two and were greeted by Jacquie, who showed them into the curate's house: their home for the next seven days. We'd put flowers on the pillows and left wine, a baguette and other little offerings, hoping that we'd done it right, that the pretty little house would make them happy.

'I told you,' said athletic-looking Hillary as she popped her head up the stairs. Tony was slogging behind with the bags. 'What's that, my love?' he gasped as Hillary went on, 'We should have booked it for two weeks.'

With the curate's house clearly a success, exhausted, we decided to relax a little and headed down to the beach the following afternoon. On our return journey we'd taken a roundabout direction and had driven through Una. It wasn't the first time that we'd passed the old mill since our departure with the mobile home. The place stood brightly lit and open for business. A couple sat outside, browsing through the menu amid the roses in the summer warmth.

'Would you like to go and say hello?' I asked Jacquie.

'They've got rid of the sign I painted,' she said sharply. 'Some other time, Rupe.'

We drove on home in uncomfortable silence, me trying to feel cheerful and wondering why such a beautiful day had suddenly become a springboard for depression. We arrived at the chapel late to find the dogs running with their usual excitement to the edge of the road in welcome. They almost never left the property; it was theirs to guard. Always together: a pair of daft, harmless, old grumbling maids.

'I've written to Jezebel,' Jacquie sighed, dragging herself from the car. 'I bet you're delighted that we're going.' She and a young French friend called Sandra had arranged a trip. Two weeks in England: time for Jacquie to see her mother and get information about diabetic courses for our holiday project. Sandra would get a tour of Norfolk and London. 'Rupe,' Jacquie sounded a little hesitant, 'I've asked Jezebel if she would like a holiday. What d'you think?'

'Sure,' I said, fumbling with the chapel keys and not feeling sure at all.

'She can come back with Sandra and me in the car,' Jacquie went on, as if selling the idea to both of us. 'She'd never be able to afford it otherwise.'

'It's fine,' I said, still unconvinced.

'We owe her one, Rupe,' she continued in a flat, no-bones-about-it tone. 'Look, she found us for one another.' I stifled back my doubts about this as Jacquie went on: 'All she does is sit there in that council house, alone.'

I agreed, as I always did when Jacquie felt strongly about something. I didn't like to share my doubts with her: I was often compliant enough to go along with her instincts and thus to encourage the idea of our mutual faith in the woman.

'Tell you what,' I said, as we walked into the coolness of the chapel and I lit the water heater that our good friends the dustbin men had given us, 'we'll put her in our bed, in the abside. It's bang above where the altar must have been.'

'She'll love it,' said Jacquie, still not particularly cheerful. 'I hope she'll be able to get into the bath.'

In the far end of the chapel I'd built a sort of grotto, making a cove in the area that was once a stable. There I'd built a huge bath with steps up to it. Frank had done the rest with his swimming-pool materials and had made it into a strange, white, druidesque pond.

We'd made stained-glass windows and fitted lights behind them, creating a spiritual effect that made it just possible to see what you were washing.

'Why are you sounding so negative about everything?' I asked. 'What's upset you?'

'Don't you get lonely here on your own all day every day?' Jacquie asked without answering me directly, as she followed me up to bed.

'Sometimes,' I said, growing curious. 'Why?'

'I couldn't bear it,' she said glumly as she peeled off her clothes, 'being alone. I need people around me, Rupe. I need people all the time.' She climbed in, watching me blankly.

'But you're not alone,' I insisted. 'You do have people around you. In fact you never stop. What about Eddy and Dorothy, Louis and Marie?' I flung my things on to the floor and slipped in under the single blanket. 'We're always doing things with them.'

Jacquie kept the solemn face, as if I'd missed the point. 'Baby,' I kissed her, 'what's the matter?'

'Nothing,' she answered, her eyes brimming.

I reminded her that at our party on New Year's Eve we'd had seventy guests. 'You must consider some of them friends.' I looked at her suspiciously. 'Are you pissed off because we went past the old mill coming home tonight?'

She rolled over, turning her back. 'Rupe,' she sighed irritably, 'please, let's not talk about it any more.'

'You know, I'm glad you're going to England,' I said dryly. Ignoring a predictably sarcastic response, I continued more gently. 'You need a break from all this, from everything, Jacq, it's getting under your skin.' Above us, glowing softly in the light of a single bulb, was the scarred and patched, cool white plaster dome of the chapel ceiling.

Jacquie eventually turned and lay quietly on her back, her eyes open, staring into space. I knew her thoughts were far away, still back at the old mill with Caroline and Jake.

16 *Jaffa*

Jacquie and her friend Sandra had been in England for almost two weeks. Since their departure, the chapel, which had not only seemed to be alive but almost breathing, now grew quieter every day. A new friend, Jaffa, had been staying there with me, helping to build the kitchen in his calm, meticulous cabinet-maker's way.

'It's not the same,' he said as, like an ape, I dragged another timber across the room. 'Without her here,' he added, 'you can feel it. The chapel starts to lose its warmth.'

Jaffa was right. I could build the place but Jacquie gave it a pulse: I knew it was she who was really at the heart of its restoration. This was slightly painful to accept, as if my own work and existence were somehow of less significance. Yet there was still satisfaction for me: Jacquie had drive like no other but she lacked direction. Together we could strive towards animating the beautiful old stones and that target seemed to have given everything about us greater purpose.

I'd met Jaffa in a *brocante*. He was slim, stubbly and painfully introverted. His love of nature and its wild gifts seemed in direct opposition to his immense self-control. A constant conflict raged within him, rooted in a painful childhood and capped under an almost silent, gentle lid. In some ways he was a typical Frenchman, passionate about food and wine, the latter passing through him as if he were a sieve, but these were small items in the vast spectrum of Jaffa's experience, which both held him to ransom and made him capable of tremendous, patient empathy.

He'd stare blankly at me as I chainsawed through parts of the floor and thumped unnecessarily large nails through undeserving timbers. Sometimes I'd scream when I hit a finger or swear blindly at a cut of uncooperative wood, and rush about stamping my feet like Skull Face, while in contrast, Jaffa never raised his voice, eyeing me as a passionate, determined, eccentric, undisciplined and often absurd bodger. He'd grown up in Paris, his father a photographer, his mother a nurse. For whatever reason, he'd eventually ended up living with his father alone. The father rarely spoke to him, leading a life of private suffering behind his bedroom door while little Jaffa, mostly left to himself, learned the way of isolation at an uncomfortably early age.

At twenty-three, Jaffa was still struggling with his father's death and the fact that he hadn't been able to save him. It wasn't the first attempt, but for Jaffa it had been too late to stop this time. He could only hold his father and watch him go, having never reached that clearing in the future that he had hoped for, the place where he believed they would finally talk.

He understood my feelings about families, about how important they were. Yet he would always argue with me on any given point. Without knowing it, he often described families like the working parts of a machine that never managed to run smoothly. A family at peace was almost as foreign in his childhood as love without distortion had been in mine. He wore his dark hair mostly short. His simple round glasses were more powerful in one eye than the other. As a boy he'd attended an anti-racist demonstration in Paris where somehow the peaceful march had turned sour. Jaffa, probably going too far with his demonstrating, had been chased into the metro and beaten over the head by a black policeman – a beating which, ironically, had corrected the vision in one of his eyes.

This was the quiet yet stormy luck of Jaffa, introverted, soft-hearted and precise. He could be strong, eloquent and painfully stubborn, but also sensitive and aware of people's pain as some are when left so alone to find the way.

17 *The Witch*

Jacquie and Sandra had decided that it would be better to stay overnight with my parents in London on the way rather than attempt the whole trip from Norfolk to the South of France in one haul. Jezebel, who lived in London, had also been invited for the evening and together they would face the long drive in our small car the following day.

Although some days she would be physically fragile, spiritually Jezebel was as strong as an ox. However, it did not help to lean too hard on her capricious nature, so giving her a minimum of stress was probably sensible. She claimed a number of woes and blamed her sufferings on the malice of spiritual enemies, on the evil that she'd fought and nobly spared others.

When I first encountered her, Jezebel had struck me as a helpless lone parent, a moderately neurotic Turkish mama, yet she was gifted with phenomenal psychic powers. She certainly had a following. Some she claimed simply to have saved from themselves. Undoubtedly these people were grateful. But there were others, she'd said darkly, who hadn't liked the truths she'd brought to light. I feel that Jezebel often drifted between two areas: in the first, with her emotional state as stable as could be, her interpretation of a possible future was often accurate, blunt, and untainted by sudden shifts of emotion. One was indeed fortunate to visit her at those times. In the second area, she became a spookier character, driving an egocentric campaign, canvassing, offering spiritual fast food for the lost living, and boasting live contact with any dead they might care to reach.

The living in search of answers were often made to feel vastly privileged. Over a cup of special coffee hope might be restored. After pouring their hearts out, she was so willing to listen, they'd leave, unknowingly having gratefully accepted whatever the chef had available. On a clear day though, Jezebel's connections with the dead were eerie and usually came with confirmation of some obscure source, occasionally from verifiable hair-raising fact.

Even before leaving her little home in West London where, she claimed, the kitchenware could fly about unaided and the letterbox frequently gushed threats of paraffin and burning matches, Jezebel feared that something was going to go wrong.

I ask myself, even now, what it must have been like for poor petite French Sandra, trapped in a small space for 800 miles with Jezebel staring at the back of her head, identifying good and evil along the way and gloomily churning out the future like fortune cookies.

Their evening with my parents ended theatrically, with Jezebel, claiming the support of the dead and the saints, almost sold out to a houseful of staunch atheists . . . and my father's tears, as he'd taken Gareth's ring from his finger and cast it away. 'There's something bad on it,' Jezebel had declared, offering sympathy even as she bathed in self-appointed authority. I was sorry that my father had felt able to trust this woman. I suppose he'd done it because he'd trusted me. She was very good, I have no doubt of that, but to convince him to remove Gareth's ring was in my view an appalling intrusion. There were warnings in my head. I couldn't identify them at the time she came to us, but doubts and instincts have a habit of being swept aside for the sake of convenience or an easy ride, only to surface with a vengeance when the accounts come in.

It was late summer, a mix of grey skies and heat. Warm torrents fell upon the mountain, followed by sun and steam. I'd been able to hear the river running again, chuckling along at the foot of the mountain in front of the chapel.

Jaffa and I were fitting the last of the door handles to the kitchen cupboards when Jacquie arrived at the chapel door. 'Home!' she said, her face glowing with relief. She tore through the door and went to hug Kansas and Yogi who were both hysterically joyful. Then, smiling brightly, she kissed me. 'Bet you guys have had a wonderful time here without me.' She buzzed about in an almost showbizzy way. 'Oh! It's beautiful. The kitchen's wonderful! You've worked the whole time!'

'How was your mum?' I stroked Kansas and Yogi, slightly lost for things to say, thinking how slowly the time had passed, relieved that she was there in one piece. She came over and put her arms around me, hugged and kissed me, then looked around in real delight. There was electricity in her movements and her eyes were bright with excitement and exhaustion from the long trip. I felt like a man rescued from a desert island.

'Mum's fine,' she told me. 'She's sent you presents; they're in the car. You'll be pleased,' she said, murdering any suspense, 'all your socks are full of holes. Oh, and Rupe, the car. I needed to put some oil in it. The light came on.'

I already knew: she'd driven that car like a maniac, every shim, every bearing, I'd guessed, would come back heated and shaken to extremes beyond any mechanical comprehension. Jacquie didn't like sitting anywhere for long and the car was no more to her than a waiting-room on wheels.

'How are you, Jaffa?' She kissed his cheek, delighting him with affection.

'Fine, thanks,' he smiled. He often seemed shy around her, yet drawn, as so many were, to her warmth and love of life.

'I've taken Sandra home.' Jacquie yawned, stretching her arms and looking at me with the same awkwardness that separation caused when we knew each other in the early days. She had lost a little weight in the short time she'd been away. A starvation party diet was probably the best way of explaining it.

Meanwhile, having wrenched herself from the rear seat, Jezebel was wandering in the garden, unfolding and looking up at the surrounding foothills, a little dazed, almost shocked. 'Oh, Rupe,' said Jacquie, 'could you get Jezebel's things?' The huge bag felt as if it had Jezebel's clone inside it.

'Ah, yes, it's beautiful,' Jezebel spoke softly as she entered the building and proceeded slowly, almost cautiously, as I showed her around. Our bed, the one we had donated to Jezebel for the duration, was in the abside. Jezebel observed that the bed's position on the mezzanine was directly above where the altar once stood. The mezzanine projected sound down from the rough plaster stone arches and into the room below. Apart from this one wooden construction, little had changed in more than 800 years. Looking at the soft light sifting through stained glass, Jezebel sat on the edge of the bed.

'You like the windows?' I looked across at my work. 'Jaffa gave them to us, they're from a prison chapel in Canada. I made them so the sun sends colours down through all the rooms in the afternoon.'

There was a silence. I smiled, feeling uneasy. 'You must be tired,' I said stupidly and pretended not to watch as she swivelled her tall, thin body around to lie down.

'Yes,' she said, 'I'll just take a little rest.'

Jezebel dressed to suit a woman of forty to fiftyish. It was hard to tell her age. Her hair was white, not grey. Her face showed strain rather than lines but all the same gave an impression of high mileage.

Jacquie was waiting at the bottom of the stairs, her hands clasped together. She looked up cautiously to the mezzanine. 'Come outside,' she whispered, and pulled me through the kitchen and around to the side of the house. 'It's Jezebel, she got weird in the car, Rupe, I mean, really nasty. She got angry, thought Sandra and I were making fun of her.'

I reminded Jacquie that most tempers could fray during a seventeen-hour drive. 'No, Rupe, this started in the beginning, on the ferry. Jezebel wanted to sit in the bar. Sandra and I went out on the deck for a cigarette, Jezebel stayed inside.'

'And that's what she got upset about?' I grabbed Jacquie and kissed her very gently. 'Because you left her in the bar?'

''No!' said Jacquie, affectionately fending me off. 'We were laughing. I don't even remember what it was about. I looked back and she was staring at us from the windows. She thought we were laughing at her.'

I asked if it was okay now, if Jezebel's good grace had returned. 'I think so. I don't know.' Jacquie bit her lip. 'She calmed down after a while, after saying all sorts of frightening things. Threatening things,

Rupe, things that she would do to us. We were really scared.' She leaned against the stone chapel wall, her face anxious. 'God, I hope I haven't done the wrong thing in bringing her here. She warned me before we left that something was going to go wrong.'

'And you still brought her! Jacquie, you believe in everything this woman says. You're always telling me to trust my instincts.'

'I know.' She hugged me. 'You believe in her too, don't you?'

'I know she can *see*, but there's something, Jacq, I don't know.' Jacquie's face fell. 'Look,' I said, 'she'll probably be absolutely fine after some sleep.'

Jacquie managed to essay a normal question about tonight's supper. 'There's chicken,' I said, seeing her smile. The look on my face explained that it couldn't compare with her own cooking.

'Did you wonder how she might react in the chapel?' I asked.

'She's so religious, it must be perfect for her. How's the diabetes been?' Jacquie's concentration was clearly all over the place.

'Fine,' I said, unwilling to discuss it. 'Come on, we'll have something to eat and you can sleep.'

'You always say you're fine when you're not,' Jacquie put her hands over her mouth and nose, almost praying, 'and just now you said Jezebel was going to be fine.'

'Well, I can certainly guarantee that one of us is unstable,' I said flatly, 'only you won't shut her up by stuffing sugar lumps down her neck.'

Waking the next morning in the bell-pull room, we heard a muffled voice. 'Jacquie,' croaked Jezebel from her bed.

Jacquie rose quickly and opened the door to look across the chapel at Jezebel under the dome on the far side. Again the faint voice beckoned. 'Jacquie!' Jezebel moaned, hardly moving, like a creature wounded and trapped.

Within minutes Jacquie descended and phoned a physiotherapist colleague. He came before breakfast, but found difficulty locating the problem. Jezebel rose shortly afterwards, came downstairs and perched bolt upright on the bench in front of the large breakfast table, her face wedged above a thick, tightly wound neck-brace scarf. With quick, doleful glances she seemed to be surveying Jacquie, Jaffa and me as a self-pitying child might. She then turned her whole body, scanning the room, looking more miserable than ever.

'How are you feeling?' I asked.

'Ssma necka,' she said, more Turkish-sounding than before, moving her shoulders and head as if she had no neck at all and showing great discomfort. 'When I wake up, I can't move, like there's something bad on me.'

'With the journey and everything, you're bound to get something like this,' I said sympathetically, as if at her age it was not unlikely. She accepted a cup of coffee, more transfixed by my face than was comfortable. I had a feeling that my thoughts were being cut open and inspected. Then, remaining silent, she began spreading butter on a fresh torn baguette. Her extraordinary hair and eyes left her looking constantly surprised. Her gaze flicked about as if to check I wouldn't draw a weapon or perhaps disappear. I felt weak, transparent, but I didn't dare go until the stares became a glazed sulk and I was left to wonder what she might have seen. 'Instincts,' I thought to myself.

I'd been taking lessons in order to obtain a French driving licence and so replace my American one. Jezebel and Jacquie dropped me at the driving school where a cluster of teenaged spare parts, recently collided with puberty and smoking like mad ever since, were hanging about outside, waiting for someone to find the key.

Summer's end was approaching. The sunlight loses its strength at the same rate as the ethnic strays pick the grapes up through France, bringing the *vendanges* to a close in the north. The Roussillon's capricious character emerges now – the mountains all but enclosing it see to that. Just as they may bless an Indian summer until Christmas, they can equally lay a snare for winter in early November.

Pepe, the waiter from Hector and Rosie's restaurant who had so kindly helped us with the electricity, and his new wife Dalida (the beautiful, crazed commis chef, recently turned hairdresser) arrived for dinner early that evening. It was only five or so, yet the shadows of the hills had fallen over the chapel.

Dalida took off her fluffy pink sweater, dropping it on the cement sofa. 'Shit, it's so beautiful here,' she said in her sand-papered voice, meaning that it didn't appeal to her taste, but we were obviously primitive or hippie enough to tolerate it. 'Rustic. That's what it is,' she compensated.

She wore her hair, as always, in a perfectly styled, young blonde version of Jezebel's candy-floss and barbed wire. It had stayed in the same style all through summer in Hector and Rosie's sweltering kitchen, sometimes tied back, but always looking fixed. Her voice, husky, begging to sing American country music, let out a soft growl as she cautiously arranged herself on the sofa. Polished nails began lovingly stroking and straightening her leopard-skin velvet leggings. This wondrous, sexually explosive bundle had unfortunately been connected to a brain so hard, aggressive and vulgar that it operated the voice and blissful carcass as if they were the jaws of a mechanical digger.

'Truly rustic,' I smiled, judging debate as hopeless and opening a beer for Pepe. I turned. 'Jezebel, I'd like to introduce you to Dalida and Pepe.'

Our guest came down from the mezzanine and greeted Dalida. Making little effort to conceal her laughter, Dalida glanced at Pepe who, showing some subtlety, pretended not to notice.

'Dalida is a hairdresser,' I added awkwardly. 'She's named after a famous French singer.'

Jezebel smiled. 'They're very good with hair in France.' She touched her frozen white floss. 'Maybe she could tell me what to do with mine. I have so many problems.'

'It's damaged,' Dalida said bluntly. 'Even with conditioner,' she tutted, putting a perfect fingernail to her lips in concentration, 'I don't know, not much.'

I translated, watching Jezebel frown. 'But I *use* conditioner,' she grumbled, 'it just grows like this.'

Dalida looked at me, making a hardened, I-got-no-time-for-this face. 'What is she?' she murmured, 'a *sorcière*?'

Many a true word spoken in jest, I thought. Yet Dalida, simple and straight to the point, was not kidding. Jezebel's eyes registered sharply as she recognized the word. Without response she walked swiftly between us and over to the grotto bathroom, sliding and thumping the heavy mirrored door closed behind her.

Pepe nodded towards the mirror. 'Nice idea, the door like that.'
Silence.

Outside the evening glowed with the almost fluorescent green
colour of storm. Gathering logs, I could hear Jacquie's chatter from
the open door and the soothing, muffled clatter of the kitchen that
one recognizes from listening to the house after bedtime in childhood.

An old friend, Stuart, arrived just before dark, a gentle, retired
Englishman with a fast brain and a liking for the adventurous young.
Public-school discipline and professional habit made him wear a tie
most days.

Another car pulled up, catching the dogs in its lights as they slunk
out of the forest in chase of a straying wild boar. John Bull, ex-SAS, a
writer with a spirited approach to life, kissed Jacquie affectionately and
handed me a bottle that I knew he'd have chosen thoughtfully. I
searched for olives while performing a frying, hissing, culinary act.
Jacquie found a bowl and filled it with grilled peppers and a little herb
oil. The dinner, as usual, would be magnificent.

Jezebel, now in better humour, almost flirted, perky across the
big square table as she sat between the two interesting older men.
Occasionally, like surf slipping back on a gentle beach, the conversation would lull and I'd find her looking at me coldly. It wasn't
something anybody else could see but Jezebel held my gaze until my
forehead wrinkled and my lips formed the word 'What?', whereupon,
satisfied, she turned her eyes away and engaged in conversation. The
fact that I was less enthusiastic about her than Jacquie was something
that I'd been trying to hide but maybe my reservations were
transparent. I didn't want any trouble but instinct had a lot to do with
the fact that she could sense my distrust. Whatever she was I couldn't
help doubting her and the way she seemed to manipulate facts. Being
manipulated as a child left me with a loathing for anyone who
deceived me, even in jest.

John Bull spoke of his experiences as an officer through Africa and
beyond. 'It was tremendous,' he went on, fidgeting with a cork,
chatting over a forest of empties that flickered green in the light of the
remaining candles, 'so few officers over such a vast continent. Had to
be resourceful,' He smiled. 'Make enemies and . . .'

Then, and I'm not sure how we managed it, we'd hardly departed from Africa when suddenly we were reliving the extermination of Jezebel's relations on a war-tortured island somewhere.

'They were animals,' she said, moving right along, drawing the company in, 'they destroy all of my familee.'

She stared at me anew, in what I assumed was intended as a show of force. Why? I wondered, while the bodies of her family, still twitching and mutilated, were figuratively thrown over the table and her eyes carried on, insistent, darting from face to face, making sure that the story had her audience by the throat. But I knew already. She could feel it. Jezebel could read me and she knew I was having none of the theatrics. I was happy to listen and even go along with some of her projections but the sane and practical Bogaerde side of me wasn't buying any of the rest.

'An' den, they take heem,' her eyes settled on the most affected guest, 'an' they cut off hees han'.' She looked around further as the room filled with scattered talk of Vietnam, Nicaragua and Northern Ireland, her eyes eventually coming to rest once again upon me. Much as I felt discomfort, I couldn't help but listen objectively: levels of carnage could depend, it seemed, on the reactions of the guests. I noticed that death itself was in remarkably short supply. However, she seemed to be having a 'special' on human disfigurement and brutalitee a la plancha, all blasted across in tortured English.

'That's nothing.' Dalida burst into life after hearing Pepe's agonizing translation of Jezebel's tale. 'You know that Elvis Presley never made it back from Korea. Uh?' Dalida's chin jutted out. 'You can't imagine,' she looked at Pepe, 'how fucking tragic that is.'

'Oh, Dalida.' The corners of Jacquie's eyes creased with laughter.

The dinner-time humour carried on, but Jezebel, having stared at me whenever she'd remembered to throughout the evening, waited until she felt she had the measure of me.

'Try taking it up over a hundred,' the driving instructor encouraged. 'These are the new ones,' he said, 'I bought four for the school, diesel. Can't stall them, it would take an imbecile to stall a car like this, but we won't say that to the boy we're picking up. You nervous?'

The prospect of the driving test had loomed large, though now, in Jezebel's shadow, it seemed less important. I couldn't stop myself from worrying about what was happening at home. Other than by poverty, for the first time at the chapel I felt we were threatened. The cheerful feeling in the building had somehow altered. Although Jacquie and I told each other that it wasn't possible, a feeling of an ugly presence was growing ever stronger. It had been three days since Jezebel had followed me into the kitchen during the last moments of our dinner with Pepe, Dalida and our two older friends.

She'd leant on the counter, blocking my return to the others, the yellow on the bottom row of her teeth clearly visible as she spoke. 'You don't believe in me, do you?'

I answered carefully, 'I'm not sure, I mean, about some things.'

'You want that I show you?' Her eyes seemed to grow bitter and sharper than ever and her cheeks began crushing up, forming huge crow's feet on the sides of her face.

I became satisfactorily alarmed. 'What? Jezebel, why are you doing this?'

''Ah ha.' She pursed her lips. 'I'm going to make you understand. You'll see, when you're punished. You'll see,' she went on as Jacquie, reading my troubled face, made her way from the table, 'something will come to you tonight, in your room, lift you in the air,' her head lifted with defiance, 'and drop you. Is that what you want?'

'Jezebel, what's wrong?' asked Jacquie.

'She wants to punish me.' I looked at the woman, who stared back with the indignation of an angry white mama. 'Because I'm not reacting the way she wants me to.'

Jacquie urged me to return to our other guests but Jezebel wasn't done with me.

'He ees evil,' the woman hissed, quietly and between her teeth.

'So what do I do?' I asked. 'Jezebel, what is it exactly that you want from me?'

'You know, sometimes I'm good,' she stared coldly, 'then there are other times. You think you can change things like this. You'll see.' She hardly blinked as she spoke, the huge eyes began to close again in a scowl. 'Then you ask me to forgive.'

'Jezebel, I'm sorry if I've upset you.'

'You lie. You and your friends, and that selfish girl,' she motioned to Dalida and Pepe, 'they won't last. He'll leave her.'

'Why is it so important for you to hurt others?' I glared at Jezebel. She said nothing.

'Rupe,' repeated Jacquie, 'go and sit down.'

As Jezebel's icy gaze was unwavering I agreed to move, baffled and angry. 'Okay, Jacquie, but I'm not bloody sorry. What do you want?' I began to sizzle on my nerves. 'Honestly, Jezebel. *Why?*'

Jacquie ushered me towards the others but I wasn't to be mollified. 'Jacquie, how d'you expect me to react? This is our house . . .' I left the kitchen, watching anxiously from the table.

'But he's good,' I heard Jacquie pleading. 'Oh, Jezebel, please, don't let it . . .'

In the night there were tears. The bell-pull room was cold, most of the few blankets we had being upon the auto-sacrosanct fiend smouldering in our bed in the dome.

'What are we going to do?' Jacquie whispered in the darkness. 'She means it.'

'She's got no way to hurt us,' I grumbled. 'She just can't stand it if you don't buy her bullshit. We're stronger than that, baby, as long as we stick together.' Strange, perhaps, that this idea which initially came from Jezebel would now be the philosophy I'd adopt to shield us from her. Jezebel, I am positive, passed on some very good things. I am equally convinced that she shopped for information in the darker regions of the spiritual world. How can one possibly come without the other?

'I can't bear it, what if she does stick pins in dolls like people say? And, Rupe, haven't you noticed the atmosphere in here? It's so cold. The air feels heavy.' It was true, the atmosphere in the building had changed, as if hatred was really in amongst us. It was something you could almost sense touching your skin, suspended in the air, like fog, the chapel walls pushing at it, forcing it out.

I tried to be flippant, light. 'I don't see any demon in the room throwing me about, unless she's going to do it.' I began to smirk. 'Of course, if she is, then she can pay for her own bloody physiotherapist tomorrow.' But then I sighed, 'We're mad to have gone and seen her in the first place. The chapel doesn't like it, babe. You can feel it.'

'It's my fault.' Jacquie started to cry. 'I should never have brought her here. You weren't sure. I should have listened.'

'Don't, Jacq, don't let her in. It's happened. We'll always be stronger than she is, as long as we stay together, and the chapel won't let anything happen.' What foolishness, one might think, the absurdity of it, but in the darkness of our little room the idea didn't seem far-fetched. The flickering of the great oak outside the window and the hiss of Jezebel's voice bounced across the chapel ceilings and around us as unhappiness took her, even in her sleep. It seemed to claw at us. We lay in the darkness, both sick with worry, listening to the troubled, gravelly voice.

It hadn't rained much that night but the sky shifted across the mountain, heavy, carrying tremendous weight. The following day Jezebel visited the physio once again. The twisted neck had worsened now and taken a claw-hold in her back. I wondered if this was not the work of the chapel itself, seemingly stamping upon the claw of the beast and trying to drive Jezebel out.

'I'm taking Jezebel to Ceret, darling,' said Jacquie. 'We're all young ones tonight, so I'll get wine if you clear up and do the table.'

'Okay.' I hugged her as, without a word, Jezebel passed me by and climbed into the car.

Tonight there were about eight of us, the majority young and male. It was difficult to translate, and the French guests were little interested in making efforts to speak English, though there was some sceptical interest in Jezebel's predictions. Hoping to loosen up, I drank more than usual. I made efforts to listen to Jezebel although my every instinct urged me to back off and trust nothing that she said or did.

From the beginning of the afternoon it had rained. Marble-sized drops turned the dust driveway into a sheet of moving silt. Water crashed down through the gardens on the mountainsides, taking the very foundations from beneath the more vulnerable houses, while the chapel stood like a battleship at speed on its rock base and the torrent carried pieces of the road down to the bridge and the bursting river beyond.

Clothes hung from every stray nail as the fireplace choked on fresh, damp wood. In the background I could hear the tumble-dryer churning away and the rising bitter wind which seemed to be throwing the rain hard at the long windows on the far side of the chapel. The sounds seemed amplified in the absence of our radio, which had burst into flames on New Year's Eve during *la danse des canards* months before and had never recovered.

I asked Jezebel about herself, hoping this would leaven her mood, but she remained mournful. 'I can see nothing for me. It's terribly sad. I see only for others. I told you, huh? Years ago.' She pointed to the white walls. 'You going to do beautiful things.'

'It's nowhere near finished,' I muttered, slightly tipsy.

'There is still another thing.' She scratched at the edge of her plate, her eyes lowered, as if this was going to be delicate. She paused, waiting for me to respond. 'It's your brother.' Her eyes turned to me.

'What about him?' I felt heckles going up once more.

At this point the humidity reached a crescendo along with the electrical overload in the kitchen from the new dishwasher. The last things I saw were Jacquie's lips, stained crimson from the heavy Roussillon red as the mains trip-switch blew.

In the light of the candles Jezebel smiled triumphantly. My dead brother had communicated, she claimed.

The wine was selling me a trip down memory lane. I found the offending circuit, flipped the trip and returned to the table.

The others laughed, making howling ghost sounds as Jezebel offered a wintry smile.

The windows rattled as she went on, as they'd done throughout the storm. 'It's him,' she said and then looked at the coffee cup between her fingers, making an apologetic solemn gesture as if accepting a grave fact.

Our guests left, politely saying goodbyes, but unfortunately keeping only some of their cynical thoughts about her to themselves.

'Your friends will die in the car on their way home tonight,' she announced vengefully even before they made it to the road.

'*Jezebel*.' Jacquie turned in astonishment. 'How could you? How can you be so unkind?' She sat down by the fire. 'Oh God, I can't believe this is happening. Why're you doing this? Why do you hate us?' Jacquie burst into tears. 'I wish you'd never come.'

'It's him.' Jezebel pointed to me. At this point I tried to get Jacquie to move, to climb to our room. 'It's you,' she hissed, 'you think I lie. Your brother was there tonight, and you turned him away.'

The driving instructor nudged me. 'Stop! This is your comrade, remember? The one who never managed to get out of second?' He opened the door as the pimpled, bespectacled lad gingerly climbed in the back. 'So! Examination day,' the instructor said with pleasure.

Later on Jacquie picked me up by the village cinema. An afternoon screening of a Bruce Lee classic was in full swing, dubbed into Italian. 'What on earth are you doing with that dog?' I asked, climbing into the car. 'It stinks in here!'

'It's for Madame Massan, I'm looking after her husband. I took the dog for her to get it a haircut.' Jacquie gave me a huge smile. 'You passed, didn't you?'

'Yes.' I grinned, staring at the mutt as it forced its head between the seats. 'So what are you doing driving round with this thing in the car anyway?'

'I was scared,' said Jacquie.

'Babe, of what?' I asked, although I already knew that this was all down to Jezebel.

We dropped Maurice the dog off at his owners' and returned home. The chapel seemed empty at first, the dim parts of the sitting-room quiet, shadowy. 'Perhaps she went out with Linda,' said Jacquie as we walked through to the kitchen.

The open-plan house stood before us, looking empty. Then Jezebel's silhouette emerged from the cement sofa as our eyes adjusted to the light.

'Oh! You gave me a fright, Jezebel,' Jacquie started. 'Did you go out with Stuart?'

'Yes.' She sat motionless. 'But I've been back for hours.'

'Did he get you lunch?'

'I didn't want any then,' she said icily, 'and there's nothing here to eat.'

'Fine, I'll make you something.' Jacquie marched back to the kitchen and picked things from the fridge in an agitated way.

'Jezebel, what's wrong?' I asked.

'You keep me here, like an animal. You said this holiday was for me, so where were you, huh, this afternoon?'

'You knew we had things to do, just for a few hours.'

'You listen, you, with your mean eyes,' she began, looking at me, 'and you, Jacquie, I should never have let you bring me here. First you introduce me to your disgusting friends and now you starve me.'

'It's not true. We've been kind to you.' Jacquie was astonished.

'You make fun of me. Very funny, huh?' Her lips tightened. 'So now we'll see how funny you think I am.' Jezebel worked her pale face into a cold, purple rage. 'It will all be ruined for you; everything, the life, all of it.'

'I don't doubt that you can see the future,' I said. Then, finding myself unduly alarmed and annoyed by her meanness, I continued, 'But you're just like the rest of us. You can't actually *change* things and what you're doing, Jezebel, it's evil.'

'I'll get you, Rupert Van den Bogaerde,' the witch pointed as she began to shout, 'even if I have to GO TO THE DEVIL TO DO IT.'

Behind me I could hear Jacquie begin to weep. 'YOU HAVE NO RIGHT,' she cried, her voice distorted with tears. 'Jezebel, how can you be like this?'

'Well, at least, Jezebel,' I said sternly, my instincts confirmed, 'you've finally shown who you are. You can get out. GET OUT OF OUR HOUSE.'

Jacquie held my hand as, hissing abuse, Jezebel turned and went to pack.

'We'll get her home on anything we can,' I stammered. Jacquie's face stayed creased in horror, as if she'd lost all control and was just standing, tight-jawed, absorbing no more.

'D'you think Linda might have her for a night or two?' I asked.

'I don't know,' she said doubtfully. 'Frank'll hate that.'

'Jacquie! They're the only people we can ask. Ol' Frank'll say yes.' She began to cry again as, profiting from the chapel's acoustics, I continued, loud enough for Jezebel to hear, 'And you can be sure Frank won't take any of her shit either.'

A distrustful Linda arrived later on in a red sports car that Frank had given her. Jezebel stood in the driveway looking at the mountain as we loaded up her things.

'Linda, I'm so sorry to ask this. We'll get her home as soon as we can.'

'I hope you can,' she said, bemused. 'I don't understand. What happened? Why d'you have to bring her here anyway? What for?'

The following morning the phone rang. Jezebel had forgotten her passport and could we bring it round. Inside, the document contained her photograph, but far more interesting was her birth date. Jezebel was just thirty-seven.

We managed to get her on a bus from a nearby campsite. It left two or three days after her departure from the chapel and carried her home to England. Frank wouldn't have tolerated many minutes, let alone days, more. I rang Jezebel's relations, but Jezebel, it seemed, had already spoken to them. 'My Auntie Jez is a good person,' the young woman said in a parrot-like fashion, sounding scared out of her wits.

'Has anything like this ever happened before?' I asked. 'I mean, does she fall out with people often?'

'She's a good person,' repeated the frightened voice, 'you must have made her like this.'

'You're scared, aren't you?'

'My aunt is a good person,' she repeated.

'Why are you scared of this woman?' I demanded. 'What has she been doing to you?'

The young woman at the other end hung up.

PART THREE

18 *Even Breaks*

When we'd managed to save a little money we went into Le Boulou and bought the first of the huge beams, which over time would replace the old and smelly railway sleepers in the chapel. We put the first and largest in late one evening. A fire was burning in the grate and the two of us heaved the heavy wooden sections inch by inch and one end at a time up the wall and into place. The clean thick pine shone in the light from the fire and the chapel seemed to come to life, free from the oppressive black of the old sleeper wood.

I dashed into the curate's house and plucked the pewter cherub from its position on the ancient oaken beam where it had originally watched over us. I returned with nails and a hammer and attached it to the bright honey-coloured beam in the heart of the chapel.

Two years passed and work for the completion of the building had become feverish. All around us it was spring and everywhere the bulbs were shooting up. Jacquie and I were finally winning the battle to breathe life into the chapel. Without the drug company funding that we had so needed it had taken us more than five years to construct, almost single-handedly, aside from the help of treasured friends. Even now it was nowhere near finished. The major part of it, however, was complete and ready enough to accommodate our first diabetic guests. All the railway sleepers and filthy make-do supports were gone, and even the wooden mezzanine floor, since the fire, had been carefully sanded and where salvageable, repaired. The clumsy stone staircase in the main part of the chapel had been replaced by a modern wooden one and there were windows, doors and bathrooms with hot and cold running water. The main floor of the chapel was now a brilliant cool white surface of large tiles with a thin cross of small dark Spanish ones, reaching to the points of the compass, each small tile decorated with a blue dragon. The cross marked the centre of the chapel, which was now open to a simple banister gallery displaying the plastered arches high above. In the curved kitchen Jaffa had finished cupboards, making their doors from the remaining floorboards and varnishing everything heavily, while I'd built in sinks and tiled surfaces with pale materials to make the best of the limited light.

Soon we'd be looking after tourists all day long, breakfast, lunch and dinner. We'd be wrapped into their lives so tightly that there'd be much less time for the moments of calm we'd known in these years of scrimping and dreaming.

The company name, Even Breaks, was an appropriate description of what we intended to offer our diabetics. We saw that the shape of the initials, EB, could form the stylized wings of a butterfly. This insignia was painted by a local artist friend, Les, on the sides of our old pick-up truck. All this was done for the incredible price of a chicken lunch and the remains of the unused paint pots that dear Les had instructed us to buy for the job.

Alarmingly Jezebel, or the Witch as we now called her, had a way of reaching out from the depths of our previous miserable encounter and scratching at us. Whenever we faced misfortune it always seemed to be her doing. Instead of bad luck, in the Witch we seemed to have discovered a reliable scapegoat. She was waiting, pins in dolls, and each time we stumbled or if we fought, we'd say, 'Let's not allow the Witch to come between us,' and we'd agree that our conflict was what Jezebel would have wanted. 'She's laughing now,' we'd say, 'the Witch is laughing.'

Big Jim put his foot inside the chapel door.

Twenty minutes earlier I'd been emotional, even tearful. Robert and Lynne, friends who had helped us finish the final part of the building, had left to continue their travels. They had spent the previous three months with us during the final push, and their presence gave the place life. With their departure I had felt unsteady and as if the wind of change had come to stay. Even Breaks, our little holiday company, had begun.

He was almost too tall for the kitchen ceiling, was big Jim.

'This is my wife, Rachel,' he said, his voice so low it made the hollow in my stomach vibrate, while his head clunked the mugs hanging from hooks in the kitchen ceiling.

'Is that your motorbike?' I asked. 'Blimey! You came a thousand miles on that!' It looked like a plane.

'An' Rachel's four months pregnant,' he boomed. 'When do the others get here?'

A bowl of powerful sangria and bottles of cheap Spanish fizz welcomed the newcomers. We'd sliced chorizo and prepared bowls of olives, nuts and crisps. 'They're flying into Perpignan this afternoon,' said Jacquie, 'you'll *all* be here by six tonight.' She dipped a cup into the sangria, scooping the slices of fruit along with the drink, and filled a glass.

Things seemed to be fitting into place. There were now four little rooms and a dormitory area on a mezzanine above the central part of the chapel. It was enough for us to make a good start and most people seemed to be happy with the arrangement. Jacquie had managed to launch it all from a pile of notepads and a telephone. We'd advertised in various papers and then she and Lynne had sat for hours, licking stamps and sending out hundreds of brochures, while Robert and I did our best to finish the last details of the building. The brochures were just a photocopy folded in half. Somehow, I believe charmed by the naivety of it all, people booked and came.

I felt tremendous pride in Jacquie, though my inability to keep up with her in the 'office' left me with a vague feeling of vulnerability. Her memory alone was extraordinary. She could carry a hundred pieces of trivial information around in her head and still find space for a shopping list and the first name of almost anyone we'd met in the last three years. In line with Jacquie's unique style we were also the only holiday organization I knew of where the traveller could barter to get in. If you could afford *most* of the cost, then you were accepted.

'I'm afraid there aren't any places left in July,' I heard Jacquie saying on the phone as I loaded the pick-up ready for a run with a group to the beach. 'I suppose you *could* come . . .' she hesitated, 'if you don't mind sleeping in the garden. No, a tent's fine.' She grinned over at me, adding cheekily, 'But in that case we might need to commandeer your car!'

The concept seemed fine idealistically, but those who'd paid for comfort and were now forced to share what little space we had were obviously going to be unhappy. 'We can't do this, babe. It'll upset all the others.'

'We can do what we want. No one will mind, just as long as it's fun. We've just got to make sure it's fantastic.'

I demurred. 'Jacquie, these are people, *real* people. It's their savings, you can't gamble with that.'

But somehow most of the time it worked. Jacquie's brilliant organization and her willingness to take giant risks with other people's dreams almost always paid off, and if it didn't, well, *that*, I learned hideously, was where equal rights ended and suddenly good old sexual stereotypes stood firm. I was expected to be manly and masterful. I remember one chap, a particularly big bloke, huge in fact, who came from London with a tuxedo in his bag. He was looking for a holiday in a place like Benidorm and had his heart fixed on ballroom dancing. He'd fallen for Jacquie's telephone voice without ever thinking to look at the photocopied details. Taking him back to the airport and paying for his flight, I got a serious earful and then came close to a smack in the mouth for his lack of enjoyment.

Such events were rare but none the less they could be unpleasant for all concerned. Jacquie's ability to brush aside the problems filled me with envy. It was as if emotionally she could reach another plane, like her nursing, and put the other reality aside, whereas I'd turn to face it, leaving her to march on and prepare for the next wave.

'After all, Rupo,' Jacquie would say with a cheeky smile, *'you're the man.'*

I began to feel like a driver on a train, rushing down a mountainside gathering reckless speed whereupon I notice that my co-driver is still joyfully shovelling in more coal. There was a tremendous excitement about Even Breaks and at this stage Jacquie and I were sharing almost every excursion. This was at the heart of the fun of it –

rushing about, flying, scuba-diving and riding, eventually sailing, water-skiing and then parascending. In time we took on the more physically perilous canyon descents inside huge gorges an hour's drive from the chapel. We'd don armoured wetsuits and climb and jump from pool to pool down the vast cracks between the mountains to arrive into the warmth of the valley below. The trip down the gorge could take up to five hours and only the physically competent were encouraged to go. We'd be armed to the teeth with glucose, pushing the diabetics to the edge. Of course there were difficult moments but our guests usually found that their confidence had reached new heights and the evenings were celebrations. Conquering fear was a huge aspect of this, no matter how great or simple the challenges.

I'd driven a group of tourists to a beautiful fortified village called Collioure, the next little port south from Argelès. I preferred it to the further-flung destinations on the winding coast roads because the distance from the chapel was relatively short.

'Kenneth says he might be going to be sick,' said a voice, so we stopped and Kenneth stepped out, oblivious to the audience in the boat.

'Are you insured for this kind of thing?' asked an accountant from Milton Keynes, looking up from a mass of bodies, like Calcutta crammed on a single bench seat. 'I mean, how many seats is this thing registered for?'

I muttered something about not being quite sure if our insurance was adequate.

'But there are fourteen of us in here,' said the accountant.

'Fifteen,' said a Kiwi girl.

'Oh?' The man did a recount. 'Fourteen,' he repeated.

'Moi boyfriend's in the back, sleeping under the boat,' hissed the girl. 'He's still there from last noight. I hope he's still aloive.'

Picnic lunches in those early days of Even Breaks consisted of baguettes, chicken, fake champagne and blood-testing equipment. We sat in the sand, half of us squeezing blood from our fingertips on to various devices for measuring blood-sugar, while the rest took insulin shots and people around gawked as if we were a convention of dieting vampires and heroin addicts. In the evenings spirits were high, floating through the summer on a cocktail of odd emotion, stretching from an appreciation of architecture to a variety of unleashed inhibitions, including the sexual. Some guests appeared to change personality entirely, while others broke down after making efforts simply to relax in an atmosphere that seemed almost always to encourage them to let go and come out of their shells.

Once or twice a week we cleared the furniture in the lower part of the chapel. This provided enough space for dancing which would often go on until the early hours. Jacquie had assembled a huge dressing-up box and those who'd come on holiday to escape sometimes leaped at the chance to be someone else. Amazing how a change of wrapping frees people's perception of themselves. A chance perhaps to select your desired character. This was really what the chapel, for Jacquie and me, was about. Inadvertently or perhaps deliberately, the old building had become a meeting place once again.

'I've always thought that we are part of some far more meaning-ful plan,' said Jacquie, dressed in a school blazer and sporting a moustache painted with a burnt cork. She'd made an incredible dinner that evening after spending hours sending out replies and booking forms, making beds and settling accounts. 'It's meant to be, Rupe,' she said, slamming a shot of tequila against the bar and tipping it down her throat. 'Look at what's happening. We're helping people.'

Jacquie returned to a man at the bar who was describing family misunderstandings. I checked to see if any inebriates were drowning in the pool; after midnight this became a distinct worry.

It was four in the morning when I packed some food in the car and kissed Jacquie goodbye. 'I'll do breakfast,' she smiled, kissing me back. 'Only two more runs like this, this week, and then they'll all be here. Be careful.' She hugged me again.

I pulled out in the darkness and headed to the autoroute and then over the pass into Spain. The flight carrying two of our tourists was due to arrive in Gerona at five-thirty. The sun would be coming up over the mountains by the time I got to the airport and for a moment I wished that I was free and driving home into the dawn alone. I was banking on their flight being on time because we'd arranged scuba-diving later that morning. If we were lucky and I drove like the wind I could be home for seven-thirty or eight, if Customs didn't stop us at the frontier and search us. Later I had the picnic to make for lunch. Jacquie should have cleared the chapel from the night before and breakfast would be under way.

'Mustn't forget the baguettes on the way home,' I told myself, 'then change those gas cylinders and vacuum the pool. Got to prepare the money for the diving trip and whatever happens make sure everyone goes to the loo before we leave; and for God's sake, this time remember to take some sugar with you. Don't forget INSULIN, for heaven's sake don't, and remember to call about the microlite flying, twelve punters are on for it, two are staying behind. Isn't that what she said?' Enough petrol in the trucks for the trip? I felt sick. Worry and a fear of failure hovered, and another feeling, one that I denied at first, that of unhappiness. My lips were swollen from yet another cold sore and I felt ugly.

The following evening, in the middle of a Bob Marley song, our generally calm neighbour, André, appeared. This reasonable man had been driven over the edge by thumping music from the back of the chapel. I was upset, knowing that this tolerant individual had probably put up with it for hours, days even, before protesting. Others on the hillside were less sympathetic and there were visits from the police who, always polite and understanding, made things as civil as they could. We'd close the doors when it got late and bring the party inside, despite the summer heat.

'Rupe, your father's here,' Jacquie announced with a huge smile, 'and there's another thing I should tell you. Now, don't be upset.' Suddenly she looked uncomfortable, the smile gone. I motioned for her to continue. 'He's got to share his room with one of the punters.'

'We're overloaded already. Darling, they're sleeping in the curate's house kitchen as it is *and* on the lawn.'

'It's only for a few nights,' Jacquie pleaded. 'The guy just turned up. I said there was no space but he didn't care. Your dad said he doesn't mind.'

'I mind.' I was irritated. 'You don't even know this guy.'

''Scuze me.' A huge creature brushed past me. He wore a little skullcap and his body had the shape of a water balloon hanging on a spike. A little man went after him, drenched with sweat, twitchy and disoriented. 'Over 'ere, Merv,' said the big one, hardly opening his mouth. He forced himself into a plastic chair and the spare flesh on his buttocks compressed, then squeezed between the holes in the plastic.

'The little one is Mervin Hipdash,' muttered Jacquie. 'He sells ping-pong balls and golf tees. They wanted a package holiday, I think.'

I asked about the other one. 'His name's Del,' she grinned. 'He's a psychopath.'

Skut, an ex-pilot and Hong Kong policeman – the man now sharing the room in our curate's house with my father – sat intimidating twin seventeen-year-old diabetic sisters at the table while unrelated twin diabetic brothers sitting opposite looked on, aghast.

'Would you mind if I mated with you both?' Skut was asking. 'I'm fabulous with virgins.' He looked up at the brothers, waggling his eyebrows. 'Of course, you guys are first in line.'

Two days later, at dawn, one of the girls woke, feeling a presence in the room. In the half-light she saw Merv standing motionless, staring down from the end of her bed. Four hours later little Merv, still sweating profusely, was put on the train back to England. I then returned from the station and loaded up with food and equipment for another day out.

Jacquie would spend the morning in our garden-shed office and then in the afternoon she'd begin changing sheets and cooking for the coming evening and the party would start all over again. These routines suited her well, but the constant excitement, the unending flow of individuals seven days a week fifteen hours a day, in all fairness, was beginning to play havoc with my diabetes and gently wear me down. I had that same feeling: as if I was back on the train with my co-driver still shovelling in the coal like nobody's business, only now the engine is thundering and the mountain track is falling away alarmingly and I'm beginning to grit my teeth and reach for the brakes.

'What's the matter?' Jacquie asked. 'I've done the picnic for you, haven't I? Look, for the first time in our lives together we're able to pay all our bills. Don't touch your face, it'll get worse. Come on, Rupe, this is a *life*. It's a party. We can be together in November. Then you can sleep.'

'November?' I bleated. 'But we haven't gone near each other since June!'

Jacquie dashed inside the chapel door and opened the oven, taking out warm croissants. Sunlight streamed through the kitchen windows, lighting the steam from the coffee as it rose in the air. Further in where the light faded a cluster of late risers sat around the table, waiting.

'Look, we've got to do this while we have the chance,' Jacquie whispered. Then, smiling brightly, she carried the croissants over to the table.

I was reminded of our first meeting with the Witch. 'You are lions,' Jezebel had said. 'Run . . . while you have time.'

'Jacquie,' I asked, 'why are we in such a terrible rush?'

On the side of the pick-up truck under the Even Breaks butterfly were the words, 'Honi Soit Qui Mal Y Pense' (*Evil to he that evil thinks*). I'd put this on the truck, not as a connection with the English royals, but because of the people I frequently saw in the south, those who had so much, every advantage, yet made such great efforts to find something to be utterly miserable about. This ancient phrase had endured the test of time. Jacquie, in her innocent way, apart from her rare, very dark moments, was the epitome of optimism and the words seemed to reflect the way we felt, especially after our dispute with the Witch.

The summer burned on. Scuba-diving and sailing days were in a way almost a retreat for me, away from the incredible confusion that seemed to be building inexorably at the chapel: the mail-shots, the hundreds of letters, departures and arrivals that I could not keep track of all stacking up inside Jacquie's head. Her notebooks were dense with reminders and references incomprehensible to anyone else. Yet her system was efficient and she seemed literally addicted to the commotion.

'Jacquie,' I'd beg, 'there are things happening every day that you haven't said a thing about. Can you at least warn me before you agree to take on any more projects? I get this feeling that we're just going to spin out of control.' And the faster we went, the more Jacquie seemed to thrive on the excitement and miraculously scrape us through.

We'd arrived back late from scuba-diving and I was slightly shaky. In the rush I put off eating anything sweet until I finished unpacking the truck. In a typically disastrous error I'd gone gently hypo, misplaced my blood-testing machine and in looking for it, pathetically, I'd fallen victim to the insulin and had forgotten why I was wandering about. While Jacquie chatted on the phone I found some soft-looking gravel in the driveway, lay down, then drifted away. It was something that was beginning to happen more and more frequently. Selfishly, I both despised it and did little to deal with it, hiding again behind denial.

'Rupert, you asleep?' said a voice. 'Do you need sugar? Rupe, for heaven's sake!' Suddenly there were hands all over me and I found myself slumped up against the wall of boulders that I'd built around the chapel. Coca-Cola was poured into my mouth and ran down my face on to my shirt and shorts. I had no intention of leaving the fortress of my mind; what on earth for? It was fucking madness out there. Someone was scooping honey into my mouth and slapping me, forcing me to swallow whilst somewhere else in my mind I could smell the fennel that grew near the chapel door and was thus transported back to the old mobile home and to lovingly building the place stone by stone.

By October we were down to seven clients out of a possible absurd but workable twenty-two. Six of them were women and the only male was gay. Almost all had one thing in common: they were looking for a holiday romance, a special man. Almost all were disappointed. I say *almost*, because there was a teacher from somewhere who seemed delighted by the imbalance of the sexes.

I pleaded with Jacquie to close for the winter. It was costing too much to run it all. Everyone around us had shut down.

'We'll run till November just to say we did it.' Jacquie gave a non-negotiable smile. I protested again that we'd earned our spurs by keeping going since May but she was not to be deterred. 'We weren't filled to capacity though, were we? Not by far.'

I shook my head bitterly and stared across the room while she pushed at her tummy. 'It's not about money, is it, Jacq? We're running at a loss. We have been for ages.' She stared at me quietly as I went on, 'It's about instant fun and disposable friends. Jacquie, the party is over, *please.*'

Ignoring the conflict, she continued to pat her tummy. 'God, I hope this baby isn't pickled.' She puffed out with a smile, brushing the previous conversation aside. 'Ho, Rupe, what a season. We really helped a lot of people this summer, you know.'

Jacquie was four months pregnant and we were both delighted. We were afraid she'd drunk too much on the odd occasion before we'd discovered the baby was there and as a nurse Jacquie was adamant that it would be free of booze and smoke. I was concerned about how we'd manage next season but the baby was something we were both utterly committed to and we'd promised one another we'd find a way to cope. It had taken a year without birth control for Jacquie's body to recover from a decade on the pill. Just as we were beginning to wonder if there might be a problem, a couple had come to stay at the chapel and the woman had announced that she was pregnant. There were happy tears and champagne. It seemed almost as if this had started a chain reaction for us.

'Baby, you're pregnant. We're exhausted and you're nursing at weekends too. Come on. We've done well enough for one season.'

'You're wrong about the money, Rupe. We broke even, not bad for a first year. You're just going through a phase. I'm not ready to stop yet.'

As I was later to find at the end of a season, there were few threads of myself left to share out and I was getting ill. Self-defence was becoming an involuntary necessity. In a rash moment of despair I threatened to leave if she chose to book another person in. We both knew that under the circumstances this was a hollow threat.

'Leave?' Jacquie retorted. 'And where would you go? We're broke, remember? And look at your diabetes.' She chuckled, adding – not without some spite – 'You're almost a liability.'

19 Saying Goodbye

It was mid-March and Jacquie, now heavily encumbered, had long since given up the winter job of nursing the ailing of Le Boulou.

The winter had been quiet, with the building work on the pool and extra rooms almost completed. During the later part of the pregnancy a friend called Fergus had offered me work, building fences in the mountains. I'd been grateful, as money was again tight. Through the colder months Fergus and I spent our time working in a burnt-out cork-oak forest above the beaches on the foothills near the chapel. It was a typical low mountain winter. Whole days were spent cutting through the undergrowth with chainsaws in the pouring rain. I learned how impassable the forest was and how hard Fergus's life could be. His friendship was special because despite his tough exterior Fergus was an optimist and his kindness was contagious. We had some laughs together on the mountain. I felt I could be myself there, no compulsion to put on my 'on-the-ball' face, or use the absurd humour that went with the nervous momentum and awkwardness of Rupert at Even Breaks.

'Oh, oh, God!' cried Jacquie, banked by pillows in her hospital bed. 'I'm so bloody uncomfortable.' Relieved it was only this, I asked if she wanted a drink.

'NO!' She threw her hairbrush down on the bed.

We'd been in the hospital for two weeks; the sheer distance from the chapel and Jacquie's fragile obstetric condition had demanded this. Only now that things were difficult for her was she sharp and quite justifiably unpleasant at times. The lid was pretty much back on the diabetes and I was feeling very optimistic and excited about the future arrival.

'You want me to call Caroline and tell her what's happening?' I asked. 'I bet she'd like to know.'

'No, but I expect Mum will. Caroline's in Norfolk, remember?' Jacquie brushed her hair, paying me no special attention. 'Anyway, why should I tell *her*?'

'She's your best friend.' It seemed odd to say 'best friend' when they hardly saw one another any more. Still, the title, in Jacquie's mind, would always belong to Caroline. The situation seemed sad. I told myself that eventually this sorrow over the restaurant and Caroline would pass.

'Look,' I went on in an upbeat manner, pulling a tattered paperback from my pocket. 'I bought this at the English bookstall. If you want I'll read to you.'

She smiled. A machine by the bed monitored the baby's heart, sending its thumping sound into the room whilst printing jagged lines on a roll of paper that cascaded on to the floor.

'The old man and the sea . . .' I began.

It was about four in the morning when for the third time in twenty-four hours we were wheeled back into the delivery suite, only this time the big bathtub was being filled up. Jacquie had chosen to have the baby in water, so when I saw the nurse turn on the taps I realized that this time was probably action stations.

There was a lot of pain. The deep breathing from the ante-natal classes didn't seem to be helping one bit and Jacquie was already noticeably weak. The room was banked with sophisticated equipment, everything bathed in calm, warm, pink light, nothing hard-edged except for the face of one of the midwives and my wife's awful pain. The lack of sleep hadn't helped. Jacquie was unruly, emotional, frightened and exhausted before things had even started to happen. She was helped into a giant bath, the warmth soothing, softening, and for a while things settled a little. About twenty minutes later another stout midwife arrived. Jacquie responded poorly, her eyelids like lead.

'Jacquelinea,' the kind but firm voice went on, 'I'm sorry, but the doctor has told me that you can't stay in there. The baby's coming,

Jacquie.' She tugged at Jacquie's hand, slapping it in an effort to draw her concentration then assisted an agonizing retreat from the bath. Jacquie was just too far gone physically – the medics quite rightly didn't want the baby's arrival to injure her, and they wanted to be able to monitor the baby properly.

For an hour Jacquie struggled on the horrid chair, looking bewildered, with me fooling neither of us about how everything was peachy. More pain followed, then howls, a variety of uncharacteristic four-letter words, and as the baby neared, a horrific delirium. I knew Jacquie had a very low pain threshold but watching the magic strength she possessed fade, I began to be fearful.

Each stage confused me. She was too tired, couldn't push. The gentle encouragement from Curly, our petite, assertive doctor, had ceased as the activity in the room began to escalate. There were electrodes all over Jacquie and pinned to the unborn baby's head. In the heat of it I hadn't noticed the machine they were joined to. I only became aware of it by following the unhappy gaze of the doctor and the others.

'Jacquie, come on, wake up. Jacquie darling, *try*.' I sprinkled her face with water.

We had chosen one of the best and safest places in France to bring our child into the world. We'd attended every ante-natal class. She'd done every exercise, read every book, and here she was, protected by technical magnificence, groaning and crapping in the chair, just as helpless and trapped and animal as has always been the way.

She hissed, straining, her face turning purple, the veins standing out like worms as I gawped, holding on to her hand, asking fate to be kind to us. Then, as she began to shout at all of us, I started secretly praying to God, like a plane full of atheists caught in a violent storm. I don't know how dramatic the whole show really was in reality but up on my oversensitive screen things were looking pretty grim.

Curly began to shout, 'Jacquelina! Push, good God!'

'I'm trying,' Jacquie began faintly. Her grip wasn't so strong and the machine that had long since dribbled its last stretch of paper on to the floor began to tell us that the baby was in trouble.

I looked at Jacquie. 'Come on, just one big try.' She responded by telling me that *I* looked pale as chalk. Then something happened, probably only lasting seconds, but I felt as if I'd been away for much longer.

The doctor had begun to snap short nervous commands at Jacquie while the midwife found a gadget nearby and plugged it into the wall. Perhaps they've forgotten to kick me out, I thought. Jacquie panted faintly, mumbling, incoherent. All of this led me to prepare for the moment when, under the strain, she'd injure herself or perhaps die. It was a notion so dark that I shut it out in search of anything, anything at all, but it wouldn't go and from then on I forgot all about the child and could only think of her.

I could describe it as an unfortunate flashback but it wasn't unfortunate. My memories, like the apricots on old Skull Face's trees (too many on one tiny branch and neglected), were responding to a past visit from the Grim Reaper. Sitting by Jacquie's side, eyes open, the horror that I was gearing up for dragged me back, for the baggage I'd left behind . . .

. . . We were trying to get into the house but it was bolted from the inside. Gareth had been there for a whole day already. His old Austin Maxi was parked in the street, so he *had* to be back from work. My father gave up pounding on the door and shouting through the letterbox. 'Maybe he's asleep. I can't hear any music,' he said.

It made sense. He was still in recovery. Away on our Christmas break both Gareth and Brock had suffered from a raging fever. Our father had taken them to the local country clinic where Brock had been given an injection. Gareth didn't seem to need it. So mild was his condition by day that he'd returned from the clinic untreated and, feeling a little light-headed, had left for our home in London the following afternoon to see his girlfriend, a day ahead of the rest of us.

Our father walked back towards the car. 'He's probably gone to sleep and forgotten about the bolts – maybe he's got his earphones on.'

It was dark by then, but still early. The neighbour had come across and told us that she'd been worried, that Gareth hadn't been out all day. She lent us a ladder, which I had held as our father climbed up and smashed the window, climbing into Gareth's room. I'd stayed gripping the bottom rungs, steadying them and wondering why Dad hadn't turned on the light.

His voice was calm yet shocked, floating out into the cold night, quite alone.

I'd climbed up and in. Funny really, I stood in the dark with Gareth lying there dead, unaware of the darkness or the time passing. Dad had knelt for a moment beside him, his voice, not like words but sounds, filling the grey before my eyes with confessions of love and failings from a father to son. His gentleness as he stroked the grey face, his pleading left me silent as he spoke for all his children. I remained silent; my eyes dry as ice. Our father ran down to unlock the front door and we were at last alone, Gareth and I.

In what seemed a large space of time I tried everything. I spoke silently through the air, hardly moving my lips. He looked like Jesus in an old oil painting – white, the bedclothes curved around his body like plastic. Following his half-sitting shape, his elbows outward, hands behind his head, I tried to look into his eyes, which had never closed, then moved to the bed and lay across him, in the hope that warmth would pass from my body to his.

There was nothing in the room there with me, nothing but the past.

The family doctor came. An ambulance arrived. Then a muster of young and older men dressed in black climbed the stairs carrying a metal-frame stretcher. It took a long time for them to get Gareth on to it. It seemed that he was just as resistant then as he'd been when he was alive. The awkward position of his arms made their progress through the house equally uncomfortable. They were unrelenting, those men, like black ants carrying a beetle along a branch. Like the Reaper himself. The stretcher struck the stairwell light, which swung, throwing silhouettes of the beetle's shape up, down and along the walls as they struggled.

Outside, once they'd put Gareth in the ambulance I stood next to one of the younger men. He wore polished Doc Marten's lace-up boots, a long black coat with velvety pocket flaps, a white shirt and black tie. All his clothes hung on him as if they were wet and his almost shaven skull seemed to shine between the bristles. He looked about my age and twice or three times as hard. We stood by the wall, staring at Gareth's old car. The lad sidled a little closer. The ambulance seemed to have gone and I'd not watched it go or said whatever I should have. I felt angry with myself for that, for not being 'on the ball'. *They whisk away your dead before there's a chance for the family to see the difference between that and the living*, an old Frenchman had once said of the English.

The young undertaker broke silence. 'I don't mean to inquoire at the wrong toime loike, but,' he then realized that perhaps a little subtlety might be in order and paused, turning away from the car to face me, 'that was yoor bruvver, uh?'

I nodded.

'D'ee live wiv you?'

'Yeah.'

'Wosn't old, wozzee? Wot 'appened?'

'I don't know. He's twenty-three, he was ill.'

'Oh, I'm sorry.' He paced a little in the cold. 'Er, the Maxi.'

'What Maxi?'

'The Austin Maxi,' he squirmed, putting his hands in his pockets, shrugging, 'was it the *deceased's*?' His eyebrows lifted up, the tight skin on his forehead bunching. 'Your bruvver's car?'

It wasn't. It was our dad's, but Gareth drove it everywhere and why should I care any more, I told myself. I nodded.

'Not meaning to be indiscreet or nuffing, but if you decide to sell it, please give us a call dahn 'ee undertaker's.'

'Of course. No, don't worry,' I heard myself say, 'life goes on.' I was actually grateful for his asking me about the car. It made me feel as if out of all the mess someone was brave and honest enough to try for tomorrow, even if he was slightly blunt.

He joined the other men and they floated away, the rear lights disappearing as the road curved out of sight. They might have been driving a hearse but it was probably an old Ford Granada with chromed exhausts, wide wheels, a jacked-up suspension and anti-friction mud flaps. The London street seemed awfully quiet then, and cold.

Little Ulric and Alice had been ushered inside and Lucilla, my stepmother, was now doing her best to prop up my father. I could hear voices and I knew we'd have to call Brock who had stayed behind, down at the little cottage with friends. I didn't want to go in. I never liked that London house but I was determined to be beside Dad when he rang and told Brock.

I remember the sound of the key in the lock the following morning and Brock bursting in, and then we were crying and hugging like little boys. 'It's just you and me now,' he'd said.

I slid back into the present, watching the midwife pump a good amount of white liquid into the drip attached to Jacquie's wrist.

'I won't go to sleep though, right?' Jacquie insisted.

The midwife held her other hand, 'No, Jacquie, I promise. The baby needs help, and you've no strength.' Curly nodded to her colleague as she applied a metal suction device with a hard rubber rim to the baby's head.

In a dramatic shouting episode the baby was literally yanked from Jacquie's exhausted body, the instrument leaving a lump about the size of a golf ball or bigger on the baby's head. I am told that the design of these devices has changed since then, thank God.

The midwife, quite calm and handling Jacquie beautifully, performed the various necessary tasks. Curly, who in order to deliver the child had needed to put one foot up against the end of the bed while tugging, now placed the baby on Jacquie's tummy.

The baby lay on its tiny belly, its head turned in my direction, no more than two feet from my face. It hadn't begun to breathe yet and the room was suddenly calm. Holding the cord, Curly counted the seconds while measuring the pulse and within moments the expressionless little face took a breath.

'I'm sorry,' Jacquie wept, cuddling the baby, 'darling, I'm so sorry.'

Only by cutting the cord myself did I realize that Jacquie was alive and the baby was actually safe. I began to cry.

'It's a boy,' said Curly. 'Papa, a boy!'

The pink lights were dimmed even more and we were left alone for a short time, the three of us. Memory of this is sharp for me because we lived those moments by sound and touch, hardly able to see for tears.

Then there was Curly's voice. 'I'm sorry, Jacqueline, but I'm going to have to put you out.' The placenta could become trapped, she explained. Then the midwife asked if I was all right.

'Perfectly okay,' I snivelled. 'Of course I'm all right! What do you think?'

I stayed for a moment as a stronger anaesthetic was found and pumped into the drip. Jacquie drifted off with a flushed, contented wisp of a smile upon her face. The hand on my arm fell gently to the bed and I left the room holding our son.

'Hello, little one,' I said, looking at him through red eyes. I had the feeling that my face had lost its elasticity and was sagging somewhere down near my chest. I seemed to be cruising around the hospital on auto-pilot.

A man wearing a tweed jacket came and took Moses from me. He worked with a set of plastic tubes, clearing airways and testing various reactions. He had a ragged moustache. His actions were abrupt and rough, his appearance alone setting him apart from the other paediatric staff. It seemed as if my very presence made him behave in an impatient, detached manner, as if the child itself was no more than a tiresome imposition. After such a humbling few hours I found this repellent. I may have been over-reacting but the man filled me with contempt and alarm.

'D'you have to be that rough?' I asked. 'Don't you get the same results doing it gently?'

He didn't answer, as if to explain would waste his time. His clenched fist turned over, flattening the baby's chest like a tube of toothpaste. Its eyes suddenly opened in alarm and for the first time Mo screamed, heaving up in pain. It was more than my battered brain could stand. Having done little but build the chapel for years, I knew I was powerful enough literally to smash his teeth right down his smug, tweedy throat.

'Do that again and I'll hit you.' With my finger I poked his skinny arm hard through the tweed. 'You've no need to be so . . .'

It struck me that the man was in fact very small underneath the padded shoulders and thick fabric and behind the moustache – very small indeed. I was actually dealing with a large, vile insect. I imagined the spider's legs, the spotty backside, it was enough to silence me. He was, in fact, a highly trained specialist but I didn't know that then. All I wanted to do was thump the living daylights out of him.

His eyes rolled up to the skies, he bundled my son up carelessly and lumped him into my arms.

'*One* of you is doing fine,' he said, pushing awkwardly out of the room.

Unsettled in every way, I returned to the delivery suite where Jacquie had regained consciousness. She'd gone very pale. 'Is she okay?' I asked.

'Now she's fine,' a voice said, 'she's flying high.'

The nurse took little Mo, and I sat quietly studying the rays of morning sunlight streaking through the blinds. There were voices, a faint bustling outside in the corridor, while beside me Jacquie lay absolutely still.

'It's wonderful, Rupe. I'm in the chapel now,' she said, pale as paste, floating on the anaesthetic as I stroked her hair, 'I'm home. I can see the walls, all white and cool, and the garden. I can smell the fennel. It's there, Rupe, *I'm* there.'

The chapel was over a hundred miles away, yet it seemed to me to be aware. A tear rolled down my cheek. Little Mo knew nothing of this love on that first day of spring.

20 *Standing Fast*

Jacquie was intoxicated, as most mothers are, with this new little life. Mo slept with his mother on a mattress in the middle of the chapel mezzanine while I ferried food up and down and cared for them both as best I could while thanking God for the freezer. She'd anticipated this and had prepared and frozen all kinds of things for me to cook for her.

She was a wonderful mother. In those early days her love for little Mo seemed to outweigh even her desire to get back to Even Breaks. Nothing stood between them. For her it was of little importance that the summer season would start three months later.

I'd built a pond in the garden, three ponds in fact, as a celebration of the new life that had come to the chapel. There were now small trees growing in the beds around it and lavender reaching out beside an older plantation of mimosas. Eddy had arrived with Dorothy to see the new baby, his practical voice ringing out, huge arms folded across his chest. 'Why make the ponds so big?' he gasped. 'Half the size would've done.'

He was probably right. Eddy's ideas were practical though when mixed with ours they often became eccentric or even absurd. If, on the other hand, the problem faced was serious, some emergency, Eddy was the one to ask: he'd nearly always know what to do.

In June most of our clients were unaware that there was a child in the house, although as the summer heightened it wasn't easy for us or particularly fair on Moses or even the clients. In the autumn we needed to make changes, find somewhere away from the madness, find a place which could become our own. The last thing I wanted to do was walk away from the chapel but I couldn't see how we could live with all those people and share the dinner-table with them and the baby at the same time. We were offering what amounted to a singles holiday centre and in the cold light of day the baby was not a major selling point. I knew we could manage for a while, sure, but not forever. Jacquie was herself sensitive about cigarette smoke and noise getting to the baby and guardedly agreed.

'I know you'll make it right,' said Jacquie, still torn between family life and the party. 'Anyway, think of all the kids that grow up in the circus. Everyone there brings them up. Don't worry, Rupe, it's great.'

'I want to bring Mo up,' I insisted. 'I don't want a bunch of transitory chefs, barmen and holiday punters doing it.'

Although we had little money, building what Eddy and Dorothy started amusedly calling the 'bijou cottage' was an imperative for me. I'd found semi-derelict construction cabins for sale in Perpignan and we'd managed to plant them around the land. One made a fine office tucked away across the drive by the trees and a further two would be the inspiration and bones for a bungalow. There were few solid timbers left in them but Jaffa, who had recently fallen in love with one of our guests, said he would stick around and help me make them into a house.

As the summer thundered along I'd relied more than ever on Jaffa. He'd drive the pick-up for us or he'd simply disappear with Mo in his arms, away from the day-to-day madness at the chapel, perhaps on an outing with his girlfriend Julia. My gratitude was tinged with resentment. 'Have a great time,' I'd say, watching them go.

In a way it was a relief to Jacquie. The workload was tough and she was finding it tiring looking after Mo while resisting the urge to get up and out. I was thankful that we'd had enough sense to start the holidays up a little later this year. Eddy and Dorothy had advised that the moment you had children you should get them used to being with other people. If someone trustworthy could help, then why not? I found this more difficult to cope with in our circumstances because the working day blended into night and the seven-day week ran away with our freedom, leaving me feeling that I was either babysitter or absent, but not really sharing our child at all. The bijou cottage was a start in that direction, I felt, and Jacquie loved the idea. We'd be close to the chapel, yet far enough away to lose the noise. The two cabins would provide only two rooms. I had a kitchen and a bathroom to build and plumb and I wanted them to be made out of stone, like the chapel. Still, in the race to find a saner base I had a slightly pained feeling that we were missing some vital point.

Jacquie made it clear: after the summer was over, we could do as we wished. We could spend more time with Mo, when the time belonged to us. It was a frustrating contradiction. She was a woman who was tremendously capable, full of excitement, who did all she could to seize the day. If you wanted it, then do it, but do it *now*. Judging from past experience, I was beginning to realize that the problem wasn't lack of time but a simple matter of priorities.

We were sitting in the 'office' – the shed – where there was now a computer and a fax machine buried under sheaves of stray letters and odd photographs. 'We'll get a manager in,' I suggested, 'when it's ticking over nicely, then we can expand the whole thing, maybe get two branches going that can meet up for excursions.'

By now many of the diabetics were going home and recommending Even Breaks to their non-diabetic friends. In fact at times there was maybe only one diabetic guest and myself. Where else could you go flying, horse-riding, sailing, scuba-diving, canyoning, wine-tasting, and eat the most magnificent food, all for the price of a mid-range bucket-shop holiday, and all in one week? 'What these people love is that we are a family, like *their* family,' said Jacquie, picking through a box of files on the table. 'We're a success, Rupe.'

'I know. So you want to keep this going just as it is?' Past the window ran John who'd been a client at Even Breaks until we'd discovered that he was a fantastic chef. We'd encouraged him to stay on and so he'd never really left for longer than a few days. He was carrying clothes pegs, a basket full of laundry on his knee and our baby under his arm.

'He's so lovely, our little boy,' Jacquie said, before I'd had the chance to speak. She kissed me, then gazed out of the window with a slightly tired face. 'John is taking the older punters wine-tasting in the pick-up while you take the younger ones up to the gorge for the day. Okay?'

Not really. The gorge was a long way away and I didn't feel like splitting the group up. Trying to entertain a small number of people can be tricky, whilst a larger group will generally amuse itself.

'And don't let Jaffa get behind the bar again tonight,' Jacquie lectured, with a knowing look. She was in absolute control and she knew it.

'Jacquie,' I sighed, 'Jaffa built the bar with me. I can't just banish him.'

'Well, he was hopeless,' she snapped. 'He demolished it himself last night and he was supposed to be in charge of it. Why did you even bother putting him to bed? I'd have just left him lying there.' There was a smile coming on her face but she was doing her best to suppress it.

'He just got a bit carried away,' I pleaded, knowing full well that Jaffa had in fact been pickled. I couldn't always keep pace with Jacquie's mercurial mind-sets. Jaffa may have had his moments but this discussion wasn't about him. This was about Jacquie and me and control of the Even Breaks machine. Since almost everything relating to mailing out was now stored in the computer, Jacquie had a tighter grip on the advertising and marketing of our affairs. Still, there was remarkably little on the computer in the way of arrival details or weekly numbers. These would be in one of the pads or on a sheet of paper or in a diary or simply in her head. The power she had with this information was staggering. I sometimes felt as if anyone coming from anywhere might walk in at any time and lay claim to a room. But my bargaining chips were limited as it was beyond me to organize such infinite detail of memory.

In the office shed people would ring and ask for details of flights booked and I'd look at the piles of notes and papers and a notion of being a co-pilot strapped in a chair in a plummeting airplane without controls would sweep sickeningly across me. If there was anywhere in the world where my unhappiness would reach a pinnacle it was the shed. No complete lists, thus no possible way of pulling the nose up should something happen to the pilot. I'd sometimes march out, slamming the door. The sheer scale of the risks taken was now beginning to escalate and torment me.

Had I been a little older I might have realized that Jacquie, even in her magnificence, was pushing her boundaries to the limit. Equally, the feeling of growing alarm was also sending me towards a form of depression and into rebellion against the restrictions of diabetes, which under the demand was becoming unsurprisingly vindictive. I needed to be free of it; I needed to speed up. I needed to be faster, stronger, brighter, quicker . . . I needed to be . . . someone else.

Sensing my resentment of her remarks about Jaffa, Jacquie decided that a careful approach would be more sensible, and softened. 'Look, why don't you talk everyone into going to the gorge and head up there in convoy?' she suggested. 'Then Jaffa can take Julia as well.'

In the early years Jaffa had given me the strength to finish the floors of the chapel. He'd built most of the kitchen with me, and the popular little bar. Even the benches and tables in the chapel had been thoughtfully constructed by him. Once or twice, when he was alone and unhappy and past the upright stage of drunkenness, his lips stained with Roussillon red, I'd carry him across the gravel in the darkness and put him to sleep on a mattress in the shed. In the same way, Jaffa would never allow me to feel shame for the mistakes I'd make but just pass me a Coke during another of my irresponsible hypoglycaemic episodes and then prop me up and suggest that we got on with our lives.

'I know what you're doing,' Jaffa would say, scratching his dark curly hair and squinting through those round glasses, 'you're finding out. You have to do it yourself. No one can tell you. You never listen to anyone else anyway,' he'd shrug.

I watched him and Julia at the gorge, as I'd watched them on the beaches, or scuba-diving. They seemed simply happy just to be together. A tiny frisson of envy could sometimes cause a shudder. I wondered if Jacquie and I had lost the plot in the race to build our chapel. The holiday machine we'd built was becoming Frankensteinesque. Something that continued at this pace could only become unsafe.

Nevertheless, I was very much in love and these upsets probably didn't matter. After all, the pressure aside, we were happy.

'Rupe, what do you think about a ski season?' Jacquie asked.

We were on a high. We'd managed to finish the whole summer and were still intact. Emotionally, as with the end of the previous summer seasons, I needed time to recover. Although I enjoyed the company most of the time, living with people for months on end, never having a single meal apart, led to an eventual feeling of invasion and tension. The bank was happy and if we were careful and worked quietly through the winter we'd have a success on our hands the following summer. This was exciting enough for me.

'But who wants to be bored all winter when we can have a clientele to ski with and a comfortable chalet to run?' Jacquie argued the ski point convincingly. 'I can't do another winter, Rupe,' she'd added, 'not cleaning stinking feet and watching people die. I'd rather do anything but that.' Very soon I was behind the whole idea.

It was to be one of our most disastrous adventures. A huge chalet, five months in winter and six months in preparation; a winter without snow in mountains declared a disaster zone.

We returned to the Roussillon and the chapel with the minibus and pick-up battered and bleeding with rust. We were thousands in debt and looking at each other with horror and bewilderment.

Another moment of wild optimism ensued. Jacquie sipped her coffee and broke into the tip of a baguette. 'It's not lost. I'll nurse and we can do the summer as well.'

To be a nurse and have a second occupation is one thing, but to be up half the night and be a mother as well is beyond all extremes. The summer season was instantly upon us and we were fairly unprepared, having done most of the summer mail shots from the mountains.

So together we hammered on. My brother Ulric, now twenty, agreed to help out as a driver and barman. With Jaffa and an extraordinary young Finnish nanny called Trudy we formed a tight team. It was a summer where the crew gave all they could, working always for friendship and mostly for nothing.

As always in those days of Even Breaks the sangria would be ready when I arrived back with the tourists from the day out. 'Will you please stop kicking the seats!' I begged while driving the last couple of miles home. 'Oh, shit! Who opened the Coke?' The sticky liquid struck the minibus windshield, then the ceiling, while the big red-faced man in the middle row guffawed. 'Couldn't you wait?' I was pissed off but trying not to snap. 'Why shake it?' Two of the women fell against each other, laughing and looking at my face in the rear-view mirror.

'Jacquie,' said a tall chap as he embraced her and walked into the building, 'is the bar open?' The others tumbled out and roared past her, shouting and singing along to whatever was playing in the bar. It didn't seem to matter what; it *all* sounded good.

'What happened?' asked Jacquie.

'Seasick tabs. I gave them one each and then they all went comatose. I had to tie up by myself. They were all stuck at the stern, all green and dead, like corpses.'

She pointed to the door as someone fell over in the kitchen, giggling. 'Corpses?'

'I got worried: they looked miserable, so I took them go-karting. Now they've gone berserk.'

'I hope they don't all flake out, we've got the toga party tonight.' Jacquie was curt. She reminded me that Ulric had the bar stocked.

'I'm tired,' I puffed. 'There was a storm: I had to reef right down.' She wasn't listening and so I focused on the evening ahead. We'd be up until half past one at least and I was already feeling exhausted and intolerant.

'Have a drink. Go and see Mo,' Jacquie suggested brightly, 'he's over there on the sofa. And Rupe,' she stopped, 'we need shopping for tonight and you'll need to go before they close.'

When I muttered something about it being a pity she hadn't shopped while we were all out, Jacquie was able to ignore, even trump, my sulking. 'I was in the office, Rupe,' she enthused. 'I've filled up almost all of September.'

I began to feel badly heart-sick. There was neither time to sit with Mo nor to finish a drink. All that seemed to matter to Jacquie was the excitement the evening would bring. I steeled myself.

'Come outside with me for a minute, Jacq.'

She followed reluctantly. 'Rupe, one of us needs to be around, to socialize.'

'Just for a second, Jacq. Ulric's there to talk to the guests. It's part of his job.' She sat on the steps and closed the door behind us, looking irritated.

'Darling,' I began, 'there has to be a more sensible way for us to do this. We'll die if we don't rest. Can't we take one week in every six for ourselves?'

She dismissed my concerns – we'd all had a long day, everyone was tired. I felt patronized but this only seemed to irritate her more. 'Okay, okay, you rest if you want to,' she said, in the tone of a bloody-minded martyr. 'I'll shop and cook dinner myself. It's okay, Ulric and Trudy can help me.' Then, defensively, she turned. 'I love these people, Rupe, I love to party. You can't deprive me of that.'

'Nobody's depriving you of anything, Jacq. You do this every night! Listen, these aren't real friends. Sure, some may turn out to be one day but most are here for their money's worth. And if you stumble, someone will be very quick to stick it in your back. Anyway, you're harder than I am. You *know* all this. I'm your friend, so's Mo. Don't sacrifice us for an extra piss-up with a bunch of strangers.'

'The supermarket will be closed.' She got up, furious. When I asked if she'd listened to anything I'd been saying she simply said she'd stay up with the clients and clear up. I reminded her that Ulric was here for that. 'We've had a beach barbecue, a Moroccan night and a pool party in two days. For God's sake,' I repeated, 'we'll die.'

Jacquie dismissed this as another diabetic whinge and to my annoyance tried to soothe me by reminding me of my special need for sleep. 'You'd better go,' she said coldly.

I hit the road and headed for the supermarket wondering how it was possible that this affectionate woman could become so deter-mined that at times nothing seemed important any more but the chapel, the party and the welfare of the Even Breaks machine. These were warning signs perhaps, but I had no notion of them. To me it was real and fast becoming a nightmare.

Dinner was a delicious spicy lamb dish. Trudy, Ulric and I hovered back and forth from the kitchen as Jacquie, exuberant, made it all look easy, inspiring those who couldn't see the holes in our bucket and mystifying and amazing those who could.

The sleepy feeling had come back and I didn't fight it. I'd probably jabbed and forgotten to eat soon enough. I staggered away from the noise and slumped on the gravel outside. 'What the hell was I doing and where was my Coke?' I talked to myself as rational thought faded into oblivion.

Then I felt honey on my face and the sticky muck being dribbled into my mouth with fingers. As soon as I'd partially regained my senses I began to consider the reasons why this was happening. What had we become? A pop-up party book. I almost smirked, drunk on hypoglycaemia and still cross-eyed as two Jacquies marched out and handed me two Cokes. 'What the fucking hell's the matter with you?' they said.

'I don't know,' I replied, now suddenly desperate with the confusion one has when coming up from a hypo. 'Why don't you just go back in?'

'Cos I'm worried. You're screwing everything up for me.' She hesitated, realizing how selfish this sounded. '. . . And yourself. And Mo,' she added awkwardly. 'We rely on you, Rupe,' she said, 'so why are you doing this?'

'I'm so dependent on you,' I scowled at her. 'And you *know* it.' As my senses returned I began to feel shame clouding my thoughts and a growing despair. A small group of stray tourists, wondering what was going on, had gathered outside the door, the copious wine lifting their inhibitions as their curiosity stopped them from having the good manners to let us be completely alone.

'What *are* you talking about?' Jacquie insisted, on her knees beside me.

'I'm committed to the babe,' I said, 'as you bloody well know.' In the face of humiliation I tried to explain myself. 'I mean, what the hell would happen if I dropped dead? You'd never cope with that, would you, Jacq?' I began to shake in the cool air because of the Coke and honey soaking my front and the nervous reaction to the hypo. 'Because you're not into being alone for a second and you *know* that any other man would throw you out if you went on for months on end like this. That is, any man that you respected enough to stay with.'

Again I could smell the fennel that grew by the chapel door and I noticed that little stones were stuck to the honey on my fingers where I'd fought suffocation as they'd smeared it into my face. 'With me by the balls,' I moaned, 'you get to do it all, endless excitement with an ever-changing cast, so the whole adventure never wears out. And I'll never leave because I'm in love with Mo and I've thrown away the bloody tools to survive.'

'Just wait, Rupe, wait until your blood-sugar comes back up,' said Jacquie. Even she, the practical professional, seemed startled by the depth of my anger. 'You don't know what you're saying,' she added.

I raised the shirt away from my chest. 'You know it's true though, don't you?' There was silence while the onlookers, feeling awkward despite the alcohol, departed.

'And you like it that way, Jacquie. You like to flaunt it, to prove that you're younger and faster. But you'll catch up with yourself and life'll get you and when *you* go, Jacquie, believe me, we'll *all* go.'

It might seem like madness, but love writes its own menu. Even after that horror we cleaved to one another, determinedly hoping to make things work. I imagined a plateau where at last we would have enough time to turn and focus on our little family. It hardly occurred to me that the plateau is a myth. Ambition and family hardly ever coexist comfortably, at least, not without the golden word . . . *sacrifice*.

The following September Jacquie was pregnant again, a pregnancy lovingly sprung by tequila and a rare siesta after a Viking party for a Finnish chap called Kristian. We'd vaguely planned a sibling for Mo, agreeing that it was unfair for him to grow up alone. Just as before, we simply left it to fate, but sadly the euphoria that had accompanied our first pregnancy eluded Jacquie this time. Perhaps the novelty had worn thin or maybe fatigue and the constant demands of Even Breaks made the whole prospect daunting.

Caroline had fallen in love with a dehydrated but aristocratic version of John Wayne, a man called Buck who ran the local ranch. We visited often with our tourists but calls to Caroline at the

The new curate's house roof, with the chapel renovation under way.
In the small courtyard between the curate's house and large buttress there are
said to be eleven of the chapel's curates buried in a crouching position against
the walls. Their number is indicated by crude markings on a marble plaque
over the curate's house door. We planted a tree, leaving them undisturbed.

Kansas and Yogi with Jacquie, autumn 1984.

Above: Jacquie cooking in the makeshift chapel kitchen, surrounded by the railway sleeper 'beams', which caught fire, destroying months of work.

Left: 11 May 1985. Near King's Lynn in Norfolk.

Jacquie and my father and stepmother on the terrace outside
the chapel in the heat of the summer.

The chapel kitchen in the early days of Even Breaks.
Me (in the foreground), Jacquie and Jaffa.

The chapel with the main roof complete. The large pond (centre), built to celebrate Moses' arrival, and (lower far left) the Bijoux cottage.

The curate's house. Jacquie is rough-plastering the stone with a sponge.

Right:
The chapel
before renovation.
View towards the kitchen.

Below:
The chapel renovated.
View towards the kitchen.

Left:
The chapel before renovation. View towards the fireplace and bathroom.

Below:
The chapel renovated. View towards the fireplace and bathroom (behind the staircase) with sliding door/mirror.

Above:
In the Alps: Jacquie with Moses on his first birthday.

Right:
Argeles sur Mer: The end of an Even Breaks summer. With Moses and Jacquie on the deserted October beaches.

Six weeks after Jacquie disappeared: a short break at my parents' little cottage on the Solent.

'Bert', our old Land-Rover, parked close to the tired south London house that became our home.

Two reasons for happiness.

restaurant were still rare and usually ended with Jacquie unhappy somehow.

Buck was a gentleman. At sixty-something he could still charm the leaves off the trees. He had a love for everything western and wore riding breeches and boots, topping the whole kit with a Hank Williams-style shirt. His passions were horses, women and guns, garnished, perhaps, with a little fascism. Much as I warmed to him as a character this aspect disturbed me.

Caroline, thirty years his junior, now spent most of her free time away from the mill in Buck's little house on the tree-covered mound in the centre of his acres. Buck was a reminder of a last heroic battle for freedom, any last heroic battle. The house, positioned like a breeze-block Alamo, held antiques from generation after generation of a North African family long gone. A large wind-up trumpet gramophone would scratch out melodies above worn chairs as Buck merrily passed sangria to guests, paying special attention to the women. Visitors propped themselves up between the antiques in the little rooms, while storming upstairs, Buck would demonstrate a priceless Winchester rifle, firing out of the window, up towards the stars.

September was usually the finest month. It was the last big push before the end of our season and with the heart of the summer in our wake, we had to face the painful reality that the disaster in the Alps had ruined us. Financially things had hit rock bottom.

If we were forced to sell, we knew we could never settle elsewhere in France, not after so many years invested in the love of the chapel. We'd have to go and look for a future somewhere else and if we couldn't find it, then we'd do what Buck would have done: we'd make a stand and fight for the chapel to the last.

Before the winter came round, we threw in the last of our money and went to Australia. We were window-shopping, Mo, pregnant Jacquie and I, searching for a fresh start. Australia had been the only other option. If we had found paradise there, we might have sold up and left France forever. We might well have found it too, if we hadn't been searching for a dream. I should have seen a shadow then of what was to come, but somehow one misses these things. Love blinds us and slowly, we adjust ourselves to fit, even if this means shutting things out.

'Can't you find a campsite where there's something going on?' Jacquie had asked. 'Let's find a place where we can have a beach party. I know I'm pregnant, but I just can't stand wasting my life like this.' In one of the most beautiful places in the world I simply could not supply the excitement she needed. The trip was a search for the pot of gold at the end of the rainbow but she could no longer see . . . that we had it already.

It had been a stick or bust trip, and having found no hope for a possible future down under, we had decided not to sell the chapel. We were, of course, going home to stand and fight.

21 *Motherhood*

The fortnight winter holiday that we ran passed by with no great hiccups. Jacquie enjoyed the Christmas celebrations in the bar and with the clientele but found a close family gathering dull. In contrast, Christmas, for me, was all about being a family, about home and comfort and private moments. While Jacquie understood this, she couldn't help but find it uninspiring.

The clients went riding on Christmas Day and our few hours spent alone were precious to me. I felt that Jacquie's past indifference to Christmas was now more like actual discomfort. We were both watching time, like sand rushing through an hour-glass, Jacquie hoping for gravity to increase and the entertainment to start up again, while I wished the sand to stop falling so we could relax and maybe both of us put the baby to bed and watch a movie. It was probably then that a sad notion came to me: I began to wonder if Jacquie was falling ever so slightly out of love.

Some months later Samuel was born at the same clinic as Moses. This time the little one came thundering into the world just after dawn, smiling, born on the floor of the delivery suite, his eyes joyfully crinkled, blinking, as though it was raining, yet with the sun beating down without a cloud in the sky. It was May, spring had already swamped the chapel in the bright yellow of mimosa, and summer was on our heels.

Jacquie stayed in the hospital for a few days; despite Samuel's relatively simple birth it hadn't been easy for her. Something had changed; it was as if she'd lost her certainty, as if the strain of it all and the months of worry had taken a grip on her senses and she couldn't work out why she was feeling this way.

Jaffa, who'd driven the minibus through every red light in Montpellier to get us to the hospital in time, had kissed the baby gently and then left like a ghost. I do not remember him going or how he managed to take himself the 120 miles home. I only remember the deed and his unconditional friendship. Conversely, I felt oddly disillusioned, watching Jacquie deal with the shock that any woman faces when the reality of parenthood kicks in.

When little Sam lay in her arms she seemed joyful with him, grateful that life had brought him to us safely. Looking at them in the hospital, with flowers all around and the blind optimism that one has when one knows that the drama of birth is over, I was happy for us, though concern haunted me. Jacquie was tired and the look in her eyes seemed distant, her thoughts concealed, as if there was something on her mind that she could not bear to share; as if she was far away and somehow so alone.

In less than a month, with the bank's gun at our heads and still massively in debt, we were back in the driving seats at Even Breaks with no one to blame but ourselves. It was harder than I ever thought it would be. We found extra help but even so, afraid perhaps of losing her grip, Jacquie decided that she felt more comfortable working than spending her free time at home with the children and sleeping. She refused to rest.

As we headed into July and August, Christine, a thoughtful, hardy girl from a large Kiwi family, was with us as a cook, working alongside another ex-client called Johnny who helped with everything. Samuel hardly had the dressing off his tummy button and we were already into seventeen clients a week and climbing. Christine not only took on the role as a worker, she also became an integral part of the children's care and would often be found with the baby under one arm while stirring a pot with Mo at her side. It was a natural thing for her. She knew what it took to look after children and her experience and patience were beyond her years.

My sister Alice had come on a working holiday; an error of judgement on my part, as she could never have been prepared for what was to happen. If I'd taken the time to think, I wouldn't have given such a responsibility to a seventeen-year-old, especially the care of a baby who now frequently cried for his mother's attention. Although she was twelve years my junior, Alice and I had always been close. Now, at a characteristically complicated age, she had agreed to the working holiday, but adolescence and inexperience were heavily stacked against her and without support she was beginning to despair.

One evening I arrived back from a visit to the Dali museum over the frontier in Spain with the minibus full of tourists to find Alice in tears and Jacquie locked in the shed, still hammering away at the computer.

'Jacq, don't you think you need a little time away from it all with the babe?' I asked, but was warned off sharply.

In the night Sam, who had not spent much time with his mother during the day, would cry. In fact, to make things worse, he cried whenever he was left alone. Those initial early times are crucial and I felt that Jacquie's ambition for Even Breaks was robbing Samuel of this. In denying her own instincts she suffered and snapped at me from what I can only now see as frustration and the burden of guilt.

'We are in a position now where we have more help than ever,' I said to Jacquie as we sat in our room. 'We got the help so you could be with Sam. It's not the money. I mean, you don't have to stay up until God knows when *all* the time.'

'Look, we are the ones that matter here, Rupe,' she warned me. 'We're the ones that make it work. We have to be there.' She sighed, irritated.

It was late and at last she had left the bar and come to bed. I was being predictable and annoying; none the less I continued, 'It's half past one, Jacq. How will you be able to get up at four to feed him?'

She muttered something about having not been able to just abandon things.

'It's important,' I pleaded, 'this is our child we're talking about. It's not like you. What is going on?'

'I can do what I want.' She became waspish. 'You can just as easily look after the baby as I can.'

While undressing, I began to put the things from my pockets where Mo couldn't reach them. He had a bigger bed now, one without safety bars, so he was free to roam the cottage in the mornings. I looked out of the kitchen window at the chapel and the warm light on its orange stones. It was a wonderful place but we hardly lived there any more, even in the winter. It seemed ridiculous that we were now housed in an extended shed beside what had once been our future paradise.

'The baby's crying,' she said flatly. I got up to deal with things.

It upset me to face it, but it seemed that Mo basked in the best of Jacquie's maternal affections, perhaps before the novelty of parenthood dimmed. It was heart-breaking to see that unconditional love withheld from Sam. Our little family seemed to be crumbling between my fingers and as far as I could see, Jacquie could justify turning her back on the children with attitudes that had become almost textbook for most fierce feminists.

'What d'you think I am?' she said. 'Here to be trapped?' We were standing at the back of the chapel because there was nowhere else to argue without being overheard. '*Alice* is supposed to be responsible for the children. I'm damned if I'm missing the horse-riding just for this. If she can't manage, then we'll find someone else. What's the point of her being here?'

I tried to be patient and conciliatory. 'She's not a mother, Jacquie. Don't expect her to be Mother. *You're* the mother.'

'I might have post-natal depression, you know,' she said bleakly. I tried to urge her to rest more and avoid exactly that scenario but her contradictions annoyed me. 'How can I stop if you're forcing me to be with the children all the time? I'd rather be at work,' she argued. 'I'm not a front-loader.'

I seemed to be trapped whichever way I went. If she worked she became exhausted, if she looked after Mo and Sam, even with Alice there too, she was miserable. A 'front-loader' was the name we gave to those tidy, organized mothers who might appear in detergent commercials. Front-loaders go to every school event. They also stay at home, bake bread and stuff their husband until he loses interest because the magnet's lost its draw. Front-loaders realize they've wasted their time living in a self-inflicted version of hell, sadly, according to Jacquie, always too late to enjoy the wonderful lives that they could have had, being free and eternally young.

'Jacquie. We have one free week coming up. Christine will leave soon if you don't slow down and without her we're dead meat. We have that one free week in this whole summer,' I begged, 'to relax and spend some time in the calm with the children. They need it, Jacq; *everyone* needs it.'

Sometimes Jacquie would sit and feed Sam at her breast in the quiet and then I could tell that her love for him was tearing her apart. He was enveloped, kissed, so much loved, yet only a part of her could be this trapped, nurturing creature and it was just as difficult for Mo. He would hold on to her, burying his head in her bosom, and I'd find her silently crying. When I asked her what was wrong she was always too confused to give a clear answer. 'I don't know,' she'd say, shaking her head in a flood of tears, 'I just don't know.'

I told her that we'd stop for the winter soon. In any case, there was no point in staying open if there weren't enough bookings later in the year.

'You really don't understand, do you? I don't want to stop. I need it, Rupe, I mean, look at me,' she said, her eyes streaming, 'look! What else is there?'

For our clients we were the model family. Jacquie and I exemplified a contagious love affair that affected most of the souls it touched. We seemed to be doing exactly as we wished in a blissful setting. Yet those who ventured to see a little deeper into the heart of it all had no envy. Concerned that we were facing both mutiny and exhaustion, I'd insisted that the sacred week should remain free. The chapel would be closed and for those six days we could spend time with Mo and little Sam, who was unsurprisingly fighting more than ever with tears for his mother's attention.

'It's not right,' said Jacquie, sitting in the cottage kitchen. 'Our own helpers are talking behind our backs. Jaffa's uncooperative and Alice doesn't help things. She gets together with Christine and they gang up and whisper about me while you're out.' The sun was beating on the thin cottage roof. 'Oh God, and this heat,' she went on, looking exhausted, 'it's unbearable.'

There were endless tasks, not only at the chapel but also at the fifteen or so other houses that we were by now managing, a project we'd set up to run alongside Even Breaks. On a tiny scale we provided houses for English tourists. There were swimming-pools to be cleaned, scores of floors to be mopped and the linen from most of the places to be brought to the chapel for laundering.

If I had understood what a wretched thing post-natal depression was, I would have taken a different view of Jacquie's behaviour, but I hadn't the faintest idea, really, that it could be so powerful and dreadful and insidious.

One of the early warning signs came when Jaffa and Alice announced that they were going. 'What is it, Jaff?' I pleaded. 'Why? Are you angry with me? With Jacquie?' I was hardly surprised at his departure but I felt I had to stick up for Jacquie, blindly pretending that perhaps Jaffa's and my sister's view of how unbearable the situation had become was wrong.

Jaffa knew that the things I loved most were my family and he had no wish to fracture our friendship. 'I'm not telling you why. I can't say.' He shook his head. 'You wouldn't listen now. You have to find out for yourself.' Then he patted my shoulder and climbed into his car.

Alice left with him, carrying a note that I'd written in wounded haste. It would make her feel that she'd abandoned Jacquie and failed me. It stabbed at her on the way back through France as she read it in a flurry of tears.

I knew Jacquie loved the children. I reasoned that we'd always defend each other, whatever the price, that the significance of a family was inestimable and its protection worthy of any action, however much sadness it might bring me or us personally. I believed that eventually, somehow, if I was as relentless as I had been in building the chapel, I would outlast the problems and things would magically improve.

The office shed was progressively turning into a battlefield, although the battles at that stage could have been even worse; my own perception of right and wrong had become distorted for reasons that I did not understand. I was now accepting things which months before I would not have tolerated. People seldom understand the altered state of those trying to maintain normality with another suffering as Jacquie was at that point.

'They'll all have to share rooms,' said Jacquie, tapping away at the computer with her usual devotion. She was speaking of a group who wanted a house to rent at a cheap rate.

'But you've put seven of them in there. Jacquie, it's a house for four people.'

'So? I warned them,' she said with a cold smile.

I repeated my concerns. 'Don't you see? It won't work like that. It'll rebound on us. They'll forget how cheap it was and only remember how squashed and miserable they were.'

The disputes would go on and on. Predictably, perhaps, as our prices dropped, so did the scruples of some of our clients. The majority were good, honest people but a few stole things from the houses we rented, while others disfigured the furniture simply for amusement. A small number must have committed bizarre sexual acts, leaving unpleasant evidence on the linen. But the worst of all were those who provoked their neighbours in the little mountain villages, who in turn entered the houses and trashed the furniture, then smashed the windows. It became, in the light of Jacquie's temperament, an extra worry that we should never have saddled ourselves with. We were trying too hard to save our chapel, so hard in fact that we had forgotten about saving ourselves.

I returned one evening from repairing someone's dream holiday cottage to find Mo wandering barefoot on the drive. The sight struck me hollow. There was no question of Mo being allowed near the chapel. It was now almost solely for tourists. The tiny, botched-together cottage had become our children's home, surrounded by gravel, nettles, the odd potted plant and dust. It seemed so absurd and wrong to me when there were other possibilities, less exotic ones perhaps, but realistic. Surely I could do building work in the winter and she could nurse and in the summer we'd do a season full-blast with a few days off every six weeks? We'd argued this point so many times. Jacquie's nursing was well paid, but this wasn't a money issue. It was the manic activity and the constant changes . . . Jacquie could not relax or slow down; Even Breaks had become her life.

My frail wedding ring had split open after a diving trip and I hadn't felt good about it. The thin metal strip clung to my finger like a paperclip, adding a physical sense of vulnerability to the growing cloudiness of my thoughts. Still, our little break was due; six whole days free out of five months non-stop. Things would be clearer after that. We also had a trip to Mo's school planned. He'd been for visits and soon he was due to start in the mornings.

'Well, you won't catch me going there looking like a bloody front-loader,' said Jacquie as she applied make-up before the bathroom mirror. 'If I *have* to be there, then I'm wearing nice clothes and my fur coat.'

'Don't be daft. All the parents will be in jeans and work clothes. You'll look like you're trying to humiliate them. You'll look silly.'

She was not to be thwarted. 'I have no intention of looking like a housewife.' She laughed dryly. 'Anyway, someone's got to show them that having children doesn't mean you have to look like a dinner lady.'

I sympathized but still, the evening was awkward. We sat on plastic chairs in the middle of a school gymnasium while a diplomatic schoolmistress gave polite instruction and Jacquie made unconscious efforts to look like Zsa Zsa Gabor. Around us, five farmers' wives, a baker and his spouse, two tobacconists and the wife of the pharmacist, all clad in down jackets and tired denim, were shooting us looks like poison darts.

'Now, don't be upset, Rupe,' said Jacquie the following weekend as I marched into the house after a run to the airport. 'I've booked some people in.'

'You've what?' I gasped. 'In *our* free week?'

'Just a couple, they'll take care of themselves.' She bustled about in a transparent effort to make the matter seem trivial. 'We just have to feed them and be around. It's money, Rupe. Don't be angry.'

I followed her about, spreading my arms out wide. 'What will we make? The whole lot of us here, everyone, for two people? Jacquie, I love you, but this isn't about *money*. This is about what? Jacquie! These months, non-stop, what's it all about? I'm too tired for this. FOR GOD'SAKE, WHAT'S IT ALL FUCKING WELL FOR?'

22 *Trouble*

In the following month I took a group across to the Dali museum in Spain. Since the elimination of our only break in many months, I had lost something of my tolerance and was not feeling sure of myself any more, not sure at all. Memories of my childhood were now torturing me. One does not get a second chance at childhood. Surely our children deserved some consideration, a weekend of our time here or there, or even a whole day? Deeply unhappy, I was confused. My feelings for Jacquie, which had been steadfast for nearly ten years, were in tatters.

Being in the holiday business, attractive women were frequently in my line of vision, but I'd been devoted for so long that having an affair seemed utterly unthinkable. Jacquie had only to look at me and I belonged. But these were dangerous days and I no longer held out much hope for change. I was also becoming angry, and loathing for the endless thrill was gathering speed.

There was a beautiful young girl called Lola staying at the chapel. She had long, dark hair, powerful brown eyes and was intellectually very fast. She was about twenty, much younger than me, and she buzzed with excitement, naive enthusiasm and an interest in me that I slowly acknowledged. It was probably the 250th time that I'd taken a group into Spain, but this time, instead of leaving my feelings at home, I took Lola and thoughts of my bitter disappointment along too.

I doubt that Lola cared about what effect she had upon me or the fact that, like a valve on a pressure-cooker, she was a release, an escape route. For Lola it was fun, excitement and forbidden fruit. She liked Jacquie, but *this* was a challenge and an adventure. For me it would be a single afternoon, an affair that died as soon as it took flight. It was a day when I could tell myself I was still a person, still interesting, had some control over my life and was desirable, human.

Almost immediately, with the challenge gone, Lola departed at my request, leaving with the words 'Don't hate me.' It wasn't a cruel parting, rather, a friendly one. Thank God she was intelligent and kind enough to see my love for Jacquie and the children as foremost. I felt shame and confusion, which never really left me, adding to a strange, emotional isolation from Jacquie. There was now a fracture in my faith like the one in my wedding ring. I was surprised and worried by my fall from grace.

I was beginning to dread the future. As I looked ahead, I felt as if I'd opened the door to damnation. There inside the Exciting Hotel of Cruel Innocence the bar was up and running and Jacquie was merrily setting up the shots in the centre of a crowd of blank yet laughing faces, the heavy make-up dripping from her eyes down the face of Jacquie at forty-five.

'Are we having fun, Rupe?' The music pounded above the general din. 'Am I having fun?' asked the mouth anxiously, while Jacquie smashed the things around her with a hammer, destroying our own possessions, pictures of our children, the windows of the chapel and our dreams. 'Rupe,' said the image of my wife, 'we are having fun, *aren't* we?' but her eyes were looking around coldly, just in case we weren't.

I was sick. I was almost convinced that I was going mad.

I *begged* for change and insisted that there was something amiss, but others just saw the same old Jacquie. They saw the same smiles, the same laughter and couldn't feel the storm coming. I asked people for understanding and too few for advice, while the champagne nights and the groups continued to thunder through the chapel doors, and with almost each and every day the early hours came and went and the threads of our marriage wore thinner.

We'd had another of those pointless 'We need money' conversations as the tidal wave of debt from the Alps reduced us to panic.

'I mean, what are you going to do, Rupe? WHAT ARE YOU GOING TO DO?'

I felt hopeless, useless, went and sat with the children and searched over and over for solutions while all the time the party went on. Like the train driver thundering along, I was looking over at my mate as she now frenziedly shovelled in the clinker. I could also see that the tracks ahead had gone into a dive and hear the engine beginning to scream. Pulling on the brake, I realized it had come away in my hand.

Jacquie's habit of keeping as many details as possible in her head served her particularly well at this stage. It was a juggling act of some brilliance and it gave her the means of control. People would arrive and depart and only Jacquie would know when and whence this would happen. It became harder and harder for me to keep track of things, though incredibly she rarely forgot a single detail.

We were having a tequila night. During these noisy evenings the baby alarm from the cottage would often be too feeble to compete, so I headed across the gravel drive to make sure things were okay with the children. Mo wasn't in his room. I found him in the bathroom clinging to the side of the lavatory. Unable to reach the pull-cord, in darkness and alone, the little chap had wept with fear, then had hidden shaking and crouching for an hour or more, in the darkness, lying in his own filth.

'We stop, Jacquie, we change course,' I said, furious, 'or this marriage is over. I fucking hate you for what you're doing to us.'

Her lips were purple, her eyes heavy. It was three in the morning and everyone had had a nice time. No, Jacquie *wasn't* drunk and I wasn't to be *miserable* and spoil it. We'd have to wait until tomorrow. Then we'd talk, tomorrow.

'I can see you need a change,' Jacquie said stiffly a day later. She kissed Mo and I fed Sam. 'I've rented a place in the village for you. I know you want to write, so go, go for a few days; take the typewriter and go. Everyone will help looking after the children, so don't worry, they're fine.'

I glared at her incredulously as the word *fine* hit the air but at that point if I stayed there any longer I'd leave her for good, and she knew it. After making sure that we had enough back-up for the kids and warning Jacquie that we had to come to a permanent agreement, I was gone.

So at the start of another week of sailing, sangria, flying and scuba-diving, vodka, horse-riding and Spanish red, I found myself alone, on the doorstep of a breakdown, sitting in an apartment above Le Boulou's thundering summer traffic, writing about France and two young people with a dream.

It's funny, how suddenly faced with demolition Jacquie tried to make things easier for me. I doubt if she ever thought I would leave, despite my threats. She knew I adored her, yet though she could be reasoned with, it was still impossible for me to convey to her that my dreams included not only us, but our children as well. It seemed to me that having had such an apparently successful childhood, Jacquie did not see the value of a family as any big deal, just as children who grow up with money often can't envisage what it would be like to be without it. Yet she'd never seemed quite so cavalier in the past. She'd had dreams too and her eventual wish for children had been so very strong. Why was she contradicting them now?

'I'm arranging something for this winter, Rupe,' Jacquie mentioned later on, 'something to slow us down. I can't take the pace either,' she said sheepishly. I looked at her suspiciously as she continued, 'I think it'll make me ill if we have no help.'

I was pleased. 'Just spend some time with me and the children; that's all I ask, just a little time.'

She agreed, joking, 'Or I'll crack up or you're going to leave me,' then sat down in the bijou cottage kitchen. 'I'm going to get a crew together for Christmas, to help us through. I'll advertise for it. And next year we'll only do one week in two.'

She seemed to be advancing unsubstantiated plans and in a way I humoured her. 'Every other week? We'll go bust.' It was quite funny how when she announced those impossible plans it was I who remonstrated about our need for dosh.

'There's the last roof to redo,' she added, 'and what about the well? That'll save us a fortune in water when it's dug out. We'll need the manpower to do that.' She had already justified the expense of this crew in her head. But we could hardly support ourselves and the children, let alone anyone else.

'Just a week off now and again, Jacq, that's all,' I smiled, 'and some time for Sam and Mo. You don't have to go mad.'

PART FOUR

23 The Coming Darkness

Sometime after that summer we met the Dodger and his wife. He was making plans to develop a centre for tourists nearby. His ideas ranged from an Even Breaks formula, which in no time he'd realized could be a winner (though he cannily saw that our handling of things was far too labour-intensive) to other schemes involving fancy equipment and trekking. He was a tall, likeable man, introduced to us through mutual friends. A large and aggressive goose guarded his house although the place already seemed to be protected like a fortress. There were gates (unlike the chapel where there were none) and wire fences, which the dreaded goose would patrol.

The charming Dodger was seasoned in the tougher aspects of the tourism industry. He knew a great deal about travel and dealing with numbers but lacked the youth, physical strength and social ease that had been such a successful cocktail at Even Breaks. Naive as we were, we quickly realized that our growing mailing list was a crucial part of this new relationship's appeal. Gradually I became aware that the Dodger's artful business ideas seemed to present to Jacquie new, exciting directions, free from the chains of parenthood and home, carrying her away from the massive financial dilemma we faced with a promise of success and unlimited adventure.

I doubt if the Dodger had the slightest idea of what was truly happening in our world. We were quite good at hiding the cracks and at doing this somehow without even realizing that the façade was deliberate. I felt some unease about the deals and collaborations he proposed but was met with disbelief and scorn when I aired them to Jacquie. She had recently become even more desperate to control every aspect of our business arrangements, making all the decisions and insisting that I look to the Dodger for inspiration.

We were sitting in the office, waiting for a fax from him about proposals for the following year. 'We're getting in too deep too fast, Jacq.' I looked at her as the fax began to reel out.

'Will you relax,' she tutted, scribbling on one of her notepads. She seemed unable to consider other things. It was as if the bargaining chips I once had were now almost worthless, as if Jacquie was gradually losing the ability to hear the voice of reason other than her own. Things were being planned with remarkable cleverness but without careful thought to the risks presented to our future. The advantages for the Dodger seemed phenomenal, leaving Jacquie with the promise of leading expeditions in the mountains and thrilling voyages with co-drivers and so on, while the threat of bankruptcy was hurtling towards us like a juggernaut. Care of the children would be left to me alone.

'The Christmas helpers, Jacq, how can we possibly afford four?'

'I've already *said*, it's budgeted for.' Gaily she went on, 'I'm putting together another ski season, Rupe, something for the spring.'

I stared at her in horror and amazement, reminding her of our huge existing debts from the last one and her need to rest.

'No lectures, Rupe. If we don't take a risk now we'll never get out of this hole. Besides,' she turned sharply, 'I don't want to sit here and be bored to death nursing all winter.' These had once been viable excuses but now I couldn't buy them. I wanted to stay put, to dig us in and fight for the chapel, finding what reliable work we could; there was no safety net left. We had children now; yet she was about to gamble what little hope there was of saving the chapel.

An English family had moved into one of the mountainside houses next to Louis and Marie-Antoinette. The two daughters, Martha and Emily, very quickly became nannies for the boys and on the odd occasion would be swept into the gears of Even Breaks. They were sensible and practical, from a Lincolnshire farming family whose greatest attribute seemed to be kindness. Just knowing they were there for Mo and Sam, taking turns, was a blessing.

Their father hadn't yet come to grips with French and so nodded over his tomato plants, tipping his cap, perhaps, at Louis and Marie who nodded back, separated by the centimetres of a garden fence and a crevasse the size of an entire culture.

We were deep into autumn. One would never know it because the leaves were still heavy on the trees, an aspect of the deceptive character of the Pyrénées Orientales. It was raining from the mountain above the chapel, weird Spanish rain, which hurled over the summits and tumbled upon us from a cloudless sky. One of Jacquie's four Antipodeans – our crew of Christmas helpers – had arrived. Don was in his mid-twenties, a traveller like the rest, doing his walkabout. He was the youngest of the 'guys' as we called them. As two more arrived, it occurred to me that four men spending a whole winter in the heart of a battered marriage might just be a mistake.

We had a post-season dinner, inviting Eddy and Dorothy whom we saw little of in the summer. Don seemed to fit in wonderfully and for Jacquie the presence of other people was always a delight. Strangely, I felt invaded, as if my relationship with Jacquie was now under obscure threat; not from the other men, but from the strength their presence gave to Jacquie. I was also aware that since I was beginning to disagree with many of the projects brought forward, I was becoming a thorn in her side. Four men, I thought, and she doesn't like family life or bringing up children any more – or the winter.

It dawned on me that Jacquie had designed her winter remarkably cleverly and as husband in any dispute I'd be isolated should I challenge her plans. Her fresh excitement seemed to confirm my fears although I don't believe that this had anything to do with unfaithfulness. Jacquie simply wanted fun, and here was old hubby threatening to turn the taps off.

'Pass me the wine,' said Eddy. 'Rupert,' he laughed, patting my shoulder as I looked gloomily at my dinner plate, 'come on. Listen, when Dorothy and I first had children, we had no help.' He shrugged, holding his hands up a little, 'Not a soul. We couldn't afford it.' Eddy had brought a couple of bottles of very good wine, as he always did.

He poured some into Don's glass and Dorothy put her hand over hers. 'We used to give our children to anyone who'd have them,' Eddy continued, 'everyone in the family, friends, they all helped.'

'I know what you're saying. That's not what I'm talking about,' I said. 'Both parents should want to be invol—'

'The answer's quite simple,' said Dorothy. 'If you don't like the way Jacquie's looking after the children, then you'll have to do it yourself.' There was laughter around the table, only partly due to Eddy's fine wine.

'It's not that I don't *like* it,' I began. 'When she does it, she does it wonderfully. But I feel like they're suffering. We need to spend more time with them.'

'I never wanted children,' said Jacquie with throw-away sincerity, possibly irritated by being discussed as if she were absent. 'I only had them because *you* wanted them. I did it for you.'

This was incredibly painful and untrue and yet bizarrely it evoked more laughter. In my whole life I'd never known my parents at peace but they'd always wanted and loved me. Not to have absolute trust in this love, in the light of the hatred and despair I had witnessed as a child, would have meant belonging to nothing, not quite existing.

In an upset and surprised tone above the laughter around the table I said, 'You're lying,' my astonishment clear. 'We both "didn't want kids" at some time or other when we were younger,' I stammered. 'You never even discussed going off the pill with me, so why did you, eh?'

Eddy patted my shoulder and said I should lighten up. I realized that as a man defending this point, I would never be credible. I also felt as though I was on a vulgar talk show, airing my dirty linen, but like most hurt fools, I was beyond caring. I was remembering the romantic moments in bed when Jacquie'd asked me for a baby, the passion and hopes, the scans and the pre-natal classes, now presented to the outside world as a joke, a lie, a farce. I was angry.

'Eddy! Did you hear what she just said?' I turned to Jacquie. 'What about Mo and Sam then? Did you consider *them* in this magnificent charitable act of yours, or did you intend to just hand them over like a bunch of flowers and then hit the road? And what about me?' I glared. 'You didn't even give me the choice.'

But my voice was drowned in more laughter. Jacquie, sensibly, was unwilling to stay on the subject. I knew she loved the children so this denial threw me into confusion. I felt betrayed – or was I going mad? Or was she now just so puffed up with self-confidence since the attractive young men's arrival? It never occurred to me that it could be anything else. I had never known her to be so cruel. I now knew, though, that I would never have another child and probably never would achieve the happiness of family life I had worked towards.

After dinner, deeply confused, I walked Eddy and Dorothy to their car. Eddy embraced me. 'I think you're letting things get out of hand,' he said kindly.

'It's not what you think,' I told them. 'Things are *really* going wrong here.'

'Why don't you come over and have a chat with Eddy?' said Dorothy, kissing me. Eddy said to call him and we'd talk. I never did make that call, believing I could sort it all out myself: a pity, a tragedy. It was one time when I would have listened to every ounce of advice Eddy offered, every single, practical, precious, sensible word.

As usual we celebrated Christmas with activities for the guests and private time with the children before preparing a special dinner for the clients. Though she participated, Jacquie again made it clear that she didn't enjoy family Christmas gatherings, not at all.

This was our third working Christmas and it was a strange time for all concerned as each and every year there were dramas of some sort. It sounds unsociable, but splitting the event with the clients and my children had more of an impact these days. It hadn't been so at first but by the second year I'd realized that Christmas would never be something that Jacquie could really embrace. For some reason we needed strangers for it to be exciting, and ironically the strangers seemed to need the trappings of Christmas so much more than we did. Jacquie was fantastic when it came to this.

The Antipodeans took care of the clients well. We'd been lucky: they were trustworthy, hard-working and kind. One of them, a slender man called Slammer, ran the bar, while Don and another called Robert helped in the kitchen. The fourth, Kurt, was due to arrive on New Year's Day.

During the days the guys drove the minibus, following me in the old Land Rover I'd bought to replace the pick-up truck which had long since retired. The Land Rover had been named Bert, a name that had stuck fast with Mo and Sam. Although the guys were wonderful helpers, in truth we were heavily over-staffed. As the weight of our numbers unbalanced the already tilted books, the fact that the man-power level would be impossible to sustain was heatedly discussed again.

'Why the hell do you worry about that?' said Jacquie. 'Bookings are coming in, aren't they? You'd better brace yourself too, there's a secretary coming in February, remember?' She adopted a slightly martyred tone. 'I'm doing this to make things easier for you.'

'But if you're using the ski reservations to finance Christmas, what will be left to pay for the skiing?' I boggled as she juggled through a desk of papers and the fax machine spat out another ski reservation. 'And if something breaks down?' I looked at her. 'Then what?'

'You have no idea how I'm preparing for things like that,' she snapped, unusually bitterly. 'You said that you wanted nothing to do with skiing, so don't get involved, Rupe. Just stay out of it. All right?'

Tired of endless rancour, I left her to do as she always did, although I remained deeply worried. With the office unnavigable, I now sensed cunning in Jacquie, which enabled her to exclude me from plans, do as she pleased and maniacally drive herself on.

Those clients who had booked for only one of the two Christmas weeks were dispatched and during the same airport run I collected the bunch that would be spending New Year with us. In holiday terms, the New Year creature, as opposed to the often emotionally bruised and sometimes homeless Christmas animal, is quite a different breed.

Among the New Year punters there was a woman called Angelica. I have no memory of how or why she and Jacquie became such friends but from the start of her holiday to the finish, this unusual, slightly older woman formed a special bond with my wife and at the same time became physically close to Slammer, our barman.

Angelica seemed to be in highly relaxed mode, away from the constraints of home. Sophistication and savvy confidence enabled her to queen it in our little world and Jacquie was there to be a new best friend, as if Angelica were warming her hands around a source of undying energy while Jacquie, in awe of this successful, experienced woman, burned brighter than ever.

We started New Year's Eve night with a delicious dinner for twenty-five.

'Robert's gay, can't you tell, Rupe?' said Jacquie, as we flew about in the kitchen. 'He just hasn't come out of the closet yet.'

'Rubbish. Anyway, if he is, why can't he come out when *he* wants to? Why encourage him to dress up like that?'

'He likes it.'

Robert appeared at that point, dressed in something that Edith Piaf might have worn and then proceeded to serenade the guests. I had to admit he was pretty good.

After dinner the guests moved downstairs from the mezzanine and the music got louder. Jacquie seemed to switch from merely excited into an overdrive that had her dancing wildly from person to person. Around half past two I found her in the bar. The party was sizzling along and she and Angelica and the boys were in poll position, drinking gin in the midst of the holiday crowd.

In the previous ten years, a part of New Year's night had always been our own, a private chance to curl up together and welcome the world and tomorrow. With all the admirers and visitors, the chance of such closeness seemed to have evaporated this year. I felt sick in the throng of smiling faces and somehow quite alone. That Jacquie now seemed so foreign to me, so unhappy with what we now were was especially poignant that night. It was as if someone had removed her feelings and separated us with a sheet of glass that I could only peer through and hear the occasional compensatory word.

At six in the morning, having slept a couple of hours, with no sign of Jacquie, I got up to go and collect Kurt, the last of our helpers, from the station in Perpignan. It seemed almost absurd to pick up yet another helper after the main part of the holiday was over but Jacquie's justifications were backed by ferocious argument and claims of bookings I knew little of, along with lucrative ventures to come via the Dodger.

It was past dawn, the sky a deep grey-blue. Walking from the cottage and into the chapel, I saw Jacquie, Don, Angelica and Slammer staggering, arms linked, across a floor scattered with empty plastic cups and other wreckage. Don was so drunk he could hardly speak, he was funny too, though I wasn't in the mood for it. His arm was draped over Jacquie's shoulder and a hand rested on her breast. I knew it was unintentional but that somehow made it more upsetting. Jovial, he staggered off to bed, leaving the others. Jacquie and Angelica laughed as they clocked me standing there alone.

Saying nothing, I walked past them and then up the stairs and along the mezzanine, finding my coat under a collapsed table. There were whispers and more laughter and then my pride took over and something popped inside my head. I picked up a chair and hurled it over the balcony, past the cherub pinned to the beam below and down on to the chapel's tiled floor where it smashed and bounced around.

'HOW CAN YOU BE SO FUCKING SELFISH?' My voice resonated against the chapel's arches.

I went downstairs as Angelica and Slammer rushed off. Jacquie stood in the trashed kitchen, swaying a little. I considered the wasted words over past months and chose to leave for the station without speaking.

As the New Year week ended, my threats of leaving were set aside, and with feverish optimism things seemed to become more hopeful although they were still pretty strained and daunting. Much of the unrest had been smoothed over by the arrival of Kurt, who had quickly been assimilated into the crew, seeming to defuse tensions as he settled in. Oddly calm, I wondered if Jacquie and I had simply run our course, as if perhaps the relationship was over and we were only staving off the inevitable for fear of breaking comfortable habits.

Angelica had promised Jacquie that she'd return in February and they'd share a party to celebrate their joint birthdays. They'd have a good time; it would all be great fun. In the meantime, in thanks for their efforts, Jacquie wanted to take all our helpers skiing for a couple of days.

'But the Land Rover,' I said, 'it's almost shagged out. Couldn't we just pay them like most people do?'

24 *The Language of the Lost*

We were in trouble. I couldn't identify exactly where in our world it was coming from but instinct told me that bad fate was stalking us.

It is a creeping feeling, coming to terms with the truth, discovering that the struggle and goals once shared have forked into different tracks. It was as if we were far out on the water in a small craft, madly rowing towards an approaching storm. It was mid-February now and the four hard-working boys were still with us. For most of the previous six weeks I had helped them on the dome roof or in the digging-out of the well or had retreated to my typewriter to work on the book I'd started the previous summer. In their presence, Jacquie's love and need of me had diminished. Subsequently I'd lost all interest in finishing the chapel.

The deals with the Dodger seemed to have taken on dimensions that on the one hand seemed reasonable but on the other threatened to rub us out effectively within two seasons. In my opinion, Dodger's promise of escape, with Jacquie leading trips to the mountains and various other adventures, would render the chapel's modest charms obsolete. Jacquie was hooked, sold, and like a mackerel chasing after a bit of silver paper she thought little of the consequences. She promised a season where every other week would be free for us to spend time as a family, a season simply to please me, a season which by its very nature would give us to Dodger on a plate and bankrupt us. I couldn't understand how she could not see the implications. Then I began to realize that those free weeks were intended for me alone. Jacquie intended to be elsewhere, on further trips for the Dodger.

For me the chapel was now losing its meaning. It no longer represented a future home for our children because the heart of it would be gone. Sadness was gradually breaking my confidence and my spirit.

In attempts to make a little money I'd done odd jobs for a retired English couple, George and Lorna, who lived in a neighbouring village. Each winter, for whatever they could afford, I'd done something for them.

Lorna, a retired psychiatric nurse, could clearly see a drama about to become a crisis in Jacquie. She'd feared trouble during the previous summer but had felt that the problem had subsided and so said nothing to alert me. Watching us struggle, she and George helped in the only way they could, finding me what work they could as our unusual friendship grew. Few people truly understand what mental illness does to those living close to it. I myself was bending to fit a world that had for some time become surreal. I was clinging on and they were becoming more and more aware that things at the chapel were not as they seemed on the surface.

In the meantime we'd survived on the cash from the sale of our car. I'd explained to the guys that we were in trouble and that things would have to change but Jacquie assured everyone that they should hang on, warning me that if I chose to ask the guys to leave, then she'd go with them. I conducted the car sale in a parking lot, not willing to take the abuse that I'd had from people who'd turned up at the chapel for the minibus sale the previous week.

We were a one-Land-Rover family now, Jacquie, our two children, our four Australasians and I. Bert, at fifteen years old, was getting very shaky.

Jacquie spent most of her time in the shed, working on her ski programme. The vision of the Alps, of being away in the jaws of excitement, seemed to drive her ever harder. As promised, Angelica had returned for Jacquie's birthday. She'd settled in with Slammer and both she and Jacquie seemed to be enjoying the build-up to their party. I felt contempt rather than envy for their closeness. Never before had I known Jacquie so obsessed with another person, with the exception of Caroline. She seemed willing to accept my continuing affection but with little sensitivity, as if her heart had gone far away and her body was simply going through the motions.

Angelica had come at a time when uncertainty had become the norm. Her ability to be anything she wished, to *have* others as and when she felt the urge, shone out to my wife like a huge season ticket to the stars. On Jacquie's climb from thirty-something, Angelica seemed to be advertising a life where fulfilment and young flesh bubbled over the horrors of commitment, leaving no visible scars. She was a shrink of some kind and had an important job in stress management for a textiles manufacturer, an expensive car and a glamorous and active single life. Her experience gave her an edge: at forty-five she possessed a powerful blend of success and good looks.

'Champagne?' Jacquie asked, pouring a glass of Spanish fizz for Angelica and passing the bottle across the little bar. Angelica took a sip and shivered. She wore a silk blouse with a collar that rose slightly around the neck. I noticed that her hands were very clean, the nails tidy, everything about her seemed groomed. She looked across at Slammer, eighteen years her junior and very athletic, offering an encouraging, almost fragile smile.

Late the following afternoon, dirty from working on the roof, I walked past the washing line and into the concealed corner of the garden, tripping on the handle of my sledgehammer. It had broken long ago and I'd replaced it with a branch from a tree. It was loose, dangerous even, but it worked okay.

Jacquie was on the office shed phone. She looked up, her eyes showing a now familiar disappointment as I passed by the front windows. My 'careful approach to life' was wearing her thin and my presence meant she'd have to do something that she didn't wish to. I went inside and studied a fax from a woman who wanted to know if we could supply an exclusive vegetarian/vegan package for herself, her husband and their two macrobiotic children. I knew it: Jacquie'd have them to stay if she could. I contemplated them sitting at the long table in front of glasses of water and bowls of berries and nuts while in euphoric mode Jacquie served a steamingly aromatic spicy lamb dish to a drunken group of braying, hope-to-get-lucky singles at the other end.

'Don't worry,' Jacquie continued, scratching paint from the

phone-stand with her clean, nurse-short fingernails as she spoke. 'Oh, you poor thing. I'm so sorry. Well, take care. I'll be in touch soon. Don't worry.' She put down the phone and wrote feverishly on a pad. Jacquie had another two of these, which contained the essentials of her ski project. There were no back-up systems and no typed information, apart from our mailing list. Her fabulous memory contained it all, supported by her ability to draw solutions from vast reserves of seemingly trivial information.

She looked up, already knowing why I was there. 'Hi.' She spoke coolly.

In the silence that followed I looked at the phone. 'Who was it?' I asked.

'Gavin.'

'Gavin?'

'He's the one I'm renting the accommodation from in the Alps. He's a lovely guy; something's happened to his father, and Rupe,' she began sweetly, 'I feel so close to him; I think I can really help.'

'You do?' I said, hovering in the doorway. 'Why do you think this?'

'Well, he hasn't got anyone who understands him.' She must have sensed my spirits fade as they had on New Year's Eve. 'Look, I know what you're thinking, but don't, Rupe. This is important to me.'

'What on earth do you expect me to think? We have two children. Aren't they *important*? The deposits we've had for the ski season are running out already. We used most of them to pay for Christmas. Jacq, you've got to help build this place up, not go elsewhere.'

'We'll pay for the accommodation when the final balances arrive. Gavin says he'll wait.' I murmured something about not being surprised and she turned sharply. 'God, you're a bastard sometimes.' She threw her pen down on the desk. I looked at her, jealousy burning, as defiantly she turned back to the fax machine where I noticed a box. 'Just *go*, will you?' She picked up a second pad and turned the crammed pages.

'What's in the box?'

'Mum gave it to me for my birthday. It's a camera. She gave it to me early, so I can use it for the children and things.' She looked away.

Barbara had left her second husband some time before and had eventually moved to France earlier in the month. She'd decided to leave Norfolk and had married our kindly, almost reclusive neighbour, André at the *mairie* in the village and we had organized it so they walked under a tunnel of baguettes as they left. Barbara seemed very happy and André, suddenly closer to the madness at the chapel than he might have wished, was adjusting to a new life more peopled than his former one.

'Jacquie, look,' I insisted, 'I've sold the minibus and now the car's gone. Last time we went to the Alps we lost thousands and thousands of pounds, which we still owe. There's no more money for this. We can't *all* go to the Alps.'

'I thought you and the children were going to stay here,' she announced. 'You could work for Skull Face and you can write,' she added nobly as if this fait accompli was doing me a favour.

Confidence is a strange thing: one moment you're managing and the world belongs to you; no matter what, you can survive and shine. Two seconds later, someone pulls the plug and you've had it. 'Jacquie,' I stammered, 'd'you think I came to France to be alone? I can't pay a nanny, feed us and run this huge place on four hundred quid a month, even if I work myself to death. The children and I will starve.'

'I'll send you money,' she offered clinically.

I kicked the partition wall gently, pressing my shoulder against the door-frame. 'How are you going to get that? And how are you going to run it all out there by yourself?'

She looked at me with an air of tremendous confidence for one about to play such a dubious card. 'I might ask one of the guys to help,' she said. Then, showing a nervousness that suggested worry about my reaction, she continued. 'Maybe I'll take Kurt – if there's enough money. The others can go and stay with the Dodger.'

Even as her plans became clear, dismay and confusion clouded my thoughts. 'That's just great,' I stammered. 'Wait a minute, you're going to the Alps with another man for months while I stay here alone with our children? That right? Is that why you got the camera? So you could take a few last piccies of the kids before you fucked off? Is your mother aware of all this?'

'Oh, God.' Jacquie sighed in disbelief. 'Of course she isn't.' There was a silence and then Martha appeared at the window in front of us, pointing to her watch.

'I'll have to go,' I said, 'the kids need someone who gives a shit.'

'Yeah, just go,' Jacquie snapped again, defending the ugliness that even she clearly felt. 'You're jealous. I'm sick of your negative attitude, always complaining.' She turned angrily. 'You make everyone miserable. You're behaving like a baby, whining like a bloody child. In fact that's what I've been doing, bringing up *three* children.'

I knew there was some truth here. I'd been weak and my diabetes, so unstable in the confusion of the summer pressure, had made things worse. Now I'd pay for it. I stood silent, watching the gravel path as Martha approached. 'I'm off now,' she smiled through the window.

'Bye,' said Jacquie, both of us projecting sickeningly polished artificial grins.

'And thanks,' I shouted, knowing she had yet again stayed late. I turned to Jacquie and spoke firmly. '*You* can put the kids to bed tonight. You haven't done it once in the last two weeks.'

She turned to the fax machine, saying she'd be over as soon as she'd sent the last three. '*I'll* send the faxes,' I said, smelling a waft of the lavender that had grown huge around Mo's pond. I wanted to tear the fax machine from the wall and throw it across the room. I began to feel sick with hatred for Even Breaks.

Jacquie turned round to face me. 'Look, Rupe, this is *my* thing. I need to reach people before they leave work and I'm waiting for a call. You can't do it. Remember; it's *all* in my head, everything. Then afterwards I've got to go over and start dinner for the guys.' I was glaring but she seemed triumphant, oblivious.

The guys could fix their *own* flaming dinner. 'You have no idea what the presence of four men in our house is doing to us,' I warned her. 'You're not even interested in your family any more. The frustrated writer and the bubbly, clever wife with a horny sparkle in her eye is *all* we bloody well are.'

'Get out, Rupe.'

Mo in his pyjamas was picking his way out of the bijou cottage about fifty yards away, barefoot on the gravel. It was almost dark. 'Please,' I begged, aware that he was on his way and that the ground around the shed was filthy. 'Go and have the children, just for half an hour.'

She began addressing an envelope.

'You know what the worst part of this is?' I said. Jacquie looked up, bored. 'The business, the loans; you know *everything* is in *my* name.' I stared at her, loathing the selfishness. 'You're like a child, you're having a ball being responsible for absolutely fuck-all and I'll be left to swing for it.'

'Yeah, well, who gets you up off the floor when you're hypo?'

'Yet you seem to feel it's perfectly safe to walk out and leave me with the kids,' I shouted as I left. 'I've been too bloody good to you.' Then, walking around the shed to the path, I turned. Jacquie stared back, her face bitter.

By my feet lay the gnarled wooden branch handle of the sledge-hammer. In slow motion I imagined I saw myself picking it up, flexing every muscle and slamming the head through the window into the fax machine and then smashing the computer, finishing it, once and for all. I guessed that no discs had been copied for ages. All the details of the clients were sitting there inside the machine, as vulnerable and neglected as our cancerous marriage. I paused to ask myself what it was that I was upset by. There had to be a logical reason for her strategy, something I just wasn't appreciating, some element which would justify her grand schemes.

Even Breaks, our wonderful invention, had become a monster. I seemed to be Son of Frankenstein by Norman Wisdom, hamming it up like mad; as if in having brought the chapel to life, I had tripped some demonic switch in Jacquie, condemning our little family; the thing I treasured. How could things be going so wrong? I'd either have somehow to adjust to fit or face losing the lot. The second 'option' was quite simply unthinkable.

Mo called, spurred on by shouts from little Sam, and hating myself for my weakness I left the hammer in its place, hearing the phone ring in the shed and Jacquie's laugh and chatter fade as I carried the boy to his bed.

Even now, and despite diabetic troubles in the summer madness, I still felt some pride. My commitment had built the chapel; we had done it the hard way over seven years, slogging part-time in the fields and taking any other work we could find. Nothing could change this, an achievement driven truly by love.

I sat and read in the cottage until the children slept and then set the intercom and crossed the gravel around Mo's pond and the mimosa. The chapel's great black silhouette stood cold in the darkness while a faint line of red-streaked high clouds hung behind the stone cross above the almost completed domed roof. When this last roof was done there would be no further need for a builder. Our battle to finish the chapel completely would be won.

I sat down on the boulders by the pump and looked up at the cross. There were birds, but not many, calling out into the cool February evening. The river chuckled faintly through the wood at the bottom of the hill while around me everywhere I could smell spring, fennel and lavender. It was so good, all of it, so very lovely. Yet it seemed that in reaching the end of the tunnel we'd lost our way in the dark. Perhaps, I thought, with the completion of the chapel we were now obsolete and God had carelessly cast us aside. Or maybe this was God's punishment for that afternoon I'd had with Lola? 'Why,' I asked, looking from the cross up to the cold stars, 'why are you doing this to us?' But I knew already the weak fool I'd been.

Jacquie was upstairs on the mezzanine watching TV with Kurt, Slammer and Angelica. She heard my voice in the kitchen, came down and for a moment we spoke alone.

'Rupe, please don't say that I don't care,' she said slightly vacantly, her fingers wrapped around the neck of a bottle of beer. Aware that anything I said in front of the guys would seem sulky or defeatist, I shrugged and changed the subject, asking when she wanted to have dinner.

'It's already in the oven.' She brightened as if this lifted discomfort in a single breath.

'I'm going to have a bath,' I said, walking away, aware of her watching uneasily as I closed the chapel's big sliding bathroom door behind me. I filled the bath and climbed in. Looking in the mirror, I mouthed the words, 'You're becoming desperate,' and lifted my hands like an Arab. 'What do I do?'

I recognized that the longer this persisted, the weaker I would become. Dismay hung over me; there would be no change, I told myself. Only I could change. Perhaps it was *my* fault. *Sure*, it probably was. This problem might go away if I took even more responsibility for the kids and let Jacquie go and be herself. And I was too straight, that was my problem – *and* I expected too much of our relationship. I had to relax, let it all happen, open my eyes.

The door rattled. 'Rupe?' It was Angelica. 'Jacquie's sent me with a beer and I've come to scrub your back.' She chuckled. Feeling awkward, I found a towel and opened the door. Angelica came in and handed me the beer. 'Get back in the bath,' she said. 'Come on, I'll do your back.'

'Did Jacquie really send you?' I asked, amazed and pretending to be comfortable. '*Really?*'

'Of course.' She sat on the edge and looked for the soap, while trying not to seem awkward I climbed back in.

'But what about the others?' I said. 'What about Slammer? What'll he think?'

'Why should he think anything? He's as independent as I am.'

She soaped my back. It was bizarre knowing my wife had sent her. I wondered if this might be a trap. I wanted to be liked by the people around me but the game seemed to be cool with everyone except me. Face it, I told myself once again, I was behaving like a prude: in their eyes, a killjoy. I *had* to make a point. I could do this stuff too, sure, without a care. I could indulge and laugh this off.

'Why don't *you* get in the bath?' I said, feeling as if I was in the skin of a stranger.

She undressed slowly. Her forty-five-year-old body was limber, almost athletic, her breasts tight and unspoilt in compensation for childlessness. Only some lines around her neck gave a guide to mileage – those and the sticky mascara around blue eyes, which seemed as unhappy as mine. Her bright self-assurance and outer toughness now seemed to mask vulnerability but she had courage, which I respected.

'Jacquie wants you to be happy,' she told me.

'And, let me guess, you're here because she loves me? So why doesn't *she* come down here?' Angelica had no answer.

I made every effort. It was a tremendous compliment after all and Anjelica was not unattractive, but it proved Jacquie's indifference and that was painful. I decided that nothing would have been better than wildly to go for it. I tried to convince myself; I could show Jacquie how little it mattered to me, but no matter how I caressed, this notion was hopeless.

We got out of the bath and I tried again . . . Nothing. Most men would have jumped at the chance but for some reason primal instinct had failed me. 'I'm sorry,' I said, finding a robe, 'you must think I'm strange but I can't handle this.'

'Don't worry.' She spoke soothingly, adopting what sounded like a professional tone.

'I want to be different,' I added, 'but I can't.'

She repeated that it didn't matter. But it did. Confusion hovered above me like a sickness, swirling and scraping at my heart. Early conditioning made me think that a weakened man is a pathetic sight. I hadn't considered myself weak before but now I was allowing the woman I loved to dismantle me.

After dinner I left Jacquie, Angelica and the guys watching TV. I felt spare in my own home. I didn't ask if she was coming to bed. Sabotaged by fatigue, I lay down, wondering what other boundaries Angelica might encourage Jacquie to cross. The bijou cottage stood silent as the early hours came and went. Things were so different now. Sometimes Jacquie'd be in at two, but with Angelica around her needs had changed and her love for me had faded for good. Enraged, I imagined my wife in various adulterous positions, decided upon one course of action, then another, always coming back to the sobering reality of the children and their needs.

I'll leave, I thought, I'll take the kids and go. Go? Go where? How will you work, here, in the poorest part of France, where there is no work? The failing business and loans are all secured in your name; you owe tens of thousands. Who would look after the children? How would you afford that privilege?

The door clicked. 'Hi,' said Jacquie, looking uncomfortable, taking off her clothes and heading for the bathroom. 'It's really late. Why are you still awake?'

'Would you have given a shit if I'd screwed Angelica?' I asked. She pretended not to know whether or not I had and I became caustic. 'You already know the answer to that. I'm sure she's reported back. The answer's "No". Why did you send her?'

Jacquie didn't respond as she climbed into bed, deep in that dangerous state of inebriation when one still imagines oneself to be coherent.

'Something's wrong,' I said, 'something really ugly is happening to us. I can't live like this for much longer with you pulling this shit.'

'Oh, come on, Rupe.' She kissed me, the taste of wine and toothpaste crossing my mouth like a stain. 'Why d'you have to be so dramatic? Listen, let's just look after each other.'

'You lie. I feel like the Witch is at our throats. I'm telling you, Jacquie, something's wrong.' Yet we turned together, kissing, moving with perfect timing as always, with the comfort of old passion hiding whatever truth neither of us could face. But even as we made love I felt as if she was waiting for it to be over, for me to believe, so we could go on perhaps a little longer, another night, another day, without argument.

Anna, the PA/secretary, arrived and was probably overwhelmed by the ramshackle outfit she'd landed into, but also happy, I believe, to be free from the pressure of her previous job. Anna would treat her time with us as a working break. She'd taken to organizing the office shed, undaunted though bemused by the piles of scribbles along with endless names and addresses that were yet to be entered into the ageing computer. We'd advertised for a helper in the free Aussie/Kiwi magazine in London and Slammer had taken a few days off to visit friends in England. It was he who had interviewed Anna there for us.

Through what had been the coldest season the guys had helped build the chapel's dome roof, putting it together in the old style with a willing patience that Australasians, more than many, wholeheartedly throw towards a cause they believe in. There hadn't been a particular schedule of work, yet there it was, a finished roof, and as it got late in the grey afternoon, down beside the little river shouts from the well rang out into the forest as the last bucket of silt and sand was lifted.

That evening Angelica and Jacquie and Slammer and I celebrated the last of the chapel's challenges. Upstairs in the curate's house we drank fake champagne and gin and tonic, sitting on a beautiful old bed that Jaffa had given us. We'd made the bed up for Slammer and Angelica. I'd always felt that the curate's house, our first home, had the life and passion of the chapel in it. It was the first part that we'd completed: the first shelter in those first years of our marriage. I loved the tiny house, which seemed to know my secrets. I felt as if it waited for us, as if the dusty stones, aged wood and earthen mortar were a shield that stood for something good, a testimony perhaps of passionate devotion and the simplicity we'd known in the past.

'Have some more.' Jacquie filled Angelica's glass and passed a bowl of crisps around. I felt uncomfortable and asked them if the four of us shouldn't join the others.

'Why? What's the matter, Rupe? They're fine.' Jacquie smiled and motioned to the chapel. 'Anna's there to keep them company. This is for us,' she added archly, 'the couples.' Then she scrunched her eyes in the corners while clinking glasses with Angelica and moving closer, pushed her legs under the duvet.

'I love attentive men,' Angelica sighed as Slammer began kissing her, first on the lips, then making his way down to her chest.

'Specially young ones.' Jacquie embraced me half-heartedly. To me the room grew colder. Before long the girls were side by side under the covers. They seemed to be laughing at their own naughtiness as Slammer lay on the far side, half on top of Angelica, while conversing with Jacquie. 'Come on, Rupe, relax,' she said as we attempted to get closer. Her eyes looked almost glazed, as if it really didn't matter what we – or anyone – did. I figured that if things heated up any more we'd have to be hip and swap women, then if I wasn't throwing up I'd get to watch my barman screw my wife. I couldn't bear it and rose, saying I was going downstairs. Did she want to come with me?

'I'll stay for a bit,' she said, unable at first to see or care how this remark would strike me.

'Sure,' I muttered, hoping to bring reality home as she watched me struggle with humiliation. She appeared suddenly to be alone in the big bed as the others writhed.

Angelica clearly relished the prospect of an audience or simply couldn't get a hold on the effect she'd had on us. In any case she was vocal. Knowing that if she stayed in bed with them our relationship would probably fall to the hounds in moments, Jacquie followed me downstairs after all. We stood in the kitchen.

'Sorry, Rupe.'

Angelica gasped through the boards above our heads.

'Like *hell* you're sorry.'

I leaned on the post in the middle of the room, confused. 'Listen, I love screwing, Jacquie, you know that, but this is madness.' She nodded in agreement. 'I just don't believe *you* want our private lives to be shared with the crew. What is this, Jacq? You freak out if I even *look* at another woman.'

'Rupe, please, I like what we're doing.' When I asked her if she'd become intoxicated by Angelica's idea of a wild time, Jacquie became defensive. 'She's my friend; that's all. We're just having fun, Rupe.' A thump came from above, a glass perhaps, falling from the bed, followed by muffled words and laughter.

'You keep on letting Slammer watch while you and Angelica lie on your backs together and then see how much he'll respect us, you and me.'

She looked at me bitterly. 'I'm going to make dinner,' she said, tying her sarong as she crossed the room. 'Just do me a favour, will you, Rupe? Please don't make a scene until Angelica is gone. Then we can do what you like, after the camping trip this weekend and my birthday. It's only a couple of days more, just the party and then she's gone.'

*

The following day Anna agreed to update and type our brochure. She and Jacquie organized the shed, working as well as they could to put order into our organizational bedlam. I asked how things were going. Anna smiled and said it was going fine, her hands still poised above the keyboard. She had a soft Australian accent.

With terrific speed she hammered all sorts of slogans into the texts, wearing fingerless mittens which permitted her to type freely in the draughty cold. 'Guess I'll have to have a rethink.' She shivered, motioning to her cashmere sweater and scarf. 'This stuff costs a fortune and I'm still freezing to death.' She looked up at the screen. 'Fruit trees and herb gardens,' she laughed, reading aloud. She was pale and had fine, straight, longish blonde hair. Clear blue eyes smiled above delicate features that looked as if they could stay calm and composed through any confusion. But it was clear that Anna wasn't by any means a pushover. 'Who writes this stuff?' she asked.

'Jacquie mostly nowadays,' I replied, not immediately seeing how different and how much better our brochure might be. 'You don't like it?'

'I love it,' she chuckled, 'it's er . . . mmm . . . artistic, love it.' I asked where Jacquie was. 'In the chapel getting the things together with Angelica for the trip to Spain. I think she wants to go soon.'

We'd organized a camping trip over the frontier where we'd spend the next day at a carnival in the Spanish seaside town of Rosas. Martha had gone home leaving Jacquie's mother to take charge of the children. Barbara had crossed the road with a mothering strength like Mary Poppins, bringing a basket of necessities, a magazine and a torch. No doubt she'd make some dinner in the bijou cottage after she'd got the children off to sleep. I felt empty, leaving the boys. Another weekend would pass without any effort being made to share time with our kids.

Crammed into poor Bert, Jacquie, Angelica, Kurt, Robert, Don, Anna, Slammer and I headed towards Spain, pulling a small trailer with the picnic and tents. We stopped at La Jonquera, a frontier village, to pick up other supplies. It was a bright, warm day; only the wind signalled the time of year. On the street there were hundreds of people, crowds after cheap Spanish meats, fruit and alcohol from the duty-free shops, which stood like heavy concrete and chrome battle-ships. The road glugged down the steep slope between the mountains in a cascade of hollow red breeze-blocks, cement, thirty-nine-franc vodka, fake pastis and fabric donkeys with plastic saddles.

Along from a counter containing 10,000 cans of sardines in every possible sauce, I chose olives and clams while one of the guys found bread. Excited, Jacquie skated about on the tiled floor, making sure that we had enough booze and any last essentials.

It was an odd moment to voice my question. 'What's with you and Angelica?' I asked, gazing numbly at a stuffed rabbit which stood on its hind legs wearing a hunter's jacket and holding a miniature rifle in its feet. 'Why *so* physical?'

'Oh, don't be alarmed, Rupe, she's so much fun. Like I said, she's going back the morning after the party so we're making the most of it.'

We made our way through Rosas, then along the waterfront, following the road around the jagged point, looking for a place, a beach perhaps, sheltered enough to pitch our tents.

'There, Rupe. There. Stop. Stop!' Jacquie pointed to a small sandy cove on one side of the road. Two or three huge boulders stood in the sand half-way up the beach and a cement staircase curled through the stone sea defences, crowded with stray cactus, crumbling and never reaching the eroded beach below.

'It's perfect,' cried Jacquie. 'Come on, everyone.' She ran down to the waterfront as the others climbed out. The wind howled off the sea. It was fine now, with the remains of the sun on the sand, but as the shadows fell, I knew we'd take a beating from that wind and voiced my doubts.

'Come on,' Jacquie shouted back, 'you might search forever, don't be a killjoy.'

We skipped stones and paddled in water which seemed every bit as cold and clear and lovely as it should in February, while Robert, Anna and the others settled their belongings in around the rocks as far away as possible from the water and wind. Beers were passed around. 'Brrr,' Angelica grinned, motioning to Slammer who passed his arm around her, 'glad I brought my heating with me.'

I fumbled with a syringe, took the shot.

We ate sitting around a fire that Slammer and Robert had made in the back of the cove. I wondered what the future held for these guys. Maybe the Dodger would take them all on. I doubted it. As far as the Dodger was concerned, Jacquie was more interesting. Vivacious, skilled and inventive Jacquie – and our mailing list.

After dinner they walked to the bars with Anna in tow. She climbed the steps, looking very tidy in her expensive white running-shoes. Slammer remained in the cove with Angelica, Jacquie and me. 'There,' I heard Jacquie tell Angelica as I searched for driftwood, 'you lie on one duvet and put the other one on top.'

I felt I was growing up. Nothing about a freezing beach in February, sand-basted chicken, the promise of bankruptcy and a coastal post-adolescent piss-up seemed appealing. No matter how poor we might be, I wanted to be on the beach around a fire with my family, getting gently plastered while toasting marshmallows or skimming stones under the moon or making love while the little ones slept. Idyllic, perhaps you might think, even boring. Others might see the concept as a joke, but life is short and you only get one go.

Those heading for the bars disappeared from sight.

Angelica lay back, smiling enigmatically as she pulled a duvet up around her neck. She shivered once again, inspecting the stars while Slammer appeared; almost a shadow. He kissed her and then went back to tend his fire, crouching like a Neanderthal in the faint light of the flames.

'God, I'm freezing,' said Jacquie, burrowing down beside Angelica. Obviously tonight there was to be no semblance of my beach day-dream. I found some beer, and sitting on the edge of the makeshift bed, handed it round.

The girls huddled close, laughing in a schoolgirlish way. Angelica seemed to be in a state of glacial rapture with Slammer on stand-by and Jacquie there to collude in behaviour that might be frowned upon in the normal way. Anything seemed suddenly permissible. I settled for alcohol and didn't much feel like talking to Slammer.

It was late when the others returned, and I was drunk, silently morose. I could not think of anything more ugly than my sad self and

I regretted that I hadn't left when I'd been sober, gone back to the chapel and packed my bags. But there were always the children to consider. I couldn't leave them, not with Jacquie like this.

I should have recognized her problems earlier, but Jacquie had always wished for more than life could give. Her love of excitement was part of what had drawn me to her. However, it seemed I was now in her way. I swam in a sea of Spanish beer and confusion, gulping back jealousy, growing angry as she flitted around on the sand with Angelica and chatted to the ones who'd made it back from the bars in Rosas. It was late, perhaps two or three in the morning, and a cold wind was cutting in sharply.

'Let's paddle,' Jacquie cried and grabbed her camera before curving around the stones with Kurt until they were out of view.

Humiliatingly I followed, finding them chatting in the darkness. Remembering her suggestion that Kurt might assist her with her ski season, I hated to imagine that she was confiding in him. I couldn't tell what was what any more and loathed myself for being unable to leave this ghastly situation without punishing our children. I felt rage.

Jacquie saw me. 'Rupe,' she swayed, wearing a childish smile, seeming just as drunk as me. She reached for the camera. 'I've just seen my fa—' I snatched the camera and threw it in the sea.

'You!' she stammered furiously, a little stunned. 'I saw my father. I took a photograph.' Her voice rose. 'Why did you do that? You fucking bastard,' she screamed, then began to cry hysterically. Kurt tried to soothe her while I stumbled about in the freezing water for the lost camera with her dead father's photo in it.

'I'm sorry, mate,' said Kurt, 'she thinks she saw her dad there by the rocks. I was tryin' a calm her down. What's wrong?'

'Everything.' I said. 'Nothing. We're both drunk.' Soon afterwards I began to shiver and drunkenly gulped down a Coke in order to have enough sugar on board to make heat. Slammer kindly rubbed my frozen feet as the others hunkered down for the night. The larger tent had collapsed, leaving only a very small one where Jacquie and I ended up, huddling lovelessly together for warmth. We were by far the drunkest and coldest of the group. Our voices floated out through the thin fabric, across the wind as dawn approached and the nightmare continued as time for sleep and hope for repair diminished.

We awoke to brilliant sunshine, many of us running on the fumes of last night's excess. We ate breakfast in a haze before trudging into Rosas to see the carnival.

I didn't see much of the girls but drifted about the streets with Don and the others. Only once did I have a quiet moment with Angelica. 'Are you okay?' she asked at some café.

'I don't know exactly,' I said. 'I'm confused. What's going on?' She murmured the obvious, that Jacquie wasn't happy, was seeking something . . . 'Then what is it? Is it you?' I asked, hoping I remained polite. And then I pointed to the guys, 'Is it *them*?' Angelica then said something about not really liking the sex stuff, which made me doubtful. In my mind, it had been a girlie fun experiment and not much more but now I was beginning to wonder. 'So what on earth can I do? How can I save it?' I asked.

Jacquie was making her way towards us in the crowd. 'Play hard to get,' said Angelica.

The sun had gone when we arrived at the chapel and the *tranmontana* hadn't yet got going, so it was a still, cool evening. 'I can't wait for a shower,' said Angelica, following the others into the chapel.

'I'll start dinner.' Jacquie picked up a few things and headed the same way.

'Don't you want to at least see the kids?' I asked, motioning across to the cottage. 'Just to say you're back? They'll probably still be awake.'

'You're going, aren't you?' said Jacquie, briefly amused by her own 'wit'. Then she sighed. 'Everyone's tired and hungry. I'm going to cook. I'll bring you some supper if you like.'

Dimly I heard Kurt call something from the doorway, but whatever it was didn't matter. 'I don't know you,' I said to Jacquie. 'Who the hell are you?'

Barbara greeted me as I brought the first things into the cottage. She was keen to get home. 'Did you have a good time?' she asked.

'Yes, thanks,' I smiled and lied.

'That's nice.' She bustled, collecting her things. 'Must've been cold. Where's Jacquie?'

'She's at the house with the others,' I said, doubting that a conversation with Barbara about our dilemma would help much just now. Barbara had seen me tearfully beg Jacquie for change before and probably saw me as weak. In any case it wasn't her problem. It was mine and I had a bitter feeling that real men were supposed to stand their ground and take it on the chin.

'How were they?' I asked.

'Fine. Mo's still awake and Sam's just gone down. I must go.' She grabbed her torch and went. 'André wants to make a start. We're away tonight an' tomorrow,' she explained.

The cottage was beautifully clean, the children's clothes put away and the sink empty. These were all demonstrations of Barbara's practical devotion to our family. I found Mo sitting half-awake in his big bed and his brother pink-faced and snoring lightly in the warm, neat room.

'Who loves Moses?' I asked.

'Daddy does. Will you tell me a Sailor Jack?'

Mo slept before long and I went to our room and sat quietly, wondering what to do next. Footsteps on the gravel finished my doze. It was Anna. 'Jacquie's sent me over with this for you. She says you need it.'

I'd noticed the can in her hand even before I'd heard the poor girl speak and my frustration got the better of me. 'I don't need a Coke, I need a wife.' Then I felt a little ashamed and apologized to Anna, trying to clear my head. 'Could you ask Jacquie to come over now, right now?' She nodded and left.

Jacquie arrived moments later and sat on the bed, leaning her back against the wooden wall, bringing her knees up and huddling her arms around them.

'I want to finish it, Jacquie,' I told her, still trusting in what I'd hoped would be a safe gamble. 'I've had enough.' But then I watched relief cross her face. Her voice became gentle again as if she were dealing with an animal that might turn and bite her. 'That's right. I understand, Rupe,' she nodded, 'I feel the same way.'

'Oh, Jesus,' I said, stunned, 'you mean you're not even going to fight for our marriage?' She mildly pointed out that I had just proposed a separation and my gamble seemed to have back-fired horribly. 'No!' I protested. 'That's the point, I *don't* want to at all.'

'No,' she said, not really hearing me, her eyes glazed, 'it's not like that.'

'Like what? You're dumping us. You're dumping your own kids!' Then it began to dawn on me. 'You've been trying to get me to do this for weeks, haven't you? So you wouldn't have to deal with the responsibility and the blame!' I couldn't see it then, but her reactions remain carved in my mind. She had become a sort of Stepford wife, as calm and soft, and with tense defences she asked me not to say such things, as if each of my words smashed into her with a force she could no longer deal with. At the time I took this as simple denial.

'How d'you want me to put it then, that you're pissing off for a chance to go skiing, then summer trekking and then shagging with the guys?' I thumped the wall, sending framed photographs of us and our children shattering to the floor. 'Or is it for Angelica?' I turned to her in a fury. 'And how come a woman? Is it because you feel that it'll drive me away?'

'Of course it's not.' Now she looked worried. I was winding up like a spring and she'd lost her control of the situation.

'Then tell me,' I ranted, 'if it were a man lying on the beach with you yesterday in Spain, would I still even be here? Is that the point, Jacquie, to demoralize, humiliate and drive me out? Make *me* be the one to leave, make me the guilty one? IS THAT YOUR FUCKING GAME?'

'Don't get upset. Shhh, Rupe, *the kids*. Come and sit down.' She motioned towards the bed.

Crazed as I was, I couldn't bear to think that she imagined that a mindless shag would solve things. But the room was softly lit and warm. Even amidst the harshness of our mood the atmosphere both contradicted and intensified our words. Glaring at her I asked her what she thought she really needed.

'I've got so much to give. I want to help people, like all those children in Kurdistan.'

'What!' I spluttered. 'What about your *own* children? Don't *they* need help?'

'That's not what I mean,' she went on, smiling dreamily. 'I want to do something, something to help so many more.'

'Like Médecins Sans Frontières or something, you mean?' Logic, I briefly hoped, might be returning.

She nodded. 'And I won't meet anyone else, not for a couple of years at least.'

Some harsh truth was returning to this insane discussion. 'Oh? Well, I'm glad to see you're thinking ahead. Maybe a doctor or something?' I met a cold gaze and couldn't stop myself. 'You're *too* kind,' I said bitterly. 'Have you thought about babies at this stage? Of course, perhaps you should wait and FUCKING WELL DISCUSS THAT WITH HIM.' She tried to interrupt but I wouldn't let her. 'You have the most wonderful home. We can do so many things from here; the possibilities are limitless. You've got two beautiful children and a husband who adores you. Please, baby,' I said softly, 'please don't throw us away.'

'You know what you want now. Don't cry.' She'd lost me in more than one respect. I didn't know what she was on about. I wiped tears away with my sleeve as she continued. 'Before it was different. You didn't . . .' Her hands opened as if in answer, 'I mean, I could *do* anything . . . And now you're strong. You know what you want.'

'I'm weaker than I've ever been,' I gasped. 'You're the one with the projects. I've done everything here to build it up for us. It's been your show and now I'm screwed. I don't have the faintest idea what I want any more. It was all for you and, and what about the kids?' I was nearly exhausted by now.

She stroked my shoulder, 'You've always been better at looking after them than me. You know that.'

I went into the hallway, pressing my forehead against the wall. Jacquie followed, clasping her hands. 'I've brought you your worst nightmare, I know. All you ever wanted was a proper family. I know it's all you were doing this for.'

I asked about the chapel as I went to sit on the floor in our room, looking at things that represented our lives together. The red striped dressing-gown that she wore when both babies were born, the pictures now on the floor, snaps of Kansas and Yogi, an old shirt worn at the start of the holiday project.

I now believe that Jacquie was quite seriously mentally ill. The tragedy is that, being so close, I could not see it at all then. She had probably been unwell for some time and I had been bending to accommodate her illness for just as long. I am convinced that neither of us was sane just then. It would take me years to understand fully what had happened and why. Jacquie loved the children deeply but illness had steered her down a path wherein her wilder personality traits had no restraint.

'The chapel's for helping people, Rupe,' she said, still sounding slightly stoned. 'You can see clearly yourself. We live in this bungalow. The chapel was never meant to be a home. It's always been a healing place. I'm going to stay here and run the holidays, bring people in who really need it,' she said. 'And you can stay too, with the children, until you're strong enough to go. The Dodger will buy you out. He and I can run it.'

For a moment I was speechless while the thought that Jacquie seemed to be calmly trying to exclude me from our home sank in. 'What!' I exploded. 'You've already spoken to him? Him! In the place we made?'

She didn't answer so I was constrained to rant on. 'Jacquie, the Dodger doesn't seem like the kind of guy that really wants to rush in and do things for free. He won't buy me out any more than he'll take you on as Mother Teresa, and you know it.' Her eyes seemed slow and tired-looking, heavy with a mixture of horror and defeat. 'Then, Jacquie, when our mailing list is on Dodger's computer and you've got completely out of hand with the fun excursions, he'll up and dump you.' It seemed as if she was going to end up giving it all away.

'There's another thing, Rupe.' Jacquie clearly wanted to change the subject and placate me as swiftly as possible. 'You know Anna?'

'Our Anna, who arrived last week?'

'I've been watching her.' Jacquie looked away, grabbing my fingers. 'She's in love with you, Rupe.'

'Oh, for God's sake. She doesn't even *know* me. We've spoken three times since she's been here. What the hell are you up to?'

'It's simple,' she went on in that ghastly calm way. 'You can stay here until you and Anna fall in love and are ready to go.' Then Jacquie began to cry. 'Only give me time, will you, so when it happens you don't break my heart.' My wife now wept in a pretty sort of way but it seemed that only part of her was crying.

I looked at her in utter disbelief. 'What do you think I am?' Silenced, her tears miraculously stopped. 'Wait a minute,' I began. 'You want to dump me and the children on Anna and before it all happens you want *me* to give *you* time to prepare for it! What's this? Is it guilt? *Here's Anna, a good replacement.* Is that it?' I snapped. 'So with that out of the way, you don't have to feel bad at all? Not one bit!'

Jacquie didn't seem to listen. She repeated how Anna really was in love with me.

'You mean, it would suit you. I'm not staying here on Death Row while you look around for someone or something more suitable. Jacquie, I love you, no one else. Please, for God's sake, for the children . . .'

'I mean it, Rupe. Don't worry, you *can* stay until you and the boys are ready to go.'

I smouldered. All night we talked. Astonishingly, you may think, we made love. Sad and lonely perhaps, but to deal with pain we all of us seek comfort. The love-making was no different, especially in a man as confused and hurt and hopeful as I was and between a couple as physical and tactile as we had always been.

In the early morning crisp light stretched over the orchard, making the long tall grass steam. The spring mornings were often sunny and still, unspoilt and free from the clawing of the wind which had ceased to blast across the valley from the still-frozen reaches of the Canigou at some stage in the early hours.

'I'll make us some tea,' said Jacquie. 'Then I must go over to the chapel and get breakfast. You can be here as long as you want. In your own time, Rupe, there's nothing to worry about. Stop crying.' She looked into my eyes as if I should feel comforted, grateful. 'I can see good things, Rupe.' Her eyes were like two maps of Birmingham drawn entirely in red. Any hope I might have had that things could be mended was smashed. 'You're going to be happy; it's true,' she went on again, 'about Anna, I mean. You're going to be a writer, Rupe, for children, and you'll live in a lighthouse,' she cried, 'you and Anna.' She gave a tired but calm and infuriating smile.

Jacquie had always been a spiritual person, but this I felt had more to do with exhaustion than clairvoyance and I even cancelled out vague thoughts of the Witch, sure that speaking of her would provoke more of the same daft conjecture.

'What are you going on about? We've been up too long.'

She wiped her nose, stuffing the tissue in a pocket. 'A lighthouse,' she repeated. 'I can see these things, you *know* I can. Because you, darling Rupe,' she sobbed again, then looked up at me, 'you're Sailor Jack.'

The whole thing seemed ridiculous. Sailor Jack was a hero in the stories that my father would tell my younger brother and sister when they were children. I put my arms around Jackie. 'We're tired, babe. We're *really* tired. You've *got* to lie down.' She didn't want to rest so I suggested that we go and sit with Mo and Sam. 'I'd say today is as good a day as any for them to wake up with the both of us beside them.'

She wouldn't move, so I got up and walked over to the window, the thin red curtains glowing in the sunlight. 'Jacquie, this is *really* happening. Do you realize what it is you're doing? Can't you *see*? Those are real children in there and you're ending it.'

'Don't be upset.' Her composure was regained alarmingly fast. 'Things are going to be good for you.' I felt like literally spanking her for the condescending way she carried on. 'You're going to live in a lighthouse. You'll be the one to *see*.' She smiled beatifically. 'There's so much you can have, Rupe.'

'You mean that there's so much YOU *want*,' I answered bitterly. 'Why is this happening? I don't understand. What's with the lighthouse crap?'

We sat together until the children woke and had a ghastly family breakfast which none of us seemed to taste. The boys played with their food. The cottage grew warm with the sun on its thin roof. Jacquie said she had to get over to the chapel to see to the helpers' breakfasts. Before going she agreed to go for a drive with me later on, to talk again. 'I meant what I said about Anna. I don't know what it is,' she said, 'it's just a feeling, but you ask her what her greatest fantasy is.'

'What do you mean?' I said, feeling exhausted. 'I hardly know her, so how can I suddenly ask something like that?'

'Just remember what we talked about and ask what her fantasy is. Just *ask*,' she said, making her way out and leaving me dangling in the husk of that new, unnerving serenity of hers.

Maybe I should have left at that point, while she was busy with the breakfast routine at the chapel. But having as a child experienced the pain of the departure of my own dad and the sometimes disturbing behaviour of my mother, I could no more walk out on my children than cut off my own hand.

I spent an hour dressing the boys and wondering what to do next. Again I thought about taking the children and throwing them and our clothes into Bert. But where could we go, without money or a place to stay? My main desire was to remain hopeful, and getting Jacquie to see sense, I prayed, was not beyond me.

Martha arrived in her father's car. 'Is it all right if I take the boys down to Argelès for the day,' she asked, already packing a handful of nappies into a bag, 'to my parents' place by the beach?'

'Sure,' I said feeling half-dead, 'and thanks, Martha. It's not an easy one today.' She nodded, probably assuming I referred to Jacquie's birthday party that evening.

I met Jacquie in front of the cottage, Bert rattling away, ready for the drive. 'Rupe,' Jacquie began, serious and almost apprehensive. 'There's something I haven't told you. I promise you, Rupe, it's the only thing I've ever kept from you.'

'So why tell now? Has Angelica just been coaching you?'

She started to speak. 'It's about Jake.' Jacquie looked at me. 'We *were* lovers, Rupe. Jake and I lived together for two years.'

I stared at her, stunned. 'But you always denied it, *always*.'

'I thought you knew, or guessed.' She searched uncomfortably for justification. 'Everyone knew,' she added as I reached inside Bert and turned off the ignition.

'Well, thanks a bunch, but I don't give a shit about your relationship. You lied. You slapped my face. Remember? Simply because I suggested it once. You told me he ripped you off and I believed you.'

'Rupe, I didn't want you to know because I was ashamed.' We hadn't moved and Martha passed by with the children in tow. We kissed them and stood until the drive was empty.

'Why on earth would you be *ashamed* of being with a man like Jake?'

She mumbled some incomprehensible nonsense about his age, which did nothing but irritate me.

'Older! Have you seen how old Buck is? You think Caroline's ashamed? No, Jacquie, try harder.'

'Look, after Dad died I got to Paris with nothing, you know, I told you about the whores and the filthy place. Jake was good to me. He took me under his wing.'

'It couldn't have happened to you at a better time. He was kind and bloody good luck for you. He was even kind to me, and seeing things as I now do I can't imagine why.'

She shook her head. 'You still don't see.'

'Oh, believe me, I do. I can't believe you kept this lie going for so long.' Considering the implications of their relationship, vague suspicions sprang into my mind. 'So were there really shares or was your cut in his restaurant a lover's gift?'

'Of course there were. It was business, Rupe.'

'If I had spent two years moulding a pretty young woman, teaching her how to hold her knife and fork, how to speak and how to dress, and paying for it, I'd expect a lot, a helluva lot, Jacquie.'

'He was too bitter and sceptical.'

'Bullshit, you cried every time we went past the mill.' I glared at her. 'So, were the tears for him or for your precious restaurant? You're such a shit. Each time you sobbed about it I bloody hated the guy. You told me he ripped you off, you made me loathe him.'

She sat on a large stone in one corner of the pond, no longer bothering to argue while I railed on. 'Finally, finally I can understand. What did you expect? Jake gave you the lot, the jackpot! Then *you* turned off the taps. Why should he continue to share things with you if you turn your back on him? Did you imagine that he was going to sit and watch you bring your boyfriends there?' I yanked at a weed curling from the stone wall and suddenly other things came to mind. 'You were jealous of Caroline, weren't you?' I added. 'You were afraid that she would get Jake and you'd lose her and your precious *bloody* restaurant. Are you looking for forgiveness or something? I mean, why bring it up now? You kept it from me this long.'

Leaving me baffled, Jacquie focused on the idea that we could suddenly adopt a relationship as old friends. As if I would simply agree, shake hands, pick up the children and leave.

'Rupe, just believe what I say about Anna,' she said coldly, avoiding further inquiry about Caroline and their scorched relationship.

'I've no interest in Anna. I only want *you*. I want *our* family. Babe, I promise, you wouldn't even have to do anything that you didn't want to. We can sell the chapel and start something else, only this time something that's really for both of us.' Anything, I thought, to keep us together.

'You know I can't *be* that,' she said. 'The chapel's important, Rupe. I'm happy with Even Breaks. Look at me: I'll never bake bread or wear long flowery cotton dresses. That's what you want, isn't it? You're looking at the wrong person.'

'Yet you cook dinner and clean for all our tourists every day and night. Jacquie, sod the baked bread and the Flake advert. Just be halfway reasonable.'

'They go,' she said, 'the tourists,' she added. 'At the end of the week they're gone and it changes.' She clutched my hand. 'Rupe, you'll see. You've been unhappy for ages. You can give the boys a good life. Just remember . . .'

'What are you going to spin me now? Some more crap about Anna's fantasy? Jacquie, Anna is not a compensation prize. You shit on us, then no excuses. Just do it, no cardboard replacements for you as mummy. *You* carry that responsibility with you. No more of your little games, Jacq.'

A thought then occurred to me: what if it were me who employed four women, then cuddled up on the beach with a man in front of my wife? Incredible, I thought, and considered how advantageous it can be for women when it comes to responsibility. A man would be punished and possibly ostracized whereas a woman is just being silly, or perhaps experimenting. Through the years of dealing with our tourists I had seen that men can be shits but some certainly win the booby prize for their absurd willingness to underestimate women.

'Progress' in Argelès, the coastal village where we had first arrived so many years ago, now filled me with a sense of grimmest destiny. It marked the closing of a door. I hardly went there now except when sailing with our tourists.

Before the construction had started, the little sandy dig which had been the port of Argelès had mustered a collection of battered shanties strewn along the waterline. These never seemed to grow any more battered or rusty, as if the aged fishermen who owned them somehow, maybe by some peasant magic, had found a way to freeze time. The whole place had been barely alive for years and yet in its own way it had great beauty and rugged integrity. It was bathed in sleep and far from the world's madness. We used to sit in the tall grass, watching the gulls and the yellow sand lizards while listening to the pinging of ropes on the masts of the local sailors' boats as they swayed quietly in the shallows. The tiny port had been one of the more peaceful places in our lives. Most of this had gone, transformed in little more than twenty months into a cluster of buildings and balconies clawing at the sea. Sand-free zones, efficient, modern and soullessly gleaming marble-clad apartments, roads, wires, fabulous fibreglass mouldings, cafés, bars and satellite dishes all standing like a mechanized cancer in the place where the reeds had once been.

Kurt sat with the sun on his back, sipping a beer as we looked across at the neat rows of boats on clean pontoons. We'd come there to get away for a while. I wanted to be detached from confusions. Kurt wore dark glasses, his short, reddish hair glowing in the brightness. We discussed the children and, of course, I wept. He even offered to stay and help me get on my feet, which was a huge offer coming from Kurt.

Kurt and Jacquie seemed to have many things in common. Both had married, had children and then realized that they could not cope with the life that unfolded before them. I wondered if Kurt was in some way offering to help in the hope of settling his own accounts. It was kind, none the less, but unrealistic.

'There's another thing,' I said. 'About Anna. Jacquie's got this idea that we're going to go off and live in a bloody lighthouse together.'

'Oh?' Kurt perked up, wiping the froth from his orange moustache.

'This morning she told me she could see it in the future. She kept insisting that I ask Anna what her greatest fantasy is, as if I cared.'

Kurt took a breath, turned it into a wry smile and shook his head knowingly. 'On the way back from Spain in the Land Rover Anna told Jacquie that her fantasy was to make love in a lighthouse. We were all talking about that stuff. *Everyone* heard, except you guys in the front. She's been playing you on that.' He chuckled, shaking his head again. 'Don't you see, mate? Your wife is trying to have you think she's some kinda psychic. She's going to have you and your kids out of the house before you've ever had the chance to work out the details. By then it'll all be too late.'

I felt anger pumping into my head like hot, steaming, foul soup.

It was late afternoon when Jacquie pulled up at the chapel with Angelica. 'Hi! We've got everything for the party,' said Jacquie.

We walked down to the orchard, or rather I stomped and Jacquie followed. 'What is it?' she asked. 'What's the matter? Why are you looking so pissed off?'

'Let's sit in the caravan,' I said, motioning to a wreck that we'd used for workers' quarters in past days.

Inside, she sat before me on cushions. 'Why did you bullshit me with the lighthouse saga?' I demanded.

'What?' she said indignantly. 'It's true. You ask Anna.'

'Jacquie, I talked to Kurt. He was with you in the back of the Land Rover so no more lies, please. I know what you're doing. You're fucking with my head.' She tried to bluster and fluster, telling me not to get angry. 'ANGRY?' I shouted. 'You were right, Jacq, the chapel *is* a healing place. It's going to heal the two children *you* leave behind, because it's *you* that's going, not us. You can take as many of your entourage as you like. I'm staying. You can survive quite easily on your own. I can't. Not that easily, not with our children to think about.'

My confidence was shot, but I had decided: no more of this madness. From now on, I would fight for everything. She could leave, go to the Alps, and she could take the blame along with her.

'I won't go,' she said defiantly. 'There's nowhere to go.'

'That didn't seem to bother you one bit when the shoe was on the other foot.'

She sat quietly, making her mind up. 'You can't *make* me go.'

I broke first. 'You'd better ask Slammer if there's a bit more room in the bed for you next to Angelica. You'll like that. And believe me, you'd better be sure what you want to do. There's no turning back. If you really want to dump us then get off your selfish arse and do it. No more rubbing my face in it.'

'I'm not dumping you.' She was able to sound wounded. 'Don't say it like that.'

'What else then? Do you want to stay for the *house*, something to keep like a piece of the restaurant? Some antique? No, Jacq; you can't *have* this place either. This house, Jacquie, belongs to our children and it was built to provide for them.'

Now, shockingly, she evinced serious concern. She looked up, shaking. 'It belongs to *us*,' she shouted. 'What happens if they turn out to be bastards?'

'What do you mean *us*? THEY *ARE* US. If they have problems it'll be mostly because we've behaved like *bastards* . . . Why should they have to live in some dump? You have the calling, so *you* hit the road. Your mother told me to be firm with you, she said she'd back me up but somehow I don't think that this is what she had in mind. You deserve it though, Jacquie; you've gone too far.' Her remark about our sons had unleashed deep rage. 'So just fuck off and take your tribe with you.'

She sat bewildered, blank-faced. Finally she began to speak, looking at me first. 'Have you said it all?'

'I've said it.'

'Then let's go and get the party ready.' She got to her feet. 'I've still got to dress up. I don't want to ruin it tonight. It's my party and I'm going to really enjoy it. I want to celebrate with my friends.'

Martha greeted me in the orchard. 'I've taken some things for the boys. We'll be with my parents. When would you like them back tomorrow?'

The party was in full swing by ten-thirty although no one had seen Jacquie yet. She'd been with Angelica in the curate's house for some hours, the door bolted. It might simply have been that our earlier discussion had required a level of counselling which was stretching Angelica's experience. Anyway, it grew late and there was no sign of them. Finally the idea that my wife was enjoying more than a caring conversation struck me. Friends and neighbours had arrived, so had the Chinese nurse who worked with Jacquie. I tried to be a good host but my heart was far away.

Charlotte, a French friend we usually kept at a safe distance because of her hawkish and sometimes bossy manner, was blasting another of her concrete opinions across the bar while Anna chatted to Kurt at the chess table that Jaffa had built. George and Lorna were there too, along with other friends. I'd shaken hands and welcomed all of them, yet felt detached, as if I was watching it all on a screen. At some stage Charlotte seemed to be instructing me on how, with her vast experience, she thought I should be handling myself concerning Jacquie. I tuned out because the idea that Charlotte, coming from a privileged background, miraculously *knew all* irritated and insulted me. All I remember is the sight of Marie-Antoinette, who after Jacquie's eventual appearance in a Bedouin outfit along with Angelica in sequins, caught the combined body language and my expression and gave me the measure of her understanding with a single look from across the room.

In the centre of the chapel, beneath the gaze of the pewter cherub, leaping from person to person, Jacquie danced – never with any one individual for more than a few moments. Her eyes flitted, avoiding mine.

'Where've you been?' I asked when I cornered her briefly.

'We can't understand each other,' she gabbled. 'You just don't see.'

'What do you mean, "I can't understand you"? It's all perfectly normal. You're taking a stab at being a lesbian and you want me to tolerate it. Isn't that it?'

'We just don't speak the same language,' she repeated, darting towards the bar and the safety of numbers where Anna sat, chatting now with Don and Kurt.

After welcoming more guests to the chapel, I was running thin on fake good humour and slipped up to the bell-tower for a while. But there was no peace. Freddie Mercury's music thumped harder. Through the stained glass and the shadows of the banisters, I watched and listened like a child as the shapes below spun about the tiled floor. It was later explained to me that Jacquie had entered the bar and presented Slammer with a bottle of water, then another of lemonade, pointing. 'That's tonic,' she'd said, and then waved at the water, 'and that's gin. So when I ask for a gin and tonic, you know what to do.'

This was the first indication that Jacquie feared that things were not quite right; something she had no wish to discuss with me. When I found out, I wondered if she was trying to seek answers by eliminating other possible causes for the strange way she was feeling.

Upstairs, after only a short time, I sat up, determined to go and face everyone, enjoy it, not let it and Jacquie's fetish for excitement beat me. I descended to chat with Charlotte.

'I don't see why you don't just let her run the business, get on with it and you have the kids,' she said, hacking away at open wounds.

Still sipping my first beer, I tried to explain things. 'So far I've done all I can to . . . oh, *forget* it. You can't see it, not what's really going on.'

'Oh, yes I can.' She nodded sagely. 'It's obvious,' she announced, as if this credited her intuition greatly, as if to let me know that she understood the entire workings of our marriage. 'You're jealous,' she told me.

'Of course I'm jealous,' I agreed. Annoyed, I made my way over towards Jacquie as she danced.

'You can't understand me,' she said once more. 'We don't speak the same language.'

'Oh, *come on*,' I bellowed, 'what d'you think I am, *Portuguese?*' Without answering, Jacquie danced away between the others and then slipped back into the crowded safety of the bar.

It was getting late. Many of the guests must have had an idea that something was up. Most of them knew us as an inseparable couple, so the simple physical distance between us throughout the evening had been message enough. Marie came towards me as she left. I began to explain but she interrupted me almost as soon as I spoke. 'You don't have to say anything, Rupe,' she said, as we walked out of the kitchen door into the cool night. 'It's obvious, I knew after five minutes of being here. Everyone can see it.' She offered a sympathetic face.

Lorna and George were also about to go when Jacquie suddenly appeared and took Lorna aside, insisting that she stay and talk. They took the steep stairs into the curate's house bedroom and I joined George by the chapel fireplace. Dressed in jacket and tie, as always he had little to say. He'd be there for me as a friend, like Jaffa, and unless asked, he'd keep his opinions to himself.

Lorna had been gone with Jacquie for perhaps half an hour and others were leaving, cheerfully wanting to say goodbye to Jacquie with that rosy, alcohol-fired warmth which produces sincere plans for future gatherings that seldom materialize.

I went into the curate's house and shouted up the stairs, 'Jacquie, come and say goodbye, everyone's going.'

'Yes, all right, Rupert,' said Lorna firmly, 'Jacquie's coming.'

'You can't understand,' Jacquie replied when I called out again. 'Lorna, please translate. *I'm* right.'

'Yes, I know, my love.' Lorna looked at me sharply. 'Jacquie's right, y'know, Rupe.'

'Lorna!' I gasped, stunned. 'How could you say that! Jacquie's destroying her own family and you're fucking *agreeing* with her?' Now I felt that I was surely losing my marbles. I turned on Jacquie. 'What have you said to Lorna?' I glared angrily. It was the first time that I'd really noticed how dark that curate's house upstairs room could be.

The stone walls seemed to be closing in and the small bedside lamps struggling and drowning in the grey-brown gloom.

'He just can't understand what we're saying, Lorna,' repeated Jacquie. 'Can't you translate, make him see?'

'Yes, Lorna,' I said sarcastically, 'why don't you translate?'

'Rupert!' Lorna patted the bedside, motioning me to sit. 'Come and I'll explain what Jacquie's trying to say. Go on, Jacquie, while I talk to Rupert, you go and say your goodbyes to the others.'

'Lorna, for heaven's sake. She's destroying everything we have.'

Lorna leaned forward. 'Has she gone?' she whispered. 'Close the door. Good, can you lock it?' I slid the bolt across the hatch.

Lorna's face had changed now and strength and softness seemed to cross her brow as she spoke. 'Listen, sweetheart,' she began, 'Jacquie is really not well. Psychiatrically speaking, I mean. It's still not too serious, at least,' she said kindly, 'I hope not. But you've got to act now. There's very little time.' She sighed. 'I thought I saw this coming last summer, but it went back under.'

I leaned on my knees, stunned. 'So what on earth am I to do to help? She wants out of our marriage. She won't even talk to me.'

'Oh, and she'll get out, one way or another,' Lorna said with grim certainty. 'But right now there's a lot more than her marriage at stake.' She put a hand on my shoulder. 'I'm so sorry, love. You're going to need an awful lot of patience. We can help her, if it's not too far on. Perhaps there's a good psychiatrist. Trouble is, they don't speak the language.'

I felt as if the ceiling had collapsed on me. I felt blinded by confusion. Jacquie and I had been like this for so long. It seemed so normal, so *Jacquie*. She was almost *always* like this. When was she sane? What was sane? How long had we been going down this path?

A scream came from the chapel, followed by a loud thumping. 'Rupert, Rupe!' one of the Kiwi guys called out into the courtyard below.

I left Lorna and ran up the chapel stairs. In the bell-tower, literally locked in Jacquie's arms, Angelica was straining, trying desperately to reason. Jacquie seemed empowered and strangely focused. I tried to grasp one of her hands but her strength was tremendous and I realized quickly that my interference would only aggravate her. Separating the two without violence seemed impossible. Jacquie could no longer hear or see me.

'No,' she implored as Angelica struggled, 'you're coming with me. We're going on a voyage together, to save the . . .'

In an effort to stop Jacquie from hurting Angelica further I asked that the guys help separate the two women. It took three of them to pull them apart and Angelica's wrist was twisted and bruised by Jacquie.

I left the room, suddenly feeling the Witch around me everywhere. It was the room in which Jacquie and I had slept when we'd given our bed to her so long ago. Jezebel would have loved to see this. Drawn out on to the mezzanine, Jacquie was then wrestled to the floor by Kurt and two others – such was the power of her resistance.

There are few things as disturbing as watching someone much adored struggle and become a casualty in a war raging within. The worst part is that no matter what attempts are made and how many favours and concessions are given, people feeding on the buzz of their mental illness can hit rock bottom and simply stay there, almost comfortable in their illness, possibly enjoying the ride. Jacquie had been on this ride for some time and I'd just realized that I'd been the co-pilot throughout.

It was three in the morning. I'd phoned the doctor when it became plain that we could do no more. Kurt was trying to calm Jacquie while Slammer had taken a deeply shocked and bruised Angelica into the curate's house and put her to bed. To this day I often wonder why she wanted to insinuate so far inside our lives. She'd come at a time when Jacquie faced uncertainty: two children not old enough for her to enjoy and a husband who had lost the depths of tolerance that she'd counted on. Angelica had shown Jacquie that she could be anything, *have* anyone. I doubt that she'd considered the cost.

I asked after Angelica. I hadn't yet had time to brood and consider her involvement. I still remember the shock on her face that day. I think she'd suddenly seen the realities, but not having had children, the full measure of our situation may never have been apparent to her. It had just been 'such fun' until now. Very early the following morning

Slammer took her to the airport. Having encouraged Jacquie to be the life of the party and wild and free and hot, Angelica would now go safely home.

'We're going on a voyage,' Jacquie kept repeating, lying on the floor, the party truly dead. 'Kurt, Lorna, the Dodger and me, in Dodger's red car. Yeah, we're going to save the world. Wait!' She stared. 'You can't go outside. The trees,' she gasped inexplicably, waving a finger.

The doctor appeared at 4 a.m. He wasn't happy about getting out of bed but he'd done it for Jacquie whom he knew well. He was the eldest of the doctors we knew, very patient, originally from the village, seemingly impervious to change.

'Have you not been sleeping?' he asked me.

'No. Things are a bit difficult at the moment.'

He wanted to give her a powerful sedative. Rather than have Jacquie suffer the humiliation of being held down (oddly for a nurse married to a diabetic she couldn't stand syringes), I suggested we lace a hot drink with the drug and then she'd go quietly, if she went to sleep at all.

'I'll send young Dr Jacques over in the morning and give him the notes,' said the doctor, patting me on the shoulder. 'There's enough of this sedative for one more dose tomorrow if you need it.' Then he said something that startled me despite what Lorna had already hinted at. 'She'll have to go in, I'm afraid.' He peeked over his lenses. I noticed their trendy frames. 'Don't look so sad. Jacques will see her in the morning.' The fact that she would be institutionalized was painful, the seriousness of it knocking me badly.

'I'll stay with her, Rupe, if you like,' Kurt offered. Helpless with gratitude and feeling utterly adrift, I left Jacquie, now a complete stranger to me, ranting to Kurt in the bell-tower. Perhaps it was the shock that made my wife and partner of ten years seem almost sinister. Shadows flitted across the coloured glass of the interior stained-glass windows while downstairs, in the heart of the chapel, I found cushions to slump on amidst the remains of the party on the tiled floor. I could watch from there, should Jacquie decide to depart in search of Eldorado in the night.

I barely slept, sick with worry, hearing Jacquie's ravings and Kurt's steady voice throughout the night. The sedative had done little to slow her down. Morning came and Barbara and André, returning from their trip, came over. I remember Barbara walking around the pond, past me and on towards the chapel door, her step quickening as she approached. 'Oh! But she's gone high!' were her first words in that Norfolk accent, as if this condition was as common as influenza. 'She's been working too hard,' she said accusingly.

'What do you mean "high"?' I asked. 'Wait a minute, Barbara, you mean the same as her brother Stephen?'

She marched past the pond and the lavender and past me with obvious distrust. 'She's overdone it.'

'Overdone it?' I blurted. 'What?' I was insulted by the absurdity of the statement and her blatant contempt. 'We've been closed for two months,' I shouted after her. It occurred to me that I had also been under strain, more than perhaps she could possibly imagine, but this wasn't something that she seemed even to consider. Still, I did not think '*overdoing it*' was any reason for Jacquie's extreme behaviour.

Moments later rain sprinkled lightly on the surface of the chapel's ponds, yet there wasn't a cloud in the sky. Dr Jacques's car pulled up. He had known us since our early days, sailed with us and dined with us before the chapel had tiles on its floor and before he'd had a clientele to speak of. He was a sympathetic, intelligent, mousy-haired man from an aristocratic family. He wore steel-rimmed glasses and was a good, clear thinker. Half of the middle-aged people in the village adored him, still calling him *young* Jacques. He took his time, chatting warmly to Jacquie on the sofa as he conducted various tests. Then he crossed the kitchen floor towards me.

'She's not too good,' he said. 'Rupert, what on earth's happened here?'

'I'm not exactly sure. But I think our marriage is over.'

He looked at me in surprise. 'She keeps going on about a voyage with some other people.' He mentioned Lorna and Dodger among others.

I explained that Lorna was a retired psychiatric nurse, English. 'Jacquie hopes that the Dodger is going to buy me out. She thinks they're all going off in his red car to save the world.' I could hear how daft that all sounded and almost expected Jacques to flicker a smile but his sympathy overwhelmed other thoughts.

'Listen,' he said, 'I know you're upset, but don't blame her. She's sick. It's not her. You'll have to put it all aside until she can handle things.'

This seemed illogical to me. How does a human being utterly conditioned to another's behaviour suddenly treat them as if they're acting differently? Jacquie was barking mad now, sure, but we'd been living on the outer limits at least since Sam was born. I knew I couldn't tell the normal Jacquie from the mildly insane and neither could our friends. I knew I couldn't explain this to a man who saw me as rational and spoke to me logically as a friend. I was disturbed, but there was nothing worthwhile left to say. His logic was only helpful for practical things at that stage. He clicked his case shut, recommending a clinic in Perpignan as he did so.

'Thanks, but she'll never go.' I shrugged. 'I doubt it. Not without a fight.'

'Rupert, she *has* to go.' He spoke kindly but emphatically. 'There's no choice. Do you have any sedative left?' I was trying to get a handle on my thoughts; this was upsetting me. Jacques patted my shoulder again. 'My friend, believe me, there is no choice.'

'Okay,' I said, confused. 'There's one more dose, but it doesn't stop her.'

'I could send an ambulance.'

'What? You mean restraints?' I frowned. 'I couldn't allow that.' Then I had an idea. 'Supposing we create her fantasy and she goes off to save the world with Lorna, Kurt and Dodger in his red car? They could get her as far as the clinic if we give her the sedative just before she goes.'

'Okay,' Jacques nodded, 'if you think it'll work. You can come round to my place and pick up the papers on the way.'

Martha arrived with the children. I made arrangements for their care then phoned Lorna and finally the Dodger, who agreed to come at once and drive Jacquie, Lorna and Kurt off to save the world in his red car. Some of Jacquie's fantasies were based on his and her combined realistic dreams, so why shouldn't he get a better view now?

Within an hour the red car pulled up beside the chapel. Lorna had come as soon as I'd called and so, with a full cast and after watching Kurt help Jacquie drink her sedative-laced hot chocolate, we set forth. Jacquie'd packed a bag of various world-saving items such as tonic, vodka, toothbrush, scented candle, etc. I stood at the door as the players in this drama walked out. Jacquie seemed stunned, a trifle slow under sedation, but she wore a faint, enchanted smile as she climbed into Dodger's motor.

At the clinic the centime dropped when the first nurse's uniform came into view. 'NO!' Jacquie screamed. 'How could you do this to me?'

She sank her teeth into the arm of one of the nurses who struggled to tow her down the corridor towards a neat, comfortable room with bars on the windows. Somehow it didn't look sinister, but she still howled and fought, clawing down the walls.

'Please,' I begged the staff, 'please don't hurt her!'

'Don't let it bother you,' said a large, jolly woman in a white uniform, 'they're often like that when they come in.'

'How could I *not* be bothered?' I replied sharply.

The woman was so conditioned to responses like mine that she hardly seemed to notice. 'Well, we're going to give her a nice sleep,' she said. 'I'm afraid you can't see her for a few days. No visits for the first week.'

'Who do I talk to?'

'You can talk to whoever you want. Talk to yourself. Everyone else does around here.'

I tried to smile and explain that I needed to know who was responsible for my wife's treatment and care. Then I waited in a reception area, watching an assortment of mentally battered and psychiatrically delicate out-patients lithium their way in and out of the building. Everybody seemed to be watching the double-locking doors which led to the in-patients section. It seemed that when people like Jacquie got restless they artfully devised ways of getting themselves through.

A woman seated next to me swayed slightly, sitting on her hands, her eyes like fried tomatoes in dreadful cried-out sockets. I felt homesick.

Then the doctor ushered me in. He was tall and thin with a moustache like Groucho Marx yet he seemed efficient. 'Absolutely no visitors for the first week,' he said. 'First let's find out what's brought this about. Tell me, has she been under any great stress lately?'

'Yes, plenty.'

'Has her work been very difficult?'

'Not her work, yes, no, not exactly,' I blithered, 'but she hasn't slept.'

'Since when?'

'She slept maybe an hour last night but that's almost it, for both of us, er, in the last three or more days. But, I mean, she *was* okay. She, she's been partying a lot, and things haven't been very nice.'

'For you?'

'For either of us. Tell me,' I asked, 'is what she's been doing for real, I mean, part of the illness, or does she mean it? Can she tell which feeling is true or . . .'

'I think you need time to yourself and a little sleep.' He leaned back in his chair in a practised way that told me he had other things to do. 'Then perhaps when I speak to Jacqueline I will see what can be done.' He nodded in a reassuring way but I was still baffled. He seemed either overworked or weary of dealing with the same old scenario over and over again. He rose to let me out.

'Thank you, doctor. Please take great care of her, she's all we've got.'

I drove home in a bizarre, almost surreal frame of mind and then phoned my family from the office shed, bursting into tears.

'How long has this been going on?' asked Lucilla.

'About two years,' I blubbed.

'Two years! Oh, Rupe! Why didn't you say something before?'

Since I moved in with my father and stepmother at the age of eleven, Lucilla had gradually become my confidante. Her gentle, sensible good nature was always there for me. She wasn't a person who allowed emotion to overrun her life, yet her capacity for love and kindness was vast.

'Thought I could fix it myself,' I told her, 'I just didn't realize.' My eyes dripped on to a letter, one of Jacquie's to a hopeful ski programme punter. 'I wanted to keep it private, between us.'

Lucilla told me that my father would be home later and not to worry, he'd ring. I felt like a fool, like a failure. Then I phoned Lorna and asked her what I should expect of the clinic. She had her doubts about help in a foreign language, however fluent the patient. A lot seemed to depend on how much attention and care would be taken over procuring an accurate diagnosis. Having seen the shrink, I had some doubts. He reminded me of all of the Three Stooges, wrapped in one expensive busy package. I just couldn't see him sparing a great deal of time for Jacquie.

'You've got to be careful,' said Lorna. 'Rupert? Are you listening to me, love? I said, you've *got* to be careful.' Lorna used the same voice she'd used when she'd told me Jacquie had lost her marbles. I remained baffled. 'I mean, my boy, that there are hawks. A lot of people could do well out of this situation. So watch your back, my love.' I was as much in the dark as ever.

That afternoon I went to rest in the furthest of the buttress rooms on the quietest side of the chapel. I felt as if I was waiting in a doctor's surgery and couldn't sleep. So I stared at pictures on the wall, the front sheets of the scores of 1900s musicals. *The Enchanted River, Over the Whistling Tree* and *Sweet Lullaby* hung silent, browning in the dry, white room. Kansas scratched at the door, then sat for a while until the *tranmontana* drove her on.

I looked out at the huge old oak through stained-glass windows which Jacquie and I had bought from an antique dealer in Montauban where we'd slept in a creepy room in a rambling water mill. Precious times. The tree stood black and grey through the tinted blue and red. Fidgeting with the split edge of my wedding ring, I felt such a great longing for the past. Later there was a knock on the door. Don and Anna had told me what to expect.

'Hi.' My brother Brock smiled faintly, hugging me. 'Dad's in the other room. He didn't want to upset you.' Brock sat on the side of the bed. 'You okay?'

'Fine,' I lied. My brother and father had dropped everything and come 1,000 miles. I felt deeply moved but even more concerned: things must be much worse than I thought.

'We've got a couple of days,' said Brock. 'Dad's worried about you.' He looked out at the mountainside, making a wry face. 'So, how are they both?'

'Who?' I said vaguely.

'Jacquie and Jacquie,' he grinned.

We spent an afternoon discussing practical issues. I would have to reimburse all of the funds taken for the ski programme. The punters would be angry. People might try to sue us, claiming that there would be no places available with competitors so late in the season, but there was no choice. Without a second thought my brother and father each offered to find the money we were short of. I was humbled and ashamed.

Then, while I slept, Jacques came round and spoke with my father. He'd brought some zombie pills for me. They came in sections: you bit off as much as you needed. Then the world around would cool right down, and emotion slipped off into the distance like launching a ship. I didn't like them, they made me feel lifeless and out of control. I finished one, then gave the rest to my father who used them to relieve a trapped nerve in his neck and phoned me a month later asking for some more.

The following day I explained about the joint venture between the Dodger and Even Breaks. 'So you'll be working half as much?' asked my father. 'And where's the minibus?'

'We needed to fix it,' I stammered, 'so I had to sell it and the car.'

'I see,' he said, resigned. 'So if the Dodger's assisting you to work half-time, he owns the vehicles which on half-time pay you'll be too poor to replace and he's got his fingers on your client list, what's to stop him from dumping you and walking away with your business?' My father seemed to be able immediately to cut through the confusion that Jacquie's enthusiasm and my own long withdrawal had blinded me to.

'We know all the activities,' I explained, 'how to run it all.'

'Where's his company based?'

'He doesn't want a French company.'

My father winced. 'You mean, it's to be *your* company? Your responsibility?' He looked at me aghast. 'What risks does he take? What happens if someone gets hurt or dies? You'll be in the firing line.'

'Dad, I know how it looks. It's all over the place. Jacquie's round there, drinking tea, making plans. He makes it all look such fun; she couldn't resist. I've never been so concerned. She makes out to me that it's a sacrifice. One week off now and again would've done. You can see now why we're fighting.'

He sat back for a moment and looked at Brock with a smile. 'Why don't we all go and have a chat with the Dodger? Just so maybe Brock and I can give you some back-up. And the guys, they're going to be working with him as well? Does he pay some of their keep?'

'They were meant to go and come back before the summer.' I didn't tell my father about that trip to the mountains skiing after Christmas – Jacquie's reward for their hard work. This alone, I discovered, had cost more than we could possibly have afforded. Why I didn't fight it remains entirely beyond me even to this day. I can only put it down to the fear of being dumped alone with the kids. My father asked why the guys were still with us, now that we were skint.

'Jacquie said she'd leave with them if I asked them to go. I was . . .' I stumbled. 'I didn't want to; we're a family, for God's sake.'

My father stared at me intently. I knew he could barely believe how I had allowed myself to become so weak and damaged. 'How's your diabetes?' he asked.

'It's okay,' I lied.

Dad and Brock took me to dinner in a restaurant down in the lovely cove of Collioure. They'd be leaving the following day and I was missing them already. My eyes were heavy, the skin beneath dark and the rest yellow-white with cold sores. They cheered me along, hiding the shock of the demolition they'd seen. We drove back and stopped in the drive in front of the chapel.

'I'm afraid,' I said. 'There's nothing left.' I began to cry. 'I'm afraid I'll fail trying to put it all right.' My father patted my shoulder.

'Rupe,' said Brock, ' you've got us on the phone. You've got to understand. I know it's awful, and we hope Jacquie gets better, but you've got to take control. Jacquie must accept that she needs to take a back seat. I mean, you've got children. If you let something happen to you . . .' He too began to cry. 'Rupe,' Brock spoke as if we were still children, 'there's only you and me.' Gareth had been on both our minds. 'If something happens to you, I . . . it's just you and me now.'

Coming into the bijou cottage, I kissed the children as they slept. Looking at them, I could not imagine how I was going to manage to do everything and make it all work. I had hope, which I have always tried to preserve. Their smiles and cuddles for Jacquie and me were endless. I wondered how they would react if in the future Jacquie did not change her view and did indeed leave me. Perhaps I misunderstood but it seemed plain that Barbara felt that I'd been weak and was responsible for all of this.

My father, Brock and I went to the Dodger's house for that little chat about the details of the relationship. I had decided to make them business partners until I could get my head into things properly. It wasn't a long discussion and the Dodger's friendly manner never faltered, but later in a fax he described them as wolves.

The following morning I foolishly lent Anna a sweater that Barbara had given me for Christmas. I then sent a message to the Dodger asking that until further notice all business should be postponed. He was upset, but better now than later, I felt. I would not take any more risks with the future so unsettled. Dealing with more practical stuff – it made me feel in control somehow – I'd asked Slammer, Robert and Kurt to leave. I'd given them money and paid for their tickets where necessary. No one was particularly happy, although perhaps they'd finally seen that without Jacquie to muffle the alarm bells of financial ruin it was inevitable. I had a family to feed, so their departure, however sad, was non-negotiable.

'Oh, for heaven's sake,' said Barbara on her way out of the chapel kitchen, heading into the cold morning, having seen Anna in the Christmas sweater, 'you've hardly given Jacquie time to get out the door.' It was an innocent mistake and I quickly found something else warm for Anna to wear. It did however slam home the reality of my situation and presage the judgements that would so easily be cast.

I'd asked Don and Anna to stay in the hope that Don's business training and good nature could contribute to a new direction. Anna could manage the office with ease and she, like Don, could be relied upon. The two were also discreetly a couple and I was relying on the fact that they'd be pleased to stick together.

'Just you watch yourself,' my father said before he went home and as Anna left the chapel dining-room. I'd mentioned Barbara's recent comments. Anna was pretty and closer in age to me than Don. The simple mathematics of this was sufficient to make Dad cast a word of warning. 'You don't want your life to get any more complicated than it already is,' he said. 'That Don is a good one. You can trust the two of them. Careful, old son.'

After my father and Brock had gone, Don and Anna handed me letters that the two had written and left for me. There was a package from Brock containing a most precious gift: our brother Gareth's watch.

I seemed to have lost my head. I was crying. We were now in debt for many, many thousands. My business had collapsed and my wife had gone mad. 'You have the children,' my father had said, hugging me before he left, 'it's all up to you.'

PART FIVE

25 Meeting the Beast

We were deep into spring. March in the Roussillon was, as always, windy, alive and beautiful. The mimosa had flowered. It still rained but the sun had shown its strength with colour flying out of the ground everywhere and peach trees well into blossom.

I'd driven to the hospital to bring Jacquie home for a weekend. Very little had changed in the two weeks since she'd gone in. She was more lucid, although heavily sedated, but still contemptuous of me.

I was ushered up to the shrink's office before being allowed to pick her up. He sat at his desk, crossing his legs and weaving all eight fingers together on top of his thigh, looking quite pleased with himself. 'How do you find her?' he asked.

'She's not exactly the same person. She's very distant.'

'That's because,' he moved his folded fingers to the desktop and leaned forward, 'if I reduce the drugs she'll go high again. That's a helluva dose she's on, you know?' He chuckled. 'Enough to knock out a *horse*. She's got incredible energy, that one.'

'Have you any idea what it is?' I asked, 'I mean, post-natal depression, everyday depression, schizophrenia?'

'I don't think we should rush things,' was all he said. I found his apparently casual attitude frustrating. I wanted to find a solution; surely it was obvious that this was in some way connected to Jacquie's brother's condition. 'Hang on a moment, let's not go throwing diagnosis around like that. She's suffered from a depression. That's all.'

'That's it? She's depressed? But she's only partially attached to the earth. *That's* depression? Doctor, there *has* to be something else.'

'Well, she certainly seems adamant about getting out of here and I can't keep her forever.'

'But the drugs,' I said, amazed at his willingness to discuss Jacquie's departure, 'they're so strong. How can you possibly tell if she's any better when she's so doped? She doesn't have much contact any more with the person she was, so how can you *know* if she's better?' My estimation of the shrink had begun to diminish rapidly. 'I really think this is something more than just depression,' I insisted.

He addressed me as if I might be ill too, which I probably was, in a way. He spoke as if I couldn't understand his reasoning or as if he resented my impertinence in suggesting that Jacquie's condition might be regulated or repaired by means *other* than drugs. He seemed to be too indifferent to the case to want to run further tests.

'So you'll just give her more drugs and send her home?' I said, disbelieving.

'It won't be as dramatic as you see it. Don't worry,' he patronized, 'she'll get stable and come here to visit.' He shook my hand while almost guiding me out, and closed the door neatly behind me.

As far as I could tell it was a good clinic. The nurses were wonderful and it was highly recommended, but the man I was dealing with had no ability to debate other than within the realms of his own views. He certainly wasn't going to waste any more of our limited insurance money to see how this English girl ticked. He was purely a French domestic model – cut a few wires with drugs and send 'em home. I found him unwilling to explore this case further and without heaps of cash there was little chance of an upgrade.

Jacquie had been waiting in her room, sitting on her bed with her bag packed like a boarding-school girl on the eve of the summer holidays. The room was a good size, comfy, with an en suite bathroom and plenty of light. For me it would have offered a chance to read, to sleep and recover. For Jacquie it was isolation and loneliness. Her need for constant change remained and although I didn't know it, she was already learning how to manipulate the clinical system of diagnosis.

'Hello,' I smiled, standing in the doorway.

'Hi,' she said. 'Let's go. I just can't wait.' Then she stopped in the doorway. 'There's just one thing. Before we go, you've got to promise me, Rupe, that you won't make me do anything that'll make me unhappy.'

'Like what?' I said, sitting down on the bed.

'I don't know, *anything*. You promise? Or else I'd rather stay here.'

'Jacq, you're coming home for the weekend. I'm not selling you to a zoo or anything. We all miss you, the boys miss you.'

'I thought you asked them to leave,' she said angrily.

'I meant our children.'

'See!' she shouted. 'You're doing it already. Making me feel guilty.'

'Never mind the kids, then. Don and Anna are still there anyway, so you won't have to talk to me all the time.'

'Like my beads?' she asked. She'd woven coloured wooden beads into her hair in long strands as she might have done years ago as a little girl.

'They're lovely.' I nodded.

'They're expensive. We have to buy them,' she said, opening an envelope filled with the coloured wooden shapes.

'D'you need money?' I fumbled in a pocket.

'No. I've still got some. I'm saving up. I've been selling things, clothes and stuff.' She beamed. 'I've made five hundred francs.'

'That's fifty quid! I'm surprised you've got anything left to go home in.'

'See? *You* can't stop me,' she added. There was an edge of spite in her tone. 'Come on, Rupe, let's go. This is my freedom we're wasting. I hate this place.' Looking very different from the neat nurse or sharp businesswoman once moulded by Jake, Jacquie followed me to the front desk to be 'checked out'.

Bert rumbled along, the gearstick buzzing as we looked out of the windows and I searched for things to say. Jacquie had lost weight since the previous summer. To me she seemed to be in perfect shape, although there were dark patches under her eyes from the effects of the medication. Every now and again she'd look as if she were about to drop off; eyelids heavy, she'd begin to fall forwards but she'd fight it.

We had lunch in the chapel. Barbara came, sitting at the head of the table. Don and Anna brought food, choosing not to sit with us, while blank-faced with her mouth slightly open, Jacquie remained silent, her gaze fixed on the wall.

The children, clearly delighted to see their mother, tore around but we were almost oblivious. It seems remarkable, but I cannot say that I noticed any reaction from them at all. They were so used to being cared for by others that the only truly constant individual now was me. In a way this was a blessing as looking at Jacquie in her withdrawn and distant state was distressing. All of her spark seemed to be gone, as if on the medication she'd become a functioning body without a spirit.

'Jacquie? . . . Jacquie, darling, are you feeling okay?' I asked, reaching across, slightly afraid even to touch her shoulder. She turned, switched back on for a moment, gave a narrow smile, then toyed a little with her food before focusing again on the wall.

After lunch she had a rest in the far room. There was no question of her sleeping in the bijou cottage with me. She seemed adamant that as little physical contact as possible should take place between us. Yet I sensed that she didn't want to be this way, that she still loved the life she'd had. But then again, I thought sadly, perhaps that was only a hope on my part. I couldn't stop loving her but I was so confused, feelings askew.

She woke at three in the afternoon and had difficulty getting up. 'I feel so ill,' she said. 'Please, Rupe, come here. Hug me. Please just hug me.' It's a horrible feeling, knowing that in a few seconds the person you're hugging will throw you away. I wondered if the worst thing I could have done was to insist that she took her medicine. Without it she was a child, a bubbling, inventive, fun-loving child equipped with the cunning of a thirty-four-year-old woman. With it she was empty, trapped in a lifeless deluded state without hope. Nothing mattered, because nothing could be felt. The doses would take months to get right, I supposed, but these first days were truly desperately depressing.

'I want to go out on my bike,' said Jacquie restlessly. 'Since I can't drive and you won't let me go into the office I think I'd like to go and see my friends. I've only got tomorrow and then I'm back in the nut-house.'

I agreed coolly: how could I forbid this innocent pleasure and release? 'I just worry that you'll have an accident. Are you steady enough?'

She eyed me venomously. 'You're just imprisoning me, aren't you? Making it impossible for me to do anything without your permission.'

'Don't be silly.' I was weary of this. 'Do as you wish. Anything you like. Go and chuck yourself off a bridge if you want. I'll even drive you.' Then I couldn't help but grin. 'Jacquie, I want you to get better. You don't have to feel trapped here.'

'You mean you want to drive me so you can keep a check on what I'm up to and where I'm going and stop me from making deals with the Dodger?' Part of that bright and brilliant brain, however muffled with dope, was still capable of tremendous manipulation.

'No! But is that what you've been doing?'

'I can do what I like,' she said, ready to go. 'There are phones in the clinic, you know. I'm not completely hopeless.' I think my voice and eyes became sad and cold as I assured her that I would never underestimate her. 'You won't stop me, and neither will that clown,' she said, seated now on the shiny red mountain bike that I'd bought her for Christmas. I asked her who she meant. 'The shrink. What a doctor! He's not interested in me, in my problems. He saw me twice last week for a total of an hour! He's just there for the money. *He* doesn't give a shit; just doles out drugs and you're left to sit in your room. That doesn't help, you know. There's a woman too, who comes and chats, like a welfare officer type of thing. She thinks I shouldn't be in there. They're so *bloody* gullible. She's practically eating out of my hand.'

Struggling with the bike, Jacquie rode out of sight.

The following morning I got the boys up and waited for Martha, then made some breakfast and went into Jacquie's room at around ten. Her face seemed even paler than I'd seen it in the clinic, her lips bluish and dry, encrusted, as if she'd been drinking a lot of heavy Spanish red. She stared at me for a long time before saying anything.

'Water,' she whispered, 'could you bring me some water?' Her eyes rolled up white as she tried to sit. I brought it and sat beside her, lifting her head as she lay limp in my arms, and very slowly she drank, taking tiny sips at first. She shook a little, an uncontrollable, slow motor shake, like an extremely fragile geriatric.

'What are these drugs for, for Chrissake?' I picked up the brown paper bag from the bedside and began rifling through the various packages. There were rather serious-looking blue capsules, white ones and a dropper with instructions. With each medicine came a list of contra-indications, which carried on for a huge paragraph or more. Of the side-effects warned of – at least of the ones I could translate – the most alarming noted the danger of renal damage. That could mean kidney problems. Appalled and frustrated, I began to consider alternatives.

If she stopped taking this medicine she'd revert to being as she was. I doubted that she'd completely lose track of reality again but there was little hope of getting her wholly back in the broad sense because she would never cope with the responsibility and drudgery of parenthood. But intellectually at least she'd be alive, and that idea seemed more promising than the look on the face of the broken soul before me.

'I've ruined everything, haven't I?' she whispered. 'All you ever wanted was a family.'

I smiled faintly. Outside the sun shone and it was peaceful. Through the blank white skylight the room glowed softly. The dogs were sleeping on the patio in front of us where a small tree we'd planted years before was now strong and in full bud.

'You've married your mother,' said Jacquie, knowing all too well that I felt my mother should have had help to deal with her struggles but had never accepted that she needed to confront them.

'You just need to rest.' I said, determined that my children were not going to see a life akin to the struggles I remembered.

Jacquie had beauty, which would help open a few doors. So many of the more brilliant creatures on this earth survive on that and the simple vitality that her drugs were burying. It would be all right for a while but hard to be locked into an emotionally arrested sixteen in her forties and fifties. I felt adoration for her, which turned, as she pushed me aside and staggered from the room, to despair.

In the afternoon she baked a cake, made the correct coloured icings and decorated it. The result turned out to be a huge, tray-shaped, chocolate sponge Union Jack. The chapel was warm with the smell of home cooking like a thousand times before. She found paper plates and plastic cups and prepared thermoses of hot tea which we took back to the clinic to share with other patients.

'I hope they let me out next weekend,' Jacquie said curtly.

'They will,' I reassured her, 'because you're going to be fine.'

'Unless *you* try and stop them,' she replied bitterly.

'I'm not going to do anything,' I promised. 'If you're well enough, you'll get out, if you rest and take care of yourself. Do me a favour though. If you make business deals from the clinic, at least let me know what you're letting us in for.'

'It's my business not yours,' she hissed. 'Anyway, I'm going to start aromatherapy courses down here. I always thought it was a good thing. I've made a list of the hospitals in England that I'm going to write to and see if I can't bring groups over.'

We sat in Bert outside the clinic and she leaned across. 'Thanks, Rupe. I've had a lovely weekend,' she lied, kissing me warmly, her eyes empty. 'Now, let's go,' she said, like a proud and brave convict marching off to face the gallows.

I helped carry things to the clinic's recreation area, setting the cake and thermoses up in front of a gathering of inmates who were lounging about before a large, wall-mounted TV. 'Hello, Jacquie,' said one. Few others commented, even though she *was* standing directly in front of the screen. 'Oh!' said an enormous young man, incredibly slowly. 'Hi . . . Jacquie.'

'Come on,' said Jacquie. 'Hi, hi!' She switched the TV off and waved her arms in front of the others who seemed so slow to respond, so *very* slow. 'We're having a party,' she announced. They all seemed to react as if they were in heavy space suits on a mission far away from Earth.

'Bye, Jacq,' I said. Even there she'd found a new excitement and could no longer hear nor see me.

At the foot of the stairs a psychiatric nurse greeted me. 'You must be Jacquie's husband?' She smiled pleasantly. 'Was it a good weekend? Did you manage?' I tried to find the right words and ended up saying simply that it had been bizarre. The nurse understood perfectly. 'Such a pity,' she nodded towards Jacquie, who was simultaneously dancing and passing out cake, 'she's nice, your wife. So sad – she's just a little girl,' she shrugged, 'just a little girl.'

I sat in Bert outside the building. Rain began to pour down, the sky above dulling the colour of even the brightest buildings in the street. The whole scene, Jacquie's bedroom with its barred windows and across the parking lot in the rain the Land Rover with the husband sitting emptily inside it, seemed to resemble a scene from an awful soap opera.

Three days later I managed to pin down the shrink. The Wednesday, two days before she came home for another weekend was the first chance I'd had. He'd seen Jacquie only once since her admission. 'She's extremely strong,' he said, 'and determined. She'll do what she wants and not much else.' He found this amusing.

'I know that,' I answered flatly. 'Can you tell me what I can do to stop her from making business calls from here? She'll bankrupt us further. Is it her illness or what? She knows there's no money. Can't you stop her?'

Still apparently amused, he felt constrained to spell it out. 'First,' he said, 'I doubt very much that this is a product of the illness.' He glanced out of the window towards Jacquie's room at the end of the hospital block. 'One has to establish if it isn't more of a personality trait, don't you think?'

'So, whether she was ill or not, this would still be happening?' I looked at the floor, then blew air. 'So I've had it, is that what you're saying?'

The doctor merely pulled a face and asked me if I thought she was any better.

'You tell me. She isn't anybody any more, not on the drugs she's taking. She's just dead, empty, and she's putting her family to death financially and emotionally. I suppose symbolically, she's already buggered off. Do you think that rates as better?' He looked at me as if I too was in need of psychiatric help. 'And yet she knows she's doing it. She's definitely not herself. Can't you give me some form of diagnosis?'

This annoyed him. I became convinced that the last thing he wanted to do was give Jacquie a diagnosis that he'd have to stand by professionally. 'I can't throw a title on someone like that. I told you, she's suffered a depression.' Annoyingly he shrugged again. 'That's all I can say.'

'So, do you think my marriage is over?'

'I'm sorry,' he said, opening the door.

Lorna had been to see me often. I was grateful for the support; she was my only English-speaking window to Jacquie's illness. In retrospect I see how much I clung to her knowledge in false hope, as if understanding the illness might bring me closer to saving the dead marriage. People often go on and on, like ghosts, sometimes in a vile or cowardly way never admitting that it's over, that they're history, that it's time to face up to it and get on with life.

'I'm warning you, Rupert,' said Lorna, 'the worst part of it isn't while they're in hospital, it's when they get out. I'm saying that, boy,' she poked me in the ribs, 'but you're not listening. Oi!' She nudged me. 'Do you hear me?' I liked Lorna. She and big Eddy were similar in that they gave immensely practical advice that I almost always stupidly ignored.

'And you watch out for that Anna,' she muttered.

'She's with Don, you know,' I explained.

Lorna looked at me with eyes that bored right through to the soles of my shoes. 'Oh, *come on*, Rupe. A nice girl, with you, alone, in your state? I wasn't born yesterday. What you take me for?' At this George, who had been wandering about trying to find something helpful to get on with, let out a short neighing laugh. 'Rupert,' said Lorna, 'smile. Come on, it's high time you went out there and threw your hat over the windmill.'

The crazy metaphor appealed to me.

Jacquie emerged from the clinic on a Saturday morning with her bag of medicine, rolls of paintings and packets of assorted beads. She also had lists of various aromatherapy set-ups and hospitals that she intended to approach for her seminars. She seemed more sedated than ever: perhaps her dosage had been raised in case her re-adjustment to outside life was turbulent.

She slept a lot, rode her bike almost every day, which worried me because with all the drugs her balance was off, and if you know anything about French country roads, you'll be aware how precarious they can be. Rarely did we discuss where she went, for fear of argument. She stayed with friends for a night here and there but it wasn't easy for her or them. Even the closest friends struggle to deal with an illness such as this, sometimes visible, sometimes not. In truth, the last thing she wanted was to be at home and faced with the children and me. I did my best to keep the children away from her but it wasn't easy. How do you separate children from their mother yet share the same house? I hated the effect it was having on all of us. I loathed the clinic for the lack of forethought given to the impact that Jacquie would have on her family in this state and vice versa.

A great deal of speculation flew around. Those who hadn't been to the clinic in March asked themselves if Jacquie *was* really that ill or was the illness a way out? Others made sweepingly painful but probably astute remarks like: 'This often happens at the end of a long relationship.'

A few people suggested that I take her to a psychiatrist in England, that we go together. I honestly would have struggled to find that sort of money, as everyone in my family had already emptied their pockets to repair the damage done by the failed ski project. I felt I couldn't reasonably ask, although I knew that for Jacquie they'd have tried anything.

There were other, far simpler reasons for not going. I was becoming annoyed and exhausted by the constant hatred and aggression. It seemed to me that Jacquie wanted everything and by being officially mad she could justify any action she chose to take, no matter how cruel or how it endangered the future of the children. Lorna had been right. When they come home it's hard going. The psychiatrist's explanation that her resentful and calculating behaviour was in part a basic personality trait and not due to the illness weighed heavily upon me.

'Well, I'm ill, aren't I?' classically Jacquie would say with a gentle, joyless smile. 'But you can't stop me, Rupe, not from being or doing what I like. It's just depression, remember? That's all the doctor said, so I can do as I like.'

I hated the clinic doctor for this, for leaving the door to our destruction open. Without official papers to prove that Jacquie was unstable, I couldn't close a joint bank account, I couldn't stop a deal that might wipe us out. She was capable enough and free to do as she wished. I could only watch my back and the garden shed.

I had never noticed the supposed change in Jacquie, instead I'd bent my own behaviour to fit. With the exception of when she was clearly mad, the personality traits and illness were so well blended that even when made aware of this, I still found it almost impossible to see Jacquie as ill and thus make allowances. Linda, her own sister, initially saw no illness at all. One sometimes couldn't tell the sane Jacquie from the *depressed* one.

I was becoming increasingly defensive. Of one thing I was sure: Jacquie could no more stop herself than I could turn her life into the amusement arcade that she craved it to be.

'If you cut me off like this, *if* you don't let me into the office, I'll go crazy, Rupe. I can't sit here doing nothing,' said Jacquie, looking out of the curate's house windows over to Mo's pond and the shed. When I told her I'd padlocked it, she airily said she'd use the cottage phone.

'Do any business on it, just try it, Jacquie, and I'll rip it out of the wall. If you do business before you're better, you do it alone and away from us.' She stared at me, defiant, and with loathing. I tried to mollify her. '*Babe*, we owe forty-five thousand pounds. This is nearly the end. I have one chance to find a way to pay it back. You should be helping us, not trying to slit my throat. This is our last chance, *please*. If I can't pay the bills this summer we're fucked, we'll lose the house. Jacq, for goodness' sake, what is it you want?'

After our situation had become increasingly unpleasant and with no progress, my father visited and agreed with Barbara and me that the only positive move left would be for Jacquie to return to England and get help in her own language. Sitting up in the dome, lost in the illness and calm, Jacquie reclined on a sofa and stared into space. I sat across from her, hearing my father and Barbara talking, planning, under the mezzanine below.

'Jacq,' I said, 'at least over there you can choose. I mean, without being influenced by me. You can stay with whoever you want,' I promised, knowing that my opinion would be dismissed in any case. 'Stay a month to find your feet and think. After that you'll maybe see if you really want to be with the children and me or not. There's no pressure. You just need to get better so you can think and cope.'

She agreed, and unsure that her motives were the same as mine, I gave her what little money I could and put her on the plane.

'She'll never come back,' I told my father mournfully.

'If it means that she gets better, then isn't that the right thing for her to do?' he ventured with savage logic.

Charlotte's car appeared in the driveway and she hovered like a hawk by the chapel door. 'Well, I'll tell you,' she suggested, applying her usual predatory spin, 'you'd have had to drag me out of this place, claw and tooth, before I'd go. She's crazy to give up what's hers like that.' I assumed she meant the children. 'I *mean*,' continued Charlotte, 'her house! Everything.'

'It's all still hers. I don't think she's quite as mercenary about our problems as that. First she's got to get well and find out if she wants it all, don't you think?'

'I don't think she knows.' Charlotte's self-assurance bordered on arrogance.

'So d'you understand why I asked her to go to England?'

'To get rid of her.'

'Jacquie always does as she pleases,' I argued, 'it's her choice. I want her to be well first; then she can make any plans she wants, providing that she doesn't make Mo and Samuel suffer. I'm not risking that. We're broke and they're confused and neglected enough already.'

Whilst I respected anyone who stuck up for Jacquie, I had a feeling that Charlotte had taken on a fight for the sake of it, for her own hawkish pleasure. My weakness made me easy pickings. Charlotte's arguments, however, fell far short in my estimation. They were about loss and gain – love and children seemed to be simply extras.

It felt strange without Jacquie. The chapel had lost its significance, point and purpose. She was the only reason for staying. She'd been its soul during ten years of reconstruction. The chapel was my gift to her and the children and her absence turned it from a burning hearth to a lifeless shell. Although I loved France, and it had been the set, the soap-box for our adventure, it seemed that the show was over and I'd been left behind to turf out the bums, sweep the floor and put the fire out backstage.

Jacquie chose to move in with my family in London. Although she did not really need to, she found work within days and once or twice a week visited a therapist my parents had found. I had the ugly feeling that in having Jacquie to stay with them, my family would become victims of any undesirable consequence. Still, aware as they were of this, their fondness for her overruled and they welcomed her.

Alex, a great friend and seven times a visitor to Even Breaks, made regular visits to Jacquie, took her swimming and phoned me to assure that things were all right. Other than this I heard very little of my wife.

Jacquie had apparently been seeing a counsellor. Perhaps this was the best thing she could have done. At least it was a start, although it had very little to do with getting her off the drugs or even regulating them. In any case I knew none of this, only that she was managing and talking to a woman professional about her illness.

Back in France our little business was struggling. Martha was helping with Mo and Sam when she could and since Jacquie hadn't been with them very much recently they weren't too affected by her absence. I did my best to look after them and felt that the boys were managing, although as a disorganized father I fretted about coping with so much at once. Still, we were lucky, so very lucky to be able to manage at all.

Worryingly, British holiday companies were cutting back and the pound had dropped from the twelve francs it had been worth when we first came to France to seven. Punters were finding cheaper places and the phones were not busy. Yet with the help of Don and Anna I was renting out houses and still hoping for a good season.

'We've got two booked down on the coast now,' said Anna in a positive tone, 'and the little house behind the casino, we'll have almost six weeks on that one.' She smiled, neatly preparing letters for the post. I looked at her and tried to understand where the strength was in her relationship with Don. During the day they hardly spoke and I was oblivious to whatever happened in the evenings. I put their lack of showy affection down to our cultural differences.

I drove with Don to Perpignan to visit my accountant, Indiana, who'd been going over our business plans. He sat behind a huge desk. The place had an air of harsh organization about it and Indiana himself, much as I liked him, appeared as an immense, alcohol-fuelled, chain-smoking, hairy, pockmarked, meatball-guzzling walrus.

'Jacquie is a good wife. She didn't fail your business, you just never recovered from the beating you took in the Alps.' He seemed unable to grasp the fact that few people would have attempted to run a business in the 'hands-on' way that Jacquie and I had. The sheer physical and psychological impact was now plainly obvious. 'I hope you'll be able to make this work.' He whacked the business plan that Don and I had brought in with the back of his hand. 'You'll be okay if you do.'

A Turkish family who had booked the entire chapel had been and gone, their holiday a success. There were sighs of relief as we set about preparing the building for the next occupants. It was odd, looking at neat graphs on the wall in the shed, showing which properties were full and who was coming when. Finally I had a degree of control. At a glance you could tell who the clients were, how long they were staying and when they were due to arrive. Don and Anna assured me that this was how it is done. My sanity was coming back, despite the lack of chapel bookings. At worst, at least I'd know when the game was up.

We'd had a call from Kurt. He was still in England but had other plans. 'I've been offered a job working over there for the Dodger, helping him build up his place. I wanted to make sure you didn't mind,' he said. I couldn't help but see him as a bad influence on Jacquie. When it came to families, Kurt seemed to be a walking Pearl Harbor that often suddenly torpedoed itself. I eventually reasoned that it was pointless to discourage him. If Jacquie wanted to run off, then she'd go.

'Why are you working a million hours a week?' I asked, sitting in the office shed during a rare talk with Jacquie on the phone. 'D'you need money?'

'I don't want you to pay for any more than you have to: you've got the children.' She refused to make an appointment to see a psychiatrist and now insisted on coming home. She had decided that she would stay in the chapel and I'd live in the cottage with the children.

I explained that I was still trying to rent the chapel out. 'You've hardly been in London a month. Why not spend some time going out with our friends and see if you can find out what you really want? Please,' I begged, 'do it for you, the children and me. If you come home like this, I'll end up bringing them up alone with you making guest appearances from next door.'

'It won't be like that.'

'You've promised you'd see a psychiatrist. You promised, Jacq. I need you to know what's wrong and to find out about reducing the junk that you have to take. Please just do that one thing. Get professional advice. Then come home.'

'I don't need it,' she sighed. 'But . . .' There was a silence while she thought. 'Okay,' she suddenly agreed, 'I *promise*.' A moment passed while I tried to work out why she had suddenly become so compliant. 'Next week then,' she said. 'Anyway, I don't see why you have to interfere. I'm doing fine on my own.'

'But darling, you don't need to work so hard. You're supposed to be resting . . .'

'I told you,' she said with proud defiance, 'I *want* my *own* money.' I was too wrapped up in the psychiatric aspects to wonder why Jacquie, living rent-free, with money coming in from me in France, was in need of so much more just now.

An appointment for the following Monday evening was fixed with a reputable psychiatrist that my parents had found. The day before, Jacquie coolly packed her bags and announced to my family that she'd taken a job with a holiday company in Greece and was leaving for the airport shortly. Stunned, they pleaded with her to stay but she'd been secretly sending out her CV for some time and new doors of adventure were opening. Brimming with excitement, she headed out. The extra earnings and the money I'd sent had funded her flight.

A talk with a psychiatrist was obviously something she'd preferred to avoid. I imagined that being a nurse, Jacquie was well aware of her condition and had no intention of allowing anyone to label her or interfere with her own comfortable management of reality. She spent the last evening with a group of our friends, celebrating her departure.

'But what about Rupert and the boys?' asked Alex.

'Let's not talk about that tonight,' said Jacquie. 'We're here to celebrate.'

My father rang me the following afternoon. 'I'm sorry, Rupe. She's gone. She's left no address, just the name of a London-based company. She said she'd call you later and explain.' He listened patiently to my despair. I thanked him and replaced the handset feeling betrayed. Jacquie, I told myself, was blaming me for her time in the clinic but now she was punishing blameless children. I thought about the psychiatrist in the clinic who I felt had dumped Jacquie back into the wild without a reasonable diagnosis. I wanted to pick him up and shake him.

Anna was in the office shed, sitting behind me and dealing with the last of the afternoon mail. I chatted for a while, knowing Martha would be back with the children soon and I'd be on duty. The chapel was quiet and bookings were down. 'I wish I were rich,' I said, 'so I could live here with the kids without tearing my guts out to survive.' Yogi lay across my foot, sighing lazily while I observed Kansas through the window, spinning in the dust, utterly barmy, chasing flies.

'I wish I could buy you a new Land Rover.' Anna smiled faintly. 'I'll help you bath the kids if you like.'

Early in the evening the phone rang. 'Rupe,' said Jacquie, 'I'm at the airport. I've got five minutes before the flight. Did your parents phone you?' In a blither I said they had, that I was crazed with worry and needed an explanation.

'This is a healing place I'm going to,' said Jacquie, 'it's especially for people with stress-related problems. I can find myself, Rupe. I don't need anything else.'

'But you're not a client there, you'll be working. You aren't suffering from *stress*.'

There was a silence.

'Okay, okay,' I said, 'so what happens now? How long?'

'Four months.' She sounded excited. 'Who knows? Maybe longer if I like it there. Maybe I can stay through the winter. I might be able to find work on one of the other islands until next season and work through. I mean, a year or so. Why not?'

'But you were going to come back in two weeks.'

'Rupe, I haven't got time. They're calling the flight. Rupe? Rupe?'

I struggled with anger and spoke coldly. 'You do what you want, Jacquie.' My head reeled. There wasn't time to think of what to say.

'I'll write to you,' she said, sickly sweet. 'Look, it's a good thing for me.'

'No kidding,' I snapped. 'Jacquie will do what Jacquie wants. So *go*, Jacq. Put down the phone.'

'Bye, darling,' said the sticky voice, sudden insecurity ringing through.

I put the phone down, then threw the first object I could find at the bedroom wall and marched out of the house. The mental picture of Jacquie sitting on a beach in Greece spilling her emotions out to an over-stressed businessman on the lookout for a holiday lay spelled: *I'd been a chump*. Of course she'd feel remorse, I told myself, but as Martha arrived with the children and I watched them – chattering Mo, Sam flushed and sleeping in Martha's arms – my sympathies edged back to despair, confusion, anger and hatred.

I told Don and Anna about Greece. They greeted the news with sorrow but not surprise. 'You got to look after yourself now,' said Don.

The phone rang again and I ran to the cottage to beat the answer-phone. It was Jacquie. 'I've got five minutes more. Rupe, listen,' said the rushed yet hesitant voice, 'I love you.' I didn't answer. 'I mean it, Rupe.'

'If you loved me you'd be in London getting help.' She went into pleading mode but I wasn't having any of it. 'Do you know how many times I've said "*Please*" to you? I've had enough, Jacquie, and now suddenly you're concerned? Why the hell is that?'

'I'll write.'

'You'll do what you want, Jacq,' I said, loathing her then. 'So far that's what you've done best.'

26 *Another Woman*

Barbara was painting. Dressed in overalls, she sat on André's bathroom window ledge looking over at me as I stood in the driveway. Their little bungalow, very near to the bijou cottage, seemed to be a victim of the English passion for spring-cleaning. 'Now what does Jacquie want to go and do a thing like that for?' she said, dabbing at tears.

'She's never going to get better, is she?' I asked. Her mother could only respond by agreeing that she did indeed need proper help. I was now faced with a bitterness that wouldn't leave me alone. I felt abused and I was angry. I'd always been very direct with Barbara. Her previous advice to me had been, 'Do what you want,' and 'Be firm,' followed by 'I'll back you up.' These words were about to come crashing down like a wall between us. Barbara showed contempt for the weak hand that I'd shown in my relationship with her daughter. I don't blame her for this but I had decided that things would change now.

In retrospect I can see how it all must have looked: the bewildered husband, the capable daughter who falls victim to strain. It seemed beyond Barbara to investigate *why* Jacquie was doing what she was, or to find sympathetic reasons for my coming defensive stance. She did not reason on the same intellectual level as her daughter though Barbara knew Jacquie well, as a mother would. It seemed to me that in Barbara's view Jacquie loved me and the illness was simply responsible for *all* the other unfortunate things. The shrink, however, felt differently. Personality traits were more to blame in his view.

I wandered back to the chapel. There was another letter from the bank, suggesting we reconsider the relationship, and a message from Kurt. He was now working at the Dodger's place. Don and Anna had gone to see him.

I found a beer and sat in my bedroom, which was also our sitting-room in the cottage. It was a lovely late spring day with brilliant light. Heat was swirling around the long grass in the orchard and the stones in the walls surrounding the cottage were white and dry. It was clear that my business was destined to collapse. It had only ever worked because of the sacrifices we'd made, and even running on adrenaline, I had no chance against the present disastrous downslide of the French economy.

In my head I flicked all the switches, turned all the knobs and sat back, staring into blank space, hoping that the auto-pilot of my childhood would cut in and I could just fly away from everything. How this was affecting my kids I didn't know. They seemed to manage happily enough, although I was blind to so many things.

That evening I felt I had to get out of the house, so Don drove me to a bar in the village. Anna had kindly offered to stay back with Mo and Sam.

We sat in Le Boulou's newest smart café, knocking back a beer or two as the late May sunshine bleached the tin tables and the fake fairground decorations while I voiced the idea of going to see an estate agent and putting the chapel up for sale. Don told me he saw no other option; the market was drying up. The owners of the properties which I'd offered to find renters for were asking why I hadn't found them anyone. Others had taken their houses from me and given them to bigger agencies. I was still rushing about trying to look after swimming-pools, etc. but Don was right, we'd had it.

I envisioned the chapel gone and starting again with the children in a house somewhere nearby. Perhaps I could be an estate agent? This idea made me smile faintly. After all, I knew enough about building. The thought of being alone frightened me. I'd be bankrupt if Jacquie didn't agree to sell and the irony was that despite all this, on paper she was responsible for nothing. Only the boys and I would go to the wall.

I asked Don about Anna. She'd been so supportive lately and I was growing fond of her. Like a dog in a manger, I wondered if they'd stay together, but Don wouldn't commit; he was younger and free-spirited, why should he be looking for more? I felt that for Anna, on the cusp of thirty, things were probably different.

Later I drove to Eddy and Dorothy's. Dorothy rushed about in the kitchen listening intently to the latest stage in my drama. Then we sat on their terrace, which overlooked the vineyards and the coast. Even in that dusky late spring light you could squint and see Argelès and the coastline. I told a surprised Eddy that I wanted to finish with Jacquie.

'If that's what you've decided,' big Eddy said firmly, 'if that's what you *really* want, well, you've got to tell her next time she rings, you've got to tell her that it's over.' He eyed me while pacing around the table. 'And that you never want to see her again and, "I'm sorry, it's terrible, Jacquie, but that's that!"'

The bluntness hit me like a mallet while Eddy poured me a hefty pastis and water, probably hoping and waiting for me to change my mind. But I wouldn't. I didn't want it to be this way but I was angry and afraid of the future.

In this frustrated and rebellious frame of mind I headed from Eddy's to meet two friends Jacquie and I had known for years. The two girls were having dinner in a little restaurant not far from the village. It was a warm evening and when I arrived they had been drinking for a while.

'Will you stay in France?' said the girl sitting on my right as her friend went off to the loo. The restaurant was practically empty, with only faint music and chatter wafting from the kitchen and the pastis that I'd had at Eddy's was kicking in nicely. I looked beside me; I'd always admired this girl but had never thought we would be anything more than friends. Strange, how others see a break-up in a relationship: there was no ill will on the girl's part. Jacquie was a friend but she apparently no longer wanted me. I was suddenly fair game and a free spirit, although I didn't feel that way. Comfort and friendship stared me right in the face.

'I want you to take me home,' said the girl. 'I'm horny as hell.' She swayed from side to side. I gulped, plonking my glass down, suddenly very aware of my Adam's apple rocketing up and down. Her friend returned to the table. 'I've really got to go,' she said, feigning boredom and fatigue. 'Do you want to come back in Rupert's car?'

The lovely creature looked at me. 'Oh, come on. You don't have to feel guilty,' she laughed. I looked at them both. The beer was finished and I felt awkward. I foresaw a little difficulty, what with my confidence blasting through the ceiling and the fear of making a fool out of myself quite near. Old Mother Guilt was there too, clasping a miniature guillotine. Then for a second I envisioned my wife sitting on the sand with some muscular geek on a Greek island. 'Sure, I'll take you home,' I said, chucking my hat over the windmill.

I left her place at three in the morning, resenting myself bitterly. She was nice; what the hell was it with me? I climbed into Bert, who burst into life on command, the only thing to have ignited all evening. Everything about me had gone limp in one sense or another. Humiliated, ashamed, virtually bankrupt and slightly bonkers and now impotent, I decided that this was as far as my confidence would be pushed.

Driving home through the warm darkness, I thought of my children. My past clicked up before my eyes, along with all the absurd things that 'people' simply can't help but do. I remembered my mother: her struggles and times in my childhood home as she'd gradually broken down. Feeling the steel of Bert's frame around me, I could almost replicate the feeling of that weird isolation.

'Where's the gun?' my mother had asked me once when I was about ten. It was the middle of the night and I was glancing nervously towards her bedroom windows.

'I don't know. I'll look for it.' I remember being slightly concerned that evening but I had no idea why. I just knew that she was afraid of something lurking somewhere outside the cottage, in the darkness. This in itself was enough to horrify.

Barefoot, in my pyjamas, I ran through the cottage to Brock's room. We used to pee on the carpet before he'd painted the walls purple and put the Led Zeppelin poster up and had lost interest in me. 'Brock,' I whispered, slightly afraid I'd be hit, 'Brock, Brock.'

I touched his arm, speaking a little louder and tugging. I was skinny and at thirteen he was huge in comparison. Old Brock could get pissed off without even making an effort. For a ten-year-old I was average or maybe smallish, kind of a runt really. Gareth wouldn't have got so angry. He just whacked you anyway and you could be sure he wouldn't miss but he had run away to live with Dad a year ago, so it was just Brock and me now.

'Gerroff!' Brock let out a slurred grumble, turning slowly back under the covers. Gone. Mum's bed was shaking audibly because *she* was shaking, more like vibrating really. It made me homesick. Light from the moon ran through the trees swaying in the wind and made shadows that flickered across the curtains.

'Can't you see?' she asked. 'Look! They're coming. I can see them.'

The bed was strewn with books like *Chariots of the Gods*, and others concerned with alien influences on earth. She'd frightened herself totally out of her wits. It was getting late, really late. I didn't have a watch but as a runt I was fairly animal and I could feel time.

'But they'll have to get through the kitchen door and the one at the bottom of the stairs,' I said, knowing the cottage door was solid. Feeling rather chilly and alone, I searched for more cartridges, only partially going along with all this. I took the four-ten and sat at the top of the stairs, pointing the barrel down towards the darkness and wishing Gareth was back and that I hadn't taken over his room and that I was asleep in *my* little room at the other end of the landing. I'd only used the gun a few times before, always with Brock, but I knew how it worked and where the cartridge went in.

If doors were no problem to *them*, then why use them at all? I asked myself. I suddenly had the horrid thought that *they* might already be in the attic. The attic was evil. I figured I could shoot anything that came up the stairs, even though I'd never hit a rabbit.

'I can hear them,' my mother said, high-strung and pinned to the pillows with fear, 'can't you? Listen. Come in here with me, you'll be safer,' the sinew and tendons in her neck were straining, 'we can lock the door.'

'But what about Brock? He's all on his own!' I blurted, not really *that* worried. I still didn't quite buy into my mother's panic. Anyway, my friend Gavin was staying, sleeping in my room, but he could look after himself, I decided. Childish logic told me that somehow friends were immune to this kind of family danger.

Yet I *was* afraid and pleaded with her, putting the gun on the bed, 'Mum, please call your friends. Please call Margaret.'

The following morning we were told not to leave the house on account of the gamma rays. We'd be going away to rest with her family for a few days, my mother announced. Gavin, as I guessed, was immune to gamma rays and so was his mum who picked him up after breakfast.

Things just weren't easy for our poor mother. If you can't handle the stress but you don't ask for help, it can't be forced upon you. You have to *want* it, but how many of us know what we really need? Somehow people muddle through.

Bert crunched along the gravel in front of the chapel. It wasn't light yet. I sat for a little while, listening to the sounds of summer dawn around me. Forget Jacquie, I told myself. You've got to survive somehow.

27 Lying for Hope

We were sitting round the table down by the pool. Ulric had arrived for a very short visit and Fergus had dropped by to see us both. It was late, perhaps eleven on a Saturday night, and we were all having a drink. I'd noticed André and a tearful Barbara race off earlier in the evening and it had given me an uncomfortable feeling. They were still not back. Tonight was Don's last night at the chapel. Tomorrow I'd deliver him to his flight in Gerona. Mostly we didn't look at each other. I was ashamed and he was astonished and hurt.

Anna sat beside him or at least closer to Don than to me. I felt as if it was all too late. I'd managed to betray a friend and typically, being the extraordinary person he was, Don had told me to look after Anna and never let her down or he'd come after me and give me a good walloping. Anna was tougher than I was; this was probably why I'd been so drawn to her. She was also very pretty, sympathetic and thoughtful. Don had known nothing until the afternoon he'd walked into my room to find Anna and me embracing on my bed.

'Oh Jesus, Don,' I'd said stupidly, 'come back. It's not what you think.' But, of course . . . it was.

It all created severe confusions. How I possibly managed to convince myself that I could enter a relationship so soon after ten years of marriage, I'll never know. I seemed to be on a panic-driven spree. This was another person's life I had thrown into the arena, a deeply selfish act. My own lies and self-delusions fascinate me. After Jacquie was gone I would have justified any action in order to make my life easier to cope with. Don, eight years my junior, had told me that I needed to toughen up. Amazing what one does when metaphorically one's ship is sinking.

Jacquie had been in Greece for only about a week. On her third telephone call I'd told her I'd had enough and that we were finished.

'What's happening there?' she'd asked. 'It's Anna, isn't it?' At *that* point Anna had yet to be kissed. But it was an advancing possibility. I asked if Jacquie was getting bored out there already. 'Don't be nasty, Rupe.' She seemed less concerned about Anna than about my decision. 'I just can't believe that you're ending it. Does my mother know what's going on?'

'Jacquie, you left of your own accord without a single thought for anyone but yourself or about coming back. Your mum doesn't know how to react. Now you fucking live with it.' There was a silence. 'I want a life, Jacq. What did you expect,' I said, throwing her words back at her, '*home-baked bread*?'

'Nothing,' she said nervously.

'If business gets any worse I'll put the chapel on the market. I've no choice, Jacq. I'll give you your share. If we don't think about it soon there'll be nothing left. Don't worry about the cash. You always take what you want, remember?' I said bitterly.

'God! Everything's happening there,' she said, her voice stressed. 'Is Mum home?'

So much had happened in the few days since she'd run off to Greece. I'd decided to stand and fight. Auto-pilot had cut in and just like the lost American space family on that childhood TV show, defensive shields were going up around me like mad.

'I've rarely seen a man so devoted to his children,' said André one afternoon, as we sat on a bench by the pool. 'But another woman so soon . . . Rupert,' he grabbed my knee and shook his head, 'this is probably a mistake, don't you think?'

I could only agree and felt a measure of shame, but like I said, I was going to stand and fight. I was going to put my faith in anyone who would believe in me. I was certainly fond of Anna but I was undeniably having trouble with *any* feelings. I couldn't be sure if the relationship wasn't simply stemming from a fear of being alone.

'Haven't you ever thought of leaving?' he went on, fascinated by my weirdness. 'I mean, I look at you and I wonder how you've managed to stay so long. In your shoes perhaps I'd just hit the road and leave them all to sort it out themselves, Jacquie, the lot.'

'And destroy the children? I just couldn't. They've no one!'

He smiled. Maybe he'd got the answer from me that he'd hoped for. André was a sensitive man and he'd watched the boys from the moment that they were born. I knew that he loved them. Barbara had also been over, helping with laundry, anything, allowing me more time to work. She had seen Don's long face sagging and had made short work of figuring out the rest. I wondered if she'd finally decided to go on a mission to save her daughter's marriage. Too late, I thought; after such emotional carnage what could she imagine there was left to salvage?

So now it was late evening around the table by the pool and with each hour that passed I'd reset my order of airports that Jacquie could be flying into. Barbara and André had been gone too long for Perpignan, so it had to be Barcelona, Montpellier or Toulouse.

Sure enough, André's car floated past and within moments Barbara's voice came through the darkness: 'Rupert, can you come up here for a moment?'

I rose from the table eyeing the others, and Anna's stricken face. I could see that Fergus might easily laugh: it was that awfulness which borders on absurdity.

'Whatever happens don't let them push you,' said Don coolly, 'don't take any shit.'

I walked up and found Barbara who seemed desperately nervous. 'Now, don't be angry, Rupert,' she said hastily. 'Jacquie's back.'

'Where is she?' I asked, trying to keep my thoughts straight.

We walked across the gravel towards the bijou cottage. 'Don't be angry with her.'

'I'm not angry, Barbara, but you could have said something before doing this.'

Inside the cottage the children were asleep in their room. The tiny kitchen was empty, as was the bathroom. I looked around and found Jacquie sitting on the edge of our bed in the dark.

We hugged one another. I felt almost dead inside, unwilling to trust even the slightest move she made. If you open your heart, I told myself, she's going to ruthlessly cut you down in the days to come. Sheepishly she moved into the light of the kitchen. Barbara pushed us together, throwing her arms about us and weeping great tears, whereas between Jacquie and I there were none.

Jacquie's face showed tiredness and remorse, her eyes heavy. I knew this look to be capable of changing within seconds and so watched her with reluctant concern. I didn't want this sudden, forced reconciliation, I told myself as we untangled. Did I honestly have any faith in this? Feeling almost detached, I addressed them both. 'What *are* you two doing?' I asked. 'What on earth do you two think you're up to?'

'I'll go,' said Barbara, 'I'll leave you alone.'

I noticed that Jacquie had bleached streaks of her fringe platinum blonde. I envisioned the party nights in Greece and the evenings by the sea and wondered how long she'd hang around here if things weren't exciting enough.

'No, Barbara, why don't you stay?' I said, irritated. 'You created this situation. You might as well stick around now you're part of it and see what happens.' I perched on the edge of the table. 'So what do I do? Don's leaving tomorrow.' I stared at Jacquie. 'So that just leaves you, me and Anna. You couldn't have timed it better, Barbara.'

'You'll have to send Anna home,' Barbara insisted.

I stared at her. Why the bloody hell should I? Not so long ago Jacquie had been determined that Anna and I were made for one another. I glanced at Jacquie as the phrase, '*Be careful what you wish for; it may come true*', crossed my mind. 'I won't do it,' I replied. 'How would you suggest I run the business alone?'

'With your wife, with Jacquie,' Barbara said indignantly.

'But she doesn't want anything to do with what I'm doing. It's too dull, remember? And Jacquie? Are you suddenly better? Goodness me. Tell me, why did you come home? For the children? For me?' There was a silence. 'Like hell,' I said scornfully.

'Because this is my home.'

'Bollocks. You came home because you stood to lose something and old Barbara there didn't want that to happen.' I turned to Barbara. 'And where were you six months ago when your daughter was sticking it in my back and you saw me in a bloody mess? You didn't give a stuff then, did you?'

'Shhh . . .' said Jacquie, 'the children.'

This rather did me in. 'Oh, as if you give a shit! Have you even been in to kiss them?' I stared at her. 'Yeah, just like I thought. You've only been away nearly two fucking months.'

'I didn't want to get involved,' said Barbara.

'So now suddenly when I fight back it's all right to do so?' I shouted. 'Barbara, I won't ask you what changed your mind, because I know. IT'S SITTING ACROSS THE GRAVEL WITH A CROSS ON TOP OF IT. Never mind the *children*, not when Jacquie stands to lose the bricks and mortar and control. Is that right?' Instantly I regretted saying this but it was all too late. Hatred would solidify now.

'Jacquie, you'd better stay with your mother tonight,' I fumed, 'while I think how to sort things out.'

Anna and I drove Don to Gerona the following day. It was an awful, silent hour, lashed with rain. I'd pleaded for his friendship and he'd departed, taking it along with him.

I arrived back at the chapel to find that Jacquie had moved into the bijou cottage and that I no longer had claims to my bed, unless I chose to sleep in it with her. She announced that she would also be taking on the children's care 100 per cent, full-time. Martha would no longer be needed. Insanely, her mother seemed to think that this was the right thing too, regardless of Jacquie's psychiatric condition. This angered me; in my eyes it appeared to be nothing more than emotional blackmail. Suddenly, for the sake of a decapitated marriage, the intrinsic value of our children seemed to be reduced to bartering chips. If Jacquie kept this up I knew she'd more than likely return to the clinic for good.

I decided to stand my ground. I would not be manipulated. If, however, Jacquie agreed to Martha helping and to getting some form of psychiatric assistance, then the door was open to debate.

Time passed slowly as Jacquie carried on with the siege, using the children to prove her mothering abilities. The result, as I had warned her and Barbara, was misery and suffering. She sat in the cottage as the children played around her, staring numbly out of the window like a tethered wild animal.

The chapel became a barbaric emotional battleground as Anna tried her best to be anywhere but in Jacquie's face. I returned from the village one afternoon to find that Kurt had been chatting to Jacquie and was on his way out somewhere. 'Is Jacquie okay?' I asked, motioning towards the cottage. He told me that she was unhappy. I felt sorrow, but I did not dare to give in.

One morning Anna and I were in the chapel kitchen when Jacquie marched through, her feet clunking on the tiles. She began rummaging for something, or perhaps nothing: here was an excuse for confrontation. 'This is my life, my home,' she said.

I knew the stand-off would have to end soon but reminded her that she should have thought about that when she was tearing it apart. With a shrink nowhere in sight the manipulative phrase, 'But I was ill,' just simply wasn't acceptable any more. She was right though, in spite of everything Jacquie deserved to be the mistress of her own home.

In the afternoon Barbara approached to put out the washing. The line ran to one side of the office-shed windows, overlooking the rougher side of the orchard some feet below. Barbara hardly looked up as she pegged up sheets and other chapel linen.

'Hello, Rupert,' she replied icily. I asked her if she was angry with me. 'I just hope you know what you're doing,' she muttered. She looked up at me with contempt. 'Jacquie's your wife, for goodness' sake, she's sick.'

Why Barbara didn't leave Jacquie in the bed she'd so cleverly engineered for herself in Greece I'll never know. Jacquie had obviously wanted to come home but again, she left me no choice. I had been expected to accept whatever decision she and Barbara made without consultation. Everyone has limits and Greece had been the final straw for me. I felt I had been reasonable for too long. It was over.

I believe that a crucial part of care for the mentally ill should be an assessment of those directly affected by the sufferer. These people are, more than likely, used to living in an altered state and are probably, as I was, deeply affected in little understood ways.

Lorna came over, fished out of the car by George after sustaining a fracture. She was now walking on crutches, her broken ankle a mass of stitches and steel pins. I could see her sum up the situation as Barbara and I separated.

'Oh my Lord!' Lorna gasped. 'When I spoke of "throwing your hat over the windmill," *this* wasn't exactly what I meant. She's got to go, Rupe. I mean it, boyo. That Anna's a right one.' As ever George said very little, quietly observing the garden.

Whatever anyone thinks of this confusing and cruel scenario, Anna should not be seen as a predator. She was a witness to the entire drama, feeling sorrow for the children and concern for us. She would never have become involved with me if she had felt that there was hope for Jacquie and me. It was only when limits were breeched to absurdity, and at my invitation that she ventured into my life, giving her support without question. My hopes were somehow to recover my emotions enough to give her something to look forward to.

I arranged for Anna to stay with Marie-Antoinette and Louis for a little while. I felt that they understood the problems, but asking this of them was hardly thoughtful. Piggy in the middle is an awful place to be and they had no wish to divide their loyalties.

'And what about Mo and Sam?' asked Marie one evening as the three of us sat quietly.

'Hard to tell. I pray it won't upset them too much,' I said blindly. 'Perhaps if I'm able to sell the chapel we'll move.' I grasped Anna's hand.

'What if it doesn't sell?' Marie asked. 'Or if Jacquie won't agree with it?'

'Then we'll go anyway, maybe. I'll declare bankruptcy and just take the boys and go. It's a sacrifice. I've made up my mind.' I tried to sound convinced and Anna squeezed my fingers.

Charlotte was coming to the house more and more. This woman, of whom Jacquie and I had always been so wary, had now become useful in an almost evangelical sense. Charlotte made no bones about it. She wanted reconciliation between us and she wanted to mastermind it. This had nothing to do with God's laws, hell no. It seemed to be almost a game to her, a battle of wills. She did not realize that the harder she pushed, the deeper in I would dig. Her attacks were destroying us, actually making whatever was left of us a source of deeper distrust.

Interfering with a battered marriage is probably the most foolish thing an outsider can ever do. I needed time to go berserk, run off with Anna if need be, to find out where normality was; time to recover and perhaps snap out of it, or perhaps not. I felt that Jacquie should have stayed in Greece until she burned her party phase out and realized how wonderful her lovely home had been for all those years. Charlotte, almost never mentioning the welfare of the children, brought only conflict and salt for our wounds.

'I'm not leaving until you call that bitch Anna and tell her that you're going back to your married life,' Charlotte announced one day. The result was a bitter fight leaving Jacquie and me cut off from one another for days. The vulgarity of the intrusion angers me still, yet Jacquie enjoyed Charlotte's visits. If I refused to comply then the guilt was mine. In a warped sense, Charlotte was offering Jacquie absolution.

Within a week poor Anna had left. I'd put her on the plane back to England and had returned to the chapel in deepest confusion. The ghastly scenes and the hatred had been too difficult for any of us to endure any longer. Selling the chapel was the only chance for Jacquie and me to do anything now, together or apart.

Without Anna there to help me I had spent my days thundering about between the office shed and the rented houses, settling disputes, floods, broken windows, taps and wells, finding doctors for clients with broken toes, massive sunburn, bouts of gout and impetigo, the odd pregnancy and other human dramas. I sent out brochures and returned deposits, organized the cleaning of the various places and, as usual, took Mo to and from the village school. Inside I was the epitome of disorder but somehow the violence of forced change was good, cruel but good.

In order to cope with the diabetes I'd become a blood-testing fiend. I'd been able to do this only because a kindly diabetic client in England who'd holidayed with Even Breaks had sent me a supply of testing equipment which, in my days of denial, I'd never used. These things were now my lead to freedom and stability. The woman who sent them never knew the importance of her gifts.

I slept in the curate's house alone while Jacquie remained in the bijou cottage and our bed. With her mother's help, we now cared for the boys between us. Our evenings together were quiet, distant and soothed along by the television, or spent in conflict and loathing following the odd visit from Charlotte, pushing at the ringside.

Sometimes we'd curl up, silent, isolated in each other's arms, bewildered. On my birthday we went to the beach and sat in a restaurant until all the tables were cleared and our candle had fallen down inside the bottle. Feeding on memories like frightened tourists, not wishing to try anything too new, we laughed, safe in the confines of the past.

'Won't you just change your mind?' she asked. I wanted to so badly just then. I decided to test the water and ask her to tell me more about what she really liked and about the travelling she wanted to do.

'I need it, Rupe, all the time.' She shrugged. 'I'm like a shark. If I stop moving, you know, I'll die.'

We wandered down the beach, she dreaming of adventure while I quietly wondered how long we'd be able to hold on to our house.

Two evenings later our accountant Indiana turned up for his occasional business and whisky session. He'd settled nicely, with a tot, chatting to Jacquie. I arrived home late from fixing a house on the hillside and was taken aback when Indiana began accusing me of not reaching the targets that Don and I had set. I pointed out that holiday companies were going bust all around us but he raised his fist in semi-drunken admonishment. 'You dirty little . . .' he said, much to Jacquie's delight. He looked round as she left the room. 'And what about your wife?' he hissed. 'How can you do this to her?'

It was dark in the cramped cottage kitchen and with her exit I realized that Jacquie had set me up nicely. We had worked with Indiana for some years and he was a friend, his fondness for Jacquie immeasurable.

He pulled me nearer, his pockmarked face strained, almost as if he were in pain. 'She's *so* pure. Not like the rest,' he scowled. I begged him to understand. 'Now, *you* listen to me,' he shouted, turning almost puce and slapping me hard across the face. '*You* just don't apprecia—'

I staggered backwards, my face numb, while almost immediately he offered some friendly apology based on love and sympathy for Jacquie.

'What the hell did she say to you before I came in?' I snapped. Jacquie was becoming ever more cunning. I left the room and took Bert for a ride.

We stumbled through the days, while I phoned Anna, lying to myself and to her about how I hoped it could all work for us and how I'd find solutions and bring up the boys without ever allowing them to suffer. The only person to hear the truth was Jacquie, who seemed to distort it and then redistribute it.

Occasionally Jacquie and I would sleep together, driven either by longing for comfort or the loneliness that comes when someone's love is no longer there but you can make believe for a while. Old friends visited and were bewildered by what they saw. It's so easy to pass judgements when you haven't been through the mangle yourself. Peter, a friend who had known us long before we were married, recalled some of the happiest days of my life, simply by describing Jacquie in days gone by. He reminded me of where my loyalties should be, and my heart sank deeper into the swamp of confusion and betrayal. Still, I was not going to shut Anna out. I felt that alone with Barbara, Jacquie and Charlotte I'd be slowly cannibalized.

It was my father's sixtieth birthday the following weekend and I'd made up my mind to be with him. Brock had arranged a party and I'd promised that I'd stay for three days and return on the Sunday. I was unwilling to leave Jacquie any longer than that. She looked tired. Her unrelenting demonstration of caring for the boys full-time and refusing help from Martha was taking a heavy toll.

'Will you see Anna?' she asked.

'Yes,' I replied, feeling dishonourable.

On the Friday I drove both of us to Perpignan to meet the bus going to London, then handed Bert's keys to Jacquie. I felt deeply concerned for her, yet wondered exactly which face I was being permitted to see. Nevertheless, the distance in her eyes seemed alarming. I was anxious about leaving her, about her driving, making her promise to be careful. Looking so sad, Jacquie waved, and I tried to keep her in sight until the last possible second. I wanted to get off the bus, but then I thought of my father and knew I should be with him there even though, more than anything, I still somehow hoped that Jacquie and I could recover the happiness we'd had.

Speeding through the darkness on my way out of the Roussillon valley, sitting in the very front, deep in thought, I gazed out over the shallow estuaries as they shimmered through the warm, moonlit evening. A shooting star fell over the oyster beds where, ten years before, half awake, having climbed from the car with England far behind, I'd seen the sun over the water and the flamingos for the very first time.

28 *Letting Go of the Wheel*

'How was it?' asked Jacquie brightly. 'How was your father?'

We talked about the party and I asked how she'd managed over the three days. Things had turned out okay, it seemed. There at the airport she wore a calm smile which I hadn't seen in months. Her face carried a look of quiet confidence which was tremendously warming.

'You've been taking your medicine, haven't you?'

'Yes, but less of it.' She gave a proud smile. 'Can you tell?'

'Sure. I know you're a little unsteady but you'll get it just right soon and be fine. You seem much better.'

We drove back from Gerona and over the frontier in the early hours. 'Did you see Anna?' At last.

I felt sick. I had promised Anna that I would make a stand and not give in to Jacquie, yet at the same time my instincts were telling me to stop this crazy affair, to stay and try for peace. Still, I was prudent, despite the apparent calm and control Jacquie displayed.

'What did you decide?'

'I don't know.' I fidgeted, passing the autoroute ticket to the man at the *péage*. 'Right now I suppose you and I should end it, we're no good for each other, we're both falling to bits.' A long silence followed as we descended the mountain into France.

'Sometimes I feel as if I'm possessed,' said Jacquie with an empty laugh, 'as if the devil's done this.' She looked neither at me nor away. 'Like he's inside me.'

I could not bear to hear this. She was in pain and I was not helping. I knew then that I could never just turn my back. The pledges I had made to Anna now seemed impossible but the recent past reminded me of just what could happen if I softened.

291

'Don't say that. There's *no* devil. It's just you and me and a big mess. Look, can't we just *not* make any promises?' I pleaded. 'You said it yourself, you can't stand the expectations, so let's just take the future one day at a time and see? No lies; please, Jacq. Just try. We just take our time. I need time to see what's what.'

'Will you finish it with Anna?'

'I can't promise anything and neither can you.' I spoke with my heart. 'I'm in a mess.' This was cowardly, but I was at least being truthful.

'I know,' said Jacquie sadly. 'You don't trust me any more.'

We arrived home before dawn and sat at the tables Jaffa had made in the chapel. I was faced with an undeniable love for Jacquie that was now forcing me into a life of utter contradiction. It was bizarre being in the building alone, the two of us, in the heat and heart of the summer. This had only ever happened when the chapel was being built. Nothing was out of place. The rough milky plaster walls glowing with the softness of the lights and the white tiled floors with the thin line of blue crossing in the centre seemed so welcome. The curved cupboards in the kitchen and the huge stainless-steel cooker, standing where the altar had once been, shone as if the house was a showroom, a front-loader's dream.

Marie-Antoinette arrived at the cottage at lunchtime. She'd often kindly bring us food, knowing how hectic our lives had become. We sat down to eat.

'I feel an awful pain in my chest,' said Jacquie, bewildered as she sipped water. 'I feel possessed.'

'I've found this marvellous woman,' said Marie, the language differences apparently making her oblivious to the dark problem that Jacquie was really describing. 'She works with the forces in the body, honestly, she's brilliant. I've had pains like that before, I pulled muscles in my shoulder and . . .'

'That's not really what Jacquie means,' I tried to explain, scooping a spoon of baked beans into Sam's mouth. 'I think—'

'I'll go and see her,' rushed Jacquie. 'I've got to get this thing off me.'

'Madame Romoon's the name,' said Marie. 'She's a radio-kinetosatisarhumbatherapist in Maureillas.' Seeing my suppressed mirth, Marie went on to justify this: 'She's got a diploma.' She tried to look serious but couldn't resist the urge to laugh. In France you have to have a diploma to be assumed good at anything. You have to have a title and a certificate. The woman in Maureillas was probably a credible physio-come-aromatherapist; I never did find out.

There was news that Kurt had moved from the Dodger's place to Collioure. He'd found lodgings with a friend of a friend.

The following afternoon Jacquie had things to get in the village. We decided to go together and pick up Mo from school first. Jacquie wasn't particularly keen on the school run but there was no real choice. If she wanted to go to town this was the only time I was able to go too. I'd had to be in several places at once that afternoon – the weakness of the pound had begun to take effect. The grapevine sang that flights to Perpignan from England would be less frequent, that the bigger holiday companies were pulling out. Our last chance, my little rental management business, seemed to be running on borrowed time but I needed to attend to it.

Months before, I'd informed the school that Jacquie had been ill. They'd often asked how the little English nurse was doing. A teacher passed. *Bonjour,*' she smiled as she saw us waiting quietly by the school gates. 'It's good to see you. It's been a very long time. Are you feeling better?'

'*Ça va,*' said Jacquie, looking strained. 'I've had a depression.'

'You poor thing,' said the teacher. 'I'm sure you'll go from strength to strength—'

'Because my husband's been having an affair,' said Jacquie. My head spun. 'It's made me *so* ill,' Jacquie went on in her best feeble tones, 'I can't manage the children.' The teacher nodded, her eyes cutting towards me like lasers. 'Things are terrible,' Jacquie insisted, 'he just left me and went off with her this weekend.'

Aghast, the schoolmistress's jaw swung open like a drawbridge, while Jacquie turned and walked long-faced to the car.

"Why did you say that?' I hissed, as Mo ran ahead with his little brother.

'I felt like it,' said Jacquie, enjoying the power immensely.

'You bitch! All these months I've said how wonderful you are and how I hoped you'd come back. I never put it about that you'd gone lezzy and berserk and dumped your husband and children in favour of a holiday job in Greece. Holy shit! You're a snake! Have you been getting tips from Charlotte?'

'Well, we're going to Charlotte's tonight, aren't we?' she said, oblivious. 'There's a circus. Charlotte says her nanny's going to take the children there while we have dinner, so you should really enjoy the atmosphere. Or you can go with the children and join your mates in the ring.'

'Very funny,' I said. 'Look. Please, Jacq, if we go can we try not to be nasty to each other tonight? If Charlotte gets into it we'll only end up miserable. Can't we just do things one day at a time? What you just did there: I mean, that was a lie, that was unnecessary.'

'I'll ask Mum for her car,' said Jacquie, tired of the conversation, 'then at least the kids will be comfy and sleep on the way back.' She looked at the boys. 'Anyway, I couldn't face the noise in the Land Rover.'

Something was still terribly wrong. Her behaviour at the school was so sudden, cruel and effective, yet she had apparently been doing so well. She'd even agreed to see a therapist and had been there twice. It wasn't a psychiatrist, but I'd had hopes. It was at least a start. The trip down to Charlotte's shop on the coast took twenty-five minutes in Barbara's little blue Fiat and I still felt dazed. 'I want it all back,' said Jacquie, as we whistled along under a huge canopy of plane trees. 'Just as if nothing ever happened.'

I looked in the mirror. Sam had dozed off. Mo sat quietly, watching the vineyards pass by with the pattern of the plane tree leaves flickering across his face. 'Jacquie, I'm sorry,' I said. 'It took such a long time for you to break me. There were lots of chances. I never turned from you until you showed me that there was no hope.'

She looked so sad. 'Can't we start again?'

'I couldn't go back, not to what we were. You're not going to change. Look what you just said at the school, and what about the boys? They'd grow up hating us.'

'We had to make money,' she snapped, suddenly sharp. 'It's not my fault that you were too weak to cope.'

'It wasn't for the money and *you* know it,' I said coldly. I was still thinking about the episode at the school and how I'd feel the next time I went there. 'And as for being weak, remember Jacquie, I fought long and hard for us. You made me beg before you lost my faith. Was that weakness?'

'Oh, FUCK YOU.' She turned sharply and gazed out the window.

'Okay,' I smouldered, 'let me tell you about Lola. Remember Lola?'

'What about Lola?' Jacquie switched her full attention to me.

'Why do you think she left so suddenly?' There was a silence, while Jacquie stared at me, waiting. I reminded her of the one week off in seven months. The week she couldn't leave free for fear that the endless party might stop.

'So you were having an affair?' she asked.

'For a day or so,' I said miserably, 'but who knows? If she'd have stayed we might even have taken the babies to the beach,' I added bitterly, 'imagine that! *Our* kids at the seaside with one of us before they grew up!' The car rumbled along, whistling a little, and Jacquie sat silent, stunned.

'Look behind you, Jacq, go on.' I motioned towards the children. 'They'll be gone before you know it, and they'll know what's what. They'll remember vague outings with Jaffa, Martha, and the inside of the bijou cottage. They'll love and stick with the ones that gave a damn about them.'

Jacquie seemed to reason this out, as if putting all the pieces of the jigsaw together. 'It's all my fault,' she said, as if experiencing a moment of terrible clarity, holding her face in her hands. 'Oh, my God.' She became sorrowful and heartbreaking in her remorse. 'I've destroyed you and me and our children,' she wept.

'I never wanted this,' I said, close to tears myself, and motioned again towards the children. 'If you could have just weathered the storm, they'll be bigger soon and it won't even be half the struggle. But you won't,' I said, as tears ran down her cheeks, 'something exciting will come along and . . .'

Wishing to save a relationship yet knowing it will destroy you is truly dreadful. My feelings were all over the place, I was sick with love and simultaneous intense distrust. We arrived, reeling, at the bustling seaside village and by the time we'd parked outside Charlotte and her husband's little shop we were as pale as dough.

'I can't get out, Rupe,' said Jacquie, 'I can't face dinner. The Witch is in me; she's inside me. It hurts in my chest. I need to go.' I looked at her with a mixture of fondness and concern. 'You know it was terrible while you were away,' she said. 'I thought Jezebel had won.'

'The Witch can never win, Jacquie,' I promised.

'I was afraid I was going to hurt the children,' she said under her breath, 'so Mum stayed with me on Saturday night.' I looked at her in astonishment. 'She didn't tell you because she thought it would make you turn more against me.'

Jacquie held my hand. We were still sitting quietly in the car as I turned my thoughts to Barbara and this well-meaning but fundamentally alarming behaviour. It concerned the safety of our children. 'What happened to the truth?' I asked. I did not think to ask *how* Jacquie thought she would hurt the children. I only understood that she meant something physical. This was outside anything that I could ever believe Jacquie to be capable of. She was a nurse, a healer. She truly loved her babies. I was deeply worried. Shouldn't we be talking to the shrink? How could Barbara let this go?

I opened the door and began helping the boys out. It amazes me now to think that I allowed myself to believe that Mo, at four years old, hadn't taken in at least part of our conversation. I smelled the sea breeze, wishing it could clear my mind like a filter, then made an effort to get moving and engage.

'Come on,' I smiled weakly, 'things are going to be okay now. Dinner will help and you can talk to Charlotte. She's your friend.' I still wanted to hear the rest of the truth from Barbara.

We sat in a little room behind the bead curtain that led to Charlotte's shop counter, while Charlotte prepared the dinner and occasionally Jacquie shot out to serve the odd punter. I was dispatched to fetch Charlotte's husband, Ferdinand, from a nearby shop and returned with him in half an hour or so.

We all moved outside and sat at a fold-up table on one side of the busy public walkway. Someone gave me a glass of wine. It was lovely, strong stuff. Jacquie seemed drowsy, I assumed from the medicine – even so, she was distracted and deeply depressed. I became anxious, deeply regretting our earlier conversations.

Charlotte's nanny edged past with Mo and Sam. I noticed that Sam looked chilly. It was July, a little after eight in the evening; the sun was in its last half hour and the shoreline breeze was slapping the ropes against the masts on the moorings as it grew cooler in the fading light. I went to the car to find Sam a sweater. Without a word Jacquie followed somewhere close behind. 'Rupe, I need the keys,' she asked as I withdrew from the car.

Behind her the children and nanny were negotiating steps on their way to the circus. 'Sure,' I reached out with the keys, 'what d'you need?'

She snatched them. 'I've got to go. It's the Witch, Rupe. It's this evil. I can't do it. It's so heavy on my chest.' She leaped into the car. 'Madame Romoon, she's the only one that can help me.'

'But that's Maureillas! You'll be gone for hours. We've just come that way. Jacquie, stop. The woman's not a spiritualist, she's a—'

I tried to prevent her from shutting the door but she'd slammed it, pushed down the lock, and begun fumbling with the ignition. 'Jacquie, don't. Please,' I begged, 'there's no need for this.' The engine connected but I carried on. 'You're among friends. One day at a time, please. *Come on*, Jacq, don't believe in the Witch.' I moved in front of the car, glancing over to find the children watching, puzzled. She accelerated and without choice I jumped aside. 'Jacquie!' I shouted.

I went back up to Charlotte and Ferdinand and explained. Ferdinand thought she'd be back in an hour or two after she'd cooled off. It seemed logical. I watched Charlotte as we talked, even partly admiring the way she, above most of Jacquie's friends, had tried to assist, no matter how maddened I had been by her intrusions. Too bad that she had condemned me so readily. The wedge she had driven had helped Jacquie and me to wreck most of what had remained.

I had no wish to borrow a car and follow Jacquie. From the episode outside the school I felt sure any intervention would only kick back on me in some unpleasant way. I was already gearing up for a wry bullying from Charlotte for being an adulterer but she held back and I in turn tried to stick to bland conversation while hoping that Jacquie would pitch up soon in a better frame of mind.

At ten-thirty Charlotte's nanny took the boys and me home. I hoped to find the little blue Fiat parked in the chapel driveway but there was no sign of it. Having tucked the boys up, I phoned Marie-Antoinette and explained. Within minutes she arrived like an angel to watch over the children, telling me not to go too fast as I sped out to Bert and began scanning the roads on my way to Maureillas.

I knew the route Jacquie would have taken from the coast, but having picked it clean, driving slowly, I discovered that even in the village of Maureillas itself there was no sign of her. Being one of the retirement-style villages, that evening, as usual, it was almost as quiet as death. Growing ever more anxious, I headed back to the chapel. Marie called Louis who drove fast down the road towards the coast. On one side the fields and little roads spread like capillaries into the black and the depths of the vineyards beyond. On the other, looming up into the moonlight, was the vastness of the Albères, the huge foothills of the Pyrenees.

We turned back more than half-way to the coast, admitting that the task was impossible, then drove up towards the Dodger's place, but I felt it was too late to drive in. There was also no sign of the Fiat, which was enough to convince me that Jacquie wasn't there.

It was three in the morning before I went to the police. Louis drove me through Le Boulou to the severe, bullet- and bomb-proof police station on the Perpignan road.

We pressed the button in the wall. Louis explained that we'd come to report a missing person. He always dealt with authority well, his army background helped.

After a long silence the duty sergeant appeared. He was tall, bearded, with a lived-in face, dark eyes and thick eyebrows, about forty and slightly bulky for his height. Pinned to his chest like a medal was a scuba-diver's insignia. He ushered us in.

The police station itself was nothing much once you were inside. There were a couple of cells to one side of the lobby and we stood in front of a large counter. Immediately behind that was a radio room. The coffee pot had the key position next to the wireless, along with scraps of paper, a couple of microphones and the odd dirty spoon. Otherwise there was nothing to suggest that humans occupied the building. I explained the basic facts and the direction of Jacquie's departure.

'Did you have an argument?' asked the sergeant.

'She was upset,' I admitted as the man made a face, which suggested that all had become clear. 'But it's not just a simple row. I'm worried because she's not well,' I explained, 'she'd be so vulnerable.'

It dawned on me that the domestic dispute would now give the police the wrong idea. Jacquie and I would simply join the ranks of all the other husbands, lovers, wives and mistresses on file who'd fought and gone to cry at a friend's for the night.

The fact that she was suffering from mental illness *had* to be got across, but like most things in France, you had to have documentation. There had to be a rubber stamp if you were to be taken seriously and I was aware that the doctor in the clinic had no intention of giving Jacquie a label. It quickly became obvious that tragically there would be no extra effort from the police. No label, no credibility. I cursed the psychiatrist. I explained about her stay in the clinic, but again, without the official paperwork it meant little.

Just as unlabelled, Jacquie could get away with murder, without a label she now had little defence against destroying herself – or wandering about and being murdered. We lived in a frontier region where people pass through all the time and a good few of them were likely to be dodgy. In her state she would be easy pickings.

'She's probably gone off to friends or something,' said the officer predictably. 'I'll contact the station down on the coast. Make sure you call us in the morning when she shows up,' he said, then added, 'Did she have anything with her?'

'Nothing. Just her clothes.' I shrugged.

'No money? What about her handbag?'

'She left it where we were having dinner. Look, I'm seriously concerned.' Again I explained that she was ill, fragile and vulnerable, but it was late, I'd already said all this and he was obviously bored. I returned to the bijou cottage and thanked Marie and Louis. It was four in the morning, probably half an hour before Louis's habitual time to knock off work. Soon it would be dawn.

I had to pull myself together. The children would be up before eight and hungry. I pricked my finger, tested my blood-sugar, not sure where the hell I was with it, climbed into bed and waited for Jacquie.

PART SIX

29 *Away from Eden*

Morning came with no sign of my wife. I was feeding and dressing the children with an awful certainty that something terrible had happened. Until recently we'd never allowed a dispute to cross the night. This was beyond anything I'd ever known her to do.

Still in the same clothes, I plodded the few yards to Barbara's and explained, dreading her reaction, then contacted the police again. Still nothing, but they'd be over later, they said, for a statement.

'You made her feel as if she wasn't worth anything,' Barbara accused. Then she added crisply, 'I don't see what she's got to come back for.' The horror of Barbara's logic has haunted me ever since. At the time I felt like simply replying, '*The children*,' but Barbara had every reason to be upset. I began calling friends, even tried the mill restaurant, but had no idea if Caroline would tell me of Jacquie's whereabouts even if she knew.

The gendarmes arrived in the middle of the afternoon. The same tall officer made his way into the chapel and introduced himself as Sergeant Jaillard. He looked around with seemingly respectful surprise. Then we sat in the little bar at Jaffa's chessboard table and he began making notes. Another gendarme followed, having searched through the other parts of the building. Since in the heat of summer most of the doors were open or simply didn't have locks, his job had been easy. He'd snooped like a weasel and mentioned to Jaillard that my clothes were all over one room, which was sixty yards from the bijou cottage and the marital bed. I found it bizarre that they could do this without asking and then not even say something like, 'I had a look around, hope you don't mind.' The power of a uniform is unnerving and I accepted this in the hope that something might be done.

I was determined that Jacquie's vulnerability should be documented but I was also protective and wanted to keep her strangeness over the past months away from the limited ideas of the village police. Primitive conclusions could be drawn and things were already bad enough with my statement flooding out, painting me in as the adulterous cad. This alone would make many simple police minds disturbingly suspicious.

It seemed that in most disappearances someone in the family is responsible and, as I'd been at odds with my wife and had also been unfaithful, I fitted the bill nicely. I was aware of this and was already concerned.

'How old are your children?' asked Jaillard.

'Four and two.'

'Don't you worry now,' he said, with a smile which did little to reassure me, 'but if anything's happened to your wife, things are going to be serious.' To this day I am at a loss to see how such carefully phrased remarks could not have been made to alarm me. It soon seemed that my 'clinging' to Anna as my marriage sank would now be the very thing that would drown me.

'So, how long were you with this Anna then?'

'A week or two,' I said flatly.

'Where is she?'

'She went back to England.'

The sergeant glanced at his colleague. I couldn't hope to grasp what they were thinking, but I guessed it would be grubby and crude, assumptions based upon tits and arse and gain. 'So you're sure your wife had nothing with her?' asked the other one.

'Perhaps she packed a bag and hid it in the car,' suggested Jaillard.

'I'm sure she had nothing, really.' It occurred to me that even the shoes she had were evening sandals; just narrow straps of leather with fake gold clasps. 'She was out of her head. Honestly. Couldn't you get a search going?'

'That's why I'm here.'

'Look,' I insisted, probably looking desperate, 'I know what you're thinking, about the other woman, but it's not like that. I love my wife.

Things just got twisted.' For a moment I imagined that they understood but I couldn't have been more wrong.

'You should keep a list,' advised Jaillard, 'of everywhere you've been since she disappeared.'

'Why? Am I going to be accused of something?'

'And no more going anywhere alone,' he added.

'*Oui*,' said the younger one. 'Maybe you agreed to meet her somewhere after she left the dinner and then got rid of her. They're going to look at everything,' he insisted, 'really, if something's happened, everything.'

George and Lorna had been visiting Barbara and came across to see what they could do to help. 'Oh, Rupert! So sorry, my love,' tutted Lorna. I asked after Barbara. 'Well, naturally she's upset. It's her daughter, Rupe.'

'It's my wife.'

'A lot of people aren't going to see it like that,' Lorna pursed her lips, 'and you know why? That bloody Anna. I ought to wring her flamin' neck.'

'Look, it's not Anna's fault. She just wanted to . . .'

'Have you got a pen?' asked George, his light voice defusing the tension. 'I'll give you a hand jotting down your movements in the last couple of days. And don't worry,' he said, very calm, 'if you need to go anywhere I'll take you.'

Some time later a familiar car pulled into the drive and a woman wearing a tweed skirt carried a bag towards the chapel. In the bag, I knew, there'd be a thermos, which she always carried on long journeys, and some shortbread. There'd be more food in the boot, along with boots and warm things, thick socks, spades for snow and those notebooks given away free at the bank. She wore sensible shoes, did my mother. I felt almost tearful that she'd come at a time like this, imagining gratefully for a moment that Mum had come to stand by my side.

'Well,' she began, kissing me absently as a wave of her unmistakable perfume engulfed me. 'I've just been talking to Barbara, she's desperate, *desperate*.' I realized then that I had misunderstood. Mother had not come to my aid. 'I have to say, you've done a nice job of it,' she began. I was thrown, accused of adultery as a genetic pre-disposition and further selfish acts until eventually I was reduced to tears. Taking no prisoners, my mother reminded me of the day my father walked out, just as she had done all through my childhood, over and over again, strangely punishing me without a thought to my own mental state. Now Jacquie was the heroine of her lifelong disappoint-ment and I, like my father, was the perpetrator.

'Typical, typical of a Bogaerde,' she continued as I began to wonder how on earth this was going to end. Mum shifted into a higher and very familiar gear. 'You can't imagine what it's like, bringing up children on your own.'

'But I have the children,' I pointed out, beginning to lose my cool. 'Mum, look. What did you come here for?' I snapped. 'Did you come here for me . . .'

'I came for Jacquie,' she said indignantly, 'my daughter-in-law, and for poor Barbara.'

'Or did you come here to punish Dad?' I asked angrily.

My mother left the following day, leaving me strangely battered and confused but also concerned for her, as always. She understood a little more of the facts by now, but still I was not absolved. For her, in so many ways, I shall always be my father's son.

I met Lucilla about two days later in Perpignan at seven in the morning. Calm, as always, my gentle stepmother sat in the railway café and we had breakfast: coffee and rubbery croissants. I thanked God that Mother was back over the mountain pass in Andorra and that Lucilla could come to the chapel without added worries. She'd just wanted to help with Mo and Sam, to be a friend, to listen with love for a little while.

'Have you heard any news?' she asked, dunking her vile croissant.

'Nothing,' I sighed, 'Jacquie hasn't called anyone. I thought that we might go up on the mountain road to the coast and search. What's happening at home, anything exciting?'

She told me with concealed anxiousness that Ulric had decided to take an epic solo voyage to India. I thought of him with his backpack and India threshing away at his fingertips. A tinge of envy, the size of a vast safe, dropped upon me, right out of the sky.

After my return with Lucilla to the cottage I was telephoned by the police and Barbara rushed across to announce the same news, that they'd found her blue Fiat.

The policeman on the phone had said that Jacquie hadn't been found. He'd demanded that I produce a medical document of some kind, anything, which could confirm her blood type. I'd rushed into the office and looked for the papers that we kept about the births of the children. They would certainly contain a record of this kind. I remember this because that morning the heat in the office, even though it was in the shade, was intense.

'It's nothing,' said the constable, 'she's had a small accident.' I badgered him with questions but he would not elaborate. 'Come down to the station and speak to the sergeant,' he instructed.

I found this worrying. I couldn't understand why they would need medical details if Jacquie *wasn't* there. The only thing I could think was that something terrible had happened to her and the sergeant wanted to break the news to me himself.

Arriving at the station, I spoke to the same young officer who explained that Sergean Jaillard was not yet back from the scene of the accident near the coast and that the car had been taken away to be examined and kept as evidence. Evidence? Evidence of what? Crime, abduction, injury . . . worse? I was assured that it was nothing but insisted on being told what *nothing* was.

'We think she got cut on some of the glass, there was some blood on the seats, that's all, but we didn't find her.'

'What d'you mean cut?' I asked, leaning up against the counter. 'Glass from what?'

But he couldn't tell me. This was confusing and deeply worrying. I imagined the car parked on the roadside. I had been told that it was somewhere behind Argelès, but little else. Time was ticking on and every minute, in my opinion, was priceless. If Jacquie had been abducted or was lying dying somewhere then time was *everything*.

*

Later the sergeant would hardly speak at all about the accident. Jacquie hadn't been found and that was that. Bafflingly, however, they were sure she had cut her hands and had superficial injuries. Barbara and I did not yet know that a judge in Perpignan, presiding over the case, the almighty, the police version of the Godfather – he who made the choices and dictated everything that the police should do – was doing virtually nothing.

'I'll conduct my own search then,' I told Jaillard when I saw how little cooperation he displayed. 'You must be able to tell me something more about the accident?'

He manoeuvred, 'They will examine the car,' and then shrugged. Apparently I wasn't allowed to see it at that point although probably I would have been able to. The fact that they suggested the accident had been insignificant led me to believe that there was no point in looking at the car. What for? Had I done so I think I would have reacted differently and perhaps changed the course of events, and no doubt this book would never have been written.

'How can you be sure her injuries were only slight?' I asked.

The sergeant replied that the look of the vehicle indicated this. 'You can do what you like,' he referred to my proposal for mounting a search myself, 'as long as you don't interfere with us.'

I'd confronted Barbara and André about not telling me that Jacquie'd feared she might harm the children and also asked why they'd failed to mention that she had been through some sort of spiritual session with a Jesuit priest in my absence. André quickly explained that this had been no religious tomfoolery. All he and his Jesuit friend had tried to do was reassure Jacquie that the *possession* thing was all in her mind and she was safe from whatever it was that she feared. Under the circumstances I felt André's approach could only have been positive. Barbara had simply not wished to rock the boat and had convinced André that they would keep quiet about both issues. I was, however, still pissed off that I had returned from the trip to see my dad and had been given no idea what I was walking into or how ill Jacquie really had been; that in itself was madness.

Again, in France, if you don't have that scrap of paper to say you're ill, then you get very little support. I also had the feeling that as a foreigner the value of my pleas for help was slight. I suggested to Jaillard that Jacquie might have gone off into the woods; after all, she was so unwell that anything was possible.

'In this heat? With no proper clothes or water?' He shook his head. 'She'd be lucky if she lasted a week,' he added. 'Have you tried to move in the woods here?' That one-week deadline stuck in my mind like a death sentence. If she was still out there wandering around we had to find her, and quickly.

I remembered my time on the mountain, building fences with Fergus, and before, clearing the woods around the chapel. The creepers that hung from the trees were the worst part; they tore your clothing to pieces. The more you fought the worse it got and the more entangled one became. It was impossible to walk even short distances in bushland like that, impossible. The whole thing seemed so unlikely but Jacquie's mental state led me to think she might have wandered off in this way. A sick feeling of shame hung over me.

Barbara and André organized posters for which I supplied photographs of Jacquie. I felt ever more hideous about the one-week survival limit that Jaillard had spoken of, as if all hope would run out on the seventh day and Jacquie would be found dead on a mountainside. The police told me that they were searching for her but it seemed to me that they were only asking questions and that no actual search was undertaken. I was not informed of any specific areas searched or of any manpower involved.

Jacquie's departure had an ugly effect on us all. Lucilla made dinner and for once, in the sweltering heat, we closed the windows to the night, then the front door and turned the key. Perhaps it was the fear of my mother turning up and setting about Lucilla as she had threatened in the past, or Jacquie returning, literally as someone else. We really didn't know why. Although I felt I understood Jacquie's struggle with motherhood, I just could not accept that she would be truly capable of abandoning her children.

The sergeant's subsequent stories about Jacquie's crash were no better than his first. There was a witness but I wasn't allowed to know what exactly he'd seen. It became even clearer that on account of my matrimonial troubles, I had lost access to a great deal of the inquiry itself. During Jaillard's explanation in the station another officer descended the stairs, the same one who'd interrupted Jacquie and me while we'd been kissing, parked in the minibus in the supermarket lot on the night of our anniversary many months before. He recognized me instantly.

'It's *your* wife who's gone missing!' He looked at Jaillard. 'Those two were crazy about each other,' he said.

A moment passed as Jaillard and the other sergeant conferred. Then nothing at all happened. *Anna*, I thought, while looking at their faces, *what have I done?*

The police seemed to be moving incredibly slowly. I told myself repeatedly that it was probably due to my lack of sleep and that my perception was off. I had no understanding of the French law machine then. I feared that things would only start to happen when it was all far too late. Searching for solutions within myself, I bought some food and drove over to Lorna and George. Their terraced house stood in shade in a quiet street in a nearby village. The stone-floored rooms were dark and cool.

'I brought you a baguette.' I handed the bread to George, with one end bitten off. Each time I came to help them, fixing the odd thing, wiring or plumbing, I'd always turn up with the same. My clothes were always rough and my face scraggy.

'Ooh,' said George, a smile spreading across his face, 'you got there first again I see.'

'And a doughnut,' I added. 'It's yours. I ate mine in the car.'

George handed me a trowel, worn steel with a scuffed wooden handle. I didn't recognize it at first. It was his way of showing me how to respect myself even if simply via my tools. He always felt that there were other things that I should have been doing and sometimes suggested that I might not look bad in a tie.

I sat with Lorna, while out of the corner of my eye George quietly devoured the doughnut. He'd have spent ages, I knew it, chipping away at my old trowel and sanding it for me with steady kindness and patience.

'You see, Rupert,' said Lorna, 'Jacquie could've lived through all this far better, perhaps, if she'd been more ruthless.' She patted my knee. 'But she loved you and those children. She was too kind. I'm sorry, love, I'm sorry for the both of you. Jacquie had a conscience. That's what made her suffer so.'

A mutter from George as he brought tea may have implied a difference of opinion here. Anyway, I tried to sit up straight and listen, their English armchair sucking me back like a sedative.

'If you're honest, Rupe, I think you know that emotionally she'd been gone from you for quite some time.' Lorna watched as a painful acceptance of sorts crossed my face.

At last I gleaned a little more from Jaillard. He took me to a room where he produced a large transparent bag with a child's booster seat in it, the odd toy and other items, all of which I recognized as coming from the rear of the little Fiat. All were smeared with blood. I felt nausea.

'Don't worry,' he said, 'the witness says he didn't notice any sign of injury at all.' I badgered him for more information while he looked as if he was considering what to tell and what to save.

'She was pulled from the car by a motorist,' he went on, 'but she pushed him aside and ran off. Somehow she got across the road. She must've climbed over the barrier in the middle. Then she ran up a track into the mountain.'

'Did he follow her?'

'He didn't want to leave her car in the middle of the road.'

'You mean she'd just stopped it and left it? Just like that; right there?' I asked. Jaillard looked uncomfortable and couldn't or wouldn't answer. 'Had she hit someone else?'

'Well, we think it was a burst tyre. She lost control. The car fell on its side.' Jaillard watched me absorb all this and then went on. Jacquie had walked up a track to an old building set quite far back in the woodland and hammered on the door. It was around ten o'clock because the man living there had just come outside to turn off his generator after watching the evening film. Jaillard looked at me sympathetically. 'You had a point when you said that she was ill.'

Then he looked almost amused. 'She asked the man if he had a gun and then demanded that he shoot her, telling him she was possessed by the devil.' Jaillard apparently accepted my claims at last. 'The man and his wife tried to get her to stay, but there are a lot of loopy, druggy people living down on the coast at this time of year.' The sergeant shrugged. 'He just thought Jacquie was another summer wacko.'

Again my heart sank. 'I told you, this isn't just any old husband and wife saga. When you finally realize that you'll . . .'

Jaillard shook his head. 'So then she went back down the track. Maybe the police were already by the car and she got frightened. The man in the house followed her a little way down. He thought he saw some lights slow down on the road. Perhaps she thumbed a lift.'

'So now d'you believe she's sick? Can I see what the people who saw her said?'

He shook his head again. 'Now we'll have to talk to her doctor and the clinic in Perpignan.'

This was agony; a waste of precious time. 'Can't you just *believe* me?' I begged. 'And what about Jacquie's mother, won't she back me up? But don't tell me,' I speculated, 'she doesn't want to admit that her daughter's got a psychiatric problem.' Again I felt that the fear of labels was going to block any useful work forever.

'We'll be talking to your mother-in-law.' He started on a new tack. 'If Jacquie was so ill, then how come you let her take the car?'

I stressed that it wasn't a case of letting her and that she had been taking her medicine properly. 'I didn't know anything about what went on while I was away, Jacquie mentioned a bit, but the rest I found out yesterday. They didn't want to tell me.' I then had to explain about Barbara and André and the saga about Jacquie's fears of hurting the children. About André's reassurance concerning her fears of possession. Jaillard's eyes widened and he barely suppressed a grin. Ironically, I could accept that.

'I understand why they didn't tell me, but just the same, you can't make proper judgements and react intelligently with only half the truth,' I told him.

'And I'll bet you didn't know your wife was full of wine too?' We'd all had a glass, I told him. 'No. See, you *didn't* know.' He looked rather pleased. 'I've been to see your friend Charlotte. She says that while you were out fetching her husband, she and your wife polished off half a bottle of fourteen-degree wine. Charlotte had a little but Jacquie, she had most of it.'

Jacquie was taking her drugs; she could take a couple of drinks maybe, no more, I told him.

'Charlotte found a note,' he went on. 'She says Jacquie left it in the till in her shop. We're having it verified, checking the handwriting. It's Shakespeare or something. Do you know if she liked Shakespeare?'

'She listens to Tina Turner and reads Sydney Sheldon, but Shakespeare! It's not Jacquie. Can I have a look? Maybe it'll lead me right to her.' I was told I could see it later.

'Why is it,' I grumbled, 'that I feel like I'm in the dark and that I'm the only one who's actually looking for her?'

Jaillard suddenly became agitated. 'Wait a minute, what d'you think we're doing here?'

'I have no idea. How am I supposed to know? You've shown and told me almost nothing. All you've done so far is contact our friends and question them about us. Half of them are terrified because they're probably working on the black.' I felt uncomfortable, fighting an urge to say more. 'You really think that *that* kind of strategy stimulates them to talk to you? Honestly! They'll all clam up. Even if they know something about Jacquie, they'll be too worried about their own skins to have you hanging around. She's been gone for a few days now, what's happening here?'

'If your friends have something to hide then that's their problem.'

'Half of the Pyrénées Orientales has something to hide,' I retorted, 'and the ones that don't are either working for the state, like you, or starving to death.' I smiled nervously and gulped. 'Don't tell me you don't *know* that?'

Growing ever more fed up with the inactivity, I telephoned a local television outfit and André did the same to enlist the help of the local radio stations. I explained that the police were not being entirely straight with me. This simple detail had been enough to enthuse a keen journalist to come to the police station and see if any dramas might unfold.

Lucilla and I pulled up in front of the gendarmarie in Bert, with the camera crew close behind. I'd brought a briefcase. There was nothing inside it except posters of Jacquie, which Lucilla and I would soon distribute. Barbara and André had been clever to have them printed so fast. The case was a fabulous prop; it added something that a police officer might interpret as power. The reporter and the crew agreed to follow us right into the station and film whatever response I got there. I had no idea if one could legally do this and left that to the journalists to sort out but I was sure that the press could get things moving.

We strode into the reception area and asked for Jaillard, who shot down the spiral stairs and eyed the camera and the briefcase with a look of suppressed horror. It was all tremendously satisfying. For a few seconds he might have felt like I did: oddly accused.

'I've come for information about Jacqueline,' I began. I wanted to hear what the witnesses had said after Jacquie'd crashed the car.

'Okay,' he said, suddenly compliant. While the camera crew waited in the reception area Lucilla and I were ushered up to a room and presented with a huge dossier. Inside were the bald facts and statements of the witnesses to date along with interviews with our friends.

There is nothing that the police loathe more, I imagine, than the teeth of the press. I was so very grateful. Without that power I'd have stayed indefinitely in France's red-tape version of the dark. 'So wait a minute,' I said, 'the car crashed into the central barrier at about seventy-five miles an hour!' I looked up at the sergeant, appalled. 'Then it slid down the road on its side . . . Can you imagine what that must've been like?'

'I think the reason she wasn't more hurt or shocked was because she was relaxed by the drink,' said Jaillard.

'Thank God. Can I visit the man she spoke to?'

'You can do what you like,' said Jaillard.

Things, I realized, were suddenly different. 'Is that because we came with the press?' I asked, expecting anything but a 'yes'.

'No,' he said, and in telling the truth, he lied again. 'You've always been able to do what you want,' he said. 'Go ahead.'

'Then how come you wouldn't let me see this when it all happened?'

If it ever happens to you, and I would never wish this situation upon anyone, first, before you get up in the morning, find out your rights. Find out where your shield lies. Find out whom you can strike within the law by discovering who can be held responsible to whom. Then make sure that the person at the top is well aware that he or she will be made to answer before the press or a higher authority; and that they will be as vulnerable as you can possibly make them.

Make sure you take notes and find the best media outlets you can, but keep some powder dry and don't fire it off all at once. Another thing to consider is that the media and the police fall into the same untrustworthy bracket; if it all goes wrong and you're horribly wrongly accused, then only those who love you and God alone will be left to help.

Keep a friendly journalist in mind and remember, the media loves a name, something to throw into the jaws of the public: a name, guilty or innocent. And lastly, never, ever go quietly. Be prepared to do anything to be heard and seen. I learned all of this too late for poor Jacquie and my children.

Human nature can be ugly and people do terrible things to others. The man down the street, the woman next door, they all do it. Policemen, priests – put a uniform or a label on them, or give them a quest or some power and they get even worse and do things that ordinarily one would never permit, because as their victim, one's confidence is jarred, one's guard is down. Rarely do they do it because they have the right. It's horrible, evil and absolutely happening – even as you read this – to some poor innocent somewhere. Justice, that wretched person will tell you, has so very little in common with law.

Although I was only briefly allowed to see it and not actually to touch it, the note written on a napkin that Jacquie had left in the till of Charlotte's shop just before her departure was, as Jaillard had described, a fragment of Shakespeare. I can only assume that these were lines she had carried about in her head from school plays or the hospital charity performances she'd been involved in years ago. The words were from *Macbeth*, Act II, in my memory set out more or less as follows:

> *Is this a dagger I see before me . . .*
> *A dagger from the heart, the handle towards my hand . . .*
> *. . . Sensible to feeling and sight,*
> *. . . a dagger from the mind?*

I felt a surge of anxiety. There was a picture of a hand and a dagger. For me the message confirmed Jacquie's view of her illness and its relentless, destructive nature. I might have seen it as a suicide note, but under the circumstances, awash with despair, booze and psychiatric drugs, I doubted that Jacquie would have known what she was about to do.

That afternoon Lucilla and I visited the house that Jacquie had walked up to after her crash. It was a bumpy trip up a steep jagged track about 500 yards long, all huge jutting stones and red earth overshadowed with woods. The house was unfinished, a mixture of breeze-block and red hollow bricks, mostly rough cement-rendered and painted white. There were cement ponds that looked as if they were once intended for other things, a swimming-pool perhaps, a project unfinished and already in decay. The place stood partly in shadow on the edge of the large wood with vineyards far off on the mountain slopes behind.

I made my way around the building looking through windows, watchful for the inhabitant's return lest I be accused of snooping. In a downstairs room I noticed cartridges on a table and a shotgun; there were rifle bullets too, but I couldn't see the weapon that they belonged to.

There were various outhouses, a chicken house and a tool shed and a wrecked car. I imagined that Jacquie could be tied up in any one of these, then tried to put the thought out of my mind. As I drove down the track I noticed a man working a field away. I wandered across, stumbling through the tyre tracks in mud set like stone in the summer heat.

He was in his fifties, with sun-wrinkled skin, short, rusty-grey hair and hard grey eyes, which were thin slits in the bright sun. He chipped away at a wall with a hammer, hardly stopping to say '*bonjour*'.

'Could you please help me?' I asked, my accent having already given me away. 'Do you know the man who lives in that house?' I pointed.

'Perhaps,' he said coldly, stopping his work and resting the hammer against his leg.

'I'm looking for my wife,' I explained, 'she went missing a few days ago. She came and spoke to the man there. He's the last one to have seen her.'

'She was depressed,' he said scornfully.

'It was you then?' I said, trying to sound friendly.

He shrugged and began chipping again. 'I can't tell you any more than I told the police.'

'You told them you spoke for twenty minutes. What else can you remember? Please.'

'It wasn't just me,' said the man. 'My wife tried to get her to come in and have coffee but she wouldn't. She asked me to shoot her. Said her life was no good.'

'Did she say where she was going?'

'No, she went back towards the road. I followed a little, but not far.'

'Did she say anything more before she left?'

'I told you. You'll have to speak to the police.' He resumed his chipping. I didn't move. Finally he lowered the hammer. We glared at each other and I turned and left. I knew it wasn't all, I was convinced that he and Jacquie'd had a conversation that had led him to distrust me. Why else would he be so hostile, unless, of course, he had something to hide.

I walked back to the main road, near to where Lucilla was wandering about. She was being very thoughtful and careful with her ideas as to what had happened.

There were still things from the car scattered about the crash site; shoes, children's clothes, a towel. I found large pieces of the car door and a sheered bolt from the wheel. Eventually, following information from the police, I was able to find the exact markings where the car had supposedly struck the barrier. There were cement posts supporting large traffic signs spaced about 500 yards apart down the centre of the road with its four lanes. The traffic was moving very fast as it rushed along the wide, newish asphalt, away from the pot-holed mountain twists of the coast road from the frontier.

Jacquie's black tyre marks were still quite clear, veering suddenly towards the barrier and a lone, solid post. Contrary to the police report, I doubted very much that this sudden swerve was accidental; there was only one post, after all, in hundreds of yards and the tyre marks led right up to it. I have never doubted this – not with such strong emotion, drink and psychiatric drugs in the mix. A moment of despair is all it takes.

It was like a Shakespearian tragedy. First the Wife, then the Husband, bewildered and shameful, then the well-meaning but bungling Mother-in-Law and finally . . . the Hawk.

Jacquie had been coming from Collioure, which suggested that she'd been visiting someone. The only person I knew in that direction was Kurt, who was now staying in the village that she had been driving from. It seemed to me that the car had climbed up the barrier and the tyre had exploded. It would have struck the huge post. I imagined that in her drunken state Jacquie had underestimated the strength of the barrier before it held, did its job and flipped the car over and away from suicide and back into the road where it had slid on its side for a tremendous distance before stopping at last.

What it must have been like to hang from the steering-wheel in a car alive with flying glass and screaming, sparking steel, while the road tore past so close to one's skin, I cannot imagine. I am only grateful that Jacquie somehow survived, although I feel uncertain about the effects of delayed shock and the horror she must have endured afterwards, walking away bleeding and alone. The wooded walk up the track to the man's house would in any case have terrified her, considering her fear of the dark.

I began looking in the mountains with friends and gave myself pointless searching missions.

I remember running along the crowded summer beaches, from lifeguard post to lifeguard post, through a sea of stripped bodies, handing out posters and explaining the situation again and again as time ticked on and my sense of powerlessness deepened.

Barbara had found a *magnétiste*: a person who, by means of a pendulum of some kind, manages to find all sorts of things or people, often working from plans or maps or any pertinent object. In Britain they're called dowsers. She had discovered the man in a restaurant in the foothills nearest to the crash. 'You know anywhere that Jacquie might have gone where there are bulls or cows with horns?' the *magnétiste* had inquired.

Jacquie had been missing now for six days. I was frantic to find her, feeling that if she were out there, still wandering on the mountain-sides, her chances of survival were very remote. Barbara, despite her great strength of character, was also showing signs of despair. She was hesitant in telling me about the *magnétiste* but eventually, as I'd begun suggesting things like this, she spoke of it. Since my experience with Jezebel I hadn't been very patient with the fortune-telling business but now we were desperate, even transparent, depressing scoops from the pool of prediction shone out like rays of hope.

'I think Jacquie hitched a ride,' I ranted once again, spoiling another of Lucilla's dinners. 'I mean, *I'd* have picked her up, she's pretty. God, what a break! Some guy picks up an attractive woman. So she's a bit wacky, who cares? He quickly realizes that she'll probably do whatever he asks, given the right encouragement, so he takes her back to his place in Spain and she stays on. He gets what he wants, till emotionally she surfaces and moves on. See?' I blithered. 'The beauty of Jacquie's problem is that you can't tell if it's there until it all goes too far.'

Lucilla nodded, letting me go on like a dog on a telescopic leash, only reeling me in if I went too far or began punishing myself by crapping on my own doorstep.

The following morning I told the police that I was not satisfied with the statement from the almost hostile man with the hammer, the last person to see Jacquie. I knew it would be futile to mention more but Jaillard was happy that I'd come in. 'I'll make a note of it,' he said.

'If there's anything more in that direction we'll be over to see him immediately.'

I had no intention of waiting. I wanted action now. I wanted to tear the man's door off its hinges, throw his guns in the sea and comb through his house and all his outhouses. I asked Jaillard if he had any contacts in the magnetism or psychic business. Remarkably, he handed me a number. 'This is the man we use,' he shrugged, 'you can take it or leave it.'

'Do *you* believe in it?'

Jaillard shrugged once again, apparently more amused than convinced. 'People find water with it. He's supposed to be good, sometimes he gets it right.' For once he seemed to make no effort to hold back a grin.

I hurried to the chapel and phoned the man in Toulouse. 'I'll get the map and give it a try,' he said. 'Give me a ring back this afternoon.'

According to both *magnétistes* (the one Barbara had encountered and the police one from Toulouse), following the crash Jacquie had headed towards Spain, via the mountains and through the woods. Again there was talk of '*toro*', the animal with horns.

'It's a plateau,' said the police *magnétiste*, 'a good hike from the wrecked car, in a straight line with the mountain peak. It all comes to a stop there.'

'What? You mean the trail suddenly stops?'

'Everything,' he insisted. 'Now, don't worry, it doesn't mean that she's dead. It could be that things got so bad for her emotionally that suddenly she shut it all out of her mind and changed tack.'

I looked at my own map. Not far from the car, a mile or more perhaps, in a line with the peak Neolus, was the Jasse de Toro, a little plateau on the corner of a mountain road. I remembered the walks that Jaffa had led with the tourists. We had taken people past that place. What would Jacquie have been doing in darkness on the jagged rock roads with the trees looming over and the blackness of the woods all around, so far away from any village? It was miles from the crash site, which meant that she would have struggled just getting there. It made no sense. 'Can you tell if she went there on her own?' I asked. 'I mean, was she taken there?'

'I can't say,' said the man. 'Do you know anywhere else where there are animals with horns, like bulls, nearby?'

'There's just one place,' I said. Jaffa had taken tourists once or twice up to the top of that mountain, to Neolus. They'd stayed in a stone shack with a steel door where mountain walkers would shelter overnight. There was a fireplace, an old table and two bunk-like rows of boards that ran the length of the room. Hikers would lie in their sleeping-bags, side by side on the rough wood, bonded by a common passion for the mountains. I thought of Jaffa, who knew all about being alone. He could go for days in the mountains. He wouldn't leave a trace there, appreciating all he saw and touched, as at home in a wilderness as he was sometimes lost in a crowded room. I missed him more than ever.

The shack stood above the clouds somewhere near the top of a forest slope. The land around it was picked clean of twigs and branches to a height just out of human reach. Hacked stumps of many small trees protruded from the ground all around the building where hikers searching for firewood had scoured the little area with the subtlety of locusts. There was a river nearby, the water drinkable, I remembered, cancelling out another necessity. Other hikers might have given Jacquie food, but what about warmth? Up there even the summer nights were seriously cold and her clothes were flimsy. She knew of the shack because we'd taken Jaffa supplies there at one stage or other, but finding it would not be easy.

If Jacquie had headed towards the mountains this was the *only* refuge that she could have reached, yet it was a vast distance on foot, madness to think she could have made it in those evening shoes. But if she'd gone into the mountains it would be her only chance. Beyond that she'd have clambered into the black heart of the vast frontier forests where I knew she would have been lost and terrified in the darkness and the search would be hopeless.

I decided that the whole thing was too far-fetched, but then remembered that all around the little building, when I'd delivered supplies to Jaffa and his group of Even Breakers, there had been bullocks and cows, their horns long and remarkably sharp, much like those of a *toro*. It was the seventh day. If she were out there in the wild, without cover, she would most likely be dead already. But in despair we decided that the little refuge *had* to be the place.

Barbara, André and I thundered up the mountain in Bert and then through the winding back roads which climbed above the cork-oaks and further up towards the pine forests. The temperature dropped as we drove on, the woods ever more dense and forbidding. I had a rough idea of the position of the hut but the forest had changed and, worse, we were approaching dusk and a heavy fog encroached as we neared a large wooden chalet on the edge of the greater part of the timberland. I shot past it and headed under a canopy of pine, which stole the light from above, the trees standing like vast pillars in the strafed brown earth.

People underestimate the Pyrenees and their vastness. Crossing a frontier here and there one has no real concept of the struggle one would face if travelling through the valleys and over the ridges on foot. There are wild animals and forests so dense that one loses all sense of direction; fear and fatigue will so easily do the rest. Our journey took us only below the summit of the low mountains above the chapel and through the edge of these vast forests, yet Bert had been climbing for close to forty minutes.

I wished that Barbara could bring herself to say something, anything. 'I brought some blankets,' I said, feeling worse than ever.

'We've got a flask and sleeping-bags and I've made a hot-water bottle,' said Barbara flatly. 'If she's there she'll be weak and cold.' I nodded.

The road curved to the right and the vaguely familiar ascent to the hut became discernible. There were many places where we could climb up. None gave me a sure feeling of the hut's true position.

It began to spit rain as the fog, or more rightly clouds, stole ground. Before our eyes the visibility halved in a matter of moments. We climbed out of the Land Rover and searched for footprints or anything in the steep, earthy, roadside bank that would lead us to the cabin, which I knew stood camouflaged a hundred or so yards further up in the woods, but in which direction, where? André and I clambered up the bank and looked into the depths, but the foliage hid the place from sight. At least the forest floor was clear of brambles, permitting us to move through it.

I realized that we were equipped for summer, and that the coming storm would entrap us if we were foolish enough to head into the woods too far on foot and get lost. People who don't understand the mountains don't realize how easy it is to become disoriented. The wind cut in harder than ever and through the sharpness André squinted in an effort to listen.

'We haven't got that much time left,' I shouted, 'it's going to be dark in twenty minutes. Let's go back to the big chalet and I'll ask for help.'

Barbara still said nothing. We drove back through the great wood to the chalet where a man gave me directions and then we drove again to the same spot. By now the fog had grown denser and a mixture of snow and rain was falling almost horizontally. I grabbed a torch and walked along the track until I found a large root, which helped me to climb the bank and reminded me of the position of the hut. I'd climbed that same root two years earlier, with the supplies for Jaffa.

'I've seen it!' I shouted, feeling every ounce of blood thundering in my head and chest.

Barbara and André followed, bundling the covers and flask up in order to climb the bank, each one of us tearing at the slope. It seemed to take forever, the longest hundred yards I've ever known. I was out of breath before time and aware that my blood-sugar level was running dangerously low. 'Shit,' I told myself, 'if you're in a bad way you won't be capable of reasoning with Jacquie. You'll have to go back to Bert and find a Coke.'

The hut was so close now. My heart pounded in my chest as though I was hitting it with a stick. I couldn't stand to turn back. I reached the area in front of the hut, past the dry stampeded earth and the scattered, hacked stumps, then gasping, I threw my fists against the steel door. I shoved and tugged but it wouldn't open.

'JACQUIE?' I pounded. 'Are you there?' I strained for breath through the thin mountain air, watching as Barbara and André caught up, puffing away.

I heard voices. A young man opened the door and I shoved my way into the room, scanning the others there.

A group of four or five startled people looked up from around the fireplace. Seven or so more were already lying asleep, almost all of them wrapped like dead bodies, sleeping, mummified in Gore-Tex on the hard boards. It was dark in there. I couldn't see much at all. The single window, covered in smeared plastic, blocked most of the dusk light. The slumbering faces were in hooded sleeping-bags. Those who were still awake sat up, squinting in the light of my torch as I dashed about.

'We're looking for my wife. She's been missing,' I gasped, feeling slightly light-headed. Unconsciously switching to English and fumbling madly with the torch, I headed across the room and began tugging at each of the occupied sleeping-bags. 'Come on. *Turn!* Let me see you, is it you?' I poked the torch into each drowsy, shocked face, hardly noticing that Barbara and André had now entered the room. 'What about you?' I grabbed at another. 'Is it you? Jacquie? *Jacquie?*'

There were shouts of confusion as the last sleeper showed her face. Barbara's cry of despair filled the little room as the onlookers absorbed the awfulness of the moment. Barbara, usually so strong, wept as André attempted to comfort her. I tore past and searched hopelessly outside.

'No, don't go,' said a kindly voice. 'Here, have something warm to drink,' said another, 'you can't go like this. It's getting dark.' Feeling sick, I walked up behind the hut to the cliff top and wondered if I had the courage to throw myself off. 'Then again,' I considered mournfully, 'if you really want to punish yourself, stay alive.'

'She's not here,' said Barbara from some distance behind in a cold tone that my sick brain translated as hatred. 'Come on, Rupert,' she said, not waiting. André had been telling the people in the refuge a little of our dilemma, I supposed, but it really wouldn't help: I knew that with the vastness of the mountains, to find Jacquie between there and the road where she had left the car would be a miracle. I stared again over the cliff edge. The mist cleared enough to reveal that the initial drop was only three or four feet into soft grass. Even head first, you could hardly call it suicide, high-velocity botany perhaps. The single thought of Mo and Sam slapped my face and tears came.

I followed Barbara down the hill, loathing the sadness of it all, loathing the *magnétistes*, the police, then Jacquie, and finally, in a pathetic crescendo, myself. Above all I felt growing regret and resentment for the simple human reactions I'd had towards the end of our relationship. Every truth warped, all mistakes I'd admitted, honestly, and each had been scandalized, even though they adhered to the naive faith that somehow telling the truth wins through. Life's winners, I have since noticed, keep their mouths shut.

I wondered how long old Bert could hold out. I'd been using the Land-Rover on the mountain fire tracks while searching through the forests like a madman. Twice, in a race to cover more ground, it had flown through the air virtually diagonally, crashing down, bouncing over the jagged stone, with the dust from the floor of the old cab clouding the air and gagging me as I went on.

Back at the police station Jaillard still had very little to say. He'd built up a dossier almost two inches thick with what I was assured added up to some sensational first-hand witness reports from villagers, some of whom hardly knew us.

'You don't think we're doing anything to find her! What d'you think all this is then?' Jaillard gestured to the folder in which the growing wedge of statements lay neatly.

'Where did all that come from?' I asked. 'I didn't know I had that many friends.' His expression told me that I didn't. 'You mean these are people who've said horrible things about us?'

'They say some interesting things,' he nodded.

'Like what? People in this village? *Our* village?' I barked. 'But Jacquie looked after most of the people we know at one stage or other. She closed the lids on their bloody grandparents' eyes for goodness' sake.'

He wouldn't amplify but I guess the message was that it was kinky sex, drugs and oh *so* much more, all happening at the chapel. We'd been rutting like animals until the early hours every night and I expect that Even Breaks was suspected of being a front for something deeply wicked. It occurred to me that some part of the village had lost a battle with common sense in favour of religion and now had a growing conviction that our downfall had come about through some kind of divine retribution.

Some win the lottery and fall prey to vices, much to the delight of the 'told-you-so' types. As far as vices go, I suppose you could say that Jacquie and I drank. Of course we drank, although in our ten years together she'd rarely seen me tipsy, and drunk perhaps twice. Sex – it was wonderful because it expressed love. In any case, sex is not a vice. Recreational drugs were out. Sticking a syringe in three or four times a day and freaking out on insulin is enough, without glugging, sniffing or inhaling another deceptive substance. A couple of beers at the wrong time could be uncomfortable enough for me and on the few occasions I'd smoked pot with Jacquie she'd gone more than strange. Once, after two puffs, she'd been convinced that our new bidet was a motorbike, which after half an hour of debate had led to upsetting scenes ending in tears, so that was that.

The single-minded vulgarity of religion is a sickness in itself and in the village it endured in epidemic proportions. People who are truly in touch with God, I told myself, don't hand out guilt or shame like red and yellow cards in a football game or look up a sin in the big book. In the village, however, this must have been very much the case and we'd openly broken God's rules by being so human and fallible.

God's punishment, however, according to the *téléphone arabe* of the huddles at the *boulangerie* and *tabacs*, had fallen upon us. So that was a relief for everyone. God had stepped in. Jacquie and I were the evil pair and here was the proof: we'd been expelled by the purity of God's very walls. The chapel had rejected even 'our little nurse Jacquelina', driven away insane into the dark unknown; punished, forced away from Eden. When I heard of this kind of infuriating, twisted, almost criminal talk I imagined the lives of the wretched people who might have said these things. Suddenly I felt better: ignorance, after all, is a dreadful prison in itself.

Later I drove round to see Buck at the ranch. Old Buck was hard hit. Caroline had given him the boot.

'It's not Jacquie's fault,' he told me, 'she made a mistake in going

326

off to Greece, simply an error.' He patted me on the shoulder. 'Look at you and me, my friend. Caroline is gone; Jacquie is gone. We are both destroyed.' With a long mournful face he climbed the stairs of his little house, a place which, in my mind, had always represented the Alamo. 'Come up,' he beckoned woefully, 'I'll show you something that's very special to me.'

In Buck's room, clipped to the mirror, was a photograph of Caroline. He took it in his hand, then sniffed a tear back as he sat on the edge of the bed. 'My baby,' he wept to the photograph, 'you don't know what this means.' He motioned to the bedside table.

Suddenly I realized the severity of the situation. A large handgun lay there on the surface, its handle shining.

'Buck! For goodness' sake,' I stammered, 'this is no way to carry on.'

'I'm finished.' He continued to cry. 'I'm old, I'm gone sixty and the love of my life has left me forever.'

'Don't be ridiculous,' I gulped, 'Caroline was a wonderful part of your life. You have no idea what's around the corner.'

'I'd prefer to die than be alone.' He slumped over in more tears.

I picked up the gun and quietly opened the revolving part that held the bullets, and shook them out into my hand.

'Buck!' I shook my head, looking at the cartridges.

'Just leave me,' he groaned, 'it's too much.'

'But Buck, listen.'

'I want to die,' he wailed theatrically as he pointed back towards the gun.

'BUCK!' I grinned. 'These bullets are blanks.'

Back home I noticed two large, dark blue police vans at the bottom of Les Chartreuses, parked in the brush up a track off the road. They were odd in that they had smoked-glass windows and markings from the Paris crime squad.

I knew that the *téléphone arabe* would have told me if there were any madmen or Parisian gangsters in Les Chartreuses, so it was safe to assume that they were there for me. I couldn't imagine anything more boring, roasting idly for days in a dark blue van under an August sun.

What on earth was going on in there? I should have taken them something cold to drink. I regretted that I didn't.

'Perhaps they're tapping the phone lines,' I told Anna, 'so I thought I'd ring you.'

'Who do they think you are?' she said, incredulous. 'Charles Manson?'

Things were getting serious, I suppose, although I couldn't understand why the police hadn't come round and searched the place or looked down the well or anything like you see in the movies. I asked this on the phone, addressing those I hoped were listening in. Of course, I may simply have been becoming paranoid.

I told her about Kurt. He'd been picked up by the police and had been told he had to leave the country. No proper papers; they'd quizzed him for ages. The questioning of Kurt often bothered me afterwards. His life had been so full of struggles concerning his own wife and children. Jacquie had faced the same dilemma: to leave or not to leave? Was it perhaps Kurt who had helped her to disappear? I was grasping at straws, any hope, clue, anything at all.

Eddy had dropped by in his big silver Citroën. The children were tucked up in their beds.

We'd had a couple of beers by the time the boys in blue decided to do a 'friendly drop-in'. Their visits were less frequent nowadays but still, each time, a jolt of electricity shot through me, along with the obvious variables. 'Your wife is dead,' would creep across the parking lot dressed in blue; 'found murdered in the woods' was another dread. But even before the gendarmes reached the house, the way they looked and picked about, or wore tired, frustrated expressions, told me that there was nothing new. It seemed odd: me, Eddy and the policemen all standing together awkwardly as if we were guests at a cut-rate gala luncheon in the tiny kitchen of the bijou cottage.

'Any news?' I asked.

'Nothing,' said Jaillard. They were long past pretending something might pop up tomorrow. 'What would you do if she turns up?' he asked.

'You mean, after I've helped you throttle her?' I said, continuing over his laughter. 'I'd find out what she wants, if she really wanted a life with us, then I'd get her a proper diagnosis and help. I've learnt a lot – too late.'

I opened another beer while Eddy chatted to the second officer. They all knew Eddy or knew of him through his business. His manner was courteous. Understandably the last thing he wanted was to be drawn into my nightmare. He was well liked and respected in the area. As such a good and thoughtful friend I felt uncomfortable for him. 'I should get myself home,' Eddy announced, and made his way out with polite goodbyes.

'We've been talking to your friend Kurt,' said Jaillard.

'I know,' I said, watching Eddy's car take the corner on to the road.

'Oh? How's that?'

'He came here,' I said, 'a couple of weeks ago, he told me he thought the same as I did.'

'Thought what?' asked Jaillard.

'That Jacquie only came home because she felt she was losing something and that it was only a matter of time before she would leave again.'

'Convenient for you,' he insinuated.

'You call this convenient?' I glowered. 'How about you? You fancy being tens of thousands in debt and bringing your kids up alone?'

He seemed to enjoy his power and my irritation. Fascist, I thought, biting my lip. In fact, Jaillard seemed an extremely reasonable, rational man. A couple of days before, I'd seen him sitting in his police van outside the supermarket, loading an enormous chocolate éclair into his face. I'd even told him how amusing it had been to watch. Aware of the spectacle, he'd laughed out loud.

'And this girl, Anna . . .' He now somehow managed to suggest that Anna had been a one-night bimbette.

'You mean my mistress?' I said wearily. 'Sure you don't want a beer?'

Jaillard shook his head. 'She got money?'

'No. Why?' I put my hands on my hips. 'What are you thinking now? If you're thinking all this stuff, why don't you check me out? It can't be that difficult, everybody knows me around here.'

'I'm not thinking anything.' He shrugged. 'Just asking questions, that's all.'

'Look,' I said, 'I panicked, okay? I freaked out when I saw that my wife was about to dump me with the house, kids and debts. I found a new partner overnight. It's animal, not logic.' I wittered on while he looked about with mild interest. 'Don't you ever read any textbooks on human psychology?' I asked, 'Don't the police *ask* you to study what makes people do things?'

'Yes, sure,' he nodded.

'Then why can't you see what's happening here? Good God! If you'd come around when this first happened I might have run off with *you*, I was *that* confused. Anyway, you're lucky. I don't go for beards.'

Another suppressed smile and he motioned to leave.

'Anna is nice,' I said, 'she cares about me and those children and she's a victim, if anything,' I added weakly. I would never be good at being alone but that in itself was no reason to encourage Anna. She deserved a life and happiness, not this mess.

Eddy's car pulled up again and he appeared at the door. 'I'm sorry,' he said, 'I got half-way home and decided I couldn't leave you here,' he whispered discreetly, 'amid the gendarmes . . . alone.'

30 *Fear*

Those who know the Pyrenees say that hikers and hunters comb the mountains constantly. 'Inevitably,' they say, 'one would stumble across some clue; a piece of clothing perhaps, or a shoe.' But I've been there. I've spent enough time working in those deep woods to know that for every tree there is a shadow and all day long the shadows move, shifting the face of the magnificent forest.

If Jacquie had strayed alone into the depths of the woods, she was undoubtedly dead. No one could survive over that length of time. If she were a prisoner, or perhaps secluded by some organization or sect, where would I begin? She might be on a boat on her way to the Caribbean or in a truck heading for a thousand other places, slightly mentally askew perhaps, but capable enough, a prisoner or strangely free but either way immensely fragile. It was also possible, as the odd psychic seemed to believe, that she'd walked into a situation where she was murdered and her body hidden.

This warped and pointless conjecture consumed the hours, making the days become desperate as they floated by. Time was passing but for me it had lost its usual rules and structure. I grew more willing, as this torment progressed, to accept even a bad conclusion, appalling though it may seem.

During her worst moments Jacquie claimed that she was possessed by the devil. In the days when I was breaking down and coping badly with the search, some of the information that I'd stumbled across initially upset me. I found it disturbing that the two *magnétistes* in their separate searches had recognized, above all else, a horned animal, the symbol of *the beast*. I find it shocking that I even permitted myself to consider this terrible train of thought and with it the ugliness and the cruel threats of the Witch. But when one becomes desperate, foolish notions take hold.

I was losing my mind. I decided to call a number that had been given to me by a client who I felt was extremely rational. He also thought his idea sounded barmy, which curiously gave me confidence.

This man, my client had promised, was one of a kind: a retired priest and a true psychic, but more than anything, this was a man who had nothing to gain by helping me. He was simply motivated by kindness and perhaps a sense of purpose. As I found out, he was not a person who did this sort of thing for kicks. I think he might have preferred to be pulling up radishes.

I rang the former priest three times, each call lasting quite a while. It was nerve-racking and left me feeling strange and wildly impressed. He asked simple questions, saying first with absolute conviction that Jacquie was dead. She had apparently been picked up by a farmer or something, then had been dropped off and later killed by someone who knew her, a blond, a hippie type perhaps. He asked if we had any enemies.

This was like being struck with a mallet, but after a moment I decided to take it with a pinch of salt. Half of anyone's friends are blond and I knew of no real enemies except the Witch.

'If you both were older there might have been a chance.' He sighed. 'Have you thought about where you might live?'

I told him that there was a house not far away that might do but he couldn't feel it.

'I see a house,' he said, 'a house surrounded by water. No, it's a boat. No – a house. There are lots of people on it.' Unprompted, he sketched the scene of the party we'd thrown on the houseboat *Esperance* before we departed for France ten years before. I listened, stunned, silent. 'Oh, what am I going on about,' he stammered, 'that was *ages* ago.'

From then on I strangely believed much, but not all, of what he said. He told me of coming struggle and something else, a threat to one of the children. I had to hold tight and be there for the boys, he said. Things were going to be unpleasant. During my three calls, never once did he make any great effort to expand on a vision, you got whatever came to him and that was that. No garnish.

'It's odd,' he said, 'her body is trapped, or perhaps buried, under leaves or water. There's water in a ravine of some kind, where two slopes meet, a sort of furrow in the hillside, and there's a plateau or a clearing nearby.'

'Where is it in relation to the car?' I asked.

'Look, you *don't* want to find her,' he insisted, 'not like this. Why?'

'I want to find out what happened,' I said. 'It's horrible, the not knowing. It's limbo. I don't belong to one side of my life or the other.'

'Can you go away for a while?'

'I'm going to England with the boys in September for two weeks.'

'To see the other girl?' he asked.

'If they let me go.'

'Well, it's not very honourable towards her,' he sighed, seeing right into my confusion, 'but perhaps you both need it now.'

'Something will work out,' I said, bewildered. I sensed that I was talking to a kind soul, though what he saw frightened me; I wanted so much to believe that Jacquie was alive.

I also wanted to be able to embrace another life and another view of things. But I am a realist at heart and the fact that Jacquie was my wife and as far as I was concerned, *alive*, was not going to leave me, nor were ten years of love, no matter how credible the retired priest seemed to be.

I sat on the floor for a while, constructing one end of a plastic railway for Mo while Sam tore the other end apart. When I thought about what I had just heard it made my eyes fill with tears and I cried silently while we played on in the warm cottage. It would be only fair, I thought, to try to make some kind of plans for their future. Moses asked the question, 'Who will be my mum?' He was being perfectly frank, it wasn't a desperate request. Fortunately Jacquie's distant stance had cushioned the boys from suffering the pain of sudden separation. For them it could only be a long and painful reckoning as the reality of her absence gradually took effect.

The Dodger and I had one last discussion about Jacquie's disappearance.

'I'm not surprised,' he told me, 'after the way she was treated when she got out of the clinic.' I had very little to say to this. His involvement with Even Breaks had been short-lived and futile and I couldn't blame him for being upset. I was sorry that it hadn't worked out. I was also sorry that he hadn't been able fully to understand the problems we'd faced. Life can seem so straightforward when you have reasonable health and don't have children. I put down the receiver, irritated. The Dodger was history.

Some weeks later I went to the police station to ask permission to take the children home to England for the holiday. I was feeling mentally unwell at this point, having searched like a madman through all the mountain roads and beachfronts. I stood at the counter while Jaillard wrote down my various contact numbers in a book.

'Are you going to see the girl?' he too asked.

I nodded. 'What do you suggest I do, pretend that Jacquie's going to rush in any time? It's been six weeks now.' I said with a frown, 'You know, I'll bet she got on a boat.' He looked neutral. 'Come on,' I insisted, 'Jacquie's a nurse, a wonderful cook and she's cute. She'd get a job on any Atlantic crossing. If so she could be in the Caribbean by now.'

'Don't you think she'll be suffering?' He regarded me coolly.

Back at the chapel I'd put my foot in it again. Barbara had been helping with the children when I'd asked her a question. She was heading back home to have tea with Linda, who had come down from Paris.

'Barbara?' I began. 'I hope you won't take this the wrong way.'

'What, Rupert?' She waited, looking perturbed.

'If you *did* hear from Jacquie, would you tell me?'

I believe that the anger and emotion of the search and our fragile state had reached an all-time low. I felt hated. I sympathized with Barbara, but she had chosen to keep quiet, first about Jacquie coming home from Greece and second about Jacquie's sufferings in the days just before she'd disappeared. Both times the results had been catastrophic. Barbara was not to blame but I needed to know where I stood and I wanted the truth, with nothing left unsaid this time.

'I don't believe it,' she started, 'you think that *I*,' she began to lose control, 'I would lie to you and those little children!' She marched away, desperately crying 'ANDRÉ!' and looking across the garden towards their house.

'No, wait, Barbara!' I pleaded. 'I only wanted to know how you felt, Barbara!'

'ANDRÉ!' she went on, in floods of angry tears. I saw André running from his garden followed by Linda who, I imagined, was switching into her ex-boyfriend Frank's kick-boxing mode.

'What's happened?' asked André, pale-faced.

'André, it's not like you think . . .' I began, wondering if he would now accuse me of being cruel to Barbara.

'What are you doing to her now?' shouted Linda. I got the feeling that soon I'd be in for a fabulous kicking from those size four tennis shoes.

Barbara pointed. 'He says I won't tell him the truth,' she wept.

'Can't you just leave her alone?' Linda snapped.

'Please. I'm not *accusing* anyone,' I pleaded. 'I haven't done a thing, I didn't do anything before. I asked her a question; that's all.' Barbara wept on, causing Linda to glare at me angrily. 'For God's sake,' I told Barbara, 'calm down. You're completely hysterical!'

Following this I had a few terse words with Linda, then she slunk back with Barbara across the driveway to their house while André took me aside. 'She hates me, André,' I said, leaning on the garden wall. 'I just wanted to know if she'd tell me or keep it from me if Jacquie contacts her. It's a reasonable request after all that's happened. I need to know if I can rely on her for the truth.'

'You can,' he said as he patted my back. 'She's just upset. The children, you know . . .'

'Barbara has always been kind to me, André, but she made Jacquie come home when I was angry. They allowed me *no* time for recovery, no time to find out what normal life is like. Anyway,' I added, 'Jacquie deserved a kick in the arse, she was cruel in the end.'

'She was ill,' he said.

'She *knew* what she was doing,' I sighed, 'and she thought that because she was ill she could get away with anything. Whether you're ill or not,' I looked at André, 'when you cut someone, they still bleed, don't they? And they don't let you do it twice. Even if it's someone you love.'

The two weeks in England were both peaceful and desperate. Anna tried hard to reach me but neither of us was able to find out what was really going on in my frazzled brain. I kept on, doing the best I could in fooling both of us that things could be all right. I had all the ingredients: the lovely girl and adorable children, but also a police inquiry on my hands and assets soon to be frozen indefinitely.

We stayed in a little cottage on the Solent where I had gone for holidays since I'd been a child. It was paradise for Moses and Samuel, a time of long walks and crab-fishing and sunshine. The wonder of children is that they can adapt, though the sadness of the search hung like a dark cloud over us all, as did the reality of returning to France alone with the children and without work or sufficient money to find help.

In the middle of our stay I heard from Kurt, who was now back in Sydney. I'm not sure why, but he was crying – either for our situation or because later that day he was going to see his own daughter and it was killing him already. He had somehow rung around until he'd contacted my sister Alice and got the Solent number.

'Tell me, Kurt,' I asked, 'honestly, do you know anything about Jacquie's whereabouts? Please, be straight with me.'

'This has gone so far. Straight up,' he said, 'if I knew anything I'd tell yer, Rupe. How are the boys?'

'Can't you see my point of view?' I asked. 'If you do know where she is you could be telling her things like that. I want her to ring and find out how they are. You were kindred spirits, for goodness' sake, I can't help but be wary.'

Having said goodbye I thought of Robert and Lynne, the friends who had helped us prepare the chapel for its first guests. They now lived in Sydney, so I dialled them. 'I've often wondered if she wasn't around here somewhere,' said Lynne. It was a long time before they got back to me telling me that Kurt's address was in a rough part of the city and that they'd tried but had seen nothing of Jacquie.

A creeping feeling that I'd somehow become transparent began to emerge. When friends called at the Solent cottage they seemed to stand back and observe me with a strange empathy, as if I were a bag of fragments of a life blown apart, then left out for display on a table in a morgue. In the midst of this poor Anna was trying to make all the bits look and function like a family.

By the time our fourteen days were over I knew I'd failed. I'd made a mess of both Anna and myself. Jacquie was either dead or somewhere so far away that I had no sense of her. In the past I'd always had a notion of her position, wherever she was – next room, next village, wherever. But then perhaps I'm simply confusing her aura with the idea that I once had of love.

Ulric phoned. I'd heard from our father that things had gone badly for him in India.

'What's up, Nod?' I used his childhood name.

'I've got a little time to myself and maybe I could give you a hand in France.'

'Ulric, I'd love you to be there. God knows, right now I really appreciate the idea. Mo and Sam'll be delighted.'

Selfishly, I felt an immense gratitude for all the awful things that had happened to Ulric in Delhi. The force of Jacquie's absence in the chapel would be lessened with Ulric there for a while, and in a strange way perhaps he and I would be doing something for each other. 'I'm afraid I'm not much fun to be with at the moment,' I warned him.

'Wait till I've told you what happened to me,' he said dryly.

On the last day, Anna and I were on our way from the cottage to London with the children when I told her that I couldn't cope any more. I just needed time, I said, sounding like a character in a soap opera. I needed to sort my life out. The words sounded hollow. Anna would remain, I knew, the catalyst in the breakdown of my marriage. Her loyalty had given me strength but the damage was such that each time we were together I couldn't get it out of my mind. There was nothing to be done and I had only myself to blame.

Confused and upset, she drove away, leaving us in front of my parents' house and me feeling deservedly hideous. I carried Sam towards the door with Mo tagging along behind. Sorry is somehow such a meaningless word.

31 Ulric

Our parents' ancient battered blue car carried Ulric, the children and me south from London over a day and a night to the chapel. Somehow the travelling seemed harder than in previous years. It wasn't the sudden vomiting from the back seats in the twists of the South Circular or the annoying rain: it had more to do with the fact that ten years had crept up and that the hours, though they sped by, were demanding a higher physical price.

'Did I tell you about the psychic and the medium and the *magnétistes*?' I began.

Holding the steering-wheel at ten and two, Ulric rolled his eyes up to the roof of the car. 'Yes, yes, we'll look when we get down there,' he groaned.

After four hours I took the wheel, Ulric sat back, opened his satchel and found a book.

'You know, it's strange,' I began, 'whenever I think of Jacquie, we're always in bed.'

Ulric grinned. 'Ah,' he said, smiling, 'comfort.'

Kansas and Yogi were on the road by the oak in front of the chapel. They tore after us, howling with joy as we pulled in. It was morning, nearly October, the sky overcast. I decided we'd move from the bijou cottage into the curate's house, back where Jacquie and I had first started. As soon as we were organized I drove Ulric up on the fire track into the foothills to the Jasse de Toro, the place that the priest had described and the two *magnétistes* had indicated on the map. There were other psychic people that I'd spoken to but I felt that this information was at least somehow half-way credible.

The Jasse de Toro was a plateau on a sharp bend in the fire track that hugged the mountainside. It tumbled over a leafy slope in some places and in others it fell away in a straight drop, down to the forest floor and the bottom of the ravine, where the leaves were broken up by boulders and scattered trees. A trickle of a stream, which in winter or in stormy weather would become a torrent, ran through the gully in the centre, just as the psychic priest had described. The torrent would come again soon and the falling leaves of autumn were also on their way.

'Rupe, you've been awake for thirty hours.' Ulric was peering over the edge, through the greenery and into the ravine. 'We should come back and search properly when there's more light. Anyway, we have to go to the gendarmerie and let them know you're back.'

'I just want to look over here. Come on, Nod,' I used his childhood name again, 'we're here. Just a bit more.'

It was raining. Ulric had observed the vastness of the mountain and saw what I couldn't possibly allow myself to see: the pointlessness of it all. What was I doing on a mountain in the cold wind looking for the body of my wife? If I discovered her there I'd be even more of a suspect. Still, I carried on, while Ulric became impatient.

I decided that the ravine would take four people a good day to search. We went to the police and checked in, then told them the plan and indicated on the map where we intended to look. Jaillard took details, making me feel more of a target for scrutiny than an innocent member of the public. 'Why would you want to find her like this?' he asked.

'I know *you* can wait,' I told him. 'You can wait forever, but I need an answer. We're all hanging on a thread here.' My words were wasted, as if he were listening but was so accustomed to people's suffering that empathy was offered only in severe cases.

I was learning it then; people like Barbara and I often become almost thankful for any outcome, even a bad one, simply to put an end to the suffering that the constant, awful, desperate searching and speculation brings. That evening I phoned Fergus and saw André, asking both of them to come along to scour the mountain and I also asked if Barbara wouldn't mind having the children. I wrote to the

Salvation Army too, one of the most successful organizations known for finding people, and asked for their help.

If I was in a mess then I couldn't imagine what it must have been like for Barbara, sitting there waiting with the children for a result which could never ease her aching heart.

'Are you sure you want to do this?' asked Ulric.

'I have to find out,' I insisted, picking at the cracks in the white plaster as I sat on the curate's house stairs that I'd built too steep.

'I know, I know,' he muttered, a little weary of listening to all this again.

'Please, Nod, I know you think I'm daft. But nobody's doing a thing to find her. I owe it to the boys.' I looked round, catching him nodding like a plastic dog in the back of a Cortina.

I was going to search the mountain, no matter what, and although I knew Ulric didn't see the use, he'd never leave me to do it alone. There was a silence while he fought with a wry smile and got up. 'Come on then,' he said, grabbing his coat and heading for the door.

Sunlight threw itself through the trees, scattering along the fire track like camouflage. Fergus pulled up in his battered jeep, sitting as usual amidst a sea of old maps, children's stickers and protruding springs. He climbed out, looking about the forest, displaying what I read on his face as grave doubt while he rolled a cigarette and chatted to Ulric.

'It's one hell of a mountain,' said Fergus, squinting in the light, 'and we're only scratching at a tiny corner.' He put on his back-pack while André sat in the shade mucking about with special socks and *exactly* the right boots, preparing himself for the descent as any self-respecting retired teacher of engineering might. We'd start high above the track and work through the ravine on the sides of the river until we hit the village.

If you can imagine a speck of dust on a blade of grass in a football field, this is what I'd asked them to help me find. They'd come for me, because I needed to prove to myself that I wouldn't give up.

'Things don't stay still in the mountains, Rupe,' warned Fergus. 'You come across a dead cow, and a week later half of it's gone, all over the forest. In a month there's nothin' left at all; there are animals everywhere.' He said it kindly but it wasn't what I wanted to hear. I don't think, despite what had been said to me, that I knew what I would have done if I'd found her.

In the last half mile, encouraged by me to jump from rock to rock, Ulric, who was less agile, slipped and severely twisted his ankle. Darkness was coming and we weren't sure of the position of the village. We followed the stream and Fergus went on ahead, always keeping us in view as Ulric hobbled on. André, unhappy about the fading light and getting twitchy, sped ahead in case we needed help.

'Well, he's outa here like a fart in an Indian restaurant,' observed Fergus as we watched André nip through the woods and disappear into the dusk like an elf. I felt tired and strangely grateful that we had found nothing. It was as if the chances of Jacquie still being alive had suddenly increased. Nothing, no matter how much I wanted a result, could stop me from hoping that she'd somehow managed to use her magical brain and had got away.

Although Jacquie had loathed the local clinic, they did a decent job on Ulric's ankle. 'Is it broken?' I asked, while Ulric sat quietly, trying to understand some of the conversation.

'Not broken, no,' said the doctor.

'You're lucky,' I told Ulric, 'there was a bus crash and they did all sorts of awful things to the poor wounded like . . .'

'I don't want to hear it,' he said softly.

'Luckily neither Jacquie nor I nor the babies ever needed to get help there,' I told him later, making him feel wonderfully safe. He put his hands together briefly and began a familiar ritual: his anti-bad luck routine which involved some very dicey facial movements and a series of praying motions topped off with flickering eyelids. I was obviously going round the twist, but *these* shenanigans had me doing a double-take every time.

'It's not broken,' repeated the doctor, 'but mangled, bashed, twisted, bruised and torn, yes.'

I requested that he give Ulric a prescription for simple pain-killing treatment, not the usual flurry of insurance reclaimable backhander products. Understanding this, he tore up the first page and began again, writing a list of only three or four items.

Clad in plaster, Ulric was shoved into the back of the Land Rover and we headed home. 'Sorry, Nod, I should never have got you or the others involved.'

'It's all right,' he lied, patting my shoulder, 'I wouldn't have missed it for the world.'

Early the following morning a Renault from the gendarmerie rolled into André's driveway across the street. I was getting Mo ready for school and had the peculiar feeling that bad luck was about to pay us a call. Without being able to pinpoint why, with each encounter I was becoming less trusting of the police and more dubious about the way they seemed to amass their information. Was it a *result* that the gendarmerie were after, regardless of the actual truth?

In asking the consulate in England if the Home Office would get involved I had begun pushing for action to be taken at a higher level. Something must have happened because I then realized, far too late, that this had only made the French authorities examine further the one suspect that they seemed to have: myself.

The gendarme arrived at the door. '*Bonjour.*' I felt my heart thumping in my throat and stood hoping for a 'Your wife's in an asylum in Normandy,' or 'She has become a member of a vodka, toga and Viking cult'-type response, anything, anything at all but death.

'*Bonjour.* We haven't found her,' said the young man, reading my face. 'The sergeant will see you later, he's coming over.' This police visit was much the same as usual except that there was a newcomer, a Sergeant Burgat, a slightly older policeman with a variety of stripes up his sleeve. This short, dark-haired man was now in charge of the case.

He was a solid member of the military civil policing establishment, but I came to see that his reasoning, decisions and hunches seemed to be based on more than bald facts. His intellect seemed far better geared to second-guessing the local peasant mentality than it was to understanding the basic truths when spoken by those from other cultures. He had a way of making assumptions rather than simply looking at the facts.

'So the parties you gave for the clients were how often?' he asked. 'Once a week? Twice?' Burgat watched my face. 'You mean more than that?' He nodded to himself.

'It depended what kind of clientele we had,' I replied.

'And you and your wife, how often did you both drink? Did you drink a lot?'

'I didn't, not that much. Neither of us were alcoholics, if that's what you want to know.'

'But you drank every night?'

'Sure.'

'And the people that came, couples or singles?'

'Singles, mostly.'

I watched a crude idea form, as if his head was transparent and its workings chugging along, visible. 'The people from the area told us that it was crazy here,' he said, 'that all sorts of things went on.'

'Are you suggesting that we ran a brothel?' I asked, testily. He went into that infuriating policeman's 'You said it, not me' mode. 'Show me anyone who witnessed that kind of thing,' I said. 'You know we weren't like that. Crazy is what this whole thing is. I lost track of what was happening in my relationship and the business fell apart, that's all; no secret wickedness.'

'If you lost track then maybe you wouldn't have known if she was seeing someone else.' He said this with a sharply aimed smile. 'How d'you know how close she got to this Australian, Kurt?'

'Look, I know Jacquie, she was lost, sick; that's all.' I leaned forward on Jaffa's table.

Burgat got up, scratched his head and leaned against the kitchen counter. If Jacquie wasn't having an affair and the chapel wasn't the den of fornication, booze and drugs that he seemed to think it was, then what on earth was happening?

'We've been given new power on this case,' he informed me. 'Judge's authority.'

I imagined that the fact that I'd admitted openly to having an affair must have sent alarm bells thundering about inside his barbecued sardine and *boules*-shaped mentality. 'The husband did it,' he seemed to be telling himself. They thanked me and on departing Burgat gazed at my face in a way I didn't care for.

In November Dr Jacques came to inspect Ulric's foot. I seem to remember having a check-up and a prescription for zombie tablets at the same time. I was still saving some up for the trapped nerve in my father's neck. The doctor sat upstairs in the curate's house amidst a sea of tax returns, looking around at the varnished stone walls, the white plaster cherubs on the wall above the bed, now coated with thick dust, and the English books.

'She wasn't *just* suffering from depression, you know,' I said.

He sighed. 'I think you were *both* living in a bizarre dream. Not only Jacquie.'

I still didn't feel that they'd done enough to find her problem in the clinic.

'They did what they could do,' he said, 'the drugs were very strong.'

I shook my head. 'The drugs were *too* strong. There had to be some other way. A proper diagnosis . . .'

'There isn't,' he said flatly. 'People have their rights.'

'Then there was no way out for her,' I said sadly.

Mother, meanwhile, had been ringing, saying that the communists were invading Andorra and that her phone was tapped by the special services. She was also almost certain that she'd seen Jacquie in Andorra and had heard rumours that she had been working in the Alps. She had also been in touch with the police who had gone all the way up to Andorra to visit her. One might get the idea from this that Mother was losing her mind but this was not the case. Some people just muddle through, unable to hear the pleas of those who love them. One has to really want change and ask for help. Mother never felt that she needed it. Perhaps it was just me; perhaps the communists *were* invading Andorra. I was sure that jolly old Jaillard and Burgat would get to the bottom of it.

All this expenditure, all those police man-hours, yet no one seemed prepared to show me where or if the police had actually physically searched for Jacquie at all.

*

There were no rents in the autumn. The chapel stood empty, clean and dark. I'd closed the pool long ago and now it had swollen with rain, its water still and gathering leaves as winter drew in. Old friends at the top of Les Chartreuses got us digging and clearing the scrubland below their house. Oddly, it was therapeutic work, but hard on poor Ulric's freshly healed foot, though he seldom complained.

While Ulric cared for the boys I worked elsewhere, putting up shelves, doing small masonry jobs, anything. I considered going back to Skull Face but we were past the days when 1,000 francs a week would do. Darkness seemed to be folding in all around.

'Why don't you just come home with me to London?' said Ulric. He would not have considered this as an admission of defeat, but for me, to leave the chapel was to confirm that I'd failed; that I couldn't even provide for my own. Strangely, leaving the house meant to me that I was abandoning Jacquie and this I could not bear. To leave would mean that it was over.

Ulric threw a log on the fire. 'There's no wood left now,' he added.

In those dark months I became convinced that I had failed Jacquie in every way and that it was I who had single-handedly thrown away our lives. This horror had crept into my very soul. I found no way of rationalizing what had happened to us any more.

There was a clearing down by the well where a tree had fallen across the river. It had been dying for ages; no one had noticed the ivy advance and strangle it. Like the events in one's life, each small growth takes grip until one can no longer find the way out or one is too weak to escape. I pulled at the battered chainsaw to start it, ripping the cord out and breaking the mechanism.

The Salvation Army told me they needed more information about Jacquie. I decided to tell them about Kurt and Australia and Jacquie's ability to adapt, and about a possible boat trip, perhaps to the Caribbean, and my thoughts about Spain and trucks. I screwed up the paper and began again and then again.

In the evenings after we'd read to Mo and Sam, Ulric and I would sit with the fire blazing and write. I'd taken to the bow-saw once more for wood and the little house was as cosy as it had been many years ago when it was all so new, except the soul of it was gone.

The copy of *The Prophet* that my father had given us on our wedding day lay on the floor beside my bed, its turned-down pages marking the sections as Jacquie had left them. I'd come to realize how desperately she'd searched to understand feelings she hadn't been able to control. The pages she had folded held the following titles: On Joy and Sorrow; On Houses, On Freedom; On Reason and Passion, and finally, On Pain. My heart grew heavy and horror and blame hung over me bitterly. 'If only I had just . . . if only . . .' The conjecture spun on through the days.

The children slept in the room I'd originally built for them, Sam in his cot and Mo with Ulric in the old wooden three-bears bed. Late, when Ulric had gone off to sleep, I'd creep down and past him. Ulric slept with his eyes squinting resembling a mole, mouth open, fingers neatly clasping the sheets up around his neck, his face white and pink with a scattering of freckles, his throat gurgling away like the last gallons of water draining from a bath. Closing the doors quietly, I went into the chapel and sat at the old upright piano that Jacquie had given me in the early years. It was true; the chapel was dead.

Jezebel's preachings shouted back at me from the cold walls. 'We would always be safe, as long as we stayed together.'

'Jacquie.' My voice bounced around.

The light above the piano made the woodwork glow, sending the kitchen and doorways into darkness. I heard Kansas wandering about, her claws clicking on the white tiles. She came to rest at my feet.

'Jacquie?' I whispered. 'You there . . . Rabbit?'

Rabbit was a name I'd given her years before, in the mountains next to Michael and Janet's château. There was nothing particularly cute about the name, although it had amused our tourists. A rabbit, when cornered, lifts its feet and strikes out, backing away wildly, smashing, tumbling, heedless of the damage that it blindly inflicts upon itself and everything it crashes into.

In the following days I had to face the fact that Mo, Sam and I would not make it through the winter. Martha and her sister Emily arrived and began packing the contents of the house into boxes while Ulric prepared the more sensitive items for storage.

It is an ugly feeling, when you know you are beaten but cannot bear to let go of the wonderful years gone by. I was deeply ashamed and stayed clear, not wishing to watch our lives being dismantled, and began to sit in the chapel more often in the late evenings.

'Hi,' I'd tell the darkness. 'You here? I'm here. Baby, what's up?' My voice bounced around the arched ceiling. I imagined Jacquie in bed; always it was a passionate scene, the perfect escape. Never did I replay the past quite truthfully. And my imagination wasn't powerful enough to take me to wherever she might have been now, though I tried again and again.

'Sometimes you're still here,' I'd lie. 'Aren't you? FOREVER YOUNG,' I'd sing, remembering my best friend Bill and the Dylan song he sang to us on our wedding day. 'FOREVER YOUNG . . . MAY YOU BE . . .' My voice echoed around the chapel, then fell dead in the horrific irony of the words.

There is something that lives in every part of the chapel, a reflection of our lives that will never leave. We will always be there together, sleeping in the stones.

In mid-December my father arrived and we loaded his car with what we thought we would need. The police had informed me that I was obliged to return for an interview with a judge in early February. I left a list of numbers with them and heard nothing more. I gathered a few last things, nappies for Samuel, my typewriter, pictures of their mother, socks. Then, feeling homesick and empty before we left, I parked the Land Rover at the side of the chapel, out of sight.

'Goodbye, Bert,' said the children.

'I'll start the Land Rover up now and again,' said André. 'We can look after Kansas and Yogi for now, but soon you'll have to do something about them,' he said bluntly.

Ulric and I had bought provisions for the dogs. I'd be back after January, I promised, and I'd find a solution. The dogs were getting old, it was cruel to leave them, but André and Barbara would care for them. After all, there was nothing else I could do.

In despair, I kissed the place with my thoughts, then the great old oak at the end of the building silently passed us by and without looking back we were gone.

I felt sorry for Barbara. Two small elements of the magnet that had originally brought her and André together were now leaving. The dream it all could have been had turned to dust in her hands. God had somehow betrayed us all, it seemed.

I sat beside my father as he drove, my eyes were filling with tears. A hand came on to my knee as I remembered the same scene in a Land Rover some thirty years before.

PART SEVEN

32 Dry Dock

If you want to grow out of a mess, survive and not *just* stay alive, then there are things you have to go through, even if your brain is jammed in a position that will only look at where it's just been, in order to recover. I have my mother to thank for showing me what becomes of those who never turn from the confines of the past. Remembering her suffering, I determined that I would force myself towards optimism and accept change.

There was something heartbreaking about returning home: not that it could have been any other way. From the first minute, when I pulled the bags out of the car in the street and carried them towards the door, my parents' house, which I knew so well, seemed somehow almost foreign.

This is where you will live, I tell myself, for a while this is your life.

Affectionate kisses and embraces are followed by tears and quiet moments alone on the bed in the attic room, where the folding metal ladder comes out of a hatch and you can just hear the boys when they cry in the night. It's all very strange: love is everywhere, yet one's heart is so empty.

On Christmas Day we had been in England for ten days. It is humbling to see your children swamped with unconditional love and kindness. It is equally strange to be looking at this through the gauze of delayed shock, as if outside, silently observing the decorations, the affection and the presents and kisses through a cold plate-glass window. Change had already come to us, yet I had not the slightest idea of how to react.

Within days I'd spoken to the Missing Persons Helpline, got Jacquie into the newspapers and had contacted Interpol, who eventually replied via the Wandsworth Constabulary, a staggering two years later. I went to my local MP and queued in the street and discussed the case with him in the front seat of his car as he'd lost his office keys. Nothing much could be done. Jacquie was long gone.

January rolled along slowly as I struggled to fill out various forms for the social security and went to see diabetic units and doctors and talked about schools for Mo and Sam. Sam at two barely spoke; Mo had a little French but in truth was as English as any other child. Both children were behind in some aspects of their development, but I imagined that with the future opening up for them once more, they would find their feet. I found I couldn't sit still for very long. Everything seemed to need attention and I didn't know how to stop and simply breathe. Strange panic set in. I wanted life to begin immediately, allowing nothing for the greatest healer of all: time. I'd been in touch with Jaffa. He had come round immediately and seen the children. We had some wine and made plans to go back to France together when I had to see the judge. He wanted to visit his family and sell his van. The arrangement was ideal: we could return to England in Bert.

'Don't worry, Rupert, there's no rush.' Lucilla's voice was soft as I tried to look for work that I would never have enough free time to accept. 'Just take it easy for a while.'

Eventually, with Lucilla's help, I found Mo a place in a school that I could walk to. I'd take him there and then wander through the market at the end of my parents' street to a café where Sam would have his bottle in his pushchair while I sipped coffee and made lists of the things that I needed to sort out. My sister Alice would often look after the boys and they'd disappear into the blue- and red-lit depths of her poster-clad room amid screams of laughter. I had missed a huge chunk of my sibling's development during my time in France. Alice was now a young woman and had inherited her mother's cool, logical, realistic nature. She had forgiven me for the scathing note I'd handed her on her wounded departure from the chapel during the build-up to Jacquie's illness.

The most serious of our problems now was the chapel. I knew that

I wouldn't be allowed to sell it until Jacquie was there to sign the deeds, which could mean never. I owed more than £45,000 and it was bearing down on me. I also needed to find us a place to live; it would be unfair to expect my parents to support us all for much longer.

However, things would have to stay as they were for the time being. Until I had encountered the French judge and he had decided what to do, we would live in uncertainty. It was entirely possible that the judge might decide that I must remain in France. A fear of being separated from the boys haunted me and kept me feeling strangely unwell. I am convinced that Mo was immediately taken into his school, which had a huge waiting list, simply because the head-mistress had listened to me blither my story and had decided to make allowances and help us. For this I was truly grateful.

Between fretting sessions there were still nappies to change, but this side of parenting never troubled me. What worried me more was the children's emotional state. I didn't know how to help them. How on earth do you repair a gash in a child's life like this? A disappearance never goes away. I did my best to conceal certain emotions, but children know. They sense far more than one gives them credit for. I would find Sam crying with little Mo doing his best to comfort him in the quiet of their room, not wishing to make things harder for their father.

Mo would spend more than the next eighteen months of his English school life either clinging like a limpet to his teacher or hiding under a classroom table. Jacquie's mental illness was cruel to all concerned but I found it hard to forgive the local French police department, who had neither the training nor the intelligence to grasp what her illness and disappearance had done to the remains of her family.

33 *Kansas and Yogi*

Seven Weeks Later

The journey down to the chapel with Jaffa was the same as the many long hauls I'd done before. His tiny van sped through the darkness over the French countryside while he patiently listened to me drone on and on. We'd left London in the early evening and were determined to drive all night.

'I'm worried about the judge,' I said. 'What the hell do I do if he decides to make me stay in France? What about the children?' Mo and Sam were in the care of my parents and hadn't liked the separation any more than I had. I'd kissed them goodbye like on a first day of school.

Jaffa turned 'Beast of Burden' down a little. 'Stop winding yourself up,' he insisted, 'it won't help. They have your parents; you're lucky.'

'I'll visit the hippie farmer guy, the last one she saw,' I muttered, 'see if he's got anything to add to his bullshit story. We could do another search maybe.'

'Wait a minute.' Jaffa looked over at me. 'How do you think that you'll manage to do *all this* in five days? And what are you going to do about Kansas and Yogi?'

It was a question that I had been worrying myself sick about. The dogs knew nothing but the chapel. The fact that I lived in my parents' house wasn't much of a comfort as far as their future was concerned, and as Jaffa had said, we only had five days to resolve all these problems before I needed to return and care for Mo and Sam. Willingly, Jaffa listened, advising on the same old problems as the miles buzzed past and the ashtray overflowed.

'When you get yourself sorted out,' he said, 'I mean, when you find a place, I'll come and stay and I'll help you. I could be useful if you don't mind the Jaffa being around.' Of course I didn't, I told him, feeling tremendous gratitude.

He told me I had to get a grip on my emotions. Like my list of things to accomplish while we were in France, my emotions were also impossible to deal with because they were still more powerful and confused than I could handle. 'I know, I know, they'll come right,' I told him. 'What will you do with your van?' I asked, changing the subject. 'You'll never sell it before we go back.'

'I'll give it to my mother to sell,' he said.

'I'm afraid that it's not going to be a very comfortable trip in the Land Rover.'

Jaffa didn't seem to care. This was an adventure. 'I 'ave 'ad far more experience sleeping on 'ard surfaces than you, my friend,' he grinned.

Kansas and Yogi bounded up the chapel drive to greet us. They slobbered madly, tearing around, chasing their tails and barking with delight. With André and Barbara to watch over them most days and Marie-Antoinette checking in they'd been all right; but even so, it had been lonely at the chapel and I felt deeply unhappy for them.

We decided to sleep in the curate's house. I knew the cold emptiness of the chapel would bring me sorrow but rather than stay with friends I felt that it was better to march in there and get on with it all. Thoughtfully Barbara had prepared the beds for us, making the arrival a little less bleak. I telephoned the police and we went over to the station. Jaillard and the slightly superior Burgat had new orders. Finally, six months after Jacquie had disappeared, these two poor wretches had been told to search my house and grounds.

'I packed the place up two and a half months ago. Why now? If she *was* hiding in the cabin by the pool she'd hardly still be alive, would she? She disappeared in July. This is February. I can't believe that she's walked all the way back here just to throw herself down the well. Wasn't a search carried out when she disappeared?'

'That was a different judge,' explained Burgat.

When I think about this judge, even now, I have an urge to

somehow find him and inflict upon him the same suffering that his lack of initiative caused.

The following afternoon we spent some time in the bijou cottage. The police were picking through the bin bags of Jacquie's clothes. I hadn't known what to do with them, so her things were just packed away. The new red bike I'd bought her had gone to Barbara.

'There are clothes missing,' said Jaillard.

'There can't be.' I looked up in astonishment.

'She could have come back and taken them,' he said. 'Look, there's no underwear, none.'

I was now being scrutinized for something that had absolutely no practical purpose. 'My father and brother packed all this stuff,' I told them. 'I didn't touch any of it. I was too upset. They've probably moved a case into the shed or the chapel.'

I spent an evening session at the police station, racking my brains as to where my wife's knickers and bras might have gone and being told that my story didn't fit. 'Why would she only take knickers and bras?' I asked Burgat. 'If she were running off with someone else, surely those would be the *last* things that she'd bother to take.'

The following afternoon the rest of Jacquie's clothes and under-wear were discovered in a chest in the office where Ulric had packed them.

The dogs spent their time close to me. They were joyful. I couldn't think how I could find homes for them, large, old and partially wild as they were. They'd been together for almost ten years, since the beginning of the chapel. Nobody wanted an animal such as this, let alone a brace. There were now less than three days to go until Jaffa and I were set to go back to England. My heart sank. I'd known it all along. There would only be one way for Kansas and Yogi to leave the chapel and this, I knew, was my responsibility.

After dropping Jaffa's old van with his mother we returned to the chapel where I helped the police in their efforts to incriminate me by reading Jacquie's and my letters out loud. I made myself useful by translating them into French while the policemen fished through books, boxes and bags. They kept the odd letter, one of the ones

Jacquie had written in the clinic. She described herself as a prisoner and I the captor. My eyes welled with tears.

What an awful job, I thought to myself, listening to endless pathetic drivel like that. A 'Sorry to have to put you through this' might have been nice though. Extraordinary how easily a title or a uniform can dehumanize the average and normally quite humane Joe.

That evening, with my soul in my boots, I was invited back for another round at the police station. They still had nothing to go on and were becoming frustrated. Some people had spoken out for me, others had enjoyed their ten minutes of fame and had said whatever came into their ugly heads. Jaillard asked me to come upstairs to the interview room where we sat and were joined by Burgat. The two sergeants adopted a friendly approach. I wondered at first if perhaps it was because they had decided that I was innocent and suddenly respected me for my dogged attitude, then I realized that this was to be just another interrogation.

'Seriously,' said Jaillard, 'what d'you think happened to her?'

'I honestly don't know,' I said.

'Look, between us,' he said with a smile, 'off the record, is there any other reason you can think of for why she's gone?'

'I've told you everything on the record.' I too smiled. 'Please, will you tell me one thing? Will the police ever let me sell the chapel? When Jacquie went, she left me in the midst of 450,000 francs' worth of debts. We're going to need somewhere to live and we will all go down the tubes if you don't put this right.'

'Your house is frozen,' said Burgat.

'Then will you also freeze the debts?' I asked, but was given no hope. 'Who's responsible for this?' I demanded. It seemed that the police would end up truly destroying us; our last asset was now in their grasp and we were penniless. 'Might I simply be allowed to sell the house to settle the debts,' I asked, 'and then you freeze the remaining money? What about all the interviews with friends you did, they must tell you something about me. Come on,' I pleaded, 'I'm telling the truth.'

'We spoke to lots of your friends,' Jaillard said.

'What about Lorna? She knew Jacquie really well, and me.'

'Yeah.' They both laughed. 'She thinks you're a saint.'

I was allowed to leave, feeling exhausted. That evening I rang the veterinary surgeon in Le Boulou. There was no time left to look for another solution.

Jaffa and George helped me load the dogs into the back of George's car. Nothing much was said that I remember. George parked outside the little veterinary surgery on the long street across from the wretched post office. 'We'll wait for you,' said Jaffa.

It was a windy, cool evening. I felt rain on my face and the only gap in the black sky I could see was in the distance, holding the last rays of the sun.

The vet's waiting-room was quiet, hot and clean. A woman holding a fat, lightly sedated poodle departed, leaving me alone. The young vet, Patrick, appeared and shook my hand, inviting me into the room with the steel table. We knew each other – we'd all been skiing together once, with nurses and pharmacists from the village. There was a desk and a couple of battered wooden chairs where we sat while I reminded him of Kansas, whom he'd stitched up once or twice after the odd dispute with the more powerful but rather dim Yogi. Patrick was not ready for what I was about to spring upon him.

'I need to find them a home,' I said, cutting the friendly atmosphere down to basics.

Patrick looked a little taken aback. 'I take it nothing's happened concerning Jacquie?' he asked.

'The police are still screwing me, that's all. I haven't heard a thing.'

'What about her mother?' Patrick suggested. 'Won't she have the dogs?'

I explained that with all she had to cope with it would be too much to ask. They would also end up driving André's many cats away. The only other choice was the pound. I knew the pound in Perpignan and I could not bear that. I knew what I wanted and I also knew that Patrick had no miracles available on that day. He begged me to leave them, saying that he'd find a place for one at least, but I refused to have them split up unless they had a fair chance. Nursing had shown me around enough farms to know: one dog would probably be put down and the other left alone in a yard chained to a pole and standing in its own shit. 'I've seen it,' I told him, 'I've worked for the peasants round here. Can you promise there will be hope for one?' I asked.

He sighed and shaking his head said a truthful 'No.'

The dreaded moment had come. Feeling strange, I asked him to put them down there and then. I could hear the words coming out of my mouth as though someone else was speaking. 'Then I'll know that they won't suffer, I can be responsible for it,' I begged. 'Then I'm to blame at least.'

'I can't do that,' he said awkwardly, looking at me as if I were slightly mad. 'You're not thinking for them.'

This was killing me. These animals were a part of me. I knew that I had to prevent the misery I foresaw. I was pleading as Patrick tried to get a grip on the situation. 'I've made terrible mistakes trying to put things right,' I told him. 'If I make a bad decision for the dogs I . . .'

Suddenly Patrick got up from the desk and searched for some equipment. 'Bring them in,' he said. Shocked and frightened that it was actually now *really* going to happen, I asked if he understood. I knew that this was against his better nature. 'You've got enough on your mind without this,' he replied.

Feeling sick, horrified and despairing, I went to the car and picked up Kansas. She knew there was something wrong and stayed limp in my arms, her eyes alert, searching me. I smelled her coat and stroked her as I carried her in and put her on the steel table. Then I went back for Yogi. I seemed to be in slow motion, as if watching a film, while very gently Patrick found a vein. I nodded and cuddled each dog in turn as they stumbled a little, then gently lay down to sleep for always. Our ten wonderful years with Jacquie were over, the moments of delight and passion suffocated me with the ugliness of this destruction.

'Yogi was Jacquie's dog,' I told Patrick proudly, my words staggering as my tears ran over her fur and I waited for her heart to stop beating. Our guardians were dead and with this I believed the last living part of the chapel to be gone, like the wind through my fingers.

'Forgive me,' I pleaded.

The judge's office was in a grand building in Perpignan across the street from a bistro where it's said the whores hang out. Before going there I bought myself a pair of leather mountain boots in the back streets. Their new soles squeaked through the long corridors of the Palais de Justice, giving the search for the judge's rooms a comic soundtrack. Jaffa and I waited on a bench outside the door as my heart thumped like hell and my mouth went dry.

I was ushered into an office with a large desk at one end. Sitting at it were two men, a young one who showed me in and another, older and bespectacled, who wore his grey beard very close-cut.

Without shaking hands the young man asked me to sit down. He was concluding a conversation about another case, I imagined. I was distracted by his age. Looking at his face it seemed that he couldn't be more than thirty-seven or eight. Intuitively, I was aware, despite the vast differences in our education and the fact that he was perhaps a maximum of six years older than me, that between the two of us, across the table, my life experience had to have been far greater.

However, I was grossly emotionally disadvantaged. My control was feeble and my faith that the law would provide a safe path for the children and me had failed me completely. I was there to ask that I be allowed to go home, yet supposedly I was innocent.

This was the new judge, the one who had been appointed to take action on the case. It was he who had ordered the chapel to be looked over and the various shenanigans over the last few days. I recognized that these actions were more of a formality than they were useful. A pity, I thought, looking at the judge. Perhaps six months ago this energetic young man might have been able to do something useful and constructive for us, but now, with Jacquie dead or long gone, he and I were both going to waste our time.

It took about an hour for me to explain the history of the case and the events leading up to Jacquie's departure. The judge scribbled notes on a piece of paper, in all only a page. I suppose he had already heard enough from Burgat and Jaillard and had read all the details but wanted to hear them from me. I imagined it was a simple way of comparing my previous statements with the one I was now giving. It made me paranoid but in truth with what I had been through up to now I was paranoid already. From this interview he would then dictate some kind of statement for me.

'There are things in your story that don't stick.'

'Like what?' I gulped.

'You said that she went off in despair, yet *she* had rejected you.'

I then had to clarify why Jacquie had changed her mind and wanted to have her family back again. Everything I said seemed contradictory, even to me.

'You were having an affair.'

'I panicked, but yes.' Heaven help me, I thought, if I have to explain what drove me to that.

Frowning, he looked at his notes. 'This woman *has* to have some kind of psychiatric problem.'

'Finally, finally,' I gasped in relief, 'someone has agreed with me. Up until now it's been seen as a depression, no more than that, and most don't understand what that means. I've been looked at as some kind of monster. I didn't even know my wife was sick until February, when I almost followed her into the clinic myself. I'd been adjusting for months to make our home manageable. I know it's difficult for you to grasp, but this couple had a life once. We were reasonable people.'

It had been almost two hours. We discussed the nature of the problems I'd faced and I was grateful to be understood and not interpreted the way that I had been by some at the local gendarmerie. Through the window I could see the sunset approaching.

'Are you sure that we've discussed everything you can think of?' he asked.

'I think so,' I said, frayed.

'Then we'll do your statement. I'll read it from my notes.' The judge left the room to find his assistant.

'Do I have a say in it?' I asked as he returned.

'You just did.' He hesitated, looking at me cautiously.

'But you could write anything!' I said.

'You can listen to me do it.'

'What about our house?' I asked. He was suddenly cold and irritable, making it clear that he didn't want a discussion on this issue. 'Another judge is handling that,' he said curtly. Eventually he gave me a name but I was never able to locate or make contact with any judge of that name.

The man with the beard came back into the room wheeling a large computer behind him. He sat down in front of the keyboard and got comfortable, then the judge began reading from his notes. As I made my best effort to listen I realized that some parts of the statement he was giving did not reflect events I had just described.

'No. Wait,' I demanded, 'I never said that.' I felt sick and confused as the story warped before my ears. 'That's not what happened either!'

'Correct it,' said the judge, giving the impression that he had better things to be getting on with. It was a game, I suppose, although I couldn't be sure. Fatigue and worry had clouded my mind so much that I had no perception any more. The judge carried on with his inaccurate version of my story.

'What is this? That's not what I told you.' I began to tremble.

'Yes it is,' said the judge. Although I felt he might be simply bluffing, perhaps to see how I reacted, I still found myself rising to the bait.

'You're deliberately telling it wrong.' I could feel anger rising. 'You don't know what it's like –' I pushed the chair away and got up. I had no idea what I would do then. I felt sure that they weren't going to let me go with an attitude like this but I couldn't stop myself – 'to feel constantly accused.'

Like a kid with the advantage of size who wants to start a fight in a schoolyard, the judge smiled, almost amused, and spread his arms. 'Who is accusing anyone?'

'Six months after Jacquie is gone you send your bozos around to ransack our house,' I yelped. 'That's not an accusation?' Tears were coming and I knew things were going too far. I just unwound there, like a bursting spring. 'YOU'VE TAKEN OUR HOME FROM US! AND LAST NIGHT I HAD TO TAKE MY DOGS AND KILL THEM.'

'No!' said the typist, horrified.

'I couldn't take them to England,' I said, eyes streaming, 'they were too old for quarantine and anyway, we have no place to go.' I stared at them. 'You *know* that. *You* have our house.' Holding my hands out, tired and confused, I pleaded, 'What is it you want? What can I do for you?'

Looking as bored with this as I was traumatized, the judge found a tissue and gave it to me. 'There'll be no more gendarmes,' he promised.

He finished the statement accurately.

Calming down, I regained my place in front of the desk. 'Can I go home to England?' I asked.

'As long as you keep in contact and we know exactly where you are.'

'Thank you,' I sighed, feeling a wave of relief and sickness hit me.

The computer excreted a copy of the statement and I read it, unable to remember each sentence as I began the next. I was aware that I was on overload and felt grateful that it was over. I almost didn't care what they'd bloody written.

'Do you think this is okay?' I asked.

'Is it?' He shrugged. 'It's *your* statement.'

'Look, I haven't done anything wrong and I don't want to get into more trouble now through a mistake. I'm not very clear in the head, that's all.'

I was encouraged to get on with it and sign and the statement was picked up and whisked away. 'Do I get a copy?' I asked, before realizing the bitter humour of the question – a statement is kept to compare with future interrogations. The men laughed and I was allowed to leave.

Jaffa took me across the street. We both needed a drink; he'd been sitting on that uncomfortable bench outside all the while. It was a comfort to know that while my brain had been frying, Jaffa's backside was numb. We ordered beers in the hookers' bar and watched as the odd, pretty, not-so-young things fished about in the last of the day's light.

I began to cry.

'I'll give you five minutes to pull yourself together,' said Jaffa.

Outside, I wondered if somewhere far away, perhaps on a warm beach, Jacquie might be watching the sun go down as well.

Thundering out of Les Chartreuses on our way back to England with the Land Rover and trailer heavy-laden with things for the children and various possessions, the gearstick buzzing and the Stones cassette back in place, I blubbed again. That time there had been nothing to say goodbye to. No dogs curled up, sleeping in the doorways, their feet no longer clicking on the tiles. I'd emptied the rubbish, chucking the last cans of their food away, feeling sick and heavy with shame.

'I want to hate her,' I wept angrily, 'but I can't.'

'I know,' said Jaffa, 'because it's not Jacquie's fault. Come on, let's get out of here.'

Sitting in the passenger seat, I combed over the days we'd just spent. I remembered that I'd passed Skull Face's place the day before and had gone in to say hello. He and his sister had built an extension and no longer lived in their parents' run-down part of the house.

'So, do you still dance the rock and roll?' Joseph had asked, putting his hands on his hips.

'Not much now.'

It had been years since I'd first cut the vines with Joseph. In those days he'd been horrified that a man would take dancing lessons, even though Jacquie and I had gone only three times. Men could either dance or they couldn't, it was natural, inherited, Joseph told me. But you could only do it with the right girl, he'd said, or it just wouldn't work. It had to be a match. You had to get it right and choose wisely; then you could do anything.

'The trouble with women is,' Joseph continued, looking no more than the 150 years old he'd seemed when we had first met, and standing skinny in the middle of his gleaming white kitchen, 'you never know what they're going to do next.'

I worked it out: we had known one another for nine years and still I wasn't sure if Joseph knew my name. Like all the other farmers he called me 'l'anglais.' Some sort of huge bone was boiling all alone in a neat white saucepan on their brand-new cooker. There were no pictures in the room and just as it had been in their parents' house, light came from a single naked bulb.

'That's why I never married,' said Joseph, scratching his scarce grey stubble. 'There's no risk of losing it all.' With a bony finger he pointed across the room. 'Did you see my new colour television?'

'We're rich,' said Yvette, shaking her head with an empty smile, 'but we've got nothing.'

Right then and there, below the naked bulb, I thought of Mo and Sam and silently thanked Joseph and his sister for the warmth I felt inside.

Jaffa was at the wheel. Rain hit the windscreen. Rain, without a cloud in the sky, and far away in London my sons were waiting.

34 Love

Certain rare events can change the way in which one evaluates every second of one's life. I tried to define what exactly it was that I felt. Was it simply the loss of love alone, or was I discovering that I was mourning years of habit and dependence while feeling ashamedly yet strangely free? There is truth in both these things.

Unlike death, when one kisses the loved one goodbye and, shattered, walks on to meet grief, a disappearance is a ticket to a grief that is permanently on hold. You watch your children, knowing they are waiting endlessly, actually physically sick in their hope, for an answer that never comes.

Outside in the London street Bert stood like a mausoleum. The posters of Jacquie beamed from each window, framed with the chapel phone number underneath and a request for assistance in English and in French. No longer in context, the posters showing the summer clothes and smiling face seemed to stand there in the winter rain like a shrine. I dialled the chapel number now and then just to listen and imagine the phone ringing at the foot of the curate's house stairs. In my dreams sometimes she'd answer it.

Lucilla offered to take the children one morning so I could get out for a while. She did this now and again and I gratefully thanked her, grabbed a coat and sped off.

I headed over Battersea Bridge to see a friend, breathing the cold air from the windows, which were open and splashed with rain. I was in Beaufort Street when I noticed the blonde hair and shoulders in the back of the taxi in front. As the head turned I thought I recognized the face; a million-to-one shot, though simply a glimpse was enough. My heart jumped. I shunted Bert down a gear and the tractor-type gearbox demanded a whole dangerous street to overtake as diesel smoke billowed into the air. Waving my hands and pumping the brakes fiercely, I eventually got the cabby to stop. He climbed half-way out as I ran back towards him, then, getting close and apologizing, I withdrew towards the Land Rover as he cursed behind me.

'She dump yer then?' he shouted, standing his ground and mocking. I looked back, annoyed, but having seen the posters in Bert's windows the man's voice had trailed off and his expression lost its edge as he himself turned and looked at the woman in the back of his taxi.

In the following weeks I thundered about, feeding children, writing letters, filling out forms for the social security and the schools and papers for Bert. My parents' house became a sanctuary, calm and slower than anything I'd known in years.

There were real holes in my memory but I felt sure they would mend. Then suddenly I'd stumble across a photograph, or even a single word in a diary written in Jacquie's hand, and the day would once more be cast away like a ship adrift, lost to me although I'd perform all the correct tasks mechanically, oblivious to time.

I was becoming more aware of how dominated my emotions had been by confusion, and the rash decisions I'd made as a consequence weighed heavily on my mind. I also could see how the highs and lows of diabetes had made this life such a struggle. Insulin is a magical product, but as a variable it can't always be in one's body in perfect, exact amounts. Taking control I would now manage far better than before.

'Is Mummy coming home soon? Is she better?' Mo was looking up from his bed in my parents' spare room while Sam brushed his hair with the spines of a plastic stegosaurus. Mo was now five years old and Sam approaching three. 'Come on,' said Mo, looking at me, his eyes following my expressions very closely in the hope that I'd suddenly change my story. 'You *know* where she is,' he nudged, with a cautious, hopeful smile.

'I don't know, Mo-Mo,' I'd plead, 'really. I wish I did, but I *don't*. Honestly, sweetheart.'

There was a single bed and a fold-away for Sam. A little sink stood in the corner and a jumble of everyone's things was strewn thereabouts. It was enough, I thought, for the boys to call their own. My parents had organized things so well.

'Why the rush?' said Lucilla. 'You still try to run everywhere. For goodness' sakes, read a book, take the boys for a walk. Rupert, honestly, boy; try to relax.'

Lucilla gave the boys a common-sense stability that I had not yet rediscovered. I hadn't realized how the healing process would work or how much time it takes. Without Lucilla's calm, love and logic the children's road would have been very much harder.

In addition, very wisely Lucilla never took over. The boys were my charge and I was at the helm. We *had* to be autonomous and I felt that for everyone's sake it should be as soon as possible. This is where months pass without apparent change, yet all the time we were gathering strength unawares. Still I was often alone, sitting in my room at the typewriter that Jacquie had bought me or with Sam at the café on Northcote Road. Without Jacquie life had stalled indefinitely and I couldn't find the mechanism to kick-start it. The chances of my finding happiness seemed somehow impossible. With my wires so jumbled I felt that I was compatible with nothing at all. I did all I felt I could to look after my boys yet I seemed to lead my life in utter confusion, cheerfully bumbling along with them, offering hope only to end up feeling dead inside.

In those early days I was often introduced to women who were comparably single. It is amazing how many parents are alone out there, making huge efforts to provide and wondering what tomorrow will bring.

Emotionally, it seemed as if each of them, like me, was bouncing around, like a pinball stuck in the top part of a machine. Almost everyone seemed to be on the rebound. Most simply wanted to weather the storm in a friend's company and let's see about the rest; another time, maybe when things get better, another place; let's see what tomorrow brings. Hopes for the future were thrown about everywhere like sparks from a Catherine wheel.

I had become a cynic about sex. It seemed to represent comfort to me. With no real understanding of how I might fall in love again, I certainly saw little reason to regard it as meaning much more. The values in my life had changed. The wounded cling on for comfort, without a commitment in sight, not for love and only vaguely for sex. This craving amongst the bewildered is often misunderstood. Running from sadness, running from failure, it's hard to explain, until you live it, that compulsion to be needed, to be something, to simply *not* be alone.

Friends and family, of course, pass predictable, pompous, and sometimes callous moral judgements and it's so easy to judge, when you're safe there, behind the glass, swimming in an uncracked bowl of your own.

'What *are* you doing?' even my brother asked. 'Can't you just stop and wait for everything to sort itself out? I mean, this is another life you're involved with.' Then the predictable tone creeps in. 'I hope you're careful.' People often don't bother to look and see what you're faced with. Things seem so easy when you're advising someone else.

All the time I would be thinking of Jacquie, comparing and subsequently feeling like a stranger. At my parents' house I'd watch our children struggle with the endless unanswered questions and cry. In fact, for the first two years it was hard to speak of Jacquie without them crying. I'd make sure that I didn't speak for long about her, yet I felt they had to know that she loved them. They had to know. At certain times I broke down and began sobbing hideously in front of my parents, part in rage and part in grief, not really knowing whether I'd been dumped or if Jacquie was dead; tears of disorientation, tears of shame.

Poverty, I feared, would lead to loneliness: the classic single-parent trap. I needed to find a job. The years at the chapel had at least taught me how to build things in the simplest, crudest sense and this might just turn out to be our saving grace.

Kind friends came forward with a variety of manual tasks, many of them more therapeutic than useful. While repairing a wall or putting on square miles of paint, I fought battles with Jacquie's ghost, over and over again. She'd disappear and I'd try to follow through the days, often finishing a job without the work registering at all. I'd come to the end and realize that hours had passed. Dragging myself from my imaginary chapel, I emerged smeared with paint from a room in Kennington. Then, while searching through the fire tracks of the Pyrenees, I'd rush through London traffic, checking every blonde head through every bus window on my way to the school to pick up little Mo.

The playground was an interesting place to be eyeballed. I felt I looked naturally odd, standing there, not fitting in with Mrs Average, nor the PTA, nor those who stood looking permanently pissed off, seeming utterly indifferent to the lives of their screaming offspring or anything else. Women in expensive deck shoes and chemists in turbans and estate agents wearing ugly ties or draped in expensive jewellery seemed to be making a far more graceful job of parenting than I was.

I was the young man in the torn bomber jacket, the one who pulled up late in the old Land Rover and was disorganized and tired-looking and so obviously bringing up his children alone. It made a good, tender story, but the reality is far from romantic. The sense of responsibility and guilt for all that had happened in France still followed me around, sick and wretched, like the spirit of the Witch.

Since time began millions of women have been stuck with the task of bringing up their children unaided. Unsurprisingly men, lacking those thousands of years of genetic programming, are generally less good at this, often because they simply can't bear to be alone and tied down. It's all rather cowardly really. As soon as I found somewhere to live I envisaged the daily struggle and the evenings as the children slept and wondered how I would cope. I never did like watching soap operas that much. The remaining friends I had in London were all at work and mostly successful and committed. There were parties but baby-sitters were expensive. Life would be quiet, I guessed, but despite missing Jacquie I still felt remarkably fortunate.

In the evenings we'd sit lumped together on Mo's bed while Sam finished his bottle and I told stories and talked about tomorrow. Tomorrow was the big one. Tomorrow was everything, just everything at that time.

'I'm afraid it'll be little,' I said, 'our new place. Maybe a flat, but it'll be lovely.'

Sam spat out the bottle. 'Will there be a garden?'

'We'll always have the park.' I patted his shoulder.

The following day I went into the street and removed the posters of Jacquie from Bert's windows. It was the first of the many things that I did to stand alone.

In the spring Fergus rang from his home near the chapel. He'd called to say how sorry he was . . . that Jacquie was dead. Horrified and apologetic, he said he'd read it in the papers and couldn't understand why the French police hadn't phoned me.

'There's a picture,' he went on, 'one of the ones you had on the posters. They've found a body that fits the description almost exactly. I'm so sorry that you heard it from me.'

I rang Sergeant Burgat who was typically unconcerned down the line, as if this was merely tiresome. 'It's not her,' he said and promised he'd call when they knew.

It was an odd day and an awful wait but Burgat never did call. Then when I called the gendarmerie the following day he wasn't there and like the French courts, no one knew anything about anything. This was agonizing. Assuming it hadn't been Jacquie, I was constrained to write to Sergeant Burgat, explaining what this experience had been like, detailing some of the more unpleasant techniques used upon me in previous months. I sent the letter by registered post to both him and the judge.

Then in the days that followed I rang to see if the letter had arrived. Sergeant Burgat picked up the phone and I could tell he was literally shaking. 'I don't want to speak to you any more. I don't have to tell you anything!' he ranted. 'Your story isn't straight.'

It was the last time I ever spoke to the gendarmerie. I decided then that if we were kept in limbo and our chapel, which was my life's work, was to be held from us, then I'd build up a campaign and record every phone conversation and finally I'd become unpredictable: I'd go to the press in England. There seemed to be nothing left to lose.

In May I telephoned the judge's office in Perpignan to find out if there had been any decision about the chapel but there seemed to be no record of a judge handling the issue. In fact the name given to me by the judge I'd seen in February did not seem to exist at all.

Our chapel was apparently lost in the workings of the French legal machine, or perhaps conveniently put aside. I couldn't find out why because again, there was no one who would talk to me. This would have been less alarming had it not been for the debts gathering like a vast storm on the horizon. Over the summer I tried repeatedly to obtain information and then, growing worried, I drafted a letter to be professionally legally translated and sent to the courts. It cost a fortune, which my father paid. No answer was ever received, though someone there must have read it. I wondered if this treatment would have been the same if I had been a Frenchman. I doubted it.

If we were able to sell the chapel we could start again. I could move us into our own place. It was either that or starting on the dole in government housing and paying debts off for many years to come. Thinking of my parents' tiredness, I knew that a decision would have to be made soon.

'Are you all right, old son?' my father would ask as he made his way out, shoving an empty cereal bowl on the table and heading for the door. I was feeding the children and there was hardly anywhere for him to sit. The door would click shut, his cup of tea on the table, forgotten. I knew that this was difficult, unfair, and for all of us it was becoming exhausting.

'No, Sam,' Mo'd say, 'Mummy's hair was like ours, yellow.'

Mo would be there to remind them both, keeping Jacquie going in his own little way for as long as his resolve would last. I felt deeply proud of him for this, for striving to understand, for his careful questions.

As time went on, having learnt from my experience with the

gendarmerie over the discovery of the body of the young woman in the Corbières mountains, I gently suggested to the children that their mother might well be dead and that we should be ready for this. In a way I hoped that this would be a release for them.

'I know,' said Mo. 'She might be an angel,' he added, while Sam cried quietly.

'She might,' I said. 'I'm sure that wherever sh—'

'She left us,' he said, forgetting about angels. 'You said she might get better.'

'That's right,' I agreed, feeling empty.

'Then why doesn't she call,' Mo's lip began to tremble, 'if you say she loved us?'

'She was ill, Mo, she really was ill. She might not even know who she is.'

There was a silence and then both boys began to cry.

'Don't worry, Daddy,' said Mo. I wiped Sam's nose, hearing my words fired straight back at me. 'Things'll be wonderful,' Mo shakily gulped through his tears while putting his arms around me, 'you just wait and see.'

Somehow, during our long siege at my parents' house, although there were struggles, the experience is locked in my memory as healing, filled with love and a powerful sense of a family's devotion, of excitement and hope. Before my father left for work one morning I'd written a note and had put it in his pocket. He'd find it at some point during the day I hoped. *We are so lucky*, I wrote, *because we have you.*

It was August now and Jacquie had been gone for over a year. Still no word had come from the courts on the fate of the chapel, which obviously, without heating or maintenance, was beginning to depreciate. This meant that for longer than a year I had been forced to continue to pay the debts or watch them accumulate at a frightening rate. I did not know when or if the chapel would ever be released to me but I was aware that with each passing month its value lessened.

In July I'd been told by a cold-sounding legal secretary in the Palais de Justice in Perpignan to wait until after August when all the judges got home from the summer holidays. 'Perhaps there'll be something for you then.' After all the letters, the phone calls and the episode at the beginning of the year with the judge, even picking up the phone to ask for answers made me shake and my heart pump like fury. 'Please,' I'd beg, 'isn't there someone who can help? I can't hold the debts back any longer.'

In September I rang again and again and was repeatedly told to call back. I began to hate the authorities. I never did speak to a judge or even a lawyer. On the last of my calls one of the secretaries was given instructions to tell me that the chapel had been released. An anonymous judge in an anonymous office had helped us. He must have finished with his holidays and for some reason had decided to agree the release papers. It reminded me of the film *Brazil*, where the state became a cruel and blind bureaucratic machine.

'Isn't there a document or something to say this decision has been made?' I stammered.

'What for?' the secretary asked. 'It's done, that's all.'

The wave of shock and relief was overwhelming. It was over; or more accurately, for Mo, Sam and me, there was finally a beginning.

PART EIGHT

35 Le Rock

Within a month the chapel was sold. My father had been right when he'd said that nothing in this world stands still for very long. For the first time in ten years I had no debts. The lawyers and the banks and *notaires* had all dug their claws in and taken their shares and we were left with far less than I'd hoped, but I was grateful. It was enough to provide us with a simple home.

It had been Lucilla who'd found the house. She was good at being able to see the wood from the trees. In my mind what we could afford was inevitably going to be a nightmare. What cheap London property could possibly size up to the chapel?

It stood empty, one of thousands of houses built after the First World War for our foot soldiers coming home. Most of the pebble-dash render had gone brown with soot and the back windows were rotten, overlooking a single apple tree, which stood alone in the middle of a good-sized garden. There was an old Anderson air-raid shelter out there and around it the remains of a variety of motorbikes seemed to be rising from the dead out of the mud.

I watched anxiously as huge, fierce Alsatian dogs in the gardens on either side of the house darted back and forth, sniffing, growling and menacing from behind overgrown hedges. Lucilla lightly dispelled the threat with the idea of a fence, although I could plainly see that she wasn't impressed. The apple tree reminded me strangely of Skull Face. It spoke to me of hope. Lightning had struck it, tearing it apart on one side, but it was still strong, standing there in a sea of buried lead pipes and shattered glass, patiently waiting, like me, for warmer days and spring.

Leaving the dogs growling, I went back into the house to look at the sitting-room which had been painted purple over wood chip. It had once been a minicab office or something, before the repossession. Above, there were three bedrooms in which previously three families had all lived at the same time. There was also a kitchen in a corridor where a mesh, steel and glass window-door looked blindly out towards the garden and the tree. Visually, it all seemed nasty, insulting, filthy and decrepit, but the building itself had life in it. I could do something with this, I thought.

I worried about the fearsome dogs for Sam and Mo's sakes. But providence and heaven's awful humour sometimes strike in the strangest ways. Magically both dogs dropped dead one after the other before I'd even had a chance to put down a deposit on the place. Old age, I was told, although I was convinced that my guardian angel was working with me here.

I'd bought the house in November and the timing was good. I could sense my parents' weariness and I worried, knowing that the continual strain of children had been far greater than they'd ever let on. It would be another two months before the new house was habitable enough. I'd put central heating in by myself and someone had given me beds for the children. We would move in after the Christmas and New Year holidays. It would be a fresh start in a new, uncharted year and the boys were thrilled and getting stronger and brighter every day. They already knew which room they were getting and arguments about who would have the top bunk had been settled.

Finally, in the last months at my parents' house, after much advice and thought, I decided to file for divorce. This was not a move taken out of malice. I was still wearing the worn-thin wedding ring, which had split open such a long time before. In times of despair and bitterness I would take it off and then later remorsefully put it back on again. Still, things were changing; Jacquie's illness had done enough. I certainly did not fear her, but I could never leave the door open to instability again. With normality all around me I was beginning to recognize just how far towards mental illness I had descended myself. I would cut myself away as best I could, promising that if she ever returned, I would be there to help her. I missed her friendship and love and the boys felt the same loss but I knew in my heart that the wonderful things I had known with Jacquie were gone forever.

Loneliness seemed to hover around, warning me to get off my backside and engage. I spent the days fixing the battered house and did my best to introduce myself to cooking, which I did badly, cursing myself for never learning enough from Jacquie. It did occur to me that I'd never seen her try to change a clutch or wire a plug and I was comforted by this. I introduced myself to our neighbours.

Grumbling through the living-room wall was a taxi driver and his family. Often they'd shout at each other over their tea but it was perfectly healthy stuff and they were always pleasant, even when I burned rubbish in the garden and covered their washing in soot. Again they showed understanding after the boys had slipped under the hedge and ripped out all their flowers, although I'm sure it made them miss their dog.

Next door on the other side was June, a tiny retired woman with a heart of gold and scars around a hole in her throat apparently caused by a particular kind of cigarette. June grunted instead of speaking and it was often difficult to catch her drift. Her companion had been the other (passive-smoking) Alsatian, and now Mo and Sam had arrived in its place.

I'd concentrate, with Sam in my arms, trying to make out what June was grunting, while Sam would reach across and try to put a finger in the dreadful unguarded throat hole and I'd try to act as if nothing was going on. June would kindly offer me tea from over the broken bits of wood where the privet hedge hadn't grown and then she'd thoughtfully disappear, back to her gas fire while I'd work, putting a kitchen together, fitting floorboards, radiators and knocking down walls, feeling both excited and isolated.

We'd fallen into a slice of what you might call 'old London'. The house was battered and ugly but we were lucky, so very lucky. I didn't sound or look like anyone in the street, although somehow we'd been labelled as 'all right', and the remains of a solid community was still there and doing what it could to look after its own.

Still, the house seemed empty at first, truly hollow. Our old furniture, which I had brought from the chapel, was piled in the middle of the purple downstairs room.

Ulric and I had hired a van and driven back to the chapel on a long weekend to pick up whatever I hadn't sold with the house. The collection of ten years of two people's lives fitted into this limited space. Many of our belongings would stay behind: the Jaffa tables, the large beds, much of the linen, crockery and kitchen equipment. I wanted change to sweep over me. I'd done almost as Jacquie's mother had done after her husband had died; I'd sold the lot, keeping only the most precious and private things.

I wanted *life* . . .

Ulric had waited in the van while I'd gone into the chapel and said my goodbyes. It was autumn then and the chapel, as before, was clean and quiet. Barbara had been in and looked after it. It had been standing uninhabited for over a year and nothing had changed. I supposed that Jacquie's and my ten-year life there was like a moment to a structure that had lasted almost a thousand years. This was a place transcending the Holy Wars, Mozart, Napoleon, the discovery of the Americas, Lenin, Hitler, the Beatles, and the terrors of African genocide. In the light of those landmarks our struggle seemed almost as insignificant as a grain of sand. But we had given this place life. 'Goodbye, old friend,' I said, admiring the pale walls.

Coming down from the mezzanine, I looked at the large beam which late one evening Jacquie and I had struggled to put into place. In the middle of the section the cherub I had brought from the curate's house so long ago was still there watching, a witness to many things and supposedly a guardian. So much for that, I thought. I glanced at the rickety piano Jacquie'd given me for my birthday. A band had played on the evening she'd brought it. Jacquie had arranged a wonderful surprise party, the sounds of which and her kisses were still with me as I stood there alone. I prised the cherub free and put it in my pocket. It was time to go.

Back at the little brown house in London tomorrow was upon us, it seemed. The months of odd-jobbing passed by and I was still trying to find ways to brighten up. Every Sunday was Pancake Day and we all helped out, even little Sam. The shortest day of the year had gone by and I was at last waking up and for the first time looking forward, instead of back, to where I'd been.

Our Christmas unfolded at the cottage overlooking the Solent where Anna and I had spent our holiday, a place where I'd spent so many days as a lad. My father and Lucilla had rented it for holidays for almost as long as I could remember and the years of our childhood seemed ingrained into every inch of the gorse-covered, windswept beaches and the holed and muddy roads around it. There was nothing there that I did not feel familiar with, nowhere in my childhood wanderings there that I could not call my own.

I had not seen much of Anna. We'd spent a little time together when I had first returned, but since then had fallen out of touch and I had left it at that. I knew I could not disentangle her from the past and I would never be able to offer her the life she so deserved.

As far as relationships go I was adrift and felt that soon I'd have to get my own life going, like a motorbike that won't start – sometimes you have to push it to get it to come back to life. Sitting there expecting to meet people is absurd and I was still in a muddle and upsetting people now and again. I wore the split wedding ring still, taking it off one day and putting it back on the next. Recently I had been trying to wear it with memories of what we were before Jacquie had been ill. This had to stop, I told myself. You *have* to move on or be left behind with your heart trapped. She either didn't care or she was dead, I admitted to myself, so get off your backside and *live*.

Women are strong; in my situation many seemed to be managing brilliantly. I hated being alone. I am simply a creature made far happier when there is someone to share the days with and to love. I was becoming aware that I would never recover from the loss of Jacquie unless love itself jolted me back. I know myself. I would need help to turn the page; pathetic perhaps, but I was not ashamed to be like this. I am only human and tears were far from over. Life, however, had become so much more serious than in naive days gone by and love and romance seemed to be in some other room, at a table reserved only for other, more carefree people.

Again throughout Christmas the children were swamped with

affection. Sam had started school and was managing well. Mo was struggling a little with it all, still occasionally hiding under his desk or clinging to his teacher, but less than before, and he now had a tribe of little friends. Mo's memory being longer and his awareness far greater at the time of all the troubles, I knew it would take thought, love and time before he would really be himself once more. For Sam this was a darker issue. He felt a sense of treachery because he could not remember his mother. He had to rely on what he heard and on the photographs I'd given the boys, along with a mental patchwork made from my stories and Moses' naive descriptions; these would be the foundations of his memories of Mummy. It was still hard for me to speak of her without reducing him to tears.

Ulric, who had taken it upon himself to dress as a pirate, led expeditions on Christmas Day to find a fellow shipmate's treasure, hidden in the water not far from the cottage. The children scrabbled with their boots, coats and gloves and rushed after him, leaving me putting on mine in the warmth and calm of the kitchen.

'I know it's a bit quiet for you, old son,' said my father, sipping at the last of his tea and picking up his old blue skipper's hat, which had washed up years ago on the tide. 'Before you know it,' he patted my shoulder, 'things will come right.'

On New Year's Eve, driving home in Bert from a dinner party, I stopped to pick up Ulric at a bash for what resembled the 'under-thirties'; quite a different venue to the one I'd just left. People were roaring and wriggling on the floor and I was convinced that someone was doing something particularly unsavoury either to what resembled a sofa or several women stuffed into the same dress.

Ulric forked himself into the passenger seat like a huge slug. 'I'm plastered,' he groaned. 'You want to go to the other party on the way home?'

We drove through the frozen countryside along the back roads and then down a long private driveway.

'How about that?' I said, looking at the white frozen grass as we rumbled along beside the fields. 'New Year's night and it's almost a full moon.' Ulric was oblivious. Moments before we'd been speaking of hopes and projects for the months ahead and now he was off in the middle of another one of his anti-bad luck routines, shuffling his fingers and rolling his eyes, probably working on a shield of good fortune for the year to come.

We pulled up in front of a huge, daunting country house and climbed out. Music was blasting from a doorway and we made our way in from the freezing night to find a couple of people still dancing in a chequered flagstone hall before a large open fire. It was two in the morning and almost all of the guests had left. A bored-looking aristocrat stared down from a portrait hanging above the hearth.

'Would you like a glass of wine?' asked one of his descendants, a pretty girl called Sophie. She was suddenly grabbed by her younger brother and whisked off to dance, so I found myself a glass and watched the two stumbling about while the fire warmed my back, throwing shadows on the sculpted ceiling and oaken banisters above.

I felt slightly shy, standing there on my own, heating my frozen fingers. Ulric had temporarily disappeared into another room and the girl before me was now in the middle of a contortionist movement with her boy brother wildly twisting her arm off. She wore a short burgundy dress and had an attractive body with a brain that seemed to be just as pickled as Ulric's. 'Ouch!' she squawked cheerfully at the clumsy brother. The wonderful thing about dancing with a sister, I remember from my experience with Alice, is that it really doesn't matter much if you stomp on her feet.

'Wouldn't it be great if I could really dance the rock and roll?' said the boy, deliberately letting go of his sister and laughing as she shot backwards in a rather unladylike stagger. The girl had large blue eyes and pale skin and I was listening to every word they were saying. I was also thinking of Skull Face and how he'd scowled at me when I'd told him about dancing 'le rock'. With this in mind the boy's words and my arrival now seemed almost perfectly timed.

'Oh, come on, Ben,' said Sophie, 'you're hopeless, get on with it.'

'Can't we do that one where you grab the other arm and then . . . ?' He struggled, still jumping about to the music.

'I can dance the rock,' I said, stepping forward and reaching out.

I was sure that old Skull Face would have approved. He'd have thrown a bony hand forward and found himself unable to stop his scrawny little body from leaping about. I think it was those eyes.

'I'll show you,' I smiled, as the warmth of her hand thawed mine.

Perhaps Ulric's little prayers had struck home.

The longest winter of my life ended early that year.

Spring. My words to Jacquie so many years ago remind me: *There has to be a winter to make way for spring.*

'Don't look for tomorrow,' Jacquie'd say, 'you might be dead. And never, *never* look back.' Today was hers. Today was who she was; and yesterday, after all, I could keep it.

Yesterday was simply someone I'd loved.

36 Epilogue

Since our dance in front of the fire on New Year's Eve six years ago Sophie and I have seldom been apart. We married and had three children. One of ten children herself, Sophie was no stranger to families. The battered little London house became one of the happiest I have ever known. Jaffa, who had initially moved in when I was alone, was eventually driven out by the sheer lack of space. He pursued his ambition to be a furniture-maker, fell in love and now has a beautiful daughter.

Time has flown past, which is in itself a sign of happiness. Moses and Sam have become their own very independent-thinking selves. Sadly little Samuel became a diabetic when he was seven, which means he injects himself twice daily and does so remarkably bravely. It was painful watching him take his first injection, not because it hurt him but because I was so aware of the insulin-connected struggles that he would inevitably endure. Sam is careful. Now a role model, I was also brought to focus harder on diabetes myself.

It was difficult for the boys, at first torn by the guilt of loving both Sophie and the memory of their mother. Postponed grief is a cruel sentence for those who should long ago have had the chance to embrace recovery unhindered. Jacquie's departure left so much unresolved. The many moments of frustration and the kindly questions became tiresome, especially when 'kindly' inquiries fired at Sophie were often little more than searches for gossip.

My mother had been in touch. She was sure that she'd seen Jacquie in Andorra. It was difficult to work out what was what and I heard, much to my amusement, that she was driving Sergeant Burgat and Jaillard to distraction.

After Jacquie had been missing for seven years Sophie and I took the children to France to visit the Roussillon and the chapel. The idea was to chase some ghosts away, to give the boys and Sophie a chance to see the life I had known. I also wanted to put the story in a real setting for them and thus destroy any unhealthy myths. Mo and Sam would stay across the road from the chapel on their first proper holiday with André and their grandmother Barbara. Ironically, it was around this time that their mother was at last found.

With memories so raw I had not much wanted to return to France before then and in any case the struggle to survive and provide for our growing family in recent times had prevented it. For me it was a trip to see it all again and perhaps close a chapter. As for Sophie, coming there was an act of bravery and curiosity.

Sadly, the discovery that summer of human remains in the wood near where Jacquie was last seen would be the start of another long bureaucratic process. A hiker or hunter had found a skull in the forests near where she had been seen for the last time and Barbara and Linda had been asked to give blood for DNA comparisons. Having known so many previous discoveries to be inconclusive, Barbara, under-standably numbed, chose to mention only the minimum during our visit. In any case it would be many months before answers were given and we were all worn from speculation.

Sam and Mo, now nine and eleven years old, spent a glorious week of games on sandy beaches, lizard hunting and early outdoor suppers with their grandmother. Barbara made provisions for their younger siblings too, her arms wide open, actions, as always, speaking louder than words.

Looking back, I am almost certain that at that time she would have been fairly convinced that the remains discovered were likely to be those of Jacquie. But endless waiting does things to make one question everything, making even obvious conclusions seem improb-able. It seems terrible but one almost believes nothing any more. Barbara carried on, shutting out her troubles, welcoming, doting on the boys, making the few days they shared as carefree as she could.

The owner of the chapel invited Sophie and me to look round. It was strange to see the way things had grown, flourishing around it, and yet I knew it would look this way. I had sold it almost lock stock and barrel and everything was still there, frozen like a photograph, almost just as it had been on the day I'd left. 'But those are your hands,' Sophie said, looking at the sculpted forearms and fingers holding up the mantelpiece in the centre of the chapel. The old piano Jacquie had given me stood silent between the simple white pillars while the linen on the beds and the kitchen crockery stared back from their original places just as before.

I was fortunate to have an opportunity to look into a window of my past – where the past had been essentially wonderful. The time in the mobile home, the curate's house and in the chapel itself sped past me, yet the spirit of the building seemed to have been asleep for some time. I missed the clicking of Kansas and Yogi's feet on the tiles. This made me sad, along with the thought of the happiness that Jacquie and I had shared. A sense of waste was heavy in my heart.

'Never look back,' Jacquie had said . . . It was time to go.

I was grateful that the place held nothing for me now. Jacquie was perhaps in every stone, maybe watching at that very moment. My only regret is that I was unable to save her from herself: this responsibility, I have always felt, was mine.

Just after Christmas in England, arriving home from a family gathering, I rushed into the kitchen to answer the telephone. Beside me, in high spirits, Moses was chasing Sam with their sisters and brother in close pursuit. It was Barbara on the line. It seemed that the call had finally come. Jacquie had at last been identified.

I now have a better idea of what happened on the night that Jacquie disappeared. I wanted to know everything but Barbara, heartbroken, had precious little to tell me. In any case, the fact that Jacquie was dead was enough to overrun one's thinking and tighten every sentiment to breaking point.

Suddenly the good things one has managed to find in life take on such meaning. One's children and simple hopes for them become so overwhelmingly precious because they are clearly so easily taken away. I felt a pain in my heart as sorrow crept in and took hold. It is hard when you have waited for so long. I wept for Mo and Sam. I wept for Jacquie and the struggles she'd faced all alone.

Since the French police have no reason or legal commitment to provide me with information I have put Jacquie's last moments together as best I can. I did this for myself, in an attempt to map out clearly and comprehend what she must have faced.

After a moment of despairing madness or, as the police put it, a burst tyre, for one reason or another Jacquie's car suddenly turned at high speed towards the central reservation and the only upright solid post in a stretch of hundreds of yards. The crash barrier, doing its job, threw the car away from certain destruction and back into the road where it slid for a hundred yards or so. By the look of the bits and pieces left on the roadside the little Fiat must have been on its side, screaming and shattering along. Jacquie was probably badly injured, perhaps internally. The raging sparks and sheer terror, the alcohol mixed with psychiatric drugs, the adrenalin and endorphins would, I imagine, have provided her with a kind of battlefield stamina, enough to support her when she was ousted from the car by a concerned motorist. She somehow pushed him aside, leaving him standing there beside the wreck while she ran across the road and climbed a jagged earthen driveway into darkness, eventually making it to the house in the woods some few hundred yards from the road.

Considering her condition, this feat alone must have been exhausting. She then begged the confused occupant and his wife to help her to end her life. In his police statement the man said he'd supposed she was another summer wacko from the many nearby beach resorts, yet he and his wife had attempted to help her and invite her in. Jacquie declined and departed, wandering back in the direction of the road. The man said he had noticed no signs of injury upon her. I was never happy with his statement. I can only assume that Jacquie never made it along the rocky drive, that in her despair, pain and bewilderment she became feeble and disoriented. I imagine she wandered through the darkness into the woods in search of the road and eventually collapsed. I pray that she felt nothing, that life might at least have accorded her this.

How it is possible that she was not found soon afterwards is something that still devastates me. I shall never accept that she was not found in time – at what I am led to believe was such close range.

Did the police ever truly search there? The simplest answers are sometimes the very hardest to find. I have lived with the endless ugly question: *Did you kill your wife?* from dinner-party gossips and the mouths of those who did not take the time to know me, all on account of a failed search, a probable lack of manpower, or perhaps, simply a lazy judge.

Jacquie was so vibrant, at times the very spirit of happiness. It seemed inconceivable and unbearable to me that she, so alive, could have simply died somewhere alone and afraid in the darkness. I shall always feel great pain and sorrow for her. Some say God has his plans but I shall never get the point of this one.

Mo and Samuel have grown up knowing what an extraordinarily wonderful woman their mother was before the illness and subsequent confusion stole her from them. Jacquie would not have wished them to feel sad; she would have encouraged them to invent, to surround themselves bravely with life and in making others feel good to create their own happiness. Not as easy as it sounds . . . but such was their mother's gift.

Finally, travelling around the countryside during our brief holiday, we stopped at Skull Face's house. His sister Yvette came down from her balcony to speak with me. No longer recognizing my face, she was immediately hostile. Eyeing me cautiously, she spat the news of Joseph across as soon as she'd felt sure that I was really '*l'anglais*' as they used to call me. Joseph, at the age of eighty-something, had got his wish. Yvette had risen one morning and found the boyish shape of her brother lying still in the quiet of his bed. Just as he had hoped, Joseph had gone peacefully in his sleep. He died in the spring of the year before we'd come. Joseph loved the spring. Spring is beautiful in the Roussillon, under the foothills, where it rains without a cloud in the sky.